*Brittany,
1750–1950*

Brittany, 1750–1950
The Invisible Nation

Sharif Gemie

UNIVERSITY OF WALES PRESS
CARDIFF
2007

© Sharif Gemie, 2007

All rights reserved. No part of this book may be reproduced, stored in a retrieval system, or transmitted, in any form or by any means, electronic, mechanical, photocopying, recording or otherwise, without clearance from the University of Wales Press, 10 Columbus Walk, Brigantine Place, Cardiff, CF10 4UP.
www.wales.ac.uk/press

British Library Cataloguing-in-Publication Data
A catalogue record for this book is available from the British Library.

ISBN 978–0–7083–2002–0

The right of Sharif Gemie to be identified as author of this work has been asserted by him in accordance with sections 77 and 79 of the Copyright, Designs and Patents Act 1988.

Typeset by Florence Production Ltd, Stoodleigh, Devon
Printed in Great Britain by Antony Rowe Ltd, Wiltshire

To Fouad Gemie
(1923–2005)

Contents

Preface   *xi*
Acknowledgements   *xii*
Terms, Abbreviations and Dates   *xiii*

Introduction: The Rocks of Brittany   1

1. *Brittany today*   *1*
2. *Birthplace and refuge*   *9*
3. *Historiography: the idea of Brittany*   *12*
4. *Brittany: a summary history*   *17*

PART I: MAKING BRITTANY

1 The Question of French Nationhood: Celts, Romans and Bretons   25

1. *Nations, nationality and nationhood*   *26*
2. *The question of the origins of France*   *32*
3. *The search for the Celts*   *35*
4. *The Celtic opposition*   *41*
5. *Brittany and France*   *49*

2 Brittany and the French Revolution   53

Brittany and old regime France   *54*
Breton nobles and Breton politics   *61*
The revolt of the third estate   *66*
The Counter-Revolution: La Vendée and Chouannerie   *69*
The formation of the Blues   *78*
Conclusion   *84*

3   Oriental Brittany 86

1   *Definitions by negatives*   87
2   *Oriental Brittany*   90
3   *The Breton specificity*   101
    Conclusion: political values   102

PART II: RULING BRITTANY

4   The Politics of Faith: Chouannerie, Religion and the Making of a White Landscape 107

1   *Chouannerie in the nineteenth century*   108
2   *A White landscape: the pardons*   117
3   *Catholic politics*   122
    Conclusion   130

5   The Politics of the State (1): People and Protests, 1830–52 132

1   *The National Guard*   132
2   *The festivals of the July Monarchy*   133
3   *The politics of bread*   140
4   *Celebrating the Second Republic (1848–52)*   149
    Conclusion   158

6   The Politics of the State (2): The Management of Democracy, 1850–1940 159

1   *Elections and politics, 1850–1940*   160
2   *The Empire*   164
3   *The Republicans*   171
    Conclusion   182

7   The Politics of Brittany: Regionalism and Nationalism   184

1   *The precursors*   185
2   *Faith and Brittany*   189
3   *The Union Régionaliste Bretonne*   190
4   *Other voices: Republicanism and socialism in Brittany:*
      Emile Masson   192
5   *After the war: the formation of Breiz Atao*   195
6   *Breiz Atao: a nationalist ideology*   199
7   *Breiz Atao: in search of a nationalist practice*   204
8   *Another protest: Dorgères and the Greenshirts*   206
    Conclusion   208

8   The End of the Road? Breton Nationalism and
    Vichy France, 1940–5   210

   Brittany and fascism   210
   Brittany and the war   214
   Clarifying collaboration   219
   L'Heure bretonne: the collaborationists of the new PNB   220
   Other collaborations   224
   Breton resistance   226
   August 1944: the Marseillaise in Brittany   229
   Echoes and legacies   231
   Conclusion   234

Conclusion: Mordrel's Children   236

Notes   240
Bibliography   280
Index   300

Preface

I began research for this book in 1998, and wrote up my findings in three bursts: I produced a vast, sprawling manuscript during my AHRB-funded sabbatical in 2001–2, then spent most of 2005 cutting sections from it and finally, in the summer of 2006, fine-tuned a few pages.

The second stage of the process proved to be far more difficult than I had anticipated. My father's health began to deteriorate in the spring of 2005. The process was not obvious at first: every piece of bad news seemed to be countered by a possibility of progress or of amelioration. However, by the summer, there was no further doubt. My mother phoned me early in September: I went back home to join her for my father's last days.

My father had little interest in Brittany. As far as I know, he only went there once, in the summer of 2004, when my parents visited Pat and me in Saint-Malo. He always seemed just a bit surprised by my choice of career, and never understood my fascination with obscure elements in French history. But I think he would have recognized some themes in this book. My father worked as a producer, translator and interpreter and – *tel père, tel fils* – this work is a translator's book: it studies some hidden aspects of Brittany's history, and adapts them into forms that an English-language reader can understand.

The last words I heard my father say were 'water, water'. Here you are, Fouad: the sparkling blue sea off Saint-Servan, the wild waves at Batz, crashing onto the sea walls, the sluggish, dark blue-green water of the Nantes–Brest canal, and grey *crachin*, the drizzle of Brest – all the water you could ever want.

ACKNOWLEDGEMENTS

I would like to thank the AHRB (now AHRC) and the School of Humanities at the University of Glamorgan for funding my sabbatical in 2001–2, and to thank the Centre for Border Studies (University of Glamorgan) for funding my six-month sabbatical in 2006.

Writing this book has been a rewarding experience: it has given me the opportunity to renew contact with some old friends, as well as making some new ones. I would, in particular, like to thank the following: my colleagues Fiona Reid, Norry La Porte, Stefan Berger and Gavin Edwards for their endless patience, goodwill and sensible advice; Ronan Le Coadic for helping me understand how little I understood and – more seriously – for giving me the confidence to speak French in public; John Barnie, editor of *Planet: the Welsh Internationalist*, for encouraging me to interview; Sarah Lewis, commissioning editor at UWP, for her guidance and encouragement; the anonymous reader employed by UWP, for some valuable reassurance; Tim Flinders for producing the map that appears on p. xvi; and in particular, above all else, special thanks to Patricia, who carried me back from Le Croisic to Waterloo International.

Terms, Abbreviations and Dates

Terms

B4/B5: references to the post-1941 four-department region of Brittany (B4), and the pre-1941 five-department region of Brittany (B5). The Loire-Inférieure, which includes Nantes, was the department which was cut from the region.

Breiz Atao: Breton nationalist paper, published from 1919 to 1939. Also commonly used as a collective term for the constellation of different radical Breton autonomist and nationalist groups in the inter-war years.

Bretonnitude: a claimed essence of Breton identity.

Celticism: the study of Celtic cultures, histories and languages; by implication, a form of study which uses concepts of 'the Celtic' as an explanatory paradigm.

Celtitude: a claimed essence of Celtic identity.

Commune, canton, arrondissement, department: the basic administrative units of France. There are currently ninety-eight departments in mainland France: these can be seen as the approximate equivalent to the British counties. Each is headed by a government-appointed Prefect. Each in turn is divided into arrondissements (headed by a Sub-Prefect), then into cantons, and finally into communes. Thus in the department of the Loire-Atlantique there are four arrondissements, fifty-nine cantons and 221 communes.

Côtes-du-Nord, Côtes-d'Armor: the department of the Côtes-du-Nord was created in 1790. In 1990 its name was changed to Côtes-d'Armor.

Emsav: the loose network of regionalists, autonomists, nationalists, language militants and cultural activists who have questioned the relationship of Brittany with France.

hobereau: a minor, often poor, rural noble.

Loire-Inférieure, Loire-Atlantique: the department of the Loire-Inférieure was created in 1790. In 1957 its name was changed to Loire-Atlantique.

Lower and Upper Brittany: the western areas of Brittany in which Breton was spoken in the eighteenth century are often referred to as 'Lower Brittany' or 'Basse-Bretagne'; the French-speaking eastern areas as 'Upper Brittany' or 'Haute Bretagne'.

pardons: annual pilgrimages to local religious sites.

Prefect: since 1806 an official was appointed by the government to each of the French departments. The Prefect acted as an overseer for all legislation; he was a key official.

Abbreviations

ADCdA	Archives départementales des Côtes-d'Armor
ADF	Archives départementales du Finistère
ADI&V	Archives départementales de l'Ille-et-Vilaine
ADLA	Archives départementales de la Loire-Atlantique
ADM	Archives départementales du Morbihan
ALP	Action Libérale Populaire: a centrist Catholic grouping in the early twentieth century
AN	Archives nationales (Paris)
CELIB	Comité d'Etudes et de Liaison des Intérêts Bretons (The Breton Research and Liaison Committee): a well-organized cross-party lobbying organization, formed in 1951
FNC	Fédération Nationale Catholique: Catholic protest organization, formed in 1924 to campaign against a renewal of anti-clerical legislation
NA	National Archives (Kew)
n.d.	no date: i.e. the publication in question is undated
n.p.	no place: i.e. the publication in question does not include reference to its place of publication
PCF	Parti Communiste de France: the French Communist Party, created in 1920
PDP	Parti démocratique populaire: centrist Christian-Democratic party, founded in 1924
PSF	Parti Social Français: a far-right group, created in 1936
PUR	Presses Universitaires de Rennes
SFIO	Section française de l'Internationale Ouvrière: the French Socialist Party, created in 1905

UDB Union démocratique bretonne
UP   University Press

Dates of French political regimes

1789   The French Revolution: constitutional monarchy
1792   The Convention: creates the **First Republic**, based loosely on manhood suffrage
1795   The Directory: restricted suffrage, republican
1799   Napoleon's coup d'état
1804   **Empire:** plebiscite
1814   First **Restoration:** extremely restricted suffrage, constitutional monarchy
1815   Napoleon's Hundred Days
        Second **Restoration:** extremely restricted suffrage, constitutional monarchy
1830   July Revolution, creating liberal **Orleanist** monarchy: restricted suffrage
1848   **Second Republic:** manhood suffrage
1851/2 **Second Empire:** pseudo-democratic; authoritarian, Presidential rule
1870   **Third Republic:** manhood suffrage; chamber of deputies and a senate; weak, indirectly elected President
1871   Paris **Commune:** semi-socialist revolt in Paris, March–May 1871
1940   Collapse of the Third Republic following France's defeat by German forces
1946   **Fourth Republic:** universal suffrage; chamber of deputies and senate; weak, indirectly elected President

Introduction:
The Rocks of Brittany

My entry into Breton studies began during a holiday in Le Croisic, a lovely tourist port on the coast of the Loire-Atlantique. One afternoon, I stood by the quayside, watching the line of cars roll slowly along Le Croisic's one-way system. In the 1990s it was easy to identify where cars came from: each number plate included the departmental number. For the Loire-Atlantique, this was 44. Predictably, most of the cars that passed me came from this department. Less predictably, most of these cars also carried little black and white reproductions of the Breton flag, stuck next to their number plates. There is something strange about this: the Loire-Atlantique has not been part of the official, administratively recognized region of Brittany since 1941. So why did these drivers choose this emblem? It was not a legal requirement, unlike the GB sign on the back of my car. Moreover, there is no mass Breton nationalist movement in this area and it was unlikely that the dozens of cars that passed me were driven by die-hard nationalist militants.

This gesture of 'soft', informal nationalist sentiment intrigued me, and eventually led me to think in terms of an 'invisible nationalism': a nationalism not orientated around state or party, without clear, rigid structures, but which was nonetheless a visible presence in this little tourist resort.

Brittany today

Brittany is a land of old rocks, like the other western European peninsulas which push out into the Atlantic ocean. It contains abundant granite deposits, which were used by the ancient, pre-Celtic peoples to make the mysterious menhirs and dolmen, the megaliths and standing stones, which still mark its landscapes. These same stones also formed the raw materials for the sixteenth- and seventeenth-century sculptors who carved the calvaries and statues still to be found at crossroads and outside churches. Such is the prominence of these rocks that they have even been used to represent the people of Brittany. Nineteenth-century Parisian visitors were shocked when they met these people who were 'as silent and as grave as the granite calvaries among which they live', as noted by Emile Souvestre, one of the first Breton commentators to describe the region to outsiders.[1] Another prominent Breton writer and collector of folk tales, Anatole Le Braz, made a similar observation in a lecture given in 1888, in which he claimed that outsiders saw Brittany as a land beyond time, inhabited by 'a race of stone'.[2] Prehistoric people had left 'a granite book' in the Breton landscape, which was both incomprehensible and unreadable, noted the mid-twentieth-century writer, Charles Le Quintrec.[3] Some important aspect of the Bretons' culture and mentality seems to be contained in this tough, resistant granite.

The stones themselves have provoked comment from the waves of interpreters, militants and commentators who have tried to present, to understand and – sometimes – to exploit this intangible sense of what constitutes Brittany. Today's postcard stereotypes of tourist Brittany often focus on the theme of rocks and seas. They portray not the gentle, warm, sandy beaches of the sunny, sub-Orientalized French Mediterranean, but the harsh clash of wind, rock and wave, signifying – apparently – a clarity, even a rootedness which today's urban tourists seem to find absent from their cities. Brittany becomes an image as bright, as clean and as real as a toothpaste advertisement. Aside from these easy clichés of waves crashing against lighthouses, the ancient, pre-historic monuments certainly still provoke a sense of incomprehension and – perhaps – even wonder.

Until the eighteenth century the ancient menhirs and dolmen were usually ignored by academic and scientific researchers who worked within the paradigms of the classical, Latinate, heritage, which valued the written and the articulate over such non-literate expressions of cultures. By the nineteenth century, however, following Romanticism's challenge to this Enlightenment legacy, Brittany's prehistoric monuments had begun to attract attention. What were they? Who had carved them? What had been their use? What did they mean? 'Speak! Speak to me!' Abbé Mahé cried to the awe-inspiring plain of hundreds of giant, irregular rock pillars at Carnac (Morbihan).[4] Often there was much confusion about what these monuments represented. Perhaps the most curious response to the stones at Carnac came, according to local legend, during the Liberation of Brittany from German occupation in 1944. At this time there were many American soldiers in Brittany and they too visited Carnac. One day, local people noted a young American soldier staring critically at the field of stones: on his face was none of the wonder felt by

Abbé Mahé. Instead, he seemed to be examining the stones with a cool, technical eye. Intrigued, the locals approached him and asked him if he knew what he was looking at. 'Oh yes', was his prompt reply, 'this is an anti-tank emplacement'. These varied responses suggest some of the problems in providing simple, neat definitions of Brittany and the Breton people. We will see, again and again, how difficult it was for both external observers and internal participants to assess material, to define their terms, and to set their programmes. Like the American soldier facing the pre-historic stones at Carnac, the more certain they sound, the more misleading their observations. Something is certainly shifting in this land of sea, wind and granite, but grasping it, conceptualizing it and describing it is more difficult than might appear.

This work studies the development of an unusual form of social and cultural identity which has evolved in modern Brittany. Its development is based upon two historic failures: first, the failure of the French state to fully integrate the region of Brittany into the French nation and, secondly, the failure of Breton political groups to devise an effective form of Breton nationalism as a counter-discourse to oppose the French state's programme of integration. The final consequence of these two processes has not been an absence of a sense of identity, but what I have termed 'an invisible nationalism', a term to be explained more fully in the next chapter. This chapter introduces the context within which these failures occurred, firstly examining the issue of Breton integration into France, and then turning to the wider issue of the representation of Brittany within France. Interpretative issues are then discussed, and the chapter concludes with a brief history of ancient and medieval Brittany.

The idea that there has been a problem with the integration of Brittany into France may well come as a surprise to some readers. Certainly, there is little evidence of this in recent elections. Generally speaking, the few political groups that advocate the outright separation of Brittany from France do not stand candidates: if they did, there is every likelihood that their score would be infinitesimally small. The main political group that questions the relationship between Brittany and France is the UDB (Union Démocratique Bretonne). This organization does not advocate separation; instead it calls for Breton autonomy within France. Such groups normally consider contemporary Spain, with its mosaic of interlocking regions, as a suitable model for the French polity. However, even the UDB cannot boast great electoral successes, and it usually stands few candidates. At legislative elections its candidates normally win less than 10 per cent of the vote, and often less than 5 per cent, although such candidates have recently been more successful in both local and regional elections, gaining scores closer to 10 per cent in the 2004 regional elections.[5]

Recent elections provide little evidence of a deep Breton alienation from France. Does the historical record suggest anything different? The formal integration of the duchy of Brittany into the kingdom of France was implemented through an awkward set of negotiations that unfolded between 1488 and 1532, culminating in the two forced marriages of Duchess Anne of Brittany (with Charles VIII of France in December 1491, and with Louis XII of France in July 1499), and the Act of Union of August 1532, dictated by Francis I of France. Outside observers considered that the integration of Brittany into France would be unproblematic. Machiavelli, writing in 1509, noted the successes of Francis I in building up his kingdom. He acknowledged that there were some significant differences between the two polities, for instance they did not have similar customs, laws and languages. His conclusion, however, was optimistic: 'In a very short space of time, the new principality [i.e. Brittany] will be rolled into one with the old [i.e. France].'[6]

Writing over 350 years later, J. S. Mill came to a similar conclusion. His ideas reflected the easy synthesis of liberalism and nationalism which was frequently proposed by mid-nineteenth-century liberals. His general principle was that each nationality had a right to self-government. There were, however, exceptions. When advanced countries (such as France) faced small, backward countries (such as Brittany), then his general principle did not apply. Mill considered the options which were available to the ordinary Breton:

> Nobody can suppose that it is not more beneficial to a Breton . . . to be brought into the current of the ideas and feelings of a highly civilised and cultivated people – to be a member of the French nationality, admitted on equal terms to all the privileges of French citizenship, sharing the advantages of French protection, and the dignity and prestige of French power – than to sulk on his own rocks, the half-savage relic of past times, revolving in his own little mental orbit, without participation or interest in the general movement of the world. The same remark applies to the Welshman or the Scottish Highlander as members of the British nation . . . No Basse-Breton . . . has the smallest wish at the present day to be separated from France.[7]

The point to stress here is the certainty expressed in Mill's evaluation: on the one hand, the glories of an advanced civilization, on the other hand the half-savage sulking on his rocks. While respecting the principle of national self-government, it seemed self-evident that such considerations should be put aside when discussing an area like Brittany. Most nineteenth-century observers shared Mill's views: it seemed almost certain that Brittany would and should be integrated into the larger French polity. Today, after five centuries of French rule, there are signs which suggest that a type of disengagement with French nationhood is taking place in Brittany. The old certainties concerning an advanced, superior, French civilization offering a primitive and subordinate culture access to modernity no longer apply. This gradual disengagement is not expressed through the ballot box but through a range of cultural manifestations; one of the most prominent of these is probably the changing status of the Breton language.

This was another subject about which nineteenth-century observers felt certain. Whether with regret or with pride, they were almost unanimous in forecasting the demise of the Breton language. The language was dying, noted the great Republican historian Michelet in 1861, expressing some sorrow at this prospect.[8] But despite centuries of administrative and political integration, despite well-focused school-based campaigns in the nineteenth and twentieth centuries which – in part – aimed to ensure the replacement of Breton with French, this language has obstinately refused to exit. Current estimates of the number of Breton speakers vary enormously. The most optimistic recent estimate is that of 800,000 which the Communist daily *L'Humanité* seemed to pluck out from the air on 25 June 1999: in other words, about one fifth of the four million people living in the five Breton departments speak Breton. Fañch Broudic's more extensive research reaches a more cautious conclusion: he suggests that in 1997 there were 370,000 people in western Brittany who could understand Breton 'well' or 'very well', but that only 20,000 of these are 'dedicated users'.[9] Stefan Moal calculates that 8.5 per cent of the 4.1 million Bretons (B5) can speak Breton.[10] This confusion concerning the number of speakers is regrettable, but inevitable, since the French government refuses to include a question relating to language use on census forms, and all estimates rely on private research. Moreover, Breton is a marginalized language: it is notoriously difficult to design reliable tests for language competence in such tongues. The broad contours of the current situation, however, are clear. A significant minority of the Breton population still has some ability to use Breton.

No one could doubt, however, that throughout the twentieth century the number of Breton speakers was in rapid decline. In 1900 – approximately – almost half the population of Brittany spoke Breton. These speakers were principally located in the western areas: in the department of Finistère, and in the westerly cantons of Morbihan and the Côtes-d'Armor. This part of Brittany was often labelled 'Lower Brittany' or 'Basse Bretagne', and it was the daily use of the Breton language which served as the distinguishing mark that separated it from the residents of Upper Brittany, who either spoke French, or a Romance dialect, Gallo, which resembled French.[11]

It is possible that in the 1980s and 1990s the Breton language's decline was arrested, and perhaps even reversed. However, more important still, there has been a change in attitudes to the language. Fifty years ago, one could be reasonably sure that speaking the Breton language would almost be a source of shame for an individual, because it marked the speaker as old-fashioned and out-of-touch. Today, an increasing number of Bretons seem to view the Breton language as a source of pride: even if this statement needs to be qualified with the often repeated observation that 'the more they speak about it, the less they speak it.'[12] One important instrument for this turnaround has been the creation of the *Diwan* ('seed') network of Breton-language schools, which offer pupils an intensive, 'immersion' training in Breton before introducing them to French. This network was created in 1978, and now organizes some twenty schools with over two thousand pupils. It includes one *lycée* which prepares students for the all-important *baccalauréat*, normally taken at the age of eighteen, which marks the end of most pupils' schooling. To date, the *Diwan* schools have not benefited from any direct state funding.[13] Rather than asking the parents of their pupils to pay, each school is supported by a network of fund-raising institutions which ensure that these private schools remain free for their pupils. This network, however, is merely one expression of a far wider fascination with the non-French elements of Brittany's past: perhaps what is happening here is a variant on the 'three generations rule' whereby the grandchild tries to remember what the grandparent tried to forget. Even among those who do not speak Breton, there is a widespread sympathy for the language. Broudic's survey showed that 72 per cent of Bretons considered that Breton ought to be available to all pupils and 16 per cent thought that it should be compulsory in schools.[14] These figures are arguably more important than the debatable estimates of language use. Broudic's survey suggests that the Breton public doubts the core beliefs of French 'linguistic Jacobinism', whereby French is actively promoted as the language of the Republic.[15] While this new-found respect for the Breton language cannot be simply equated with Breton nationalism, it is an important indication of changing political and cultural attitudes in contemporary Brittany.

Another prominent Breton cultural assertion is in the field of music.[16] Breton – or Celtic – folk music has become astonishingly successful. After an initial period of experimentation by pioneering artists such as Alan Stivell in the late 1960s and early 1970s, there was a real, commercial, boom of interest and sales in the 1990s. This wave is given its most concrete representation through concerts and performances. Most Breton towns and even villages now hold regular *festoù-noz*: informal concerts of Breton dance music, in which participants perform traditional line and ring dances. Aside from the small, usually locally based *festoù-noz*, there are the bigger and more prestigious festivals. The pioneer of these is the Festival Interceltique (or 'FIL'), held annually at the port of Lorient (Morbihan) since 1971. From its beginnings as a small, traditional folk music festival, the event has grown each year. In 1999 it included fourteen separate stages, and was opened by a parade of three and a half thousand musicians, singers and dancers, who took four hours to pass through the streets of Lorient. During the festival itself, some four hundred thousand people listened to four and a half thousand musicians and singers.[17] The FIL has played some role in creating a sense of Celtic community, with visiting groups from Galicia, Scotland, Ireland, and Wales. A younger cousin to the FIL is the 'Vieilles Charrues' (Old Ploughs) festival, held in Carhaix (Finistère). Begun by students as a form of summer entertainment in the 1980s, this has grown into one of Europe's biggest music festivals, second only to the Glastonbury festival in size. In 1996 twenty thousand attended, and by 1999 over one hundred and fifty thousand were present. While the FIL is fairly solidly rooted in acoustic, traditional folk music, the 'Vieilles Charrues' is a festival for young people, and offers an eclectic mixture of rock, reggae and Celtic music at a very low price.

Many commentators are sceptical about the real significance of these big festivals and the associated wave of Celtic music. To some, these events can appear as clichéd and as unthreatening in their Celticism as the dire tartanry of the Scottish Kailyard tradition.[18] The thrust of these events is essentially non-verbal: the stress is on the *rhythm* of dance music, the *sight* of the parades, the *sound* of the songs. When lyrics are sung, they may be in Breton, French or English, but it would be difficult to be certain of the extent to which the audiences notice them, in whatever language they are sung. Therefore, argue sceptics, identifying the political or cultural significance of these festivals is difficult, if not impossible. What is certain, however, is the pride that the Breton people take in them. The FIL and the 'Vieilles Charrues', the *festoù-noz* and the *Diwan* school network are all signs of some significant shift in Brittany, and in particular of the relationship of Brittany to France. 'Brittany is trendy' notes Jean-Michel Le Boulanger,[19] and evidence for this can be drawn from the simple point that French people are now coming to Brittany, some as tourists or festival-goers, others as permanent migrants.

Some twenty-five thousand people moved to Nantes (Loire-Atlantique) between 1990 and 1999. Three of them, all migrants from Paris, were interviewed in *Le Monde*. They talk of the social misery, the stress and the pollution that they encountered in Paris. Nantes, on the contrary, appears to them to be a town which is 'big, but not too big'. Life is lived there at a slower pace. There are fewer contacts (i.e. e-mail and phone messages), and more real meetings. Nantes' disadvantages? The rain and, perhaps more worryingly, the uniformity of the population: less ethnic variety, and more 'people like us' – which appears to mean white. The demographic balance for the whole of Brittany (B4) during the 1990s shows the same positive pattern: some two hundred and thirty thousand people left the region, while three hundred and six thousand moved into Brittany. In particular, the demographic exchange between Brittany and Paris is now overwhelmingly in Brittany's favour. In the 1990s some one hundred and ten thousand Parisians left for Brittany (B4), while only about sixty-five thousand Bretons made the opposite journey.[20]

These cultural and political shifts have emerged towards the end of a long cycle of economic development. The Breton economy still includes a substantial agricultural sector, which provided 16 per cent of the region's jobs in 1999 (B4).[21] Despite the continuing Breton public loyalty to the ideal of the family farm, the process of agricultural modernization meant the concentration of farming on fewer people: in 1970 there were more than one hundred and fifty thousand farms in Brittany (B4), in 1988 there were ninety-two thousand, and by 2000 the number had reduced further to fifty-one thousand.[22] In 1999 Brittany (B4) produced 58 per cent of the pigs reared in France, 50 per cent of the chickens, 20 per cent of French milk products and 15 per cent of the cows.[23]

Brittany has also been at the leading edge of developments in the French telecommunications industry. In 1958, following lobbying by CELIB members, the prestigious Centre national d'études des télécommunications was located in Lannion (Côtes-d'Armor).[24] In January 2000, 45 per cent of French research in this area was based in Brittany; this included twelve training schools.[25] This 'hi-tech' edge of region become known locally as 'Trégor Valley'. This sector offered some of the highest salaries available to Breton workers, and though it was affected by the world-wide slide towards economic depression in the last quarter of 2001, it remained an impressive indication of the technological shift in the Breton economy.[26]

A scheme to label certain products as 'Produit en Breizh' (or, 'Made in Brittany') has also proved moderately successful. In 2001 there were 117 enterprises affiliated to this association, mainly drawn from the department of Finistère.²⁷ The lesson to draw here is obvious: Brittany sells; it has positive connotations for both Breton and French consumers.

The various trades connected with tourism are often necessarily seasonal, and many Breton industrial and commercial enterprises are significantly smaller than their French counterparts. These factors mean that salaries in Brittany are still noticeably lower than in France. In 2000 one study considering levels of pay ranked Brittany as the twentieth of the twenty-one official administrative regions of France. On average, Bretons earnt 9,000 francs per month, compared with a national average of 10,255 francs for French workers.²⁸

The easy assumption of French superiority, neatly captured in Mill's remarks (quoted above) concerning the savage Breton 'sulking on his rock', is clearly no longer valid. Indeed, at times one gets a sense that the cultural centre of France seems to be shifting, looking outward from Paris to Brittany as a model of conviviality and authenticity, or as a type of cure for the pathologies of modernity. While this has not been accompanied by a dramatic or statistically significant rise in Breton nationalism, there are more subtle signs of important changes in Breton political culture. One is the slow rise of left-wing parties in the region since the 1950s. Accompanying this are some distinctive political attitudes: Bretons are more likely to adopt pro-European Union attitudes than other French people, and significantly less likely to vote for the far-right *Front National*.²⁹

Birthplace and refuge

We will return to these themes in future chapters. For the moment, let us consider some of the most common ways in which Brittany has been represented within French culture over the past two centuries.

One persistent trend is for Brittany to appear as a type of beginning-point. Once one looks for these moments, it is astonishing how frequently they occur. Flaubert's *first* full-length text concerned his walking holiday in Brittany.³⁰ The name of Fortuné de Boisgobey is less well-known than that of Flaubert: however, in the late nineteenth century he was a popular novelist, who published some sixty novels. His first work was a collection of travel-writing texts (like Flaubert) concerning Brittany, which remained unpublished during his lifetime.³¹ Gauguin's *first* serious artistic studies depicted the sights of rural Brittany.³² The *first* novel of Balzac's remarkable literary cycle, the ninety-text *Comédie humaine*, is *Les Chouans*, which concerns the activities of Counter-Revolutionary guerrillas in Brittany during the French Revolution.

Significantly, Balzac presented in this novel a clear dichotomy between Brittany and the course of development followed by France: 'Brittany is like a coal which remains dark and black in the middle of a raging fire', he wrote.[33] Michelet's magnificent, lyrical introduction to the socio-cultural geography of France, his *Tableau de la France*, makes Brittany the subject of its *first* chapter. 'The eldest daughter of the [French] monarchy,' Michelet wrote of Brittany, 'our first study must be this Celtic province.'[34] Wyndham Lewis's *first* book-length work, his *Wild Body*, was a set of short stories: many of them were set in pre-1914 Brittany.[35] Literally translated, Finistère, the name of the most westerly Breton department means 'the end of the earth', but looking over what might appear a strange chain of coincidences, one wonders whether it might not be appropriate to reverse this term, and rather to think of Finistère as the *beginnings* of France, rather than as its end.

Of course, this list of 'firsts' is not a string of coincidences. One element in an explanation relates to Brittany's new-found nineteenth-century prestige as a 'Celtic' region: a point which will be explored more fully in the next chapter. For the moment, however, let us briefly consider how this 'Celtic' status might operate within the broader field of French culture. Writing of the relationship between Ireland and Scotland with England, Katie Trumpener has argued that

> English literature, so-called, constitutes itself in the late eighteenth and early nineteenth centuries through the systematic imitation, appropriation, and political neutralization of antiquarian and nationalist literary developments in Scotland, Ireland and Wales.[36]

Trumpener's work is an exhilarating combination of political analysis, cultural studies and literary scholarship; there are clearly some significant parallels between the processes which she identifies and the relationship between Brittany and France. Applying her ideas, we could suggest that the pioneering works listed above represent a form of colonial exploitation of Brittany's cultural resources. There are, however, also some important differences. The first of these can be stated quite bluntly: Brittany has never had a Walter Scott, nor France a Scott-land. No single author monopolized and then universalized the Breton experience as successfully as Walter Scott did for Scotland. While the authors listed above – Balzac, Flaubert, Michelet – certainly include some of the greatest names from the French literary-political canon, none of them became identified as *the* Breton author. Brittany's 'Celtic' status certainly attracted those searching for the origins of France (a point to be explored in the next chapter), but Brittany never acquired the same pivotal role in French literature which Trumpener ascribes to the UK's Celtic fringes.

Instead, our explanation for the activities of these literary tourists may be drawn from a simpler argument. In the nineteenth century, Brittany offered a young Paris-based writer or painter, a Boisgobey or a Gauguin, a *cheap* exoticism. While not as impressive as the distant Orient uncovered by the great travellers (such as Lamartine, Chateaubriand or Nerval), it was still satisfyingly different from the metropolis. Relatively unexploited, Brittany allowed a young writer the space to develop cultural and aesthetic reflections on the nature of modernity, of civilization and of community, without undertaking an expensive journey far from the Parisian centre.

When not a birthplace, Brittany has often featured in French history as a *refuge*. Indeed, even its very name was created as a result of a flight of refugees: during the fifth and sixth centuries groups appear to have left present-day Wales and Cornwall, probably pushed by Anglo-Saxon invasions from the east, to reach Brittany. The old Roman term Armonica vanished surprisingly quickly from written documents, to be replaced, initially, by 'Britannia'.[37] During the ninth century, as Irish-based Vikings attacked Britain's western shores, refugees once again fled southwards, over the Channel, to arrive in Brittany. In 1870, as France was attacked from the east by the Prussian army, military authorities considered a withdrawal west, into Brittany. During the mounting tension concerning the international situation in the late 1930s, the Breton writer Louis Guilloux felt relatively secure: surely Brittany would be safe from any future conflict with Nazi Germany?[38] In May and June 1940, as the German army advanced from north-eastern France, de Gaulle refused to accept that the military defeat of the French army was definitive. He considered the idea of re-grouping French military units in Brittany as a basis for an immediate fight-back. In the 1950s, Brittany became the chosen site for the popular Astérix cartoon series, featuring a plucky little Gaulish community who, alone, resisted the Roman invasion. These Gauls followed the druidic cult and were portrayed – albeit anachronistically – carving menhirs.

One simple point needs to be stressed about these clear, evocative images of birthplace and refuge: they do not only define Brittany in relation to France; their logic can also flow the other way, and actually define France in relation to Brittany. This type of two-way relationship will be explored frequently in the chapters that follow.

So far we have briefly evoked some attempts to portray or to conceptualize Brittany over the past two centuries: from granite rocks through anti-tank emplacements to the development of the French telecommunications industry, from sulking savages through beginning-place to refuge. One straightforward point can be drawn from these varied and contradictory images: a sense of the intensity of a debate. 'The Breton Question' has never been an innocent one; Breton 'exoticism' always implied an interrogation of the standard which was set by France as the 'norm', and defining Brittany always raised reciprocal questions about defining France. To return to the quotation from Balzac's *Chouans*, one can only notice the single dark coal by reference to the fire raging around it. Furthermore, there is a persistent dissident sub-strand in these debates, which significantly re-sets some of its terms. The idea of Brittany as the birth-place for France suggests that we are looking at something more complex than a banal process of polarized 'other-ing', in which Brittany supplies the shade to balance the light of France, the feminine opposed to a masculine France, and so on. Instead these themes suggest something closer to an asymmetrical but reciprocal process, a swirl of political cultures and cultural politics spinning between the two sites, Paris and Brittany, producing and re-creating identities for each of the partners.

Historiography: the idea of Brittany

A number of previously published works consider relevant themes concerning Breton history. These can be divided into four principal categories, plus one important sub-category.

Antagonistic-political

Contemporary Breton nationalism seems to possess a marvellous capacity to incite fury and indignation among critics. Two recent authors have been particularly virulent in their attacks. Neither is a professional historian, but in both cases their works raise issues relevant to the historical analysis of Breton identity.

The first of these is Maryon McDonald, whose *We are not French!* was published in 1989. As this work continues to structure and inform English-language debates concerning Brittany, it is worth considering this book in some detail. McDonald is an anthropologist who aimed to write a social-anthropological study of a contemporary ethnic grouping, the militant Bretons of the cultural-nationalist movement. Her work has some successful aspects: McDonald certainly has a gift for lively description, and this is one of the rare academic publications which has the capacity to make the reader laugh out loud. Such mirth, however, is cruel in nature; McDonald is aggressive and dismissive. The Breton movement is, she argues, a purely negative phenomenon, which 'requires external opposition against which to define itself'.[39] Militants live in a self-circumscribed 'world of intellectual creation';[40] they ignore the 'blunt fact' of the popularity of the French language.[41] They create a 'hollow unity, theoretical and abstract in origin'; this is 'pursued by the Celtic enthusiast, and [filled] with words and deeds, with birth, copulation, and death'.[42] The political cultures which such movements create are termed 'ethnic', but in reality they are no more than 'racialism'.[43]

In the last analysis, this argument eats its own tail. No consideration is given to the important occasions on which the discourse of Celticity has become more than a hermetic discourse of a minority of zealots. No explanation is given for why apparently well-educated, intelligent and caring people should be inspired by such a movement. In McDonald's eyes they are just mad or bad – or both. A glance at the publication date perhaps explains the origins of this analysis: 1989 was the high tide of Thatcherism. McDonald's aggressive and dismissive polemic resembles the attacks that the populist, right-wing press launched against the 'loony left' and the 'race relations industry'. It signifies a refusal to debate with those who stand outside the established political system, and a contempt for those who raise awkward questions about power, identity and oppression. The aim of the publication is to dismiss, not to understand.

Just occasionally, one finds that McDonald does act like a well-trained anthropologist. For example, there is a charming anecdote, at once eloquent and witty, in which McDonald relates that while living on a bilingual (French/Breton) farm, she noticed that the mother used Breton to speak to the dog, but French to the cat. When questioned, she explained that the dog was a farm dog, therefore a working animal, and to be treated like the other workers – so addressed in Breton. The cat, however, was a pet, and therefore to be addressed politely – in French.[44] Significantly, this example is presented merely as a footnote, and it demonstrates the most curious aspect of this book: how rarely McDonald writes as anthropologist. If nothing else, such scholars are supposed to feel some empathy for their subjects. One has to search very hard through this work's 330 pages to find any trace of empathy.

More recently, Françoise Morvan has voiced similar scepticism about Breton nationalists. Her work is entitled *Le Monde comme si* (2002) – the 'let's pretend' world, a phrase which echoes some of McDonald's views. Morvan, however, is a more serious and substantial critic. She is a Breton speaker, a participant in the *Diwan* movement, an author, a translator and an editor with an established record in the recovery of the Breton oral literature tradition. She has considerable inside knowledge of the movement she criticizes, and for that reason deserves to be taken more seriously than

McDonald. Morvan notes the reified nature of the new standard Breton language which is taught in the *Diwan* network, and the separation between the Breton militants and the mass of the population. She writes of the young Breton-speaking pupils who are far more likely to be radically hostile to the provision of Breton-language classes in schools than their French-speaking fellows and who, above all, wish to leave Brittany.[45] More than McDonald, Morvan stresses extremely strongly the involvement of Breton nationalists in collaboration with the Nazi occupation of France, a topic which will be discussed in chapter 8. She goes so far as to create a teleology around this theme, arguing that 'fascistic leanings' were inscribed in the Breton nationalist movement from its beginnings in the 1830s.[46]

However, her arguments have similar weaknesses to those presented by McDonald. We learn very little about what motivates this minority of nationalist militants, beyond one throw-away comment that they have created 'a lucrative business'. One can be absolutely certain that many militants could quite accurately reply that if they had wanted to get rich, they would not have chosen to learn Breton.

A quality which these two works share is their myopic concentration on a tiny minority of militants. At one point Morvan raises this as a question: how can such a small grouping have acquired such authority?[47] She intends this remark as a type of rhetorical flourish: because they attract so few followers, their actions must be illegitimate, and only a fool would take them seriously. But one can turn this question round. Why is it that so many Breton people have, in certain circumstances, shown sympathy for the themes propounded by the minority of militants? Why do the cars of Le Croisic have Breton stickers?

In a limited sense, Jack Reece's older work, *The Bretons against France* (1977) shared some of these faults. This book has none of the aggressive, polemical characteristics of the works by McDonald or Morvan: it presents a coherent and observant analysis of organized political tendencies. However, it has the same tendency to reduce Breton nationalism to the activities of small, formal, political groups. My intention is to interrogate this point more closely: I wish to question the extent to which such small organizations should be seen as central to the development of an identity movement.

French-neutralist

The dominant viewpoint within French historiography remains a Paris-centred, political perspective, in which a modernizing nation-state drags the rest of French society into modernity. Eugen Weber's *Peasants into Frenchmen* (1977) is probably the most articulate expression of this interpretation. Such analyses can be written on a smaller scale, in which the region is presented merely as a sub-section of a larger whole. Within Breton scholarship, Jacqueline Sainclivier's well-researched, detailed and informative works are the clearest example of this interpretation.[48] The idea that Breton society might, on occasion, be capable of acting with a limited autonomy is simply ruled out: issues of identity are ignored, often even submerged, beneath a wealth of statistical and empirical data. Such works also fit well into French university syllabuses, which usually demand that France is seen as a whole, and that therefore any smaller territory can only be approached as a sub-section. Political Breton nationalism is usually not confronted or criticized in such works: its relative lack of appeal means that it can simply be ignored.

Such works are certainly valuable sources of information, but they fail to consider important issues in the lived experience of many Bretons – issues which may well grow more important as France's national identity crisis grows more pronounced.

Breton-nationalist

It is easy to be dismissive of writers inspired by Breton nationalist ideals. To quote one example from my own experience: after giving a paper in which I rehearsed the extremely convincing evidence that – at most – about half the population of Brittany spoke Breton in the mid-nineteenth century, I was criticized by one listener who told me that she believed that the whole population must have spoken Breton. Morvan's taunt of the 'let's pretend' world certainly seems to make sense at such moments.

It is important to see the relative poverty of many Breton nationalist works in context. This is a movement without a strong academic base, beyond a foothold in some language departments. It lacks resources; there are few strong counter-institutions. Historical writing, which demands the slow, patient study of a broad selection of often quite intractable documents, is probably particularly unsuitable for this movement. Where the Breton nationalist movement has excelled is in some genuinely thought-provoking polemics. Works such as Morvan Lebesque's *Comment peut-on être Breton?* (1970) and Erwan Vallerie's *Nous barbares locaux* (1997), which combine both passion and insight into the Breton situation, are absolutely essential reading for a proper understanding of this region.

Furthermore, there is a genuinely academic fringe to the Breton nationalist movement, which forms the sub-category noted above. Jean-Jacques Monnier, who holds no university post, has written analyses of a complexity and depth to rival those produced by any professional historian: he may well be a unique figure. Alongside him are a series of academics with one foot in the world of the university and one in the Breton nationalist movement: people like Alain Croix, Michel Denis, Jean-Yves Guiomar and Ronan Le Coadic (see bibliography). The difference between nationalist and the academic is neatly illustrated by the contrasting definitions offered by Monnier and Denis of their subjects in their respective contributions to a work concerning Brittany's experience during the Second World War. Monnier, analysing Breton nationalist militants, writes of people who 'whether Breton or not, were conscious of the Breton identity and who worked to promote it in the cultural and/or political field.'[49] Denis, addressing a similar issue, produces a more nuanced definition of his subjects: 'those who refuse the pure and simple integration of Breton society into French territory, starting from the observation that [Breton] society has, at all levels, whether economic, political or cultural, particularities and specific interests to protect.'[50] The difference between the two may appear slight, but it is important: while Monnier proposes a single identity for his land, Denis's language is emphatically pluralistic; and while Monnier's vision is predicated on the idea of a putative nation, Denis holds to the more subtle concept of a society.

Inevitably, all these scholars can tell their own stories of how they suffer criticism from their two audiences. To the most militant they seem insufficiently committed, and to the wider academic world, they seem obsessed with a tiny, insignificant region. But something important emerges from these studies: a willingness to go beyond the easy answers of the French establishment and the Breton romantics, and a questioning of the previous myths of identity. It seems likely that works produced by such scholars may well grow in importance in succeeding decades. Brittany, for so long dismissed as a mere periphery to French power and dynamism, may now assume a different role: a privileged observation post, from which to watch and analyse the painful decline of a once-proud French nationalism.[51]

Interactionist

The most inspiring historical analysis of Breton society to date is Caroline Ford's *Creating the Nation in Provincial France* (1993): I see my own work as a development of Ford's original research. The key point which I draw from this earlier work is the concept of an interaction between Brittany and France. Here, Breton identity is not analysed as created by itself, in a process of immaculate Celtic conception, or simply through a refusal of outside interests. Instead, there is a dialogue – even if, at times, it resembles what the French call *un dialogue des sourds*, a dialogue between the deaf. Moreover, Ford is scrupulous in noting the rationality and even the humanity of the actors involved in this historical cycle: like E. P. Thompson in *The Making of the English Working Class*, she seeks to rescue the poor, be-clogged, Breton-speaking Catholic clerical rioter from 'the enormous condescension of posterity'.[52] She explains that she wishes to study the process 'by which individuals and social groups define and redefine themselves'.[53] Furthermore, Ford's work concentrates on popular culture: the great battles of church and state only matter *if* they acquire some real, popular resonance.

The only significant flaw in *Creating the Nation* is the manner in which the subject matter is framed. Ford's entry point is through the politics of religion, and the book is oriented around the clash between church and state, Brittany and Paris in 1902–5. In adopting this approach, Ford firstly underestimates the importance of a regionalism – maybe even merely a proto-regionalism – which had developed in Brittany during the nineteenth century, and of which the clashes were merely one episode. Secondly, Ford's work fails to consider some more long-term consequences of the early twentieth-century clashes, principally the development of political nationalism and other forms of protest politics. My work seeks to add this longer, wider dimension to Ford's original insights, through the analysis of the history of concepts of Brittany.

At first sight, this may sound like a type of intellectual history, centred on great novels and sophisticated political analyses. Only a few people have expressed their ideas of what constitutes Brittany in coherent, published forms: a work which concentrated on these rare books would certainly be an example of intellectual history. My areas of interest are different: I seek to examine how Bretons have represented themselves in great, popular expressions of identity.[54] These are discussed principally in chapters 4, 5 and 6; they are primarily the religious *pardon* and the Republican (or liberal) political festival. Records of these events provide coherent documentation concerning wider social and cultural attitudes which are relevant to the evolution of concepts of Brittany. Thus this work will certainly examine the key theorists of Breton politics, but it will constantly contextualize them within the wider sphere of popular culture.

Brittany: a summary history

Choosing a point at which to begin a historical narrative is always awkward. Aside from the obviously arbitrary nature of any chosen date, there is the other, more subtle point that different topics evolve at different rhythms, and that as histories evolve, it is almost as if they circle round their own pasts, in millennia-long spirals, which throw distant epochs into contact with each other. Maupassant once fell into conversation with a Breton peasant and found that he talked of Caesar as if he had met him earlier on the same day.[55] Something similar has happened in this work. The formal beginning of the narrative could be dated to the mid-eighteenth-century revival of interest in Celtic identities marked by the publication of – in England – William Stukeley's *Stonehenge, A Temple Restor'd to the British Druids* (1740), in France Simon Pelloutier's multi-volume *Histoire des Celtes* (1740–50) and in Scotland the three volumes of MacPherson's *Ossian* (during the 1760s). More directly significant than any of these works, however, was Jacques Cambry's *Voyage dans le Finistère* (1799): a work which synthesized eighteenth-century scholarship into a distinct sense of Breton particularity. The formal end of this narrative is marked by the creation of CELIB in 1951. The issues covered in this study, however, range far more widely in time. Like Maupassant, we will listen to both earlier and later voices.

In this section I will provide an introduction to some key themes in ancient and medieval Breton history.

Prior to the arrival of the Romans, the Gaulish (or Celtic) peoples living in the area we now know as France were grouped into sets of rudimentary social networks.[56] One of these stretched along the north-west coastline of France, from the estuary of the Loire to the estuary of the Seine. According to Roman sources, this region was termed 'Aremonica', meaning the area facing the sea. Like other Celtic communities, its decentralized economy was principally agricultural, with a small warrior-aristocracy. There were no towns, but some temporary fortified camps and a few permanent settlements. Its people have left no written records: they were probably almost entirely illiterate. Its craftsmen produced metalwork that echoed the swirling, intricate beauty of the style which has since been labelled 'La Tène', and which has been seen as a distinctive sign of Celtic civilization.

The Roman advance into Gaul started in the second century BC, with the first Roman victories in the south. Julius Caesar then led the Roman advance north in 58 BC. There was no protracted military campaign in the western regions, beyond a major naval battle in the Bay of Quiberon in 56 BC. Instead, Roman rule was implemented and institutionalized through the development of a new elite, who built villas and dealt in cattle. Their rule led to some significant changes in the area; the peninsula's economy was integrated into the wider Roman economy. The three major Roman roads, running east–west, were the region's most important routes before the *routes royales* designed by the duc d'Aiguillon in the eighteenth century. There was little attempt to impose either Roman religions or languages on the natives, but Roman customs possessed all the prestige of an elite culture. During the period of Roman occupation there were some minor rebellions, which were repressed with the help of mercenary soldiers from mainland Britain.[57] In the third century AD the Roman occupation ended as it began: there was no dramatic battle, but a gradual withdrawal of soldiers and resources out of the peninsula. Evidence suggests that the withdrawal was accompanied by a commercial collapse. In the same period new walls were built around the small towns of Rennes, Vannes and Nantes, suggesting a fear of attack.

The following centuries are among the most confused in Breton history: the absence of coherent written sources means that there is little reliable evidence. Discussing the reasonably convincingly demonstrated migration of refugees from Britain over the Channel to the peninsula, Henri Hubert, one of the greatest of French Celtic scholars, remarked that: 'the history of Celtic Brittany is even vaguer than that of the emigration. Legend tells more about it than history.'[58] Another illustration of this absent evidence can be drawn from the history of Quimper. In the third century AD a small Gallo-Roman town existed on the left bank of the Odet. In the tenth century, another settlement was present on the right bank of the Odet, at the confluence of the Steir and the Frout. What had happened to the previous settlement? Why did it decline? What was its relation to the later settlement? There are still no clear answers to these questions.[59]

Important questions concerning post-Roman Brittany also remain unanswered. What language did the indigenous peoples speak in this period? A variant of Gaulish: in other words, a Celtic tongue? Or one of the many European derivations from Latin? What was their religion? The new immigrants probably came from present-day Wales and Cornwall, and they brought with them Celtic dialects, Christianity and – eventually – the name of 'Brittany', which was in use by the sixth century.[60] Whether their entry into the peninsula should be understood as a military occupation, or as the peaceful establishment of a new group in an almost empty land, or as the more-or-less happy fusion of two similar peoples is again unclear. The numbers of colonists and their social status are not known; certainly, groups of soldiers were prominent among them. No new central administration developed in the area; instead, it was divided between several rival chiefs.

Different Celtic dialects spread across the peninsula: some linguistic evidence suggests that it was northern Brittany that was most strongly influenced by the newcomers.

Meanwhile, to the east, a new power was developing. The Carolingian Empire dominated those areas that now constitute northern France and Germany, and it seemed probable that Brittany would quickly be incorporated into this new entity. Military expeditions against Brittany, directed by Charlemagne (768–840), took place in 786, 799 and 811, but did not achieve a decisive result. The rival Breton chiefs led several small revolts and so, in 830, Nomenoë was sent to pacify the region by Louis the Pious, one of the kings in Charlemagne's empire. This decision had some far-reaching consequences: in designating an area to be controlled, Louis had also produced 'the formal recognition of Brittany as a single political entity for the first time'.[61] However, the project back-fired. Taking stock of the area under his control, in 843 Nomenoë instead decided to lead a Breton revolt against Carolingian authority. His forces quickly seized the major towns of Nantes and Rennes. Fighting between the two powers continued into the 860s, to be ended only when the threat of Viking incursions set both rulers other priorities. The area loosely controlled by the Breton duchy actually expanded in the succeeding years, to reach its maximum size in 866.

One must not understand these early medieval conflicts as marking the birth of the Breton nation. Instead, these messy, opportunistic conflicts were largely apolitical battles for power and prestige, fought out by warrior elites who had no meaningful support from the mass of the population. To some extent, Charlemagne and his successors could be seen as possessing some type of political consciousness. They were inspired by their distorted interpretation of the Roman legacy, and so wished to act to implement some form of legal and political unity on their territories. But, like all medieval rulers, their powers were severely limited by a simple lack of resources: lack of trained administrators, lack of professional soldiers, lack of educators, lack of literate supporters . . . One could read back into these conflicts the vague, distant origins of present-day cultures of identity, but there was no equivalent, among either Carolingians or Bretons, of a sense of nationhood. Wendy Davies's neat phrase is probably the best available description of the irregular patchwork of local authorities which constituted early medieval Brittany: 'a range of miscellaneously controlled territories'.[62]

With establishment of the duchy of Brittany in the tenth century, feudalism developed in the region. As elsewhere in Europe, this system was based on a decentralized network of warrior-aristocrats, each owing various services to the duke, and each in turn demanding customs and services from their followers. By the late twelfth century there were about forty great nobles in Brittany, and several thousand minor nobles. These nobles were usually French speaking, and their courts tended to imitate the chivalric values which were set by the French courts to the east. Many of them participated in William the Conqueror's invasion of England: in 1086, about a tenth of English land was owned by Breton nobles.[63]

In the tenth and eleventh century the question of Brittany's relationship to the power of the French monarchy continued to provoke conflict. Breton rulers only ever claimed the status of 'duke', and they recognized the French king as a superior power. As Michael Jones notes, Brittany was only 'a partly independent duchy'; it remained 'somewhat apart' from France.[64] French royal ordinances applied in Brittany; the Breton courts were subordinate to the highest French court, the *parlement* in Paris. Significantly, the business of administration and politics was carried out in French and Latin. Jones cites a telling example to illustrate the status of the Breton language in the fourteenth century. For the *whole* of that century, only two examples of written Breton have been preserved: a six line scatological poem, and an official report which quotes two phrases to illustrate slogans shouted during a riot in Vannes.[65] Defence of the duke's powers against the political advances of the French monarchy could be seen as the first, primitive, expression of 'an explicit Breton political ideology'.[66] The two powers drew up rival histories which, following the dream-like fantasies which dominated medieval historiography, put forward competing claims of their Trojan origins. (We will return to this point in the next chapter.)

The factor which probably saved medieval Brittany from French domination was the rival power of the English monarchy, and its interests in Gascony (in south-west France). Brittany, with the port at Brest, was a vital staging-post for ships sailing from England to the south. For several centuries, Breton rulers were able to play off the interests of the two great monarchs against each other. Brittany was largely neutral during the conflicts of the Hundred Years War. Moreover, Bretons themselves were actively involved in maritime trading, taking salt and canvas to England, and so established cross-Channel links. As this commerce grew, so the urban centres of Brittany developed: by the fifteenth century Nantes and Rennes both had populations of between thirteen and fourteen thousand. In 1434 building began on a magnificent new cathedral in Nantes, and in 1461 the city became the site for the first Breton University.[67]

In the fourteenth and fifteenth centuries, with a population of about three-quarter of a million people, the duchy of Brittany began to develop some of the attributes of a modern state.[68] Its capital was Nantes. Duke Jean III drew up a series of constitutional regulations in 1334–41. Some aspects of these regulations appeared distinctively different from French practices, due in part to the English influence on Breton politics. Regular meetings of a representative political structure, the Estates of Brittany, had begun. In 1441, there was a Breton Concordat with the Pope. A small permanent army, controlled directly by the ruler, had also been formed.

This bundle of political and constitutional practices survived surprisingly well after the enforced unification with France (1532). Early modern France was still a federation of provinces rather than a unified nation. Brittany continued to possess its provincial administration, based on the Estates, which represented the church, the nobles and the biggest towns. The mass of the rural population was entirely unrepresented. These Estates successfully protected the province from many French royal taxes, including the *gabelle* salt tax. (These points are discussed in more detail in chapter 2.) The economic growth of the late medieval period continued, with the coastal areas in particular expanding. However, even in the seventeenth century, Brittany was not yet 'an integrated economic unit'.[69]

How should we characterize the cultural identity of this fast-changing region? Many commentators have unquestioningly assumed that the phrase 'Celtic' is the most apt description of its cultural identity. Wendy Davies, in her well-researched monograph on a tenth-century Breton community, sounds a note of caution: 'they do not look distinctively Celtic (or Frankish) and will have shared as many characteristics with cereal-growing communities throughout western Europe'.[70] We will return to this point in the next chapter.

The chapters that follow are divided into two parts. The first, 'Making Brittany', surveys the intellectual, political and cultural debates concerning the status of the region within the French nation-state. An essential step in this process was the political and social experience of the French Revolution (chapter 2). However, the main focus of these chapters is the intellectual and cultural developments which led to a coherent image of Brittany. The second part, 'Ruling Brittany', analyses the rival attempts of organized interest groups – the church, the state and political parties – to direct the region. This is a cruder process of power politics, and for this reason we will turn away from printed texts to examine government initiatives and popular culture.

PART I

Making Brittany

1

The Question of French Nationhood: Celts, Romans and Bretons

A brief guide to walks in Brittany, published by the weekly *Nouvel Observateur*, starts with the comment that 'the spirit of the Celts is still alive here'.[1] Such observations are typical of the manner in which Brittany is treated in today's tourist literature, and they have become so common that they do not seem to merit comment. In fact, such naive observations are the product of sustained and complex historical developments. For these reasons, it is worth making explicit some implications of the *Nouvel Observateur's* observation. First, this 'Celtic' quality is clearly seen as something positive and attractive about Brittany. It is – presumably – also something that distinguishes the region from the rest of France. Secondly, however, it is principally identified as a 'spirit' [esprit]: an intangible and unseen quality, which is to be *felt* by the individual visitor, rather than a quality which is made manifest in – for example – a building or a painting. Lastly, this quality is automatically linked to a past: it is 'still' [toujours] present in Brittany.

These ideas are a by-product of the process of national identity-formation in France. Often, France is seen almost as a textbook example of a successfully unified polity: from the Jacobins in the 1790s to de Gaulle in the 1960s, leading French political actors have stressed the virtues and the necessity of national unity. When we consider the specific issue of the relationship of Brittany to the French polity, however, we can note some of the inconsistencies and contradictions inherent in the process. In particular, 'the Celtic' proved to be a particularly awkward component to integrate into French national culture.

Before discussing this point further, we will first consider the formation of national identity in Europe.

Nations, nationality and nationhood

Most of us live within the structures of nation-states. For this reason, it is often difficult for us to see what is distinctive about them as they have become 'normal' features of our mental and cultural landscapes. Before considering recent debates on the nature of nationhood, let us start by briefly noting the perspectives of two outsiders.

Rabindranath Tagore (1861–1941) was an Indian radical who was concerned that India would merely imitate and adopt the structures of the west; nationalism in particular worried him. He produced a number of thought-provoking definitions of nationalism.

> A nation, in the sense of the political and economic union of a people, is that aspect which a whole population assumes when organized for a mechanical purpose. Society as such has no ulterior purpose. It is an end in itself ...
> The Nation ... is the organized self-interest of a whole people, where it is least human and least spiritual.[2]

For Tagore, the concepts of nationalism and nationhood represented the most mechanical, materialist and undesirable aspects of western culture.

Frantz Fanon (1925–61) was a psychiatrist from the French Caribbean who became a leading member of the Front de Libération Nationale – the revolutionary organization which fought for the liberation of Algeria from French colonialism from 1954 to 1962. He took a far more positive view of nationalism. For Fanon, it allowed the transition from an unthinking condition into lucidity. Nationalism, according to Fanon, has an ability to clarify, to awaken and to liberate.

> The developing conscience of the entirety of a people is the living expression of the nation. It is a coherent and enlightened praxis of men and women. [Nationalism is] the collective construction of a destiny, it is the acceptance of the responsibility of history.[3]

Therefore, nationalism, for Fanon, is the achievement of a type of political adulthood.

Both writers treat nationalism as a powerful form of mass organization, but while Fanon welcomes nationalism's political potential as an instrument of liberation, Tagore warns of its dangers. These two distinct views, which respectively applaud and criticize the concepts associated with nationalism, alert us to some of the complexities of this topic.

Over – approximately – the past two decades, the linked topics of the nation, nationhood and nationalism have been the subject of a long-running interdisciplinary debate that has stimulated some immensely valuable contributions, of which Benedict Anderson's *Imagined Communities* is one of the most significant. In recent years, despite Fanon's evocations of 'lucidity', the debate seems to have grown uncertain, with each new work announcing in turn that it is difficult to provide comprehensively applicable definitions and concepts. One reason for this is obvious: nationalism has radically different meanings for different people; it is a contested concept. However, more significantly, it seems possible that the concept itself is inherently contradictory, at once 'obscure and obvious' according to Michael Billig.[4]

Within this work we will be encountering four types of nationalism which, while distinct, also overlap with each other. The paragraphs which follow identify each of these forms by certain key characteristics which can be seen as Weberian 'ideal types'. It is not my intention in this section to provide watertight definitions, encyclopaedic surveys or definitive analyses of the many manifestations of nationalism, but merely to note and to explore the simple point that nationalism has a history, and that it grows and develops.[5]

Type A: Republican nationalism

This is the form of nationalism identified by most of the leading researchers as the first fully-formed version of modern nationalism.[6] Anderson locates its genesis in the eighteenth-century revolt of South American colonies against imperial Spain.[7] John Breuilly considers similar movements which developed in early modern England and France as a platform for opposition to the absolute monarchies.[8] In a more compact review essay, Stuart Woolf raises the intriguing possibility that perhaps the first successful prototype nationalism may be that which arose among Greek rebels in the Ottoman Empire in the 1820s.[9] There is no need here to attempt to assess which (if any) of these theses is correct; instead, we can note some common features. Each identifies a self-consciously oppositional movement, that attempts to mobilize the bulk of the population against a ruling elite which is portrayed as illegitimate, corrupt and sometimes also as alien. The vocabulary of classical Republican virtue comes easily to these young radicals: they imagine a world of austere, noble-minded people, linked by transparent bonds of community, whether or not they envisage a Republican political constitution as their goal. A second, linked, key concept is that of fraternity. These young patriotic radicals typically present themselves as brothers, engaged in a struggle against an iniquitous patriarchal authority.[10] Questions of ethnicity, of identity and of the legitimacy of a future national authority seem either irrelevant or easily solvable at this stage in nationalism's growth: any political problems can safely be blamed on the existing oppressive power; the nation faces forward, and nationalism writes in the future tense.

Type B: state nationalism

After a period of glorious and impetuous youth, nationalism reaches its corpulent middle years. Whether created by the state enlarging its power over an initially apathetic society – recall Massimo d'Azeglio's famous comment 'We have made Italy, now let us make Italians' – or by a spirited minority pushing and re-moulding a state into the form of a nation, this is now an official state-movement. To varying degrees, it is a *compulsory* nationalism: a nationalism usually based on passport, flag, national anthem, mass conscription and school curriculum. When this process is implemented effectively, nationalism becomes part of daily 'common-sense', and even words as simple as 'we' or 'here' become vehicles for a sense of nationhood.[11] Historians tend to cite Britain and France as the principal examples of this form of nationalism, with Italy and Germany representing slightly different and later variants of the same. At its best, this movement is broad and inclusive. It promises equal rights to all members of the new national community. Previously marginalized groups can be offered access to this space: in France, young women become state schoolteachers, in Germany patriotic women's groups were formed.[12] A similar process is initiated among ethnic minorities who, as J. S. Mill pointed out, are offered the chance to exchange their lonely rocks for entry into a modern community (see introductory chapter). This communitarian aspect of nationalism also has an important role in compensating for some of the socially dislocating effects of early industrialism.[13]

To date, these first two types of nationalism together form a standard model of national development. In the twentieth century, however, two significant variant forms of nationalism emerged.

Type C: hyper nationalism

Among these patriots, the strength and nature of attachment to the nation varied. A dissident strand of nationalism emerged in the late nineteenth century, which proposed national unity as the over-riding political value, and which went on to conceptualize the nation-state as an independent being, with rights of its own over the individual and over other communities within the nation. Such ideals were expressed powerfully in the writings of the Italian fascists.

> The nation is not simply a sum of individual beings, nor is it an instrumentality of parties for attaining their own goals. It is rather an organism made up of an endless stream of generations whose individual members are but transient elements. It is the supreme synthesis of the material and immaterial values of the race ... Fascism reasserts the rights of the State as expressing the real essence of the individual.[14]

Such ideas imply the effective collapse of the private sphere. Fascism used the concept of the closed national community as an ideological instrument to identify and then to stigmatize outsider groups. The logic of domination, exclusion and extermination was an intrinsic and necessary aspect to this authoritarian conceptualization of the nation: the systematic racist violence of the Third Reich was a logical consequence of such thinking.

Type D: neo-nationalism

In recent decades a fourth variant on the nationalist theme has emerged. Any judgements on this new form have to be provisional, for in areas such as Wales, Catalonia, Brittany, Palestine and Kabylie this form of nationalism is still developing and changing. Quite possibly, in future years, it may be necessary to unpack this parcel further and re-classify its tendencies more exactly. However, neo-nationalism has two distinguishing features. First, it expresses a rebellion of a minority against an already-formed nation-state. It therefore immediately suggests problems or short-comings in the Type B nationalism outlined above. Indeed, in the hands of a master-analyst such as Tom Nairn, neo-nationalism provides a uniquely privileged vantage point through which to understand and evaluate the older state-nationalism.[15] The simple existence of a Type D nationalist movement raises fundamental questions about the status of the nation: for example, if Spain is a nation-state, can Catalonia exist as a nation within this structure? The Spanish government's solution to this problem has been to define Catalonia, the Basque Country, Galicia and other regions as 'autonomous communities' within the Spanish nation.

Significantly, Erwan Vallerie, a skilful, articulate Breton nationalist militant, explicitly argues against the sloppy, polemical rhetoric which proclaims that Brittany today forms a nation. He argues that without any institutional or political vehicle to express this sense of nationhood, Brittany cannot yet be categorized as a nation. However, Vallerie concedes one might logically state that Brittany has a 'vocation' to become a nation.[16]

The second distinctive feature of neo-nationalism is its self-reflective dimension. This is because all neo-nationalists must go through the process of presenting a case for their re-configuration of existing national identities. This normally involves portraying their new national identity 'as a community with which individuals can identify': a claim which, of course, implies that such individuals experience some significant difficulty in identifying with the existing nation-state structure.[17] Many are inspired by the struggles for national liberation by colonies, and even aspire to the achievement of a 'post-colonial' autonomy. Often this is understood in a metaphorical rather than a literal sense, meaning the shedding or transcendence of feelings of inferiority towards the central power.[18] While some neo-nationalists put forward absolute claims as sweeping as any put forward by previous generations of nationalists, they are usually accompanied by others who present a more considered discourse, often specifying how their claim to full nationhood is qualitatively different from previous claims, and how therefore it will avoid the problems associated with the older national forms. Indeed, at times this strand of neo-nationalism seems closer to a post-nationalism which transcends the limits of older concepts of nationhood.

There is a conceptual problem with all four descriptions of nationalism outlined above. Each of them resembles a description of a bicycle: we learn that the wheels are so big, there are so many gears, the metal used is composed of these elements, the brakes work thus; but we are not told that if you sit on the bike in the right manner, and push down on the pedals correctly, it moves. Alongside its many other qualities, nationalism is above all a dynamic, which is powered by the support of individuals. In other words, it only exists because it has some strong appeal, on an individual basis, to significant sectors of the population. For example, when Peter Burke writes that Europe is an idea, rather than a place, he is implying that individual Europeans need to make a specific effort to re-think their understanding of the place in which they live, in order for the concept to have any validity.[19] Smith is most convincing and most challenging when he asks why nations 'generate so much passion and such strong attachments'.[20] His answer is to suggest that nationalism draws its strengths from pre-modern, ethnic roots: a response which, as we will see, raises more questions than it answers. Smith is, however, correct to stress that this second, individual-emotional aspect of nationalism may well be expressed through symbolic, rather than explicit, forms of discourse, for this is an arena in which the symbolic constitutes 'a central component of identity creation and maintenance'.[21]

There are therefore two hubs to nationalism: a political-institutional dimension, normally or ideally based in the institutions of the state, and a subjective, psychological, cultural dimension, located initially within the consciousness of each motivated individual, and then structured according to the larger contexts of class and community, gender and ethnicity. Fanon noted the importance of both these aspects when he wrote that 'nationhood does not exist except insofar as it is present in the programme elaborated by a revolutionary leadership and consciously and enthusiastically taken up by the masses'.[22] It is the shifting relationships between these two aspects that gives nationalism its distinctive range of different variants and its different cultural and political stresses, for even within the four forms outlined above, one can encounter significantly different combinations of state direction and individual participation. This second aspect is particularly important for research on Breton identity politics as, for most of the past five centuries, Brittany has lacked strong centralized political institutions.

Few researchers have considered this second element. Prominent among this small group who debate the psychology of nationalism is William Bloom, who uses elements from psychoanalytic theory to identify the process through which first individual and then group identities are formed. Bloom's argument is that this process of identification is intrinsic to all forms of social existence: it is 'a prerequisite for an "adult" participation in society'. Nationalism represents a new stage in this process but, like other more elementary forms of identification, it becomes deeply rooted in the psyche of each individual. Events which challenge this bond are serious: they are experienced as 'a threat to survival'.[23]

Jean Bethke Elshtain speculates on some of the political consequences of the psychological bond expressed through nationalism. Like Tagore, she notes the mechanical and anti-humanist aspects of nationhood, and she argues that the constellation of values associated with modern nationalism are most clearly revealed in moments of war. Nationalists normally manipulate images of a female mother country: 'the nation is home and home is mother'. These bonds are immensely powerful. 'The child's will-to-sacrifice flows from embodied ties to both parents that project outward into a more generalized relationship to a feminized mother land, a masculine sovereign state.' Elshtain realizes the futility of simply trying to imagine away the nation, but speculates that we can reform nationalism by moving towards a 'post-sovereign politics'.[24]

Elshtain's and Bloom's arguments are interesting in their own right: however we should, provisionally, note one shortcoming. Bloom and Elshtain tend to assume a static model: children are socialized into the forms of national discourse of their parents. What of migrants? What of those living in 'new' nations? And, more relevant to us, which factors might lead a group to disengage from one particular form of nationalism, in order to participate in another? We will return to these questions in later chapters.

As Benedict Anderson perceptively argues, nationalism is not another political ideology, like marxism or liberalism. Instead, in the period from approximately 1850 to 1950, it acted as a foundation for all modern political ideologies, it formed the space within which they developed, and it contributed to the vocabulary that they exploited.[25] Even if we can today begin to debate globalization's potential to transcend the national, such ideas are still merely rudimentary, for the nation has not yet died. The potential combination of a strong exterior authority and a vibrant, personal desire to participate makes the nation one of the most powerful political concepts created in recent history. Unlike many modern political ideologies, successful nationalisms normally exert a tremendous power directly within daily life. They provoke the 'politicization of culture':[26] banal elements of ordinary existence can be called into question. Activities such as speech patterns, music, dress and leisure can become invested with intense political significance.

A further important aspect of the process of nation-building is the construction and elaboration of a narrative of national history.[27] In the preliminary Type A version of nationalism these are heroic stories designed to rouse an often apathetic population to action; in Type B state-nationalism they become the basis for history lessons in the school curriculum. Schöpflin's comments neatly capture the potential importance of memory to forms of nationhood: 'A society without memory is blind to its own present and future, because it lacks a moral framework into which to place its experiences.'[28]

The question of the origins of France

Within France, national historians have faced a particular dilemma: is France to be situated as one of the 'Latin' nations? The concept of 'Latin' can carry a variety of meanings. It can refer back to the imperial legacy of the Roman Empire: significantly, French colonial literature on Algeria often noted parallels between the actions of the French and Roman civilizations.[29] It can also refer to an intellectual tradition which privileges individual, rational thought, as exemplified by the intellectual tradition of the eighteenth-century Enlightenment. Voltaire, for example, considered that France had taken on Rome's role as an intellectual centre for the world.[30] Religious qualities can also be invoked: within Catholic cultures, France is frequently proudly referred to as 'the church's eldest daughter', meaning that France was the first major country to convert to Catholicism. Lastly, reference to the Latin tradition can be used to imply some quality of biological, racial or ethnic inheritance: a point frequently made by Charles Maurras, the theoretician and leader of the proto-fascist group, Action Française.

These 'Latinists' were usually quick to assert that 'Latinity' represented a type of unbroken bond, connecting France directly with the glories of the Roman world. However, such arguments ignore significant shifts in French cultural identity.

Medieval monarchs throughout Europe only had extremely vague ideas about the cultural or ethnic identity of their realms, and made little attempt to manipulate or manufacture identities. The concept of the nation was occasionally used in a sentimental or symbolic manner to signify a common birthplace, but it was never used to represent a unified polity.[31] However, as part of the oft-started process of creating a more coherent, more centralized polity, monarchs did understand the use of history as a propaganda tool. In particular, there was a common pride among European medieval rulers in being able to claim that their kingdom was the repository of Roman traditions, as the Roman Empire still set the archetype for rule and organization. The continuing domination of this legacy can be seen in the practices of the Church: during the medieval period, Church Latin continued to be the only language which could be understood across Europe.[32]

A series of historical *Chroniques* were produced in France from the thirteenth to the sixteenth centuries. The first series was written by Benedictine monks, while the later series were produced by secular bureaucrats.[33] They portrayed French history as a saga dominated by the actions of kings, assisted by the barons and princes who were the only market for these fantastically expensive manuscripts. On the question of the origins of France, these *Chroniques* were unanimous in following an idea which originated in the eighth century. They could not claim that the origins of their country were to be found in early Rome. However, the French ruling aristocracy, drawn largely from the descendants of Frankish invaders of the fifth century, claimed that they originated from the Trojans. This claim seemed to function within medieval historiography as an acceptable substitute for a Roman inheritance. It therefore established a form of political and social legitimacy, based on the idea that a successful conqueror had the right to rule a beaten country.

This paradigm began to be challenged in the sixteenth century. In part, this was simply a result of Renaissance scholarship, which produced a better knowledge of Latin texts, particularly of Julius Caesar's *De Bello Gallico*. The arguments concerning France's Trojan origins, as put forward by the *Chroniques,* were no longer credible. Furthermore, the spread of the printing press meant that historical works could circulate among a far larger audience than kings and aristocrats: there was no further need for historians to orientate their writing solely towards these privileged circles.

New debates started in the same period concerning the French language. Those who took pride in France's Latin identity wished to prove that French was a legitimate development of the Latin language, rather than a type of degenerate slang Latin. In putting forward such arguments, however, they raised further questions about the influence of other languages and cultures in the creation of France. International politics were also a relevant consideration. Stressing France's Latin inheritance meant associating France with other countries in Europe which laid claim to the same origins: this could suggest a united Latin-European community, with France peaceably linked to the patchwork federation of the Holy Roman Empire. On the other hand, finding some alternative form of identity could be a means to claim a particular, distinct identity for France: a useful tool for the emerging absolutist state of the sixteenth century. Such particularistic developments ran parallel to evolving concepts of identity which developed elsewhere.

These debates grew livelier in the eighteenth century. By this stage, history had already become a politicized arena, in which competing groups commissioned works to justify rival ideologies.[34] There were three significant claims concerning French national identity, which could, on occasion, overlap. First, the nobility, particularly the conservative nobility, generally still accepted arguments about their Frankish origins and their right, as conquerors, to rule France. Writers such as the comte de Boulainvilliers continued to rehearse these theses.[35] Secondly, the new voices of the Enlightenment tended to stress the value of reason, and rejected the argument that a conqueror had the right to rule. Exploiting the characteristic devices of Type A nationalism, this second group used the language of nationhood and patriotism to advance their claims, and so also attempted to create their own sense of the history of the French nation. They valued qualities such as communication and debate, and admired what they saw as the purity of the French language, and so tended to stress France's Latinate identity. Lastly, a minority, dissident current asserted the influence of Celts in French history. The multi-volume *Histoire des Celtes* written by Simon Pelloutier (1694–1757) could almost be read as the manifesto for this last current.[36] He presented the Celts as an enlightened people, with a humanistic and tolerant form of religion: a perfect foil to the alleged excessive intolerance of the Catholic Church. There was some interest in these topics among the reading public. During the eighteenth century there were about a hundred works published on the Celtic presence in France.[37] This was 'an explosive debate'.[38] The difference between on the one hand, the first and, on the other hand, the second and third views of France's origins was politicized in the last years of the *ancien régime*, with the patriot radicals of the Third Estate repudiating the Frankish conquerors' elite status in French society, and claiming a 'Gaulish' (i.e. Celtic) inheritance.[39]

Interest in the Celts was growing across Europe during the early modern period. For example, in Britain in 1582, Buchanan suggested that the Irish and Scots were descendants of the original Celts: a point which raised questions about their incorporation into the developing British polity.[40] *Stonehenge, A Temple Restor'd to the British Druids,* by William Stukeley, was published in 1740: as the title suggests, he – incorrectly – credited the construction of Stonehenge to pre-Roman druids, and thus asserted the Celtic origins of British identity. MacPherson's three-volume *Ossian* was published in Scotland in the 1760s.[41] This work, a largely (but not completely) spurious imitation of old Celtic stories, was widely translated and discussed across Europe. It portrayed a type of heroic-warrior society, and the work pre-figured the Romantic sensibility of the nineteenth century.

Questions about the origins of French national identity, about the French language, and about French social structure had all been growing in significance from the sixteenth to the eighteenth century. Each, in turn, led to further considerations concerning the Celts. These references, however, raise another question: who were the Celts?

The search for the Celts

Identifying the Celts is a singularly difficult task.[42] As Timothy Chapman has pointed out, none of the ancient peoples now identified as Celts ever applied this label to themselves.[43] For much of the claimed existence of these peoples, they were illiterate. For historians, they often appear as a 'silent people'. According to Duhamel, ancient Celtic Brittany did not produce a single painting, statue or book.[44] Much of our knowledge of their early existence comes from the records of other literate contemporaries: principally Greek and Roman authors. These classical civilizations were certainly interested in the Celts. Indeed, following a successful Celtic attack on Rome, in 391–90 BC, Latin writers were left with a Celtophobia which lasted centuries.[45]

The first references to the Celts come in Greek texts from the sixth and fifth centuries BC. These works attempted to survey and to identify the peoples of the known world: the Celts appear as people on the outer edges of civilization. The observations about their culture and society clearly played a pivotal role in allowing the construction of a Greek self-identity, for such authors 'in naming the "Barbarian" ... helped create the classical'.[46] From the Greek texts, one gains some impression that over the centuries this group was expanding from an area north of the Alps, and that in particular they were moving westwards. However, the scattered references are unclear, and have provoked protracted historical and archaeological debates as to what conclusions should be drawn from them.

Roman authors give more detailed accounts. While they use a different term to designate these peoples – 'Gauls', instead of Celts – there is a clear continuity from the Greek to the Roman accounts. Roman authors were fascinated by the differences between their own civilization and these peoples to their north and west. Their texts suggest a simple fear of these 'giants of violent pathos', capable of moments of great rage.[47] It is clear that this group was positioned by Roman writers as 'others' to the norm set by Latin civilization, for 'the first European barbarians [that] the Romans knew were the Celts.'[48] By positioning the Celts as inferiors, such writings suggest a clear sense of racial hierarchy, and so implicitly condone the institution of slavery.

Roman authors noted that the Celts could not write, did not live in towns, and that their religion was 'an imprecise and abstract worship of natural forces with no seeming emphasis on one prominent god'.[49] Such negative images reached a type of climax in Caesar's propagandistic work, *The Gallic War*, which records the Romans' conquest of present-day France and Britain in the first century BC. This work makes fascinating reading. Caesar's purpose was to confirm the grandeur he gained by conquering these peoples: by emphasizing their savagery, he justified their conquest; by highlighting their strengths and power, he claimed greater glory for his victory. According to one recent study, his work was a 'prodigious myth-making machine'.[50] One can read in Caesar's works some of the typical traits of imperialist culture. He depicts the Gauls as fickle gossip-mongers, and contrasted their primitive, irrational cultures with the clear-sighted planning of Rome: 'Such stories and hearsay often induce [the Gauls] to form plans upon vital questions of which they must forthwith repent; for they are the slaves of uncertain rumours, and most men reply to them in fictions made to their taste.'[51] Within his work are some of the most detailed written descriptions of Celtic society and religion available to historians and archaeologists. According to Caesar, the Celts were ruled by two elites: druids and warriors. Caesar explicitly states that the druidic religion was common to both the peoples living in the British Isles and to the Gauls on the continent, but – curiously – he never refers to the inhabitants of the islands as 'Gauls' (or 'Celts'). He also claims that the Druids conducted human sacrifices, and that their religious culture was preserved by rote-learning.

The nature and legacy of the Celtic presence in Brittany has been subject to considerable debate. Nineteenth- and twentieth-century Breton nationalists often wished to assert the strength of the region's Celtic culture. One stage in their arguments was to claim that the Roman Empire had relatively little effect in Brittany, and that it did not put down deep roots.[52] This claim has some force to it: the Roman Empire was not Stalinist Russia or Nazi Germany. Without the benefits of modern technology, it could not enforce a linguistic policy or a programme of political indoctrination on any people. In fact, Roman rule relied on the foundation or co-option of local elites to serve central interests.[53]

Historians wishing to suggest an unbroken legacy of Celtic history and culture, however, move on to develop a second stage to this argument. They suggest that it was religious groups such as the druids who maintained Celtic cultural unity during the period of Roman domination.[54] A presence, an identity was preserved: 'like Poland, it survived conquest'. Instead of a blending or interplay between two cultures, for these historians there was an autonomous Celtic continuity: 'the Gallo-Romans mostly continued to be disguised Celts'.[55] This is far less likely. First, although Roman cultural technology was rudimentary, their society was still orientated around the written word. One could logically expect that this vital, modernizing feature would give them the edge in any cultural contest with the Celtic peoples.[56] Significantly, Nora Chadwick suggests that the Gaulish language died out in Brittany during the period of Roman occupation.[57]

Many Celticists add a supplementary argument at this point in the historical narrative: acknowledging the long-term effects of the Roman occupation on indigenous cultures, they note the emigration of peoples from the British Isles to Brittany. (It was from this process that the region acquired its current name.) For some, this movement amounted to a 're-Celticization' of the region. Professional historians are more cautious in their judgements.[58]

There is an aspect to Celticist and nationalist arguments concerning Brittany's ancient identity which is profoundly worrying. Their arguments assume that there is some vital essence which demonstrated, like a passport, the identity of the Celts. In other words, it raises the question: what is a Celt? This is a difficult question to answer because of the fragmented, disparate sources available. Historians and archaeologists can refer to:

(a) texts written by Greek and Roman observers;
(b) material evidence, particularly that which gives some indication of religious cultures (i.e. tombs, burial mounds, etc.);
(c) linguistic evidence relating to the presence of Celtic languages;
(d) fine art work in the Hallstatt and La Tène styles.

In each of these media, the term 'Celtic' can be usefully deployed in a way which successfully illuminates the material uncovered. It is a term that allows trends to be identified, and it encourages some constructive comparisons between material from different places and ages. One objection might be that the people being surveyed probably did not consistently apply the term 'Celtic' to themselves. This is of relatively little importance: Mary Wollstonecraft never described herself as a 'feminist', but this does not invalidate the appropriate application of the term to her by later historians and researchers. If a term helpfully illuminates debates, its use is legitimate.

The bigger problem, however, is that when the totality of this material is compared, it is more or less impossible to synthesize these strands into a coherent presentation of a single, unitary Celtic identity. Attempts to do so fall apart almost as soon as they have been written. Consider, for example, the following passage by Myles Dillon and Nora Chadwick:

> The attempt to present the Celts in history as one people, with a common tradition and a common character, is new, and in some degree, experimental. It seems to us to have been justified beyond our expectations, inasmuch as there does emerge in the history and institutions and religion, in the art and literature, perhaps even in the language, a quality which is distinctive and is common to the Celts of Gaul, of Britain and of Ireland. We hesitate to give it a name: it makes a contrast with the Greek temperament, it is marked by extremes of luxury and asceticism, of exultation and despair, by lack of discipline and of the gift of organizing secular affairs, by delight in natural beauty and in tales of mystery and imagination, by an artistic sense that prefers decoration and pattern to mere representation. Matthew Arnold called it the Celtic magic.[59]

This mish-mash of evocations and oppositions is unacceptably vague as a definition of a key concept in a work written by two professional historians. The single useful point that can be drawn from these one-and-a-half hundred words of nonsense is how frequently 'the Celtic' is defined as un-definable. Like Roman and Greek authors before them, Dillon and Chadwick position 'the Celtic' through its opposition to dominant norms.

A second response to the contradictory strands of evidence is to privilege one particular source of evidence. Miranda Green appears to be following this type of argument when, in studying Celtic art, she argues that such artefacts are fundamental to Celtic identity in the illiterate Celtic societies. 'This very lack of written communication . . . may have elevated Celtic art into a kind of visual language.'[60] Peter B. Ellis provides another variant on this theme. For him, it is the linguistic evidence which provides the indisputable proof of the Celts' presence: 'Certainly no Celtic scholar would identify a Celtic people in any other way.'[61] While these are both understandable reactions to the fragmented nature of the evidence, they simply sidestep a fundamental dilemma. How do we analyse these peoples if, as often happens, linguistic or artistic evidence is not available? Worse still, what happens when the evidence of the artwork contradicts the evidence uncovered by the linguist or the anthropologist?

A third possible response is to express frustration with the whole concept. Professional historians studying these themes in recent years have grown increasingly annoyed by the forms of half-mystic, New Age silliness which have been attached to Celtic identities. For example, Patrick Galliou and Michael Jones complain that considerations of Brittany's enigmatic stone monuments (which pre-date the presence of Celtic peoples) have 'created in many minds a fairy-tale view of a Celtic twilight zone existing on the periphery of an otherwise rational and dynamic late twentieth-century state.'[62] This hostility to sensationalist and romanticized interpretations has led to 'Celto-scepticism'. Writers following this line of reasoning argue that the category 'Celtic' is an invented one. The 'Celtic' is a sloppy and misleading concept, whose original purpose was simply to project 'an outsider's sense of uniformity upon diverse societies.'[63] When modern scholars attempt to apply the term, it is argued, their studies become hopelessly muddled. 'The "Celtic World" is a pastiche,' writes Andrew Fitzpatrick, 'an unchanging rural idyll which has been characterized as traditional and timeless.'[64] Applying the term to the ancient world confuses our understanding by blurring important cultural, social and historical differences. Above all, reading back a modern-day sense of nationhood into the rudimentary social networks of the pre-Roman peoples is particularly misleading. 'There is never likely to have been a "Celtic Nation"', notes Colin Renfrew, 'if that term implies an association of populations speaking different Celtic languages and possessing some coherently-unified social organization.'[65] Arguing at his paradoxical best, Simon James suggests that if we wish to find the 'real' Celts we should look, not for roots in the ancient past, but to modern senses of ethnic identity, for 'the modern Celts constitute a real and legitimate "ethnic group".'[66] Applying the term to the ancient past runs the danger of creating an ethnic, even a racist, vision of history, and a justification for an authoritarian 'Fortress Europe' policy.[67]

This 'Celto-scepticism' can be seen as a post-modernist intervention into the debate. Like post-modernists, Celto sceptics refuse the grand narrative of the Celtophiles, and stress the invented, constructed nature of these categories. There are, however, some differences between the two strands of thought: most Celtosceptics accept that a rigorous and scholarly treatment of evidence from the past can create a meaningful re-construction of past cultures; they do see a world beyond the text.

The last significant contribution to this debate was made by Patrick Sims-Williams, whose essay begins with the observation that 'the terms "Celt" and "Celtic" have become a battleground'.[68] Sims-Williams attempted to synthesize some of the themes which had emerged in the debate. On the one hand, he noted the sloppy, over-unifying use of the term, which has reduced disparate cultures and peoples into a single common bloc. This was clearly inaccurate. 'Self-conscious Celtic solidarity cannot be traced back beyond the modern period.' Moreover, there is a permanent problem with source material which cannot be resolved, so 'professors and cranks alike are principally dependent on the same ambiguous classical sources'. Maps of the speakers of Celtic languages do not easily match maps of the presence of peoples who have been labelled Celts by art historians and anthropologists: in other words, language is not an indisputable test of *celtitude*. On the other hand, Sims-Williams noted some important features of the way in which Celtic Studies had developed: it is an inter-disciplinary field of study, and as such, it resembles other similar fields in that it is difficult to construct coherent transdisciplinary concepts and definitions. Sims-Williams's final word was to recommend a cautious pragmatism: 'There is no problem so long as we do not use the concept "Celtic" unthinkingly as a short-cut from one discipline to another, or from one region to another, or from one millennium to the next.' If the word is used with sensitivity, each discipline in turn could still use the term Celtic to identify discrete topics.

Sims-Williams's arguments lack the transcendent 'magic' of what one might term hard-core Celticism, which throw the reader into some time-defying vortex that connects the Celtic present to the ancient Celtic past.

His arguments also have none of the peculiarly intellectualized destructiveness of the post-modernist scholars, who consider that they are capable of busting a different paradigm each week. But, for the moment, this cautious pragmatism probably represents the most realistic academic approach. Invention or not, the term does have some limited validity. The conclusions which I draw from this debate are that, first, we should consistently link the term 'Celtic' to plural entities. In other words, we should talk of 'Celtic peoples' rather than of the Celtic people. Such groups constituted 'a fluid network of autonomous societies speaking a set of related languages' rather than a single bloc.[69] Secondly, we should be sceptical about claims of trans-historical continuities, which link millennium to millennium, and we should acknowledge, without scorn, the significant contribution to the *making* (not *re-making*) of Celtic identities by eighteenth-, nineteenth- and twentieth-century antiquarians and cultural militants.

The Celtic opposition

Let us return to eighteenth-century France. The revolutionary regimes drew their political language, their sense of history and their symbolism largely from the Latinate cultural values of the Enlightenment. 'In the revolutionary view of history', explains Lynn Hunt, 'the republicans of Greece and Rome had invented liberty, and the mission of France was to bring that good news to all men.'[70] The new rulers of revolutionary France commissioned statues to symbolize the new public virtues: these resembled the older sculptures of Greece and Rome. Like the Romans, they built triumphal arches to celebrate military victories. However, within the revolutionary discourse, there was also some renewed interest in the Gallo-Roman past. This was not evident in the first years of the Revolution: neither the Salon of 1789 nor that of 1791 included any depictions of Celtic themes. But in 1795, the new rulers re-discovered the Celtic heritage as a means by which to define France's natural frontiers. The most prominent indication of this tendency was the later creation of Académie Celtique in 1804.[71] Napoleon, a keen reader of MacPherson's *Ossian*, was concerned to develop the territory controlled by the French Empire.

Academics and scholars, however, were intrigued by some more intellectual lines of enquiry. Once again, the French language was debated. Was the French language merely a degenerate form of Latin? Or was it a development from the pre-Roman, Celtic or Gaulish, languages that had thrived in France? In terms of the vocabulary and structure of the French language, the Celticists were on weak ground. As the debate progressed, however, scholars turned their attention from semantics and grammar to examine French literary production. Here, there was a more evenly divided contest. Southerners saw the songs of the medieval troubadours as the first examples of a proper literary French production. Northerners, however, referred to the rich legacy of Celtic legend which, they argued, had produced epics such as the King Arthur and the Round Table.[72] In turn, the debate divided Classicists, interested in stressing France's Latinate heritage, and Romantics, who were more concerned with some of the shortcomings of both the revolutionary regimes and their associated rationalist individualism, and who were open to other ideas concerning France's origins.

A different type of challenge to previous literary-anthropological research was suggested by the methods adopted by the Académie Celtique.[73] Beyond the critical texts by classical authors, there were few printed works to which the *académie* could refer. As we have seen, these classical works were invested with a great prestige. Indeed, few researchers would even consider challenging the authority of the established Greco-Roman authors; the underlying purpose of much previous academic research had been precisely to establish a continuity from these ancient authors to contemporary France.[74] The *académie's* members took the revolutionary step of looking away from these standard sources of academic knowledge, to sources of evidence such as folk culture, rituals, traditions and monuments. Of course, they were not the first to do so: for example, in the seventeenth century there had been studies of superstitions.[75] However, the purpose of such previous research had been to demonstrate the foolishness of popular beliefs. Researchers had studied in order to condemn, not to understand. The Académie Celtique followed quite different lines of enquiry. By studying the savage, they believed that researchers could gain material by which to understand the distant past. In particular, the *académie* was quick to see actually existing peasant customs as authentic survivals from the distant Celtic past. Such lines of enquiry certainly conflicted with the previous Enlightenment stress on the value of written, articulate sources.

The introduction to a short story by Emile Souvestre, published in 1849, gives some idea of how the *académie's* members worked: while his interests were different from theirs, he nonetheless followed many of their methods. First, the researcher had to visit farms, because 'it is above all in the countryside that we have tried to re-discover the popular tradition. There, among isolated families with fixed lives, away from the great events which disrupt their conduct, without books, the traditions of story-telling has been preserved.' He must then question the older peasants, and overcome their suspicions of outsiders. Should he persuade a peasant to co-operate, he must listen without questioning, for 'the story-teller that one questions grows nervous, and then stops speaking'. The researcher must be motivated by passion and must be prepared to search everywhere.[76]

To many observers, there was something bizarre, even demeaning, in the *académie's* interest in the rituals of illiterate villagers and the songs of crude peasants. This is one factor in explaining the rapid demise of the Académie Celtique in 1814. Another important factor in their fall, however, was the *académie's* often uncritical and unscientific admiration for all that they considered Celtic. For example, one of the principal members of the *académie*, Jacques Cambry, applauded the 'sublime, marvellous religion' of the druids of ancient Gaul, which – he claimed – was based on a knowledge of nature, astronomy and chemistry. In the same passage, Cambry went on to claim that within living memory, druidic customs had been practised in Brittany. Elsewhere, he told readers that 'no conquest' had altered the Bretons' customs or ideas.[77] Such claims provided easy targets for critics. Merimée scoffed at the Celtic researchers of Lesneven, who could not accept that local ruins were Roman rather than Celtic.[78] Souvestre was only exaggerating slightly when he laughed at Celticists who attempted to prove, by reference to the Bible, that Adam and Eve had spoken the Breton language.[79] Such thinking was quickly condemned by hostile critics as 'Celtomania'.

A few years later, however, some of the *académie's* ideas no longer seemed so unacceptable. European culture was changing. The novels of Walter Scott were a particularly important part of this process. They showed a new way of representing the past and of drawing values from it. Significantly, Scott's books quickly became popular in France.[80] His novels are too rich and complex to be reduced to a single formula: they both 'depict the process of cultural erasure under the violence of history' *and* they celebrate the historical process of development.[81] The interest in Scott's work was encouraged by the new Europe-wide culture of Romanticism, with its keen interest in the emotions, and its assertion of the value of the heart over the qualities of the mind. Romantics began to rethink *celtitude*: they interpreted past history in such a way as to suggest that France's Celtic ancestors had lived in an organic, spiritual society. This was then opposed to the largely Latinate political culture of the Revolution, now depicted by the Counter-Revolutionaries of the restored monarchy (1814–30) as cold, technocratic, and cartesian.[82] Celtic culture could be an instrument for the conservative right to use against the revolutionary legacy.

Surprisingly even liberal opponents of the restored monarchy, such as Guizot, would identify themselves as inheritors of a Celtic or Gaulish culture. Dietler has recently argued that, with the creation of the more liberal July Monarchy in 1830, 'this movement permanently established the Celts as a primary ethnic foundation for the modern French nation through the popularization of an essentialist racial vision of Celtic identity and French history'.[83] In fact, as will be seen, this is something of an exaggeration. But there can be no doubt that, increasingly, official proclamations began to assert that France's ethnic identity was 'Celtic' or 'Gaulish'. In other words, as the French government entered phase B of nation-building (state-nationalism), memories of a Celtic past were deliberately revived or created.

The climax to this new wave of state-national commemoration was the sponsorship of archaeological research by Napoleon III, the authoritarian ruler of France from 1851 to 1870. In particular, he supported and paid for an archaeological excavation of the site of a Celtic fort and the associated battle at Alésia (Côte-d'Or), in eastern France.[84] This battle featured prominently in Caesar's *The Gallic War*, in which it is described as marking the final defeat of the Gaulish rebellion of 52 BC against Roman power. In the early nineteenth century there were a number of different claims for the location of this battle. Napoleon III's excavation ended doubts about Alésia's status. More importantly, it also fixed the date as a turning-point in the making of French nationhood. Significantly, the excavation was accompanied by the Emperor's own two-volume study of Caesar (published in 1865). These activities also 'created' the figure of Vercingetorix, the leader of the Gaulish rebels, who was commemorated by the erection of a six and a half metre high bronze statue and the establishment of an accompanying museum on the site. But, it must be stressed, such discoveries did not mean any imperial sympathy for Breton scholars: in fact, Napoleon III abolished the Association Bretonne in August 1859, a point to which we will return in Chapter Seven.[85]

This second achievement – the creation of Vercingetorix – was perhaps more impressive than the physical work of opening up the site: it represented an 'archaeology of the imagination', in the words of Buchsenschutz and Schnapp.[86] A complex and ambiguous message was being portrayed through these images. First, what was being the commemorated? The victory of the Romans, or the defeat of the Celts? The focus on Vercingetorix suggested an identification with the defeated forces, and his statue portrayed a handsome, noble, muscular man, with his now-famous long moustaches. Yet if Napoleon III's intention was to celebrate a Celtic legacy, why choose to focus on this defeat? Instead, a more complex message was being formulated. France was founded from this meeting of the Celtic and the Roman. The defeat of

Vercingetorix's forces was a necessary part of nation-building. Significantly, in Caesar's account, Vercingetorix is silent at the moment of defeat, which is recorded in brief, terse phrases: 'Vercingetorix was surrendered, arms were thrown down'.[87] His adventure belongs to pre-history, to the history of peoples before writing, before civilization. There was an obvious comparison to be drawn between the defeat of these primitive forces and the defeat of native forces in the areas which France was colonizing in the nineteenth century. Such defeats were not to be 'celebrated', but they were to be understood as a necessary part of the process of civilization.

In the late nineteenth century, school history textbooks began to start with the now-famous phrase 'our ancestors the Gauls'. The first chair in Celtic Studies was created in France in 1876. Such processes of identity-formation were given added impetus following the French defeat in the Franco-Prussian war of 1870–1, after which successive French governments wanted to emphasize the significant differences between France and Germany. The part played by Charlemagne's Empire in the formation of both nations was therefore downplayed: the stories of Vercingetorix, the Gauls and Rome were more appropriate. Alésia became a site for patriotic pilgrimage, and Vercingetorix was compared to Joan of Arc.

Do these moves mean that the French government had now re-defined France as a Celtic nation, as argued by Dietler? It is important to remember that this official cult consistently spoke of the Gauls, not the Celts. In other words, by using the Roman term, it stressed the interaction of these peoples with the Roman Empire, not their autonomous development. Secondly, Dietler overestimates the extent to which this argument dominated. A contrary view can be found in the work of Charles Le Goffic, a prominent early twentieth-century popularizer of images of a romantic, Celticized Brittany. He is generally an unreliable witness, but he comes closer to the truth than Dietler when, with reference to early twentieth-century Brittany, he argued that 'our education is Latin, while we remain Celts'.[88] The French academic system remained (and remains) thoroughly committed to classicist, Latinate values and culture. Reference to the ambiguous moment of Latin/Gaulish/Celtic contact was a useful propaganda device to differentiate the French nation from Germany, Britain and other rival nations, but such references were deliberately formulated in such a way as to short-circuit any substantial assertion of France as a Celtic nation.

Little of these discussions specifically concerned Brittany. The most significant archaeological sites suggested that the Celtic heartland of France was either in the eastern department of the Côte-d'Or, or in the south-central region of the Auvergne.[89] Even in the early nineteenth century, observers still doubted whether there was any necessary connection between the Breton language and France's Celtic past. For example, J.-F. Brousmiche, a tax official in Finistère with a real talent for recording and interpreting social and cultural change, was frankly sceptical of recent linguistic speculations claiming that the Breton language was related to the language of the Ancient Gauls.[90]

The celebrated early twentieth-century Celtic historian Henri Hubert produced a more subtle and dialectical interpretation of the interaction between Brittany and France.

> Brittany has never ceased to look towards Britain, bound to it by its resuscitated shipping, until the day when it found itself in contact with the very body of France, a France which was no longer German or Celtic but was France, and absorbed Brittany naturally and without a struggle.[91]

In other words, rather than promoting a sense of Brittany's cultural specificity, this 'Gaul-ization' of French culture was, according to Hubert, merely a stage towards the establishment of an authentic French identity, which would then absorb and integrate Brittany into the nation.

Among some writers, however, the Romantic interest in the Celtic past did stimulate a specific interest in Brittany. Some of these were Paris-based outsiders, others were born in Brittany. The chart below lists some of the most significant texts of the early and mid-nineteenth century.

Jacques Cambry, *Voyage dans le Finistère* (1795, published in 1799)
Honoré de Balzac, *Les Chouans* (1829)
Jules Michelet, *Tableau de la France* (1831, revised edn 1861)
Emile Souvestre, *Poésies de la Bretagne* (1834)
Emile Souvestre, *Les Derniers Bretons* (1835–36)
Théodore Hersart de la Villemarqué, *Barzaz Breiz* [Poems of Brittany] (1839; revised editions in 1845 and 1875)
Auguste Brizeux, *Marie* (1840)
Emile Souvestre, *Le Foyer breton: contes et récits populaires* (1844)
Auguste Brizeux, *Les Bretons* (1845)
Ernest Renan, 'La poésie des races celtiques' (1854)

Chapter 3 will identify and debate some of the key features of these works. One point that can be made immediately, however, is to note the variety of forms of writing listed in this chart, which includes full-length novels, travel-writing, political anthropology, short stories, collections of folk tales, and volumes of poetry, but not works of history. This range suggests the unformed, experimental nature of the discourse which was being elaborated. No one literary genre was the vehicle for presentation of *bretonnitude* to the wider public.

Of these pioneering innovators, the most original and – eventually – the most influential was undoubtably Villemarqué's *Barzaz Breiz*. The first edition of this work contained fifty-three song lyrics. It was bilingual, presenting readers with a Breton text and a French translation. Villemarqué's claim – which was later vigorously disputed – was that these texts were accurate copies of the lyrics of songs currently sung in Brittany. In the twentieth century this work was celebrated by Breton cultural nationalists. Per Denez has described it as being 'at the origins of Brittany's literary renaissance'.[92] If the work is seen in the long-term context of the development of Breton literature and the Breton language, then such comments may well be justified. However, in some ways, they are misleading. There can be no doubt that Villemarqué's intentions were quite different from those suggested by Denez's observations. Mary-Ann Constantine correctly notes that it is 'an astonishing book', and Jean-Yves Guiomar is not exaggerating when he observes that Villemarqué intended 'nothing less than a complete renovation of European culture and civilization'.[93] Unpicking and identifying Villemarqué's aims for the *Barzaz Breiz* is a complex task: we will start by simply listing five of them. The *Barzaz Breiz* presented the following claims:

(a) an argument for the creation of a Catholic, conservative, social France, to lead Europe;
(b) this France would be rooted in Celtic tradition;
(c) exemplified and preserved specifically in styles of life still present in Brittany;
(d) which were expressed through its existing oral literature;
(e) accurately recorded in the *Barzaz Breiz*.

Let us examine each of these points in turn. Villemarqué's politics are difficult to define. It is easy to label him as 'conservative': the son of a Breton Legitimist deputy during the Restoration, his Jesuit education, avowed Legitimism, sincere Catholicism and aristocratic family connections all seem to mark him as a simple reactionary. Even his youth seems to link him to another of the stereotypes of the Romantic revolt: he was only twenty-four when he first published the *Barzaz Breiz*, at his own expense. Such labels are undoubtedly too simple. Before placing Villemarqué in the reactionary camp, we should recall the political trajectory of his Breton compatriot, fellow Social Catholic and near-contemporary, Lamennais, who moved from the Counter-Revolutionary right to an unusual form of Social Republicanism in 1848.[94] Both men had been disillusioned by the experience of rule by the last Bourbon monarch, Charles X, who reigned from 1824 to 1830.[95] (Like Lamennais, Villemarqué stood for election as a Republican in 1849; unlike Lamennais, he was not elected.) We should also bear in mind that the very form of Villemarqué's researches took him far from aristocratic culture: like the Académie Celtique, he lauded the works of folk poets, mere peasants. He studied 'popular poetry; the poetry of the uncultured, the savage and the ignorant'.[96] Many of the verses of the *Barzaz Breiz* depicted the cruelties of the nobles. The verses, in turn, were an inspiration to many on the political left: George Sand, for example, compared them to Homer's writing.[97]

Unlike most of the Legitimist right, Villemarqué rejected the traditional arguments concerning the Frankish warrior-elite's right to rule, and based his political values on an idealized concept of Celtic society. This provided the *social* dimension to his Social Catholicism: he dreamt of an organic order in which the bard, the noble and the people were united in a common cultural community. Villemarqué certainly joined the Legitimists in attacking those forces which aimed to centralize and modernize the nation: the Université, the Napoleonic tradition, the sceptical spirit, and so on.[98] But his solution was significantly different. He did not aim for mere decentralization, which would grant the conservative nobility a greater degree of freedom from liberal Paris. Instead, his fight was for a reorientation of French culture: a cultural and spiritual *recentring* of France, with Brittany to be the focus for the new order, for it was in this region that the essential qualities of the anti-liberal Celtic spirit had been kept alive. For Villemarqué, this was the region's unique characteristic. Brittany was the missing link which could join liberal France to the wonders of continental Celtic culture; it was the place in which 'the Christian faith could be grafted onto the Celtic oak'.[99] The importance of the verses in the *Barzaz Breiz* therefore went far beyond mere literature. They were presented by Villemarqué as works of almost-Biblical importance, 'precious and instructive',[100] certainly demonstrating great skill and fluency, but more significantly expressing codes of morality and spirituality which would inspire the French people to 'return' to a Celtic and religious mode of being. In other words, Villemarqué was not aiming to initiate a neo-nationalist movement, but to reconfigure French state-nationalism.

Villemarqué's ideas can be understood as part of the European-wide Romantic critique of the developing liberal order.[101] And, just as conservatives had felt some scepticism about the Romantics' innovative literary and cultural themes, so they were also hostile to this project to reposition Brittany. Once again, Brousmiche, our Breton tax official, provides an invaluable critique of Celtic Brittany. His comments can be found in his two volumes of travel-writing concerning the department of Finistère. He described the *menhir* at Plouarzel, which was then seen by both *Celto-manes* and orthodox opinion as a Celtic monument. Brousmiche commented:

> The antiquarian will be amazed by this monument. He will be inspired to dream of those far-away times in which the heroes celebrated by Ossian shone in all their glory. He will think of those bards who captivated an entire people with the war-like sounds of their harps. [Such commentators] accept a quite hypothetical concept of the past. They allowed their imaginations to run riot in order to embellish the past. They dream about the druids, who they see as legislators for the peoples who lived in Brittany, but they all too easily forget that these priests were ministers for merciless gods, who wanted human blood . . . It even seems likely that [such commentators] regret [the druids'] passing, and that they prefer them to the brave and fervent men who tore [ancient Brittany] from idolatry and who sanctified it by the sign of the son of God.[102]

Brousmiche's comments are important, for they demonstrate the distance between the new ideals of *celtitude*, represented by writing such as the *Barzaz Breiz*, and more orthodox conservatism. He expressed a number of important doubts. Firstly, Celtic ideas are pagan – a quality which Brousmiche immediately associates with cruelty. Secondly, they are based on guesswork rather than proper historical research. It is unlikely that Brousmiche knew of the extent to which MacPherson's *Ossian* was a forgery – such knowledge did not become common until the 1860s – but if he had learnt of this, he would no doubt have considered that this merely confirmed his suspicions about the ill-defined Celtic research. Lastly, Brousmiche evokes a certain attitude: the 'antiquarian' is depicted as a dreamer, a fantasist. Such people, for Brousmiche, are escapists: their ideas are as much to be criticized for the cloudy, weak-willed mental irresponsibility that they encourage as for their historical content.

Brittany and France

Villemarqué argued that there was some unique quality of great value that had been preserved in Brittany. For many reasons, this idea would have amazed many contemporary readers. There was a long history of Parisian scorn for

Bretons. Even in the thirteenth century, satirical Parisian literature mocked the Bretons. While the Bretons were certainly considered to be physically strong, they tended to occupy the most humble of positions: they carried the water; they cleaned the latrines. Their clumsy efforts to speak French also provided hostile caricaturists with an easy target.[103] There are few signs of any significant Breton fight-back. Perhaps one could consider Anne de Bretagne's decision to commission the production of a history of Brittany in 1505 in this light.[104] Significantly, however, it is from later decades that one can date the first trace of Breton particularism: a Breton work of history from the 1580s, which suggests some criticisms of the French royal tradition.[105]

Villemarqué's collection of verse from Brittany was intended to overturn this accumulation of negative stereotypes, and to place Brittany at the centre of a renewed concept of French nationhood. His work certainly stimulated considerable new interest in Brittany, but there were few signs of any immediate success for his wider project. Indeed, Auguste Brizeux's picturesque images of a 'soft Brittany, laughing and innocent' were – initially – far more successful than Villemarqué's grave Celtic Catholicism.[106] When Théophile Gautier saw Breton artists at the Salon of 1847, he immediately compared their work with that of Brizeux, not Villemarqué.[107] (We will examine this question more thoroughly in chapter 3.) As our conclusion, however, some evidence can be cited to demonstrate the continuity of hostile images of Brittany into the late nineteenth century.

As we have seen, a new interest in heritage developed during the early nineteenth century. The July Monarchy (1830–48) carried out one of the first surveys of historic monuments and sites. Prosper Mérimée, who was later to write the short story 'Carmen', wrote detailed reports for the Minister of the Interior. He was sceptical about the status of Brittany's monuments. 'The near-complete absence of historical information condemn[s] our researches [on these objects] to remain almost entirely fruitless' he commented to the Minister of the Interior.[108] In 1846, 934 historical monuments were officially recognized in France; only sixteen of these were in Brittany.[109] This evidence certainly suggests that Brittany was not seen as a key source of the French historical identity. A second example on the same theme can be gained by consulting Bruno's classic textbook *Le Tour de la France par deux enfants*, aptly described by Jacques Ozouf and Mona Ozouf as 'the little red book of the Third Republic'. This work was first printed in 1877, and by 1901 more than six million copies had been distributed through the schools of the Republic. Bruno's description of Brittany would have disappointed Villemarqué. First, there was no mention of any special Celtic or spiritual quality. Secondly, Bruno's Brittany was still clearly that of the eighteenth-century traveller. Nantes, Brest and its naval academy were all mentioned. Brittany's contribution to the French navy, and Nantes' exports of vegetables and sardines were also noted.[110] But the Breton language, the prehistoric monuments, Celtic culture and the difficult relationship of the region to the rest of France were all quietly side-stepped.

Villemarqué had failed to refocus French culture. Instead, he had inadvertently initiated an interpretation of 'the Celtic' which ran quite counter to the now-official government cult of 'our ancestors the Gauls'. One thought-provoking example of how this new oppositional cultural Celticism might function has been identified by Mark Antliff.[111] In the years before the First World War there was intense debate among avant-garde artists connected with the Cubist movement. Maurras, the leader of the quasi-fascist Action française, was attempting to capture this movement for his far-right cause. His analysis of Cubism stressed its compatibility with the classical tradition. Against him, Albert Gleizes wanted to preserve Cubism as a left-leaning movement. He consequently made use of 'an alternative definition of national identity allied to France's revolutionary tradition' – in other words, he referred to a version of Celtic identity. Bergson was re-interpreted by Gleizes as a 'bard' in the Celtic tradition. The Cubists' debate was not unique. The association of Celtic/Gaulish qualities with popular or left-wing causes continued into the twentieth century. Brittany would sometimes be placed at the centre of these oppositional currents.[112]

Conclusion

'Official', governmental 'Gaul-ism' is still alive and well today. Its health can be gauged by the popularity of the 'Asterix' series of cartoon books, which identify France with the plucky little Gaul and his village of colourful stereotypes, and by the rivalry between the 'Parc Astérix' and Eurodisney. The official Asterix web-site informs us that Brittany represents the quality of resistance.[113] On a more serious note, we should remember Mitterrand promoted the Celtic site of Mont-Beuvray and, like his predecessor Napoleon III, was willing to claim its Celtic heritage for his own immediate political advantage.[114] A more recent development of this official Celticism has been its evolution into an emblem of European unity.[115]

Celtic ideas have significantly contributed to all four types of nationalism identified at the start of this chapter. In Type A, Republican Nationalism, *celtitude* could act as a counter to racist and ethnic myths of Frankish warrior aristocracy. The powerful images of Vercingetorix were at the centre of the culture of French State-Nationalism, leading to the myth of 'our ancestors, the Gauls'. While Type C, Hyper-Nationalism, has not been discussed in this chapter, we can note in passing the collaboration of certain Breton nationalists with both the Vichy authorities and the occupying German forces during 1940–4. (It should not be forgotten, however, that there were also many Bretons active in the Resistance: this point will be discussed further in chapter 8.) Lastly, there are movements and cultures alive in Brittany today which are attempting to create a neo-nationalist force.

The quality of *celtitude* remains intensely difficult to define or characterize. At first sight, one notes the scarcity of reliable evidence. Recreating the history and cultures of these ancient peoples is like trying to guess the meaning of a thousand piece jigsaw of which one only possesses fifteen pieces. It is clear, however, that this very absence of evidence has aided professors and cranks, militants and romantics, to devise their own Celticisms, cut and tailored to their own political or cultural needs. The persistence of these uncertain rumours, echoing through the centuries, is genuinely astonishing.

2

Brittany and the French Revolution

In the previous chapter, debates by writers, politicians and philosophers on the place of Celtic identity in French history were analysed. As was seen, by the end of the eighteenth century, a small minority were arguing that Brittany might make some special contribution to the development of French identity. In this chapter, we turn to examine a more concrete issue: the experience of Brittany during the French Revolution. The first sections of this chapter will survey existing historical research on pre-revolutionary Brittany, and the second half will then analyse the new cultures, both revolutionary and Counter-Revolutionary, which evolved in Brittany. As will be seen, none of these new political cultures had any direct link to the discourse of Celticism.

The issue of Brittany's role during the French Revolution has been discussed in a long-running and sometimes acrimonious debate. To simplify, one can distinguish three approaches to the topic. Chapters 6 and 7 will show that first historians of the revolutionary years analysed the region as forming a stubborn, conservative opposition to the revolutionary values of progress and modernity. In reaction to this, a new generation of political and social historians in Brittany have produced a series of extremely important qualifications to these easy assumptions. Two works produced during or shortly after the bicentenary of 1989 illustrate this revisionist tendency. Alain Droguet's edited collection of essays, *Les Bleus de Bretagne* (1991), provides a wide-ranging survey of the various Breton groups and tendencies who celebrated the Revolution of 1789. While never arguing that these groups were dominant in Brittany, Droguet's collection does correct some of the clichés about the backward west, for it convincingly demonstrates the existence of deep-rooted, long-lasting and influential 'Blue' currents within Breton political cultures. Michel Denis's *Rennes, berceau de la liberté* (1989) presents similar arguments in a more forceful and provocative form. While this work is focused on a single city, Denis makes some far-reaching claims which could change our understanding of the whole region. He suggests that the Revolution actually began in Rennes on 10 May 1788, not in Paris on 14 July 1789, and that the clash on the streets of Rennes in January 1789 between students and servants (employed by aristocrats) was 'the first revolutionary conflict'.[1] Denis's arguments are carefully phrased: he avoids exaggeration and rhetorical claims, and – in most cases – his aim is not so much to suggest that Rennes constituted France's leading progressive city as to argue that it is in Rennes that one can see most clearly the tensions and opposing forces which produced the violence of the Revolution.

The third interpretation of Brittany's role in the Revolution is still waiting its presentation in a substantial form. However, historians inspired by Breton nationalist ideals, such as Loeiz Ar Beg and Alain Pennec, have presented short analyses of the revolutionary decade. The significant contribution of their work is to open up the question of Breton public opinion: here, the quest is to identify a 'real' Brittany, which had been disguised or distorted by both 'Blue' revolutionaries and 'White' Counter-Revolutionaries. Thus Ar Beg considers that 'the Breton peasantry, both Gallo and Celtic, WAS BRITTANY in 1789. But it did not realize this, and so it could not play its historic role.'[2]

The points discussed in this chapter are slightly different from the concerns of each of these three historiographical strands. Here, we will concentrate on how the new political cultures debated the nature of Brittany. While it is undeniable that a substantial Counter-Revolutionary movement did develop in Brittany, one can question and qualify the extent to which this should be interpreted as a specifically Breton movement, let alone as the dominant political tendency to evolve in the region during the Revolution. The new generation of Republican historians have made a useful contribution to the debate by mapping the range of Blue influences in Brittany but, with reference to these cases, it is instructive to see how frequently these groups constituted themselves as tiny minorities of dedicated militants rather than as mass movements. Lastly, in response to the Breton nationalists, I will be arguing that there was no true, authentic voice of Breton nationalism in this period and, moreover, that there could not be one.

Brittany and old regime France

France at the end of the Old Regime was not a united nation. It had no single, coherent law code, no uniform currency, no nationwide market, no single, shared language, no national system of conscription and no coherent system of political representation. Even the Catholic religion could not be used as a building block for an inclusive French nationalism: there were at least one million Protestants resident in France, plus several tens of thousands of Jews. Furthermore, Catholicism was – arguably – an international religion, with its centre in Rome, not Paris. Was there no quality which united this patchwork of duchies and regions into a single polity? One response to such a question is to consider the position of the absolutist state, led by the king: this was clearly one institution which worked to produce a greater social uniformity. It was guided by a new political ideal: the active ruler who did not simply interpret old laws, but who devised new laws.[3] This meant that the state became a more active force in the seventeenth and eighteenth centuries. This development did not, however, automatically create a patriotic unity. One common reaction was actually increased antagonism to the state. The new laws were frequently interpreted as being made for the benefit of the rich and powerful: hence the common toleration of salt and tobacco smuggling in Brittany and the frequent refusal to speak to police officers.[4]

Alongside a stronger relationship with the state, all French people probably shared another quality: a common admiration or grudging respect for Parisians.[5] This could be just an acknowledgement that Paris was the centre of cultural and social life, and the city with the most highly paid workers and the most sophisticated lifestyles. Certainly, this was often little more than a vague feeling, and few people in France ever travelled to this far-away centre to see if their assumptions were accurate. But it was also a two-way relationship. While outsiders admired Paris, Parisians commonly considered 'the provinces' as a zone of backwardness. Brittany appeared to them as more backward, more savage than the other areas;[6] Bretons 'were the most scorned of all the provincials'.[7] What were the reasons for these attitudes?

Certainly, there were few signs of economic development in Old Regime Brittany. The region's economy was declining. In particular, the policies initiated by Louis XIV and his minister Colbert took trade away from many of the Breton ports. Their protectionism produced high tariffs on incoming goods, and their empire-building sparked off the frequent wars of the late seventeenth and early eighteenth centuries: both these changes hampered Brittany's maritime commerce.[8] Brittany's agriculture showed similar signs of decay. In 1700, approximately two thousand horses were sold at the annual fifteen-day horse-fair at Le Folgoët, in present-day Finistère, but this number was lower than the number of sales in previous decades, and was to continue to decline throughout the eighteenth century.[9] Older trades such as canvas manufacture and rope-making were following a similar path. In these cases, the economic dislocations caused by the revolutionary wars were the last blows which finished them off. Population levels from the eighteenth century confirm these impressions of a general decline. In the 1670s the region's population was probably slightly under two million people: about nine or ten per cent of the total French population. This increased unevenly during the next decades until the 1770s, when it fell sharply from about 2.3 million to about 2.2 million – or approximately eight per cent of the total French population.[10] The sudden falls in population in the early 1740s and the mid-1770s were caused by the spread of typhus, which came to Brittany through its ports. In the 1770s the epidemic had devastating consequences: it spread through a population which was already weakened by malnutrition. Records from particular localities reveal steep falls in the numbers of inhabitants. In 1703, 8,900 people lived in the little town of Guérande (present-day Loire-Atlantique), but only 5,300 in 1781.[11] A similar profile can be seen in the southern port town of Vannes (present-day Morbihan): 1,830 taxpayers were registered there in 1704, only 1,492 in 1783.[12]

Why would an eighteenth-century traveller choose to travel from Paris to visit Brittany? Its capital, Rennes, had few prestigious inhabitants and little commerce. It existed primarily to serve the surrounding farmers and to host the two-yearly meeting of Brittany's principal representative institution, the Estates of Brittany. According to one visitor, Rennes's only distinguishing feature was the prodigious number of rats and mice to be found there.[13] Such unattractive images were repeated by many other visitors. In 1698, an *intendant*'s report described the Bretons as 'poor, neither industrious nor hard-working'. The same report noted their habitual drunkenness.[14] In 1787 Arthur Young visited the small rural town of Combourg (Ille-et-Vilaine), which was dominated by the château owned by Chateaubriand's family. He commented that it was 'one of the most brutal filthy places that can be seen; mud houses, no windows, and a pavement so broken as to impede all passengers.'[15] Brittany had no spa towns, few celebrated inhabitants and it was a 'cultural desert'.[16] Brittany's universities were mediocre; its nine old episcopal towns were badly built, over-crowded and crumbling, and among its churches were no prestigious examples of the Gothic artwork which was growing in popularity. The great, Catholic, reforming impulse of the Council of Trent (1545–63) had run its course: Brittany's priests still taught their parishioners the values of a fixed hierarchic order in their weekly sermons.[17] The numbers of students attending its colleges were stagnating, if not actually declining: there were about a thousand pupils in Nantes in 1700, about six hundred in 1770 and only three hundred in 1785. The same tendency can be seen among Brittany's printers and bookshops: there were three bookshops in Brest in 1701, and only one in 1759.[18]

This generally gloomy picture, however, does need some qualification. The simple statistics of demographic stagnation do not tell the whole story. Within the region, there were two great demographic movements during the seventeenth and eighteenth centuries. These firstly drew the population away from the region's interior, out to its more commercially minded coasts, and secondly, to a lesser extent, drew people away from the northern coast, which was most affected by the military conflicts of the period, to the southern coast. The great naval port at Brest, its attached Marine Academy, and the linked southern port at Lorient were both localities which won genuine admiration from Parisians. Brest was fast becoming the principal French centre for ship-building. Writing in Morlaix in 1794, Cambry noted that this land had once been covered with woods, and that Brest's industries had consumed them all.[19] In the early eighteenth century the port employed between fifteen hundred and three thousand workers; their numbers grew steadily in the second half of the century, from 2,157 in 1771, to 4,658 in 1776, to reach 9,360 in 1783. Their numbers were supplemented by the city's notorious prison-workshop, opened in 1749, which housed between two thousand and three and a half thousand workers in the late eighteenth century.[20]

Brest typifies this countervailing socio-economic tendency: while Brittany's agricultural and rural economy declined or stagnated, some ports developed innovative new specialisms. In the early sixteenth century, the port of Saint-Malo had pioneered cod-fishing off the north-eastern coast of America. In the late seventeenth century, some fifty to eighty ships sailed across the Atlantic each spring, to spend the summer months fishing off Newfoundland. They then followed a complex, three-cornered route. In the autumn, they took their catches, dried and preserved with salt, to the great cities of Catholic Europe: their cod would be sold for consumption during the following Lent. It was exchanged for wool, ironware, wine, oil and soap, and the ships then finally sailed back to Saint-Malo.[21] In the seventeenth century, this port was the principal point of entry for southern American silver into France. But it was in the 1670s that it developed its most notorious specialism: the launching of privateering ventures to supplement the weaknesses in French naval policy. Between 1688 and 1713 some 947 privateers, approximately fifty per year, left the port. They captured about two thousand enemy vessels.[22] Sailors were recruited – and sometimes even conscripted – from a broad range of parishes around Saint-Malo, stretching up into Normandy. The last privateers were still operating during the Napoleonic wars.

Nantes, a southern port city, was more protected from the ferocious military and commercial antagonism with Britain which affected the northern coast. Like Saint-Malo, it developed a distinctive economic role. In the sixteenth century a network of small maritime traders evolved in Nantes, dealing in wine, fish, salt and grain. They were generally unadventurous: for many, the main aim of their commerce was to buy land and a château, and then to attempt to climb into the ranks of the nobility. Their failure to take initiatives led to the domination of the city's more profitable long-distance trade by outsiders: major Portuguese, Spanish and Dutch trading houses were established in seventeenth-century Nantes.[23] The salvation of the city's shipping came with the establishment of French colonies in the West Indies. In the 1620s and 1630s the first Breton ships left Nantes for the islands such as Saint-Christophe. They carried tobacco and silverware, and soon also began to take 'engaged men': workers who would provide the colonists with three years of labour in return for the payment of their passage to the islands.[24] In 1688 the trade grew more elaborate: in this year, the first ship from Nantes left for Africa to pick up a cargo of black slaves for the French islands. The city grew rich on the slave trade, drawing in a network of thirty-five smaller nearby ports. By the early eighteenth century, Nantes was the principal French port involved in the slave trade. In the 1770s, there were about a thousand black slaves living in Brittany.[25] The slave trade's profits provided the economic base for the new group of about twenty rich families who directed the city's commerce in the late eighteenth century.[26]

The examples provided by these three port-cities reveal another side of Brittany. While more old-fashioned ports like Vannes may have stagnated or decayed in the eighteenth century, these three ports were booming. In each case, distinctive trading activities supported the development of a new elite group. Thus, writing of the seventeenth century, Alain Croix considers that Saint-Malo was one of the rare Breton cities to develop 'a real commercial bourgeoisie'.[27] In each case, the port in question developed a particular relationship with the absolutist state, requiring state contracts for ship construction in the case of Brest, subsidies and the loan of warships for Saint-Malo and the granting of commercial monopolies for Nantes. The lifestyles of the port-based elites also represented a significant change in the nature of the elite groups who dominated Brittany. This was not necessarily in the form of a direct challenge to the aristocracy: often these traders still wished to buy up land and to join the aristocracy. The young, aggressive captains of privateers in Saint-Malo would wear swords, take up gambling and fight duels: all conspicuous signs of an aristocratic lifestyle, at variance with the sober utilitarian calculations of their merchant fathers. In June 1709, Louis XIV even awarded noble status to two brothers from Saint-Malo: one a shipping merchant, the other a privateer captain.[28]

This port-based 'Breton bourgeoisie' was probably rather more limited in its political importance than it might appear. While Saint-Malo recruited sailors from parishes as far away as Normandy, and while Nantes became the centre of a network of thirty-five local ports, these merchants and traders did not operate on a larger, regional level. Their commercial activities actually drew them away from the region, to Newfoundland or the Caribbean, and threw them into negotiations with the French state. In each case, the language of their commerce was French: Saint-Malo and Nantes had never been Breton-speaking, and Brest was a port-city of migrants. For these reasons, the merchants and traders formed highly localized groups, and were therefore unlikely to provide a type of Breton revolutionary leadership. Significantly, it was the administrative city of Rennes which probably played the most prominent role in the revolutionary years, not these port-based bourgeoisies.

One last qualification needs to be made to the more general picture of Breton social and cultural decline. While educational and cultural resources were generally shrinking, there were some signs of Breton participation in the debates of the Enlightenment. In the small northern port of Morlaix, a debating society was formed in 1778.[29] In Rennes, two new Masonic lodges were created in the late eighteenth century: La Parfaite Union and then, in 1768, a lodge specifically for artisans, La Parfaite Amitié. Members of both lodges regularly made use of the new Sabbatine library, opened in 1775, which subscribed to twenty-three periodicals and contained three thousand six hundred books by 1789.[30] Lastly, there was an important change in Breton local administration in 1691. Previously, each of the region's thirteen hundred irregularly sized parishes had, in theory, been run by a decision-making body named 'le général' or 'la généralité', which was supposedly open to all male inhabitants. In practice, few attended, and servants and workers were usually excluded. The reform of 1691 replaced this older tradition with a body of twelve named local officials, usually recruited from among the non-noble landowners, and therefore including some relatively well-off peasants.[31] During the course of the eighteenth century, these bodies grew more experienced and more professional. While these innovations are clearly not evidence of some mass cultural shift, they are important, for they explain the origins of many of the militants and activists who would bring the Revolution to the region.

In what sense did 'Brittany' exist during the Old Regime? There was a Breton legal framework, which was supervised by the Parlement at Rennes, and there was a Breton representative structure, the Estates of Brittany (to be discussed below). But it seems unlikely that these institutions encouraged any form of mass character with Brittany as a culture or an identity: at best, Brittany was a specific legal status.

There was little idea among eighteenth-century writers and scholars that Brittany was a distinct area with an identity of its own. Officials studied geography or economics in Brittany, observes Catherine Bertho, they did not write the geography or the economics of Brittany.[32] Bretons could not even be identified by a distinctive style of clothing: the *coiffes*, large hats, baggy trousers and embroidered waistcoats which make up the currently accepted stereotypes of Breton regional dress all seem to date from the early nineteenth century.[33]

One could raise an objection to this argument by referring to the Breton language. The Villers-Cotterêts decree of 1539 had established French as the official administrative language of the nation. One might therefore expect that eighteenth-century Parisian travellers and officials would have taken note of the prominent existence of Breton language. Such arguments are based on a misunderstanding of the linguistic and cultural policies of the absolutist state. As Paul Cohen has noted: 'linguistically unifying its culturally diverse realm by royal fiat was simply beyond the state's means'.[34] Use of the officially approved, orthodox version of the French language was a signifier of elite status: no eighteenth-century French government attempted to make all French people adopt such codes. Therefore, officials and travellers expected workers and peasants to speak differently from them, and often found lower-class speech incomprehensible. Whether this was because the ordinary people spoke with a pronounced accent, or used a distinct dialect, or spoke an entirely different language, was of little interest to the Parisian observer. In this respect, Brittany was no different from any other French province, and in eighteenth-century reports and travellers' texts, the Breton language features only as 'an unimportant phenomenon'.[35]

One key characteristic of eighteenth-century Breton society was its variety: while its economy was backward and often declining, it did contain some pockets of extremely dynamic and enterprising commercial activity. While it was largely a rural region, it included some prominent and significant towns.

The single most important social group in its social hierarchy was the aristocracy. We will now turn to examine how this group acted during the Revolution.

Breton nobles and Breton politics

The nobles were the first group to assert a specific form of *Breton* politics. There were many reasons for this. The treaty of 1532, finally codified and regulated in the Constitution of the 1580s, guaranteed them a privileged position in the region, in both economic and political terms. The nobles were exempt from most taxes, as were nobles across France. But, more importantly for our purposes, they came to dominate Brittany politically. The Breton Parlement was established in 1554 by Henri II: like similar bodies elsewhere in France, it was not a representative institution, but a type of high court, or a final court of appeal, with an additional responsibility for registering and debating new legislation. It also worked as an arena in which French and Breton elites met and – over time – fused with each other. In the seventeenth century, the Parlement could still serve as a channel by which a few lucky commoners joined the nobility. After 1672, it became more exclusive. Non-nobles were not allowed to serve in the Parlement: its one hundred or so officials were all nobles.[36]

Alongside the Breton Parlement were the Breton Estates, organized, like the estates in the other French provinces, into three groups: the church, the aristocracy and the commoners, principally represented by the towns. At the 1608 meeting of the estates, these three groups were represented accordingly:

first estate: 7 bishops, 5 abbots, 8 cathedral chapters;
second estate: 146 nobles;
third estate: representatives of 30 towns.[37]

The absolute numbers of the representatives was of little formal importance: each estate was supposed to present a single, unanimous opinion, and thus in the final discussions there were not 146 votes from the assembled nobles, but just one voice from the second estate. More significant than the absolute numbers of representatives was their social composition. No peasants were present: they were supposedly represented by the aristocracy. No workers or artisans were present: they were supposedly represented by the towns. Very few merchants or traders were present: they too were supposedly represented by the towns.

In practice, the meetings of the estates did not function in the manner that their rules suggested. While only a limited number of nobles were allowed to vote, *all* were allowed to attend the meetings. In 1700 there were about four and a half thousand noble families in Brittany: they constituted about one per cent of the region's population.[38] Not all of them attended the estates, but during the eighteenth century, more and more of them came: 689 were present in Vannes for the meeting of the estates in 1689;[39] about eight hundred and fifty attended the estates in Rennes in 1732, and over twelve hundred were present for the estates' last meeting in December 1788.[40] (After 1732, estates meetings were fixed at Rennes, and were held every two years.) The nobles' presence often seemed to dominate the entire city for the weeks in which the estates met. The richer Breton nobles imitated their Parisian cousins' lifestyles: they owned two houses, and wanted their urban residences, ideally in Rennes, to be designed according to the latest Parisian styles.[41] When the estates met, the nobles filled the city's cafes; they ate, drank and swore, they crowded out onto its streets. This regular, biennial meeting gave them the opportunity to develop a sense of group identity, and allowed them to gloss over the differences between the super-rich noble elite, who could afford to attend the King's court in Versailles, and the lesser nobles, some little more than peasants with swords, fighting to retain the prestige of their family names. The poorest nobles were usually unable to afford the costs of transport and accommodation in Rennes.

Chateaubriand's description of his father, a reasonably wealthy noble, gives us an insight into the Breton nobles' culture.

> He was miserly, hoping in this way to allow his family to return to its original glory, arrogant when he met other nobles at the Estates of Brittany, tough with his serfs at Combourg, taciturn, despotic and threatening at home. When you saw him, you felt afraid.[42]

This was the social group who became the most stubborn defenders of Breton privileges at the end of the Old Regime.

In the eighteenth century, the nobles dominated the two most important political bodies in Brittany: the Parlement and the estates. These nobles set themselves the task of defending the Breton Constitution, which contained many privileges for which the bulk of the Breton population could feel grateful. In general, taxes were significantly lower in Brittany than elsewhere. As there was no salt tax (or *gabelle*) levied in the region, salt sold in Brittany cost only one thirtieth the price of salt sold elsewhere in France: a situation which encouraged the widespread secondary trade of salt-smuggling.[43] Bretons were also exempt from ordinary conscription, although some were required to serve in a new coastal militia created in 1716.[44] The nobles made themselves into the guardians of this privileged situation, and would forcefully resist attempts by the King and government ministers to devise new forms of taxation. The most militant of all, it was frequently noted, were the poorer nobles, who formed 'the Bastion': a type of hard-line, no-compromise faction within the nobility.

In 1718–20, following the royal decision to exile a number of *parlementaires*, there was even a rebellion among the nobles. The Marquis de Pontcallec created a sort of league of nobles, with a few hundred members. This organization led a tax revolt. The affair grew more serious when Pontcallec even appealed to Spain, at that time an enemy of the French government, for aid. One representative of the conspiracy made two journeys to Madrid to negotiate with Philip V's government. In 1719 seven ships sailed from Spain to Brittany but, following a storm, only one reached the peninsula of Quiberon. It carried some three hundred soldiers, who disembarked. When they found that nobody was there to meet them, they returned to their ship. In 1720, seventy nobles were arrested, and the government decided to make an example of their leaders. Four of them, including Pontcallec, were decapitated in a public square in Nantes: a form of execution usually only reserved for commoners.[45] While few other nobles followed Pontcallec into open revolt, his movement can be seen as part of a series of anti-governmental rebellions, which involved serious political clashes between the Parlement and the Crown in the 1760s and 1780s. These incidents meant that Brittany acquired a reputation as a kind of rebel province before the Revolution, at the forefront in defending the interests of the ordinary person against the greed of the absolutist King and his government.

There were, however, some important limitations to the nobles' defence of the Breton Constitution. Defending Brittany's tax privileges obviously meant that peasants and labourers paid less in tax: this, in turn, meant that they were able to pay higher land rents and other charges to the largely aristocratic owners of seigneuries. There were 3,905 such properties in Brittany in 1710.[46] In general, their aristocratic landowners contributed little to the region's economy. A few pioneered the little mines and forges that processed mineral deposits from their land, and some joined institutions for the scientific study of agriculture, but such innovators were exceptions to the rule. The Breton Constitution allowed the aristocracy a privileged position: they defended this with great zeal, but they did little else for the well-being of the people of the region.

During the eighteenth century, aristocratic arguments in defence of the Breton Constitution grew more sophisticated. On the one hand, each protest would look back to the Treaty of Union of 1532, and would defend this as if it was a sacred text which could not be amended. On the other hand, echoes of the modernizing thinking of the Enlightenment were also inserted, in incongruous fashion, into their petitions and public letters. The Parlement's *Remonstrance* of May 1788 contained references to the concept of the social contract, natural equality and to Rousseau's idea of the 'General Will'.[47]

In 1788 the aristocracy continued to defend Brittany's privileges against royal tax proposals. Such initiatives were usually popular. When twelve such noble critics were arrested in July 1788, it led to a prolonged protest campaign. In September 1788, the twelve were released from the Bastille: a crowd of more than six thousand people cheered their return to Rennes, and fireworks, bonfires and illuminations continued into the night.[48] This was perhaps the last occasion when Breton opinion seemed to accept the aristocracy as genuinely representing Breton interests. By December 1788 the Breton aristocracy was facing real opposition from within Brittany (to be discussed in the next section), and needed to consider some new tactics.

In many ways, the nobles' response to a changing situation was disappointing and unimaginative. In August 1788, estates from across France were invited to elect representatives for a meeting of the Estates General in Versailles in 1789 to discuss reform and representation. The Breton aristocracy refused to participate. They even locked themselves into the meeting hall for the Estates of Brittany in January 1789. Their main tactics at this point were, firstly, a call for a Breton patriotic defence of Breton institutions against the Crown and, secondly, an appeal to the poor of the third estate to act against the lawyers and merchants who represented them. In January 1789, nobles paid for the publication of ten thousand copies of anti-bourgeois pamphlets, with seven thousand copies in French and three thousand in Breton. It accused the urban bourgeoisie of preventing the Breton Estates from working properly.[49] The estates were, however, finally abolished in November 1789. In 1790 the aristocrats' ideas were summed up with admirable clarity in a pamphlet by the Comte de Botherel, a member of one of the oldest aristocratic families in Brittany, and a key official of the Estates of Brittany.

The first point to note here is the unusual nature of this document. Normally, aristocratic political culture was not expressed through formal argument or written documents: aristocrats were loyal to intangible ideals, not to philosophical investigations. The fact that Botherel had been forced to resort to the literary weapons of his opponents, the urban bourgeoisie, is an indication of the degree to which political culture had changed in Brittany within the space of two years. Botherel quickly passed judgements on the rapid constitutional and political evolution of France since 1788: it was merely a decay, brought about by the aberrations of a few wild minds and the lethargy of many.[50] Against this decline, Botherel presents a new idea: *la patrie*, or the fatherland. Once again, we can note a sharp distinction between Botherel's concepts and those of his pro-revolutionary opponents: the nation and fatherland were both new ideas in 1789. For most of the new generation of patriotic activists, even in Brittany, these terms referred to the French nation. Botherel was unusual in applying the word to Brittany.

Botherel deplored the speed with which fourteen centuries of governmental tradition had been destroyed. The ancient provinces of France had been replaced by 'a mass of separate little administrations', with no direction or ethic to hold them together.[51] Within this strange new situation, a new ruling class was forming. In the past, 'Brittany governed herself', but now: 'How can a few isolated men, often chosen just to please a faction, [or chosen by] the intrigues of a deviant crowd, present, research and defend the interests of a province about which they only know a few points?'[52] This strange new situation offered nothing worthy to the Breton people.

> In the place of that ancient body of magistrats, all fundamentally related to the Breton Constitution, in the place of a sovereign court, the upholder and guarantor of our contracts . . . whose regulations developed a constant, uniform jurisprudence for the whole of the province, in the place of those magistrates whose incorruptibility was recognized by the whole of France . . . small courts have been established with judges hired by cabals and factions who can dismiss them at whim.[53]

Botherel ended his pamphlet by an appeal to the lost, aberrant Breton people to recall their true interests. The third estate should not hold itself above the other two estates, but should work with them in an orderly and conciliatory manner, in order to create a single will.

This pamphlet provides us with unambiguous evidence of the difficulties which the older nobility experienced in adapting to the new conditions of the Revolution. They simply could not understand the new systems of rule and direction. Instead of criticizing the new institutions from a political perspective, and so raising questions about their possible efficiency, Botherel simply dismisses the new strata of administrators and representatives as corrupt and illegitimate. His whole argument rests upon the intangible, unproven right of the aristocracy to represent and to govern Brittany. For these reasons, Botherel – and the aristocracy he represented – made poor nationalists.

Botherel had no sense of how to appeal to the people, and no respect for their right to choose their own representatives. Indeed, he had little clear sense of the interests of the mass of Breton society. Above all, his conception of Brittany strikes one as remarkably limited: he had no idea of Breton culture, of a Breton ethnicity and certainly made no reference to the Breton language. At the heart of this aristocratic radicalism is a dry, legalistic concept of Brittany as a specific lawful entity.

The revolt of the third estate

As Michel Denis has argued, the social tensions of eighteenth-century France quickly became obvious in pre-revolutionary Brittany. One striking point is the speed with which new, critical ideas spread across the region. Part of the procedure for calling the Estates-General in Versailles was the drawing up of *Cahiers de Doléances* (literally, complaint books) by each parish. Over seven hundred were produced in Brittany. In some places, peasant *cahiers* were drawn up for them by urban lawyers and merchants but, more often, peasant delegates were surprisingly confident and articulate in presenting their own concerns.[54] In rural Trégor, for example, approximately half the rural parishes produced their own *cahiers*.[55] In such debates, the poorer peasants' and day labourers' concerns were often ignored by the richer peasants, but the key point that still emerges from rural *cahiers* is the deep, widespread anger that was felt against the seigneurial system, coupled with the peasants' faith in the capacity of the king to introduce deep, structural reform.[56] Peasants also routinely demanded the end of such practices as seigneurial monopolies on windmills and ovens.[57]

In places, there remained some affection for the privileges guaranteed by the Breton Constitution. For example, in April 1789 Joseph-Michel Pellerin, a lawyer, was elected to represent the third estate of Nantes. In November of that year he spoke in the National Assembly: here, he defended the Breton Estates on the grounds that they were older than the Frankish estates, which could only be dated back to the fifth century, and that the Parisian National Assembly could therefore not abolish them.[58] Normally, however, any loyalty to the old Constitution by members of the third estate was qualified by a deep scepticism about the nobles' ability to defend the Constitution in the people's interests.

The urban *cahiers* stressed some different issues. Commonly they called for the end of royal customs houses at the edge of towns: such tolls were an irksome reminder of royal power, and prevented urban economies from growing. Half of the thirty-three towns in Brittany were actually owned by seigneurs, and so urban delegates could sympathize with the anti-seigneurial anger of the rural *cahiers*.[59] In Rennes, new young radicals demanded the exclusion of all nobles and all officials who worked for nobles from their meetings before they elected delegates and drew up their *cahiers*.[60]

These procedures marked another step in the increasingly deep split between, on the one hand, the third estate and, on the other hand, the nobles and the upper clergy. The nobles simply boycotted these elections. Many of the lower clergy, principally rural priests, did participate, but the upper clergy – mainly aristocrats – followed the nobles in their boycott. In the spring of 1789 forty-four Breton delegates for the third estate and twenty-two delegates for the first estate were elected. The forty-four third estate delegates were mainly lawyers or other legal officials: thirty of their number worked in such professions. They also included seven merchants or maritime traders, five farmers, a doctor and a landowner.[61] One point to note here is the social origins of this so-called 'revolutionary bourgeoisie': in Brittany, as elsewhere in France, the Revolution was led by lawyers. The merchants of Nantes and Saint-Malo certainly participated, but it was the legal professions of Rennes who dominated. Of course, activists drawn from the legal professions knew the nature of the seigneurial system inside-out, and were often deeply committed to its liberalization. Many of them had a deep, sincere faith that the free market was the best replacement for the monopolies and privileges that characterized both absolutism and seigneurialism. But they were not traders, and on other occasions would show ethical concerns about the unregulated free market.[62] Secondly, one also notes the under-representation of the rural people: approximately 85–90 per cent of the Breton population lived in the countryside, but more than 90 per cent of the third estate delegates came from the towns.[63] While peasants were able to draw up *cahiers*, they were less successful in putting themselves forwards as political representatives.

As *cahiers* were discussed and delegates were elected, political debates continued. One clear example of the new political culture of the third estate was written by Jean-Marie Glézen (1737–1801), a lawyer from Rennes. His magnificently polemical response to the aristocratic defence of the Breton Constitution was published in Rennes early in 1789. The pamphlet was clearly designed to be read aloud – or shouted.

> How dare you support a constitution in which the dignity of man is insulted and his rights are ignored to the point that millions of men are subordinated to the whims and the greed of a privileged class, a constitution which allows a handful of individuals who have set themselves up as despots, granting

themselves the shameful privilege of exemption from taxation, and making the people carry the burden for them, a constitution which is alien to the concept of the good, because to make it work would need fundamental reform – reforms that will never come, because those that claim to be the masters, those guardians of the constitution, crush the best intentioned citizens . . . how dare you suggest that such a constitution provides for the well-being of this great province and that all Bretons must honour it?[64]

The ideas that circulated among the third estate in Brittany were as radical and as hard-hitting as those anywhere in France. One reason for this militancy was the relatively well-organized and militantly conservative aristocratic opposition to social and political reform in Brittany. The representatives of the third estate saw clearly that they had a fight on their hands: they had no illusions about the nature of the aristocracy. On 16 July 1789, in Rennes, patriotic activists appealed to soldiers to join their revolution. Many responded, and a national army was swiftly formed, with young radicals and professional soldiers patrolling the city's streets.[65] In this case, it is clear that events were moving as fast in Rennes as they were in Paris: in the capital, the patriotic National Guard was formed on 13 July 1789.

These factors meant that in the summer of 1789 the Breton delegates of the third estate were among the clearest-thinking and best-organized politicians in Paris. They formed a type of political caucus, the Breton Club: soon third estate representatives from across France were attending its meetings. One should note the contrast between the two types of political culture identified so far. On the one hand, there was the nobles' defence of the Breton Constitution: a backward-looking, sentimental discourse, rooted in the concepts of the region's unique, particular privileges, and aiming to preserve social inequality and economic exploitation. On the other hand, there emerged a Breton interpretation of the revolutionary ideals: clearly hostile to the inequality of the seigneurial system, but somewhat vaguer on broader political questions. As yet, there was little criticism of the monarchy: in fact, Bretons of the third estate tended to show a renewed faith in their reforming King. Such activists had no sympathy for the old Breton Constitution, and joined other third estate delegates in voting against it in the second half of 1789. Their attitude was neatly summed up in a line from a pamphlet by Laurent-François Legendre (1741–1802), who was elected as a third estate representative for Brest. They had defended the Breton Constitution against despotism, but they would not defend it against liberty.[66] Added to this, there were passionate commitments to forms of equality, particularly tax equality, and to a fairer system of political representation, but not necessarily to democracy.

It remained to be seen how their region would be integrated into these broader programmes.

Above all, the Breton representatives of the third estate were committed to the exhausting, exhilarating processes of political debate. Joseph Delaville-Leroulx (1747–1803), a third estate representative from the southern port of Lorient, wrote 373 long, detailed letters back to his electors from April 1789 to August 1790.[67] It would be easy to dismiss these pamphlets and speeches as just so much hot air, but such judgements underestimate the nature of the new political culture of revolutionary France. These speakers and writers were committed to their cause. Their words burn with an almost religious intensity; they are an integral part of the construction of a new mentality or a new spirit. Very soon, this new generation of political activists would need to back their words with actions.

The Counter-Revolution: La Vendée and Chouannerie

If one can make the claim that the French Revolution started in Brittany, then it is also possible to argue that the Counter-Revolution started in the same region. There were many points of rupture. The savagery of anti-seigneurial violence in the countryside took many urban politicians by surprise: they urged caution, and told the rioters to respect the wise decisions of the National Assembly.[68] With hindsight, we can see that this rural violence marked the beginning of a profound split in the third estate, suggesting that there were actually two separate revolutions unfolding in Brittany.

A second, clearer, point of rupture developed in 1790, when the National Assembly passed a proposal to reform the Catholic Church, transforming it into a national institution, with its priests and bishops paid by the state, and with the boundaries of ecclesiastical administration consistent with the secular boundaries of the eighty-three new departments. To finance this measure, and to pay off the debts accumulated by the Old Regime state, church property and lands would be sold off. In Brittany, this meant the reduction of the nine old dioceses to five new dioceses in the five newly formed Breton departments of Ille-et-Vilaine, Loire-Inférieure, Côtes-du-Nord, Morbihan and Finistère. The delegates of the National Assembly had expected priests to support their proposals, but across France they aroused controversy. In fact, only approximately half the priests in France swore an oath of allegiance to the new church. In Brittany, rates of refusal were even higher.

Some points need to be stressed about this data. First, one frequently comes across the assumption that the more westerly, largely Breton-speaking

Table 2.1 Proportion of priests refusing to swear an oath of allegiance to the Constitutional Church, 1790–1.[69] (per cent)

Department	Percentage refusal
Côtes-du-Nord	75
Finistère	75
Ille-et-Vilaine	83
Loire-Inférieure	75
Morbihan	85.5
Approximate regional average	80

departments were more hostile to Parisian laws than the easterly, largely French-speaking departments. The data in the above table clearly contradicts this idea: westerly Finistère was showing the same degree of opposition as the easterly Loire-Inférieure. The department with the highest rate of opposition, the Morbihan, was later to be the base for a more substantial Counter-Revolutionary movement. What were the reasons for this widespread refusal? Some of the more aristocratic churchmen had been concerned about the threat to the church's autonomy prior to the Revolution. In May 1789 Pierre-Joseph de Clorivière (1735–1820), one of Brittany's leading Jesuits, noted that 'Religion will be lost if its concerns are placed, without qualification, to the votes of an assembly and if the clergy is not the unique judge of such matters.'[70] In 1790, one pamphlet spoke of the new laws as being imposed on the church, without any consultation.[71] These points are more important than they might seem. For the revolutionaries, the National Assembly was sovereign: if its deputies voted through a law, then no further consultation was required. Our clerics were suggesting another logic, thinking of France as a collection of institutions, each with their own autonomous, decision-making processes. The government should not be allowed to legislate for the church.

The revolutionaries were surprised by the lukewarm response to their proposals. In May 1791 a compromise law was finally passed, which allowed for individual churches to be divided between constitutional and non-constitutional priests: significantly this law was often not applied in Brittany. A process of political polarization had already started. The radical, politically aware patriots of the towns were suspicious of opposition, and were not prepared to tolerate dissidents. A pamphlet by Pierre-Jean Le Breton (1752–1829), a third estate representative for Vannes, warned priests of the dangers of opposing the Civil Constitution. The reforms would lead to a better church, closer to its original simplicity. The opponents were motivated by 'greed and pride'; they merely 'borrowed the language of piety'.[72]

In many rural parishes, however, the constitutional priest was seen as an unwelcome outsider, and met with open hostility. In February 1791 the priest of Plumaugat (Côtes-du-Nord) intended to take the constitutional oath. The devout women of the parish were horrified by his action: they invaded his church, pushing past the National Guards who had been sent to protect him, hitting their commanding officer, and then forced the priest to retract his oath.[73] As the months passed, this rural discontent seemed to grow stronger. In October 1792 the furniture of a priory was offered for sale at an auction in Locmaria (Morbihan). Local people protested, and threw themselves at a detachment of twenty soldiers. The soldiers fought back, firing their weapons at the crowd. When the day ended, four protestors and one soldier had been killed.[74] More generally, many rural districts, perhaps even the majority, refused to accept the new revolutionary calendar, with its ten-day weeks and meteorologically-orientated months. 'They're not getting used to the new calendar', reported a municipal official in Vitré (Ille-et-Vilaine) in 1793, 'all the citizens rest during the old festivals, listed in the old almanacs . . . The shops stay shut.'[75] Watkin Tench, a British naval officer held prisoner in Quimper in 1794–5, observed the struggle between the Sabbath and the *décadi* continuing. He noted that on the *décadi*, the flags were flown and the clerks had their day off, but it was on Sundays that most of the shops seemed to be closed.[76]

One further sign of how the political tide was turning is provided by the Breton Association organized by the Marquis Tuffin de La Roüerie. He was a prominent noble: he had been one of the twelve tax rebels, imprisoned in the Bastille in 1788, and then welcomed by the crowds on his return to Rennes in September 1788. In May 1791 he began to collect members for a secret association which – unusually – accepted non-nobles as well as nobles. From October to December 1791 he toured the coasts of Brittany, evaluating points which would be suitable for landing soldiers and weapons from Britain, and also forming twenty-two secret committees. His supporters were largely landowners and old professional officers, critical of the new revolutionary army. Among their ranks were a handful of peasants: a sign of future Counter-Revolutionary opposition.[77] His conspiracy was uncovered in the summer of 1792, and La Roüerie was guillotined in Rennes in October 1792.[78]

The paragraphs above outline some of the signs of tension which, with hindsight, we can see suggested the clash that was to come. However, in each of these cases – aristocratic pamphleteering, peasant discontent, religious conservatism and aristocratic plotting – no substantial social movement emerged. While there is every indication that many villagers were growing alienated from the revolutionary process, as yet there was no clear break.

The issue which finally split Brittany was conscription. War broke out on France's eastern border in April 1792. The new government organized hastily created mixed units of regular conscripts, patriotic volunteers and National Guards, and won some stunning victories against professional armies. In the spring of 1793, however, it became clear that such improvised forces were no longer sufficient. A general conscription of three hundred thousand young men was ordered in February 1793. The new administration expected some significant reluctance to serve: even some outright refusals. Even in patriotic Rennes, the conscription announcement led to a 'worrying agitation'.[79] In parts of the west of France, however, specifically in the departments of La Vendée (to the south of Brittany), of the Maine-et-Loire (to the south-west) and in the Loire-Inférieure, young men did not simply resist conscription, but fought back against the soldiers and National Guards who were sent to enforce the orders. While war was being fought out in the east, the government could ill-afford to send soldiers on police duties in the west.[80] Yet on 15 March 1793, the little town of Redon (Ille-et-Vilaine) was reported to be attacked by countless bandits, and the department itself was 'threatened from all directions'.[81] For many weeks, the government continued to underestimate the problem. Soldiers from the affected areas were sent away to guard ports while the rebellion gathered support. This coincidence of events may be the explanation for the transformation of a series of anti-conscription riots into a full-blown Counter-Revolution. The rebels initially only faced small groups of ill-trained National Guards, fighting far from their home towns, and who were quickly demoralized when faced with a determined attack.

To make matters worse, when the Republican soldiers did win victories, they showed no mercy to those they considered as traitors. On 19 March 1793, Republican soldiers re-took the small town of Chateaubriant (Loire-Inférieure), which had briefly fallen into the hands of the rebels. They captured ninety-six prisoners, all of whom were promptly executed.[82] This type of vicious, bloody repression set the tone for the battles of the succeeding months: it made compromise impossible, and pushed the rebels into a position of no return. Atrocities were committed by both sides.

The fighting took two forms. During the summer of 1793 there were a series of attempts by young aristocrats to convert these untrained bands of peasant conscription rebels into something approaching a regular army, which took the title of the Royal Catholic Army. Fifty years later, one Breton Republican could still record his surprise at the sight of this force: 'We saw, there on the plain, not battalions, but a mass of men preceded by countless priests, crosses, banners, flags and standards.'[83] In the summer of that year, the peasant insurgents achieved a type of control over the rural areas in the departments of La Vendée, the south of the Loire-Inférieure and the Maine-et-Loire. In all, rebels were present in ten French departments.[84] However, the towns resisted their attacks and, if they were captured, the Vendéens rarely were able to hold them for more than a few weeks.

Following a serious defeat at Cholet (La Vendée) in September 1793, the leaders of the rebel army embarked on a new strategy: in order to defeat the Blues, they had to have British weapons, particularly artillery. But for this to be landed, a port was needed. The entire Vendéen force crossed the Loire, and marched up to the Channel. At this point, they were no longer an army, but a collection of old men, women, children and rebels, perhaps a hundred thousand strong in total, with approximately thirty to forty thousand fighters.[85] Given the savagery of the fighting, no one could be left behind in the villages. Despite attacks on the Channel port of Granville, and on the towns of Angers and Le Mans, the Vendéen force was unable to find a base for the winter. They then turned southwards, to suffer a second crushing defeat at Le Mans in December 1793.

This improvised force was then transformed. While Counter-Revolutionary officers still planned to create a regular army to oppose the forces of the Republic, the fragments of the army scattered to hide out in the hills and forests. Here they began to make good use of the bocage landscape which dominates this area, and which was eloquently described by the widow of the Marquis de La Rochejaquelein, one of the youngest and most charismatic of the Vendéen generals.

> This land is full of hills, covered with trees, crossed by many gushing streams. Narrow, muddy tracks lie deep in the ground, bordered by high hedges and by trees. There are no highways or navigable rivers . . . and there are many huge rocks. Much of the ground lies fallow: they plant broom bushes on these fields, and then they leave them for as long as ten years. These can grow into impenetrable forests.[86]

The key point here is given by the word 'impenetrable'. This was a landscape in which it was difficult to ride horses or to move artillery. Even large, regular units of marching soldiers would only be able to move slowly. But to those who knew the area, who knew each track and hill, it was almost ideal as a refuge. The small groups of Vendéen fugitives found many hiding places in its hills and forests.

A new term came to be used to describe the second form of opposition which was begun by these fugitives: they were Chouans. This term was drawn from a signal used by smugglers before the Revolution, who would imitate owls' hoots. The term suggests an element of continuity in the region's politics: just as Breton peasants had tolerated the illegal activities of salt smugglers, so they felt a degree of sympathy for the Chouan cause. Significantly, well into 1793, Republican officials continued to describe them as 'brigands', suggesting a refusal to see any specific *political* content to their actions.

The presence of the fugitives changed the climate of the many rural districts. As we have seen, in the first years after the Revolution, there was a type of low-level hostility to the pretensions of the new rulers. The Chouans gave a focus to such discontent: they formed the link between aristocratic rebels, conservative Catholics, non-constitutional priests and disgruntled villagers. When the new authorities attempted to clamp down on these rebels, often their own weakness became obvious as they struggled with the massive passive resistance of the rural people. For example, in October 1795 it was estimated that there were some sixty-five illegal, non-constitutional priests in the arrondissement of Redon. By May 1796 only four of them had been arrested: another four had fled abroad.[87]

Table 2.2 Actions by Chouans in the arrondissement of Redon, July 1794–July 1796.[88]

Action	Number of incidents
Robberies from farmers who had bought church property	30
Thefts	20
Murders	11
Ambushes	3
Destruction of liberty trees	2
Theft of weapons	2
Preventing travel	2
Fights	2
Taking prisoners	2
Violence	1
Anti-tax riot	1
Total	76

Table 2.3 Victims of Chouan violence in the arrondissement of Redon, July 1794–July 1796.[89]

Target group	Number of murders
Municipal officials	2
Ex-priests	2
Judges	1
Farmers owning ex-church or ex-aristocratic land	1
Jacobins	1
Postmen	1
Weavers	1
Charcoal burners	1
Ex-soldiers	1
Total	11

After each Republican victory and succeeding political repression, Chouannerie flared up again: in 1795, in 1799, in 1813, in 1815 and even after 1832 (a point to be discussed in chapter 4). To an extent, Chouans began to develop their own forms of political culture: when a white flag was placed on the Gravelle road in Vitré (Ille-et-Vilaine) in March 1794, all of the Republican officials knew what it meant: it was not simply a sign of a Chouan presence, but also a threat, to them.[90] However, this improvised, inarticulate movement never produced any manifesto or leading philosophers. To those involved, the meaning of Chouan actions was self-evident.

The research by Monique Souben allows us to gauge the strength of this movement. From July 1794 to July 1796, Chouans in Redon arrondissement were responsible for seventy-three illegal acts, including eleven murders. It is clear from Tables 2.2 and 2.3 that the first and most noticeable feature of Chouannerie was violence. The cycle of attack and counter-attack, begun with the war in the La Vendée in 1793, now continued on a smaller, local scale. On occasion, this was aimed at symbols of Republican authority, whether municipal officials or artefacts like the 'Liberty Trees' which had been planted in 1789. On other occasions, Chouannerie acted almost like a counter-police force. Armed bands, who could be anything from five to sixty strong, toured the villages and hamlets at night, demanding non-cooperation with the regime, and punishing those who showed sympathy for the Blues: hence the presence of the charcoal-burner and the weaver on the table above.

In the affected areas, their actions were surprisingly successful. Witnesses refused to identify individual Chouans and there was a 'wall of silence' when the police asked questions.[91] But the most lasting effect of Chouannerie was to divide communities: it 'was the visible manifestation of a countryside that was seriously fractured' notes Donald Sutherland.[92]

Because so many were eventually arrested, some information is available about the type of people who joined the Chouan bands. Their ages varied enormously: they included grandfathers and teenagers. Monique Souben estimates that their average age was 33.5 years old. As might be expected, almost half came from agricultural trades, ranging from day labourers to tenant farmers, and a significant minority were rural artisans. A handful of women were arrested along with the Chouans: they had served as assistants or lookouts.[93] Sutherland cautions against seeing Chouannerie as a movement of the poor: it was, rather, a movement led by peasant notables who had grown disappointed with the Revolution.[94]

One final point needs to be made about the nature of the movement. The desperate anti-conscription rebels of 1793 constituted a popular movement: there is more than an element of truth in the romantic tales that circulated about peasants demanding leadership from isolated aristocrats who had thought that the Revolution had beaten all opposition.[95] But with each successive wave of Chouan violence, the aristocratic leaders imposed stricter direction on the movement. There were some real tensions between these two poles. For example, when British ships arrived at Carnac (Morbihan) in June 1795 they brought with them twenty-seven thousand guns and about fifteen hundred aristocratic exiles. The plan was that these Counter-Revolutionary forces would join with Chouan groups active in Morbihan. In practice, the aristocratic Counter-Revolutionary leader, the Comte d'Hervilly, was dismayed by the sight of the desperate, ill-disciplined, hard-drinking Chouans, and refused to work with them.[96] In later years peasants grew more sceptical about these aristocratic leaders. In May 1815, when the nobles summoned them to fight against the returning Napoleon, only a few peasants responded, and they showed little enthusiasm: this war was senseless, they realized.[97]

Chouannerie was widespread in Brittany during the revolutionary years. It must be stressed, however, that it did not cover the entire region. Roger Dupuy has tried to gauge the extent of Chouan support in 1794. He estimates that they were active in roughly 60 per cent of Brittany: in nearly all of the Loire-Inférieure and Morbihan, in about half of the Ille-et-Vilaine and about a third of both the Côtes-du-Nord and Finistère.[98] Once again, it should be stressed that the three predominantly Breton-speaking departments, out to the west, were not the most likely to support this rebellion against Republican rule.

For some conservative Breton nationalists, there was an unbroken line of development from the aristocratic conspiracy of Pontallec, through the aristocratic Counter-Revolutionaries and Chouans of the 1790s, to the first nationalists of the early twentieth century.[99] We will re-consider this argument in chapter 7. For the moment, however, let us examine whether these movements are the roots of a modern sense of nationalism. First, it is clear that none of these movements could properly claim to represent the entire region: these aristocrats made poor populists, and were usually unable to present their political ideals in a form which attracted the majority of the population. Instead, these movements seem only loosely connected to Brittany: aristocrats looked to the Spain court in the 1710s, to German princes in 1790 and to the British government in the late 1790s. Moreover, the movements were limited geographically and socially. Lastly, these movements had, at best, a weak sense of Breton identity. Brittany was simply a good recruiting group for Counter-Revolutionary activities: Bretons were rarely presented by these militants as a people with a history or a culture of their own. In many cases these reactionary movements overlapped with other areas of France: this is most clearly revealed by the Chouans, a movement which was started outside of Brittany, in La Vendée.

Rather than beginning a nationalist tradition, these Counter-Revolutionary movements represent the start of a nineteenth-century form of conservatism, which defended a regional 'pays' against the modernizing state. An essential part of this political culture was the idealization of social relations in the 'pays'. La Rochejaquelein included a romanticized image of Vendéen society in her account of the revolt:

> The people are fundamentally gentle: they are stubborn, hospitable, good, trusting, brave, happy and extremely devout. They are full of respect for the priests and nobles. They approach them carefully, although they are always sure that they will be warmly welcomed: then, in an instant, this timidity changes into familiarity, and you could say that they approach their *seigneur* like children approach their father: with respect and fondness. These peasants are pure and simple; they live comfortably, without being rich, and they are very happy ... What a fine *pays*! How could one not love you? Alone in France, you never changed, you never made a single mistake.[100]

Chateaubriand wrote about La Vendée in similar terms, arguing that 'God seemed to have preserved this model of society to teach us how a people to whom God has given laws is stronger than a people who legislate for themselves.'[101] Of course, neither of these images accurately depicts social relations in the Chouan areas: one point worth remembering is the *cahiers* written by these same happy peasants in 1789. They were often vigorously anti-seigneurial.[102] Later conservative historians would attempt to blur the distinctions between the participants in the Counter-Revolutionary rebellions: for example, Barthélemy informed his readers that Bretons and Vendéens could not be separated.[103] But it must be stressed that La Vendée is not Brittany: the two areas had different histories. Chouannerrie was certainly an indication of social problems in Republican France, but it was not a proto-nationalism.

The formation of the Blues

Republican groups in 1793 were not concerned about subtle distinctions. For them, a simple dichotomy had been created by this conflict. 'Against the Republic, which was progress and the future, Brittany in 1799 was the past, ignorance and the rejection of the Enlightenment.'[104] Opposition in Brittany, La Vendée and the west was conflated into a single act of deliberate betrayal.[105] While the forces of the Republic were slow to act, it was clear that they saw the issue as first and foremost a military confrontation, and they refused to consider negotiations. In March 1793 fifty thousand soldiers were sent to the 'La Vendée militaire', the area of conflict around La Vendée. By December 1793 there were seventy-five thousand soldiers in the area.[106] Such initiatives marked a significant change in the nature of Blue political culture. Previous initiatives, if not exactly democratic, had been based on the assumption that the revolutionaries were acting for the benefit of the majority of the population, and that they could count on their support. Thus Jean-Marie Jézéquel, a Republican activist from Morlaix, begins his account of the revolutionary period with the statement 'I was a patriot; as was the land [pays].'[107] Roger Dupuy provides a succinct summary of the new attitude of 1793.

> Patriotism could only be imposed with the support of an energetic administration that was able to enforce its will: in other words, with an effective armed force, a professional army. But such units were rare and so, finally, it was the active and relatively large units of the National Guard that imposed patriotism on the recalcitrant.[108]

This point is vital for our analysis: (French) patriotism was not simply imposed on Brittany by a law being passed in Paris. It was imposed by a

Table 2.4 Political clubs in Brittany, 1789–95.[109]

Department	Proportion of communes with a club (%)	Clubs per 100,000 habitants
Côtes-du-Nord	7.7	5.8
Finistère	11.7	8.4
Ille-et-Vilaine	6.6	4.7
Loire-Inférieure	9.7	6.4
Morbihan	13.8	8.0

significant minority of local Breton people, acting with energy, bravery and imagination in the most difficult of circumstances.

The astonishing point that comes across from the documents of this period is how quickly a deep sense of revolutionary community emerged among this new generation of activists. In 1789 and 1790 Joseph Delaville-Leroulx, busy writing his 373 letters, may have seemed almost like a madman. In these crisis years of 1793 and 1794 this communicative activity suddenly became the basis for a substantial movement. At the centre of this new culture were the radical political clubs that spread across France. P. Gervais has attempted to quantify the spread of such clubs in Brittany. Gervais estimates that 78 clubs were to be found in the predominantly Breton-speaking west, and only 67 in the predominantly French- or Gallo-speaking east. When Barère made his now infamous speech to the Committee of Public Safety in January 1794, stating that 'federalism and superstition speak Breton', he was factually incorrect: Breton-speaking areas were slightly more favourable to the Revolution than the French and Gallo-speaking areas.[110] Clubs were most frequently formed in towns and ports: only 20 of these 145 clubs were based in settlements smaller than a cantonal head-town, while about 40 per cent were located along the coast. French nationalism flowed along the roads and coasts to existing centres of communication: the first task of these clubs was to watch the roads and to receive the mail. Their most basic daily activity was the passionate reading aloud of journals and letters. In fact, sometimes the age-old tension between town and country seems to constitute the basis for the great political divide of the revolutionary period. 'The towns' example will persuade the country folk that there is only one way that they will be happy', reported the municipal official in Vitré (Ille-et-Vilaine), 'they must destroy all their old prejudices and work together for the maintenance of the Republic's prosperity.'[111]

Table 2.5 Ages of members of the Republican Society in Vannes, November 1794

Age	Proportion of members (%)
17–30	17.11
31–40	28.18
41–50	33.22
51–60	16.10
61–70	5.36
70 and above	1.34

Bertrand Frélaut has analysed the membership of the Republican Society in Vannes, which was active under different names from 1791 to 1795. A list compiled in November 1794 gives some details of the club's 285 members. The information in Tables 2.5 and 2.6 allows us to understand the basis of the Blues more clearly. These activists were not young hot-heads: the majority of them were married fathers in their thirties and forties. By and large, they were educated, professional people. They already worked in offices or ran workshops. Their militancy was a natural development of their accepted social status. On the other hand, they were far from the 'revolutionary bourgeoisie' of Marxist mythology: this data suggests that Blues were as likely to be lawyers or artisans as they were to be merchants.

In general, the clubs expanded in the years from 1789 to 1795. Their expansion was fastest in reaction to Chouannerie: from September 1793 to August 1794, Gervais estimates that no fewer than sixty-seven new clubs were created. They worked to build up a reliable, effective network of militants and activists across Brittany. Their letters and publications frequently

Table 2.6 Social composition of club members[112]

Social sector	Proportion of members (%)
Legal professions	16.60
Military and police	11.60
Church, teaching and medicine	12.80
Administration	16.90
Commerce	19.00
Trades and artisans	22.80

show the importance that they attached to such matters. When the municipal official in Vitré estimated that he could only find 'reliable men' in four of his district's forty communes, he was not stating some sort of idiosyncratic personal preference, but making an important sociopolitical judgement concerning local resources.[113] Without genuine support, it would be hard to save the Revolution in this area.

When faced with opposition from conscription rebels or Counter-Revolutionaries, these activists felt no sympathy or hesitation. This is, perhaps, the significance of their repeated use of terms like 'brigands' or 'fanatics': they refused to recognize any legitimacy in the protests. The departmental administration of the Ille-et-Vilaine issued the following declaration within days of the first signs of trouble in March 1793:

> Urgent action is needed to stop the deadly effects of agitators' plots and to disperse the many conspirators' meetings which are ruining this department: we need prompt and exemplary punishments of those who carried weapons to these meetings and of those who are convicted of joining in their disorders.[114]

When they won such battles, the Blues showed no mercy. Conan, a Republican soldier, recalls capturing a Chouan near Guingamp one night, and then touring the town in order to find a prison for him. When it was clear that none was available, they simply killed their captive.[115] Jézéquel recalled the victory of his National Guard unit at Fouesnant: 'We treated the land as if it was a conquered territory. The cows, sheep, birds, butter, fruit and women were seized and we made good use of all of them.'[116]

The first result of the conflicts of 1793 and 1794 was a profound, lasting sense of polarization. 'Two civilizations fought each other' notes Jean-Clément Martin.[117] This may have started as a political disagreement, but it was quickly supplanted by a record of violence and counter-violence. Each side could point to the atrocities committed by their opponents as a justification for further action. By 1803, the Guingamp Sub-Prefect (Côtes-du-Nord) could assume that this situation was almost the norm in his territory. 'What land [pays] does not have its Chouan militants, and its partisans of the regime of 1793? They are like the weeds which grow in the best-kept earth.'[118] The Blues had devised a political ideal which resonated in the regions for decades. During the 'Hundred Days' of Napoleon's return (March–May 1815), groups of armed, anti-royalist 'fédérés' were promptly formed in Rennes. They were clearly directly inspired by memories of the experiences of the 1790s.[119] Writing in the 1840s, Jézéquel was still moved by the ideas of his youth. 'Patriot! People laugh about it. The nation is in the cash-till. Even the rich man says he's a patriot! . . . Oh, poor France of 1789, what's happened to you?'[120]

It was because of the strength of their beliefs, and their certainty that the nation had reached a crisis point, that the Blues were prepared to accept some of the bloodiest aspects of the Revolution. The policy of 'terror' was launched in the summer of 1793 as a means to surmount the multiple military, political and social crises that the regime faced. 'It implied something more akin to a political version of martial law, administered by the government, in accordance with rules that placed the supposed interests of society above those of the individual,' explains Norman Hampson.[121] In practice, it meant that improvised courts dispensed quick justice to those who were unfortunate enough to find themselves arrested as suspects. The regular criminal court in Rennes tried 327 suspects from March to July 1793: it condemned 24 of them to death. It was then supplanted by a revolutionary commission, run by Brutus Magnier, which examined 399 suspects: 224 of them were executed.[122] Carrier was also sent to Rennes to enforce the terror. Thankfully, he saw his priority in this city as purging the administration rather than eliminating opponents. His report leaves us with some telling images of his motivations.

> We have dismissed all the royalists, feuillants [members of a royalist club], federalists and moderates. Positions in food supplies, estates and registrations have been purged. Only the hospitals have escaped our reforms, but this is only a temporary delay. All those old health officials stink of the aristocracy, and the young ones are fops, pretty boys, royalists and federalists who have slipped into their places so that their delicate, beautiful bodies escape service at the frontiers. We will ask a commissar to recruit some tough Jacobin fathers in Paris: they will do a lot to maintain the public spirit in Rennes at the level we have placed it.[123]

Nantes was Carrier's priority. This great port was a target for British influence: like the southern French port of Toulon, it could be seized by the Revolution's enemy. There were 144 executions in the city in November and December 1793, but still Carrier thought this was too slow. He organized a secret police to identify suspects more swiftly. Thousands of Vendéen prisoners also arrived in Nantes: from mid-December 1793 to mid-February 1794, some two thousand six hundred were executed. Sometimes two hundred were killed on a single day. The most sinister note of all came when Carrier announced that he still considered the rate of executions to be too slow, and demanded that more efficient means be found. The result was the infamous *noyades*: prisoners were trapped in old boats, which were taken out onto the Loire, and sunk. Between seven and eleven of these dreadful actions took place; between about two and four thousand died in them.[124]

Not all the region suffered such terrible violence. In the port of Saint-Malo, approximately a hundred died. In Finistère there were only about seventy executions.[125] In Saint-Brieuc there was no 'purging' of the administration and no new revolutionary tribunals.[126] Cambry gives us a pleasant little sketch of life on the island of Sein (Finistère) in 1795. 'The Revolution has changed nothing in this quiet, poor land [pays]. The bells ring at 5 pm, and everyone goes to prayer. The priest, a brave man, has not left his parish. He probably knows nothing of the divisions and schisms of his brothers.'[127] Renan, discussing the Trégor area of the Côtes-du-Nord in the early nineteenth century, made similar observations.

> In fact, the Revolution [of 1789] never came to the world in which I lived. The people's religious ideas had not been sullied. The congregations reformed; the sisters of the old religious orders became school-mistresses, and gave girls the same teaching as before.[128]

These varied images demonstrate a range of experiences, from conflicts as severe and bloody as anywhere in France, particularly around the eastern cities of Rennes and Nantes, to the relatively less severe forms of repression in the western areas.

Breton Blues participated enthusiastically in the formation of the National Guard units and in the development of political clubs. But they felt deep misgivings about the Terror: Brittany lacked any real equivalent to the militant Parisian *sans-culotte* movement. The more moderate Girondin Republicans attracted widespread sympathy in Brittany in 1793 and – significantly – were not persecuted as severely here as they were elsewhere.[129] Even a passionate defender of the Republic, such as the municipal agent for Vitré, criticized the actions of arbitrary soldiers who were sent to repress Chouannerie, but who terrorized and even shot innocent citizens, and who stole cattle and fish.[130] Leperdit, the mayor of Rennes, did what he could to stop executions and – later – his actions were celebrated by the city's inhabitants.[131] By the late 1790s, officials were noting how a certain tolerance of unauthorized priests and *émigrés* seemed to be accepted.[132]

There was another aspect to Blue political culture which strengthened it and helped it to last into the nineteenth century and – arguably – to the present day. Alongside their demand for revenge, the Blues also constructed a new social framework. The Breton landscape itself was being transformed by the Revolution. For example, the small rural town of Montcontour (Côtes-du-Nord) was a base for 'Blue' politics, which it imposed on the surrounding countryside. Its council enforced de-christianization, closed chapels, changed street names, executed Counter-Revolutionary suspects and attempted –

unsuccessfully – to replace the traditional seven-day week with ten-day revolutionary *décadi*.[133] Watkin Tench noted the new statue of Liberty standing over Quimper market place, while Cambry, coming across a Liberty tree in Morlaix, imagined succeeding generations gathering beneath it to discuss the heroism of the Revolution.[134] When the municipal official in Vitré wanted to combat 'brigands' hiding in wooded areas, he hired five hundred workers to cut through the woods at Pertre.[135] His comments on electricity in April 1794 are extremely revealing of this new mindset: 'We must electrify the fanatical communes which lie close to the towns: we must inspire them with love for the nation, respect for the laws, the hatred of tyrants and scorn for all the objects that their superstitions hold dear.'[136] Bearing in mind the ill-understood properties of this new source of energy – one thinks of Mary Shelley's *Frankenstein*, published in 1818 – these lines suggest a surprising and deliberate modernism, a proud espousal of the values of science, seen as a force which in itself was on the side of the Republic.

The new nationalism was part of this pride in modernity. Many Breton Blues thought of themselves, without qualification, as French. 'We are Frenchmen of the 14th July' stated the Jacobins of Brest. 'We're ready, and the 150 leagues [from Brest to Paris] can quickly be crossed.'[137] Within the political culture of the Blues, there was no space for arguments concerning Breton particularism. And yet: one can detect a lasting 'Breton-ness' in some of their ideas. Their limited social programme, ferociously anti-seigneurial, but with few other social reforms, reflected the reality of a region in which the aristocracy had held great social and political power. Their astonishing ability to organize and to inspire was shaped by their status as a minority within Brittany.

Lastly, the Republican governments demanded better knowledge about French society. One aspect of this was the first census, conducted in 1801.[138] Another was Cambry's description of Finistère, written in 1794–5 and published in 1799. Cambry stood at a meeting point of many intellectual currents: he was Breton, moderately Republican and a Celticist. His attempts to understand Brittany within these three frameworks aroused little interest at the time of the publication of his book, but his work does foreshadow some of the great debates of the nineteenth century.

Conclusion

Was this really a period in which two civilizations battled with each other? Certainly, the desperate, bloody clashes of 1793 and 1794 produced as clear and stark a social and political polarization as it is possible to imagine: this episode of Breton history would affect the region's evolution for decades. But, if one accepts this image, it is surprisingly difficult to reduce these two forces to two neat terms. Of course, it is relatively simple to identify the Blues: they were clearly the best-organized force in Brittany during the 1790s; they possessed a functioning network of political institutions, and while rooted in urban elites, they also had some capacity to appeal to artisans, workers and peasants. Most important of all, they devised their own myths, within months of their creation, and these in turn evolved into a convincing world view. Surprisingly, their minority position gave them a sense of group discipline: they developed little sense of factional loyalties to the moderate Girondins, the radical Jacobins or the statism of Napoleon.

But who, exactly, were their opponents? The Chouan guerrillas possessed few ideas beyond a deep resentment to the imposition of revolutionary values. It remains unclear if they were primarily defending a vision of the church, a vision of a reforming monarchy or merely their own relatively privileged position within the micro-world of villages and hamlets. There were real tensions between these peasant rebels and their aristocratic leaders who were hardly the most perceptive or analytic of political thinkers, but who were able to think long-term, and who attempted to direct this anti-conscription rebellion into a force for political change. Here, too, there was only the most limited concept of Brittany as a region with a culture and an identity.

The Celticists were actually quite different from both sides. Just occasionally one hears echoes of their ideas.[139] When Barère fulminated against the Counter-Revolutionary exploitation of regional languages, he did trace the Breton language back to the Celts. Apart from the great battles between town and country, church and state, aristocracy and Republic, there was another process beginning here. This was the debate that would finally place Brittany on the map: we will return to their ideas in the next chapter.

Rather than seeing the 1790s as years marking a clear, binary political polarization, it would be better to recall the terms used by Legendre, the third estate delegate from Brest. He spoke of despotism, the Breton Constitution and liberty: a three-cornered contest. None of the movements or political cultures that emerged in the 1790s provided a convincing conceptualization of the qualities which constituted Brittany: that process was still to come.

3

Oriental Brittany

A bizarre encounter is recorded in the August 1999 edition of the UDB's (Union démocratique bretonne) monthly journal, *Le Peuple Breton*. In a guide to introductory works on Brittany for tourists, they recommend Pierre Loti's celebrated *Icelandic Fisherman*. Why should this well-organized, realistic and relatively efficient left-autonomist grouping, the largest of the regionalist, autonomist and nationalist organizations in Brittany, cite Loti's peculiar, sentimental, sub-Romantic drivel as a useful introduction to the region? One might have thought that the UDB would have shared Tzvetan Todorov's summary judgement on Loti: 'Racist, imperialist, sexist and sadistic'.[1] The appearance of Loti's text in the UDB journal leads us to debate the role of disciplines such as Celticism and Orientalism in defining Breton identity.

This chapter will draw together the arguments presented in chapters 1 and 2, where we saw a growing intellectual interest in Brittany's potential contribution to a sense of French national identity. However, this initial sympathy was tempered by the violence of the revolutionary process, which polarized Breton political cultures into 'blue' and 'white' camps. Here, we turn to another form of analysis: the Celticist representation of Brittany.

Edward Said has suggested that 'Orientalism' can be seen as a self-indulgent, anti-rationalist romantic protest against the culture of European industrialism.[2] While the new urban-industrial landscape grew to dominate the French nation, readers and politicians were increasingly attracted by shimmering, dream-like portrayals of the Orient in literature. Romantic and voluntaristic themes were popularized in new forms of mass fiction, which in turn often provided moral justifications for colonialism. Something similar can be seen in nineteenth-century writing about Brittany. At first, many writers and commentators saw Brittany simply as 'other' to France: they defined the region by what it lacked, what it failed to possess. Cambry's *Voyage* certainly contains writing in this mode alongside some other themes. Almost every second page of his work complains about the lack of squares, promenades, fountains and docks in Breton towns. But others went further than this, and often their commentaries suggest that Brittany appeared similar to that other great dreamscape, the Orient. This chapter will debate this 'orientalization' of Brittany, and question to what extent representations of Brittany and the Orient can be compared. We will conclude by considering some political implications of these arguments.

Definitions by negatives

Many travellers who visited Brittany emphatically and vividly recorded their impression of the filth, dirt and muck that they encountered. In 1636, the first town on Dubuisson-Aubenay's voyage to the region was Châteaubriant. He found it 'filthy and unpleasant'.[3] Of course, such filth could be found in any region of France, probably in any village. What is more significant is the manner in which such qualities became used almost as a cipher to indicate Brittany: a region distinctively marked by an *absence* of civilization.

Mérimée's rejection of the status of Brittany's historic monuments can be seen in this light (see chapter 1). One can add his frequent despairing comments concerning specific sites: for example, 'I know no monument in Saint-Brieuc which merits a description.'[4] While Stendhal's imaginary 'touriste' admired Nantes, 'a great city', he scorned the smaller Breton towns and villages. When he got off the coach at La Roche-Barnard (Morbihan), 'everything I saw was ugly'.[5] In 1839, Fortuné de Boisgobey, a young student, set off from Paris to Brittany. On his way there, he stayed overnight at Blois. He was awoken during the night by fleas in his bed: 'A foretaste of Brittany!' he noted in his diary. Later, while in Vannes, he recorded his impressions of the town: 'An ugly, filthy town. Everywhere there are dirty streets with no distinctive mark other than their filth.'[6]

Such expression of a simple disgust with Brittany reached a type of climax in the work of Hippolyte Taine, famous for his contribution to the development of 'scientific' racism within French thought. In the 1860s he served as an examiner in France's military schools and, in this position, travelled across France. He produced two volumes of travel-writing which recorded the sights he encountered. His comments on Brittany are memorable. In Rennes he noted 'morality remains extremely primitive here. Breton families come into the town once a week; they go into a *cabaret* and drink all day long. They are all completely drunk.'[7] The implicit moral judgement in this passage was then developed further:

Of all the regions of France, it is Brittany which supplies the greatest numbers of recruits for Parisian vice. In the countryside, brothers and sisters sleep together, and the consequences are easy to guess. At fairs and at *pardons* drunkenness is everywhere; everyone loses all control; and you can see many young men and women in the ditches.[8]

Brittany was a country of 'miserable cottages, emaciated, pale, mystical or idiotic people . . . and sixteenth-century savages'.[9]

Some themes within Taine's comments are worth stressing. First, note that 'the Breton' is defined by negatives – by the absence of morality, of cleanliness, of modernity – as an absolute 'other' to the urban modernity of the newly Haussmannized Paris. Secondly, as was the case with some of the writers cited previously (such as Stendhal), Taine suggests a sharp division between the town and the countryside. 'The Breton' is out there, in the villages; these Breton families come into the towns on market days. Thirdly, Taine's writing also suggests a type of malign, negative inversion of Villemarqué's ideas, which had proposed that Brittany constituted a moral model for the rest of France. Taine, on the contrary, saw Brittany as a reservoir of immorality which was in danger of infecting the rest of France.

There are indications that such negative images were prevalent during the nineteenth century. William H. Dawson was a British tourist. For him, too, Brittany was characterized by its lack of cleanliness: 'Dirt and squalor meet you everywhere in the rural districts of Brittany: they seem the natural element of the *paysan*.' He expressed some surprise that there had been no cholera outbreak at Dinan (Ille-et-Vilaine).[10] More significantly, such stereotypes may even have been internalized by the Bretons themselves. Jean-Marie Déguignet's *Mémoires* are a rare example of a Breton peasant autobiography. Written in 1904, he reflected on events over the previous seventy years. Déguignet makes a particularly interesting observation in his account of his military service. Having travelled to Lorient, on the day before reporting for service he made some effort to wash and tidy himself. Why? Because 'you had to try to enter the barracks looking clean, otherwise you would be treated as a dirty Breton, a Breton pig.'[11] Déguignet's comment suggests that such clichés were common: they certainly circulated in the Belle Epoque press.[12] While these scattered references hardly provide us with definitive evidence of a paradigm, they are telling indications of cultural inequality. We will return to this point in later chapters; for the moment, let us note in passing the important argument produced by Fañch Elegoët, who links the production of these hostile stereotypes of the Bretons with the eradication of the Breton language. For Elegoët, these developments resulted in the internalization of a 'negative identity' by Bretons.[13]

The significance of these negative images is that they extend beyond a simple impression of dirt to generalizations about the Breton people, their culture and their character. J.-J. Baude, writing in the prestigious *Revue des Deux Mondes,* was not hostile to the Breton towns – but neither was he impressed: 'Rennes is just a satellite of Paris', he commented dismissively.[14] Châteauneuf and Villermé produced an interesting image of Breton folk dances:

> Their songs have no grace, their dances have no life. They present a fixed image of a long line of men and women, holding each other by the hand, ceaselessly moving in and out, with slow paced steps: it has no charm, no nimbleness, just like the instrument which accompanies it, that type of bagpipe called the *biniou*: a tiresome and irritating thing.[15]

Here, it is clear that these two Parisian authors have taken current Parisian dances as their norm: Breton folk dances are condemned for their failure to follow Paris fashions.

More directly, Baude commented on the Bretons' political culture. The Breton was: 'the enemy of innovation: his first reaction is always to refuse'.[16] Victor Hugo, with his gift for exploiting a cliché, uses similar images at the start of his novel *Quatrevingt-treize*. The scene is a Republican sergeant interrogating a peasant woman during the repression of the Chouans in 1793. He asks her to which nation [patrie] she belongs:

> 'The Siscoignard farm, in Azé parish.'
> 'That's not a nation [patrie].'
> 'But it's my country [pays] . . . Now I see, sir. You're from France, while I'm from Brittany.'
> 'Well?'
> 'It's not the same country.'
> 'But it's the same nation!'[17]

Hugo's point is that the Bretons lack a proper sense of nationhood; he has no intention of suggesting that they form a separate nation from France. Instead, as was seen in previous examples, Bretons are being defined by what they lack.

There were, however, some important variants on this simple negative image of Brittany. Let us return to Cambry's pioneering work of travel-writing.

> Imagine the filth, the smell, the damp and the mud which form these underground dwellings! Imagine the water from the dung-heap barring your entrance, and leaking into the cottage: add the filth, and the inherited scabies

of the parents and their children – the filth of people who never bathe, who never wash, who have come from the ditches, the marshes, the sewers into which their drunkenness has pushed them. Imagine their flat, long hair, their thick beards, their faces streaked with dirty scratches, their short waist-coats, their baggy breeches, their little buttons, and their clogs which form their costumes, and you will have an idea of the Breton peasant.

Do not judge these people by their appearance. Usually they are hospitable, intelligent and quick-witted. They think clearly, they calculate accurately, and they have got strong imaginations. The priests have abused them. You will see in the rest of my book the excesses of their superstitions, and how their dreams dominate them. They live among shadows, demons, fairies, ghosts and witches. They see them at night and in the day; they see them when they sleep, in the corners of their fields, in the sky, and in the clouds. They have added to the tales of the Catholic religion and the practices of Rome, material from the druids' religion.[18]

Cambry's writing adds a vital new element to our analysis. Alongside the simple negation of the validity of Breton culture, there emerges a second theme, suggestive of an important ambivalence. Cambry remains fascinated by these people and their cultural potential, and is therefore reluctant to dismiss them completely.

Oriental Brittany

Cambry's peculiar mixture of attraction and rejection is curiously reminiscent of the cultural and political discourse which has been identified by Edward Said as 'Orientalism'. Put simply, Said argues that:

(a) the eighteenth- and nineteenth-century discourse termed 'Orientalism' was based on the assertion that valid generalizations could be made about peoples and cultures from Morocco to Japan;
(b) there was a clear connection, perhaps a kind of symbiosis, between this cultural discourse and the powerful colonial drive which followed it;
(c) such discourses locate Arab and other people at the bottom of a cultural, sometimes racial, hierarchy;
(d) the positions within this hierarchy are fixed: the Arabs were unable to assimilate to Western modes of behaviour and culture. If they should attempt to do so, then they risked losing the essential qualities which made them 'Arab' without acquiring any positive new identity.

In the pages below, I will survey images of Brittany, first collecting data which suggests that a comparison between Orientalism and Celticism is valid, and then noting some shortcomings in this argument.

Direct comparisons

The first, and probably the most simple, link between Orientalism and Celticism is that many authors explicitly compare the two discourses. Even Walter Scott, an important (if distant) inspiration for many French Celticists, stated that the morality of the Scottish highlanders was that 'of an Arab chief'.[19] A character in Balzac's Brittany-based short story 'Un drame au bord de la mer' claims, during the action of the narrative, that now she understands 'the poetry and the passions of the Orient'.[20] In no other country, 'even Africa', could one find the depth of superstitious beliefs that one encountered in Brittany, wrote Cambry.[21] Souvestre stated that he aimed to write a *Thousand and One Nights of Brittany*.[22] The Breton language was 'as incomprehensible as Arabic' for one British tourist; it was similar to Hebrew, according to two Nantes-based liberals.[23] In a short story, Octave Mirbeau described the fatalism of the Bretons in the face of the threat from typhoid: 'There is something Oriental about these anaemic Celts, something Muslim about these Catholics who, in their minds, pray to the Mecca of Sainte-Anne-d'Auray.'[24]

Our student-writer, Boisgobey, came close to making a similar comparison. Travelling through Brittany, he searched for suitable images to evoke the strangeness of the countryside. The dryness of the earth around Poullaouen (Finistère) reminded him of Spain, or perhaps Corsica: 'How often the old and primitive land of Armorica shows physical similarities with other countries which are still as savage.'[25] Balzac reaches for similar means to register Brittany's strangeness: for him, its people are like Red Indians or Mohicans.[26] Sometimes comparisons could flow the other way. André Cochut, one of the regular writers for the prestigious *Revue des Deux Mondes*, noted in an article published in that journal that without French rule, Algeria would be like Gaul without Julius Caesar.[27]

Aside from these direct comparisons between the two dreamscapes, there was another literary point of contact. Many prominent nineteenth-century writers chose to write on both Brittany and the Orient. The best example of this tendency is Pierre Loti, one of the most successful of the French nineteenth-century Orientalists, author of *Le Pêcheur d'Islande* [The Icelandic Fisherman]. This work was extremely popular; it went through 266 editions between 1886 and 1905, and in 2002 seven separate French-language editions were in print.[28] Chateaubriand, Flaubert and Renan also all wrote on both Brittany and the Orient: their works concerning Brittany were less phenomenally successful than those of Loti but their wide literary interests still suggest some direct comparison between the two zones. We can say now that an overlap, if nothing more, connects the two forms of writing.

Timelessness and primitiveness

For Orientalists, the 'East' existed in a type of timeless vacuum: visiting Arab countries was supposed to give direct access to the cultures of the ancient, even pre-historic, past. Celtic cultures have often been analysed in this way, as bridging 'the difference between the past and the present'.[29] This first generation of writers on Brittany often shared similar viewpoints. Cambry considered that the Bretons still practised Druidic customs. Edouard Richer, visiting Le Croisic in 1822, commented that Brittany was 'the most intact remnant left from the Celts'.[30] Villemarqué argued at some length that the structures of oral culture in Brittany were capable of preserving a song or poem, essentially unchanged, from the sixth to the nineteenth century.[31] E. Fleury felt that when walking in the countryside near Brest, 'it seems as if one has travelled back several centuries; everything reminds one of the antique and the savage: one could almost say of Druidism.'[32] According to Souvestre, in the Breton countryside there were:

> pagan temples, feudal towers, holy monasteries, symbols of all the ages and all beliefs! It is as if these monuments of the past had been caught, at random, in the corner of Time's tunic, and then this debris had been allowed to fall, lost in the green valleys.[33]

In 1830, the towns of Brittany still resembled those of the fourteenth and fifteenth centuries, according to Renan.[34] Little had changed in Brittany for fifteen hundred years, considered the bishop of Saint-Brieuc.[35] Luzel recorded that while walking near Plouharnel (Morbihan), he passed a peasant woman on the road who was 'tall, straight, and wearing almost the same clothes as the wife of a Gaulish chieftain'.[36]

By the early twentieth century, such observations had become clichés. Both Charles Le Goffic and Anatole Le Braz described Brittany as 'the land of the past'.[37] Le Braz elaborated: Brittany is normally seen as:

> A very old land, whose poetry, charm and attractiveness come above all because it is as if [this land] has been held immobile on the banks of time ... This is what many of us like about her, this is what those from outside,

artists and tourists, come here to find: it is above all the sights and senses of older times, it is the exoticism of history.

Surprisingly, such ideas have even influenced some recent histories of Brittany. Nora Chadwick, for example, writes that 'today, as we cross the narrow sea from Southampton to St-Malo, we are conscious of passing not so much into a foreign country as into a past age'.[38]

Another similarity between the two discourses, the Orientalist and Celticist, is that the only register through which historical change could be noted was that of decline and corruption. At one time the East may have been great, but now, argued Orientalists, the Arabs had been humiliated by the scientific advances of the West. Villemarqué considered that linguists and philologists urgently needed to work on the surviving Breton poetry, for often those who sang the words had forgotten their precise meaning. 'Through these rags, shine threads of gold from a past splendour', he wrote.[39] The more straightforwardly conservative commentator Keranflec'h noted that the abbey had been replaced by the *cabaret*.[40] Luzel, a dedicated collector of Breton folk-theatre and a one-time rival to Villemarqué, made a similar point. Following the decline of the chapels and Breton-language culture, 'no one believes in anything'.[41]

Just as in the case of Orientalism, such observations could be turned on their head: the region could then be valorized *because* it was primitive and therefore 'authentic', a healthy counter-point to the excesses of modernity to be found in frenetic Paris. Brizeux commented: 'those who feel so proud but so ill at the centre of the most advanced civilization, will feel happy at the sight of the calm of these primitive cultures.'[42] What had first appeared to be ignorance could also be praised as examples of an attractive, naïve spontaneity. Often commentators praised the 'natural' quality of Breton poetry: for Brizeux, it was a healthy verse, 'born from the soil'.[43] Villemarqué distinguished between a number of different poetic modes, some of which were the result of study and research. However, within these modes there was also a current of popular poetry which he admired: 'uncultured, savage and ignorant; a child of nature with the full force of that term'. Such poets composed songs: 'like the birds who throw notes to the wind'.[44]

Mary-Ann Constantine's comments on the nineteenth-century discovery of Breton folk poetry are pertinent to this point. Constantine speaks of 'an artless art':

> To the enthusiast it acts as a short-cut to that realm of pure expression and integration with the natural and human world which eighteenth- and

nineteenth-century Europe came, under the broad label of Romanticism, to locate variously in mystical/religious experience, love, madness, childhood – or, more pertinently, in the untrained state of the savage. The domain, in short, of all that is not 'reasonable', and which via Renan . . . has come to be seen as the prerogative of the Celt.[45]

The rapid development of tourism in Brittany during the late nineteenth century, in which the region was marketed as both healthy and exotic, was an important stage in the evolution of images of Brittany.

Sexuality

There are sexual themes in many Orientalist works: sometimes in a crude explicit form, at which point Orientalism becomes another vehicle for pornography, sometimes presented more subtly, in the form of romance. Rana Kabbani finds that in Orientalist discourse the East was a place of 'lascivious sexuality' and 'inherent violence': 'Europe was charmed by an Orient that shimmered with possibilities, that promised a sexual space, a voyage away from the self, an escape from the dictates of the bourgeois morality of the metropolis.'[46] The celebrated art historian Linda Nochlin has made imaginative use of Said's ideas in a review of French painting. She identifies a similar type of Orientalism: for artists, the Orient: 'existed as a project for the imagination, a fantasy space or screen onto which strong desire – erotic, sadistic, or both – could be projected with impunity'.[47] Such themes were certainly present in Loti's novels on Japan and on Arab countries. Are they also to be found in literature on Brittany?

Our initial response is negative. Loti's highly popular novels *Le Pêcheur d'Islande* and *Mon frère Yves* [My brother Yves] are innocent tales principally concerning all-male sociability.[48] While other novels portray issues of sexuality and marriage in a more aggressive manner, there appears to be no equivalent to the sub-pornographic depictions encountered in Orientalist discourse.[49] On the other hand, one does find constant reference to the Breton wife's submissive status. Brousmiche, our Legitimist tax collector, is one of the first observers to include detailed descriptions of women's experience of marriage in Brittany:

> Women's destiny, throughout the countryside, is to be a slave to men's domination, to bring forth children, to take care and responsibility for them. Thus almost all of them are old before their time; unity reigns in their households, as women are accustomed to it from their childhood. Adultery is extremely rare in the cantons of Armorica, because it always results in dishonour.[50]

Conservative writers used such evidence to suggest that Brittany constituted a model domestic utopia for France. For example, J.-J. Baude praised 'the patriarchal simplicity of [Breton] families, the peace which reigns in the countryside', which he contrasted to 'the envious, greedy agitation of our towns.'[51] As French commentators grew more concerned about the nation's declining birth-rate in the late nineteenth century, a second aspect of this patriarchal utopia is stressed: the Catholic, Breton family was often cited as a model of patriotic fecundity.[52] By 1891, only 21 per cent of French families had more than four children, while 31 per cent of Breton families were of this size or larger.[53]

Thus, while there is no direct Breton equivalent of the Harem fantasy, there were nonetheless certain sexual assumptions inherent in the depiction of the 'typical' Breton household and family.

Religion and the romantic unconscious

Orientalists usually ignored evidence of Arab sciences or studies: Arabs were therefore seen as unschooled, uncultured people, and to be compared to children. Islam was treated correspondingly; it was depicted as a type of pseudo-religion, an excuse for fanaticism. Similar observations were made about Breton religious culture. Cambry, predictably, considered that the peculiar literal and superstitious aspects of the Bretons' Catholic faith could be explained by the Druidic origins of their religious practices – an analysis which was repeated by Stendhal.[54] As noted in the first chapter, there was (and is) little 'hard' evidence about ancient Celtic religious practices. This silence provided a space within which commentators could develop fantasies about the rituals which had taken place. Armand Guérand, a student from Nantes, visited Carnac in 1845. Like many tourists, he was amazed by the sight of the stones, but then fell to pondering on their uses: 'What human sacrifices must have defiled this ground!'[55] Mérimée was more prudent, but he too was influenced by such fantasies. Examining the enormous *menhir* at Dol (Ille-et-Vilaine), he recorded that one local legend told that it had been built by Caesar, while another suggested that it had been constructed by the Devil himself. Was it really a burial place, or was it used for human sacrifices? wondered Mérimée.[56] Brousmiche was scathing and dismissive about these aspects of peasant religious culture, noting how clusters of legends, superstitions and 'absurd tales' concerning fairies, ghosts and other forms of enchantment would develop around particular historic sights.[57]

Commentaries on Breton Catholicism were hardly more positive. Balzac noted the twisted forms of Catholicism that evolved among the Chouan bands.

'These ignorant creatures' religion – or rather their fetishism – stopped them feeling remorse for murder'.[58] Souvestre noted that Bretons 'adored' their priests.[59] Even Serbois, a quietly conservative tourist, felt uneasy in the face of the Bretons' extravagant piety:

> The Breton is as localistic in religion as he is in politics: he feels a piety for his local saint that one would call excessive ... Such piety degenerates into a superstitious faith for everything which concerns the saint or that is connected to his flag, his statue, and the illustrations of his life ... Nowhere else has the clergy so much influence on the people; nowhere else are the parishioners more trusting, or the pastor more devoted.[60]

This stereotype of 'priest-ridden' Brittany was an important element in the liberal and Republican historians' analyses of the Chouan rebellions. Thiers, for example, described the Bretons as 'entirely subjugated to their priests' influences' in his history of the Revolution.[61] The same image also featured in hostile caricatures of Bretons, to the point where antipathy to Breton culture became an accepted vehicle for expressing anticlericalism.[62] Anti clerical critics stressed the role of the church in encouraging a fatalistic spirit of submission among the Bretons. Mirbeau wrote a number of satirical texts on such themes. In one, a Parisian lady searches for a Breton maid: 'In Brittany, the people are virtuous, loyal and they hardly eat anything: they're servants like before the Revolution [of 1789]!'[63]

On the other hand, conservatives could take the same themes and present them as positive advantages. For the bishop of Saint-Brieuc, Bretons were 'the people of the faith'.[64] We will return to this point in the next chapter.

Reformers' target

The Orient was a permanent challenge to the West: observations of Oriental societies or cultures often portrayed them as almost *demanding* reform or repression – or both. There was a similar vein in the commentaries on Brittany: the government had to intervene. From the first commentators, such as Cambry, observers of Brittany constantly noted the need for agricultural improvement, for the rationalization of the excessive numbers of fairs and markets, for a targeted programme of industrialization, for urban renovation through the building of squares, public fountains and promenades, for better roads, and – usually – for more schools. A similar line of reasoning can be found in Balzac's *Les Chouans*. While the text rehearses similar exotic-negative images of the Bretons, Balzac explains the political logic inherent in his novel in a comment in its preface: 'May this work make true the wishes of all friends of the nation for the physical and moral improvement of Brittany!'[65] In the Breton peninsula, 'men, animals, earth – everything needs to be improved', commented Châteauneuf and Villermé.[66]

Baude's comments on the Breton language illustrate how this 'modernizing' aspect of writing on Brittany could be developed:

> People admire the energy and the simplicity of the Breton language. While scholars have been wrong to claim that it was spoken after the fall of the Tower of Babel by Gomer, Japhet's son, and that it is the common ancestor of all Celtic languages, there can be no doubt that it is far older than the languages derived from Latin. Whatever noble titles this tongue can claim, when it has no literature, no ability to express new ideas, when it is unintelligible to all outside a narrow circle, then this language closes these people in, it limits their intellectual horizon and creates, within the country, barriers which are inconvenient for those on either side. A common language, on the other hand, is one of the most solid and most agreeable links that can be established between men: a point which is just as important for individual's benefits as for the unity of the state. In the last twenty years, the French language has won from Breton more ground than it gained in the entire century before. The useful dispersal of the country's [*pays*] youth in army regiments, and the stationing of regiments in the peninsula, the improvements in communications which encourage men to leave their homes – all these factors have been as powerful as the energy of the Université.[67]

This passage begins by echoing some of the arguments which we have already seen: Brittany, the Breton language, are characterized in purely negative terms. The *Celtomanes* are then easily dismissed. What is more significant, however, is that Baude, writing during the political crises of the Second Republic (1848–52), makes explicit the political implications of such thoughts. The response suggests a vigorous reform programme, imposed from above, to drag the Bretons into (French) modernity.

Once more, we can note a clear similarity between the Celticist and Orientalist discourses: for all their appearance of innocent romantic descriptions, there were some tough political implications to these writers' words.

Scientific discourse

The Orient was also a favoured field for scientific endeavour, and the discoveries made by linguists, archaeologists and historians flattered a Western sense of intellectual superiority. The key argument that developed here was that the Orientals were not capable of managing or exploiting the cultural, spiritual or economic riches that their lands contained, and that therefore a colonialist intervention was justified. The most dramatic example of a Western scientific advance in the field of culture was probably Champollion's translation of ancient Egyptian hieroglyphics: he was praised for his contribution to the 'glory of French science', for his work demonstrating the ability of Western academics to make the East speak.[68]

Did science play a similar role in the field of Breton culture? Some commentators thought so. In 1907, distinguished Celtic language expert Joseph Loth wrote a study of the rivalry between Celtic and Latin languages in ancient Brittany. His essay started with the comment 'since Celtic studies have followed the scientific path' – although he did not state *when* this transformation took place.[69] Of course, the work by linguists, who identified and analysed the links between the Celtic languages spoken in Brittany, Wales, Cornwall, the Isle of Man, Ireland and Scotland, certainly constitutes a major corpus of social-scientific investigation. But while these advances are important, their success in driving forward a distinctive sense of Breton identity are open to question. Referring back to Déguignet, our peasant autobiographer, it is significant that he writes that the Bretons spoke 'a language without an equivalent in the world': he had certainly learnt little from the Celticists' linguistic studies.[70]

Rather than constituting a zone defined and marked by scientific research, *bretonnitude* seems instead to be constituted as a quality which was inherently hostile to rationalization. Le Goffic made this observation with typically romanticized clichés: 'there are two [enigmas] which we will never come close to understanding: the heart of a woman and the soul of a Celt'.[71] However, it is our student-writer, Boisgobey, who produces the most arresting statement on this matter: 'Today, Brittany is like a vast museum without a guidebook ... a museum where almost everywhere you have to look without understanding, but not without admiring.'[72]

Essence

Celticist and Orientalist forms of writing were both clearly 'essentialist': they asserted that there was some fairly clearly identifiable 'soul' or other expression of identity which was common to all inhabitants and all authentic cultural expressions of their respective areas of study. By the mid-nineteenth century, observers were almost unanimous in attributing Brittany's distinctive features to some particular Celtic quality, though interpretations differed as to the exact nature of this quality. In this respect, one could judge that Villemarqué's pioneering work had won some acceptance.

In turn, this belief in a type of essence of Brittany fuelled lively debates between commentators, each claiming in turn to have uncovered the true, real, authentic nature of the Bretons. Souvestre wrote a particularly forceful rejection of certain Parisian portraits of the Bretons, which he considered were based on nothing more than eight days observation from the seat of a post-carriage.[73] The title of his first full-length work on this topic – *Les Derniers Bretons* – can be read as a pun: it could be translated as 'the last Bretons', but also as 'the latest Bretons', in the sense of the latest delivery. Such comments are a good indication of the manner in which academic and political rivalries developed amongst scholars of Brittany. None of them contested the idea that there was some peculiar, vital characteristic which exemplified Brittany; instead rivalries developed concerning who had best grasped this quality.

This particular quality which made the Bretons unique and distinctive was, predictably, difficult to name explicitly, let alone debate and analyse. We frequently find commentators assuming the existence of this quality, and referring to it indirectly, in a manner which raises more questions than answers. Thus Boisgobey confidently dismisses the *paludiers* (salt-workers) of Guérande (Loire-Inférieure) as not being real Bretons, but at Elven (Morbihan), he is delighted to find 'the true Breton'.[74] Serbois also stated that he felt some admiration for the 'real' Chouan, the Counter-Revolutionary idealist, whom he distinguished from the mere bandit.[75]

Others do put forward more reasoned arguments. Renan imagines a traveller entering Brittany from the East, and going westwards until 'he enters the true Brittany, that area which merits the title by its language and its race'.[76] Michelet makes a similar distinction, claiming that the western half of Brittany is: 'the real Brittany, Breton-speaking Brittany, a land which has become foreign to us, because it has remained too faithful to our primitive [i.e. original] condition'.[77] Le Goffic and Luzel followed the same line of argument, writing of 'the true Brittany, Breton-speaking Brittany' and of visiting 'Brittany, by which I mean Breton-speaking Brittany, Breiz-Izel [Lower Brittany]'.[78]

The references in the last paragraph show that one of the most commonly cited qualities of this 'essence' of *bretonnitude* was the ability to speak the Breton language. A second quality was residence in a rural area, a point which was usually demonstrated by reference to urban culture. 'I will say nothing of Brest', wrote Souvestre, 'as the only Breton quality it possesses is its name.'[79] Michelet saw 'true' Brittany as surrounded by four French towns: Nantes, Saint-Malo, Rennes and Brest.[80] Henry Blackburn, another British tourist, considered that Rennes was French rather than Breton.[81] There was little distinctively Breton about any of the towns in Brittany, thought Yves Kano.[82] Serbois proved surprisingly eloquent on this point:

> All traditions, legends, rituals, language and costume are more resilient [*vivace*] in the country, and resist more effectively and longer the movement of ideas and new fashions. In the town, everything is hidden or disguised, all the doors are closed, all pride is gone: everyone lives by themselves, for themselves, and they leave the traveller to explore the buildings or to walk the streets [by himself]. All originality fades: people dress, talk and think more or less like everywhere else . . . [Provincial towns resemble] what Paris was six months ago, a year ago, ten years ago . . . Today's towns, we regret to say, are only made different from each other by their past, their monuments, and their history. Once a church, a town hall, even just a simple house had a particular character, a type of originality [which reflected] its land [*pays*]. But everything made in the last century seems exactly the same, from the east to the west, from the north to the south: the same black suits, main streets, gaslights, prefects and train stations.[83]

Correspondingly, Serbois told his readers that neither Vannes nor Lorient counted as 'Breton' towns.[84] Flaubert made similar observations about the towns of Brittany, and concluded by inventing the neologism 'de-bretonization' to describe the process which he saw taking place there.[85]

These forms of argument had a surprising consequence: much of Brittany, including the greatest concentrations of population and most of the eastern half of the region, was then described by writers and commentators as not really Breton. What must be stressed here is the ease with which such distinctions were made. Even young students like Boisgobey and Flaubert felt certain that they could identify the 'real' Brittany, and correspondingly were swift to dismiss the towns and much of the eastern areas as somehow being inadequate, artificial or false.

Provisional conclusion

There can be no doubt that there are substantial similarities between the Orientalist discourse identified by Said and the Celticist discourse which developed in the early nineteenth century. Indeed, the two forms of writing are often so alike that one could take many passages from Orientalist texts, substitute the term 'Celt' for 'Arab', and then read them as descriptions of Brittany. An indication of the compatibility of the two forms of thinking can be seen in the writings by Bretons on the 'Orient'. It is possible to see some Breton writers as showing a particular sensitivity to issues of cultural oppression and colonial economic exploitation. Bernard Hue, for example, presents this type of defence of the works of Auguste Pavie concerning the Khmer people of south-east Asia.[86] Other Breton writers, however, clearly participated willingly in the French Orientalist discourse. Chateaubriand could be legitimately described as one of the inventors of French Orientalism.[87] Muriel Desfontaine's comments on the travel writings of the Breton aristocrat Odette du Puigaudeau are particularly relevant. While Puigaudeau participated in the Breton nationalist movements of the 1920s and 30s, her *bretonnitude* seemed to vanish when she reached Africa. Here 'she thought of herself as French. She argued that she was Breton when she was in Paris, but she was clearly French in the colonies.'[88]

When we turn to consider the political instrumentalization of Celticist and Orientalist works, however, differences emerge.

The Breton specificity

One key difference between the Celticist and Orientalist discourses concerns the questions of 'roots'. While specialists might occasionally refer to the East as the cradle of civilization, there was no following proposition that the study of these areas could shed light on the origins of French – or western – civilization. The Orient represented a stage which western societies had definitively transcended. Studies on Brittany, as was shown in the previous chapters, developed within a different time frame. If it was accepted that the distinctive features of Breton society and culture were the result of its Celtic inheritance, then it was possible to argue that Brittany constituted a type of starting place for France, as it was an area, even *the* area, which had best preserved the 'roots' of French culture. Rather than simply being the 'Other' to France, Brittany played a more complex role in the construction of French national identity.[89]

Secondly, one by-product of these nineteenth-century Celticist texts was a renewed interest in the nature and status of the Breton language. Villemarqué's *Barzaz Breiz* was originally published in a bilingual edition, and some argue that his publication played a vital role in the preservation of the Breton language into the twentieth century. Orientalists often – but not always – studied Arabic and other vernacular languages and, sometimes, encouraged academics and even colonial administrators to do the same, but they had no intention of aiding the survival or development of these languages. No popular or successful Orientalist texts were published in bilingual editions. Again, on this point there seems a sharp distinction between the two discourses.

One of *the* constitutive characteristics of Orientalism was its role as the study of an 'Other' civilization. Putting this point bluntly, white researchers studied the cultures of black, brown and yellow peoples. However, in the case of nineteenth-century Celticism, often these studies were carried out by researchers who claimed that they, too, were Bretons. In the passages above, we have read observations by several authors who either were born in Brittany or who lived there: Brizeux, Brousmiche, Cambry, David, Fleury, Le Braz, Le Goffic, Kano, Keranflec'h, Renan, Richer, Souvestre and Villemarqué. Rather than strangers to their object of study, they asserted that they were speakers for Brittany, often with the subtext that they could be playing a vital role in political mediation between Paris and the West. At times, one can identify some differences between these born and bred Bretons and outside observers. Certainly, the outsiders tend to be more aggressive in their descriptions of the ignorance and the dirt which they found, more dismissive concerning the character of Breton religious piety, and more likely to welcome the decline of the Breton language. However, the difference between 'insiders' and 'outsiders' is only one of degree: their writings share most of the distinctive features described above.

Lastly, for all their muddle-headed Romanticism, for all their backward-looking praise for the Celtic soul, these writers are – arguably – the forerunners of the modern Breton regionalist, autonomist and separatist movements. Once again, there is no comparison here between the Orientalists and the Celticists. No Arab nationalist movement has made sustained use of Orientalist images: all have shown pronounced and clear hostility to such images.

Conclusion: political values

The discourse of Celticism positioned Brittany as a type of provocation: its very existence was a challenge to the French state, which was almost obliged to act to free these people from their backwardness. Such forms of thinking were common in the nineteenth century, and can be found among a wide range of reformers, whether liberal or conservative. Indeed, as I have noted elsewhere (n. 89), the establishment of a national schooling programme, including the provisions for free and obligatory primary schooling for all children (1881–4), was only achieved through the laborious construction of a concept of popular ignorance by social scientists and cultural commentators. To paraphrase Blake, schools were built with bricks of ignorance.[90] The urban working class, and particularly the potential political threat of the organized proletariat, were generally the first target of reformers' zeal. Not far behind, however, came this ill-understood mass to the west, in that area where La Vendée and Brittany seemed to merge to form a single, stubbornly reactionary bloc, and then, further away, the 'savage', misunderstood societies in Arabia, Africa, Asia and America. In each case, as Todorov has noted, the definition of these societies was constructed by identifying what they lack.[91]

It is also clear that the Celticist discourse, with its stress on the unknown and unknowable, was unlikely to be a vehicle for academic research. Unlike Orientalism, the contribution made by scientific research to Celticism was negligible, with the one significant exception of the linguists' contribution. Like Orientalism, however, Celticism could function as an escapist protest against the mundane qualities of debate and representation; it expressed anti-modern, anti-urban sentiments in the name of vaguely evoked transhistorical values. Should we therefore understand Celticism as contributing to a type of postcolonial cultural autonomy in Brittany? Here, our response must be more nuanced.

Both Celticism and Orientalism were anti-modernist ideologies, at times raising some genuinely challenging points about the nature of modernity, but more frequently leading to an ugly tendency to reduce societies and cultures to pre-determined racial groups. The Celticists generally wished to define the Breton people through an imagined historical inheritance. Both Celticists and Orientalists tended to take as their model for understanding social development a type of community in which qualities of identity were inherited, fixed, and not open to development.

However, there are also differences between the two discourses. Their romantic and idealistic rhetoric led most of France's Orientalist writers into clear connections with strands of right-wing thinking, in particular with the ideological ferment of the racist 'new right' in the 1890s and 1900s. It is common to see these early Celticists as similar, and to note for example, Villemarqué's espousal of social Catholicism as an example of their inherent right-wing drift.[92] The material discussed here suggests a different trajectory. With the possible exception of Le Goffic, the nineteenth-century Breton writers inspired by Celticist ideas usually moved towards other political values.[93]

(a) *Legitimist-Bretonists*: writers like Brousmiche and Keranflec'h accepted the idea that there was a specific positive quality to be celebrated in Breton culture, but identified this as a particular form of Catholicism, which was threatened by the pagan legacy which the Celts had left

Brittany. In other words, their interpretation of *Bretonnitude* was Roman rather than Celtic;
(b) *Republicans*: commentators such as Baude, Hugo, Michelet and – to a lesser extent – Taine and Flaubert, were willing to accept that a 'Celtic' influence had formed modern Brittany, but then argued that the contemporary deficiencies of Breton society were a result of this legacy. As they accepted the essentialist logic of the discourse, such Republican writers could not conceive of progress through the amelioration or modernization of Breton culture, but only through its assimilation into French–Republican culture;
(c) *Bretonists*: writers such as Luzel, Souvestre, Brizeux, Le Braz, and – with some qualifications – Le Goffic, who began the process of reinterpreting Villemarqué's research as an expression of a Breton *regionalist* ideology. Despite their personal contacts with legitimists, these writers were often, broadly speaking, Republican, or even left-of-centre in their outlook;
(d) *Tourists*: outsider observers such as Boisgobey, Serbois, Dawson and Blackburn, who accepted, with little questioning, ideas concerning the Celtic nature of Brittany. Tourist guides marketed Brittany's Celtic character to this increasingly important audience.

There was, however, a turn to the far right in the 1930s: a point which will be addressed in chapter 8. In each of these four nineteenth-century variants of Bretonism, ideas concerning the relationship of France to Brittany, and Brittany to France were vital. Each geographical space acted as mirror to the other, allowing and provoking the identification of particularities and specificities.

The UDB's approval of Loti's work is a sign of a wider cultural weakness. The Breton left, from Republicans such as Le Braz to contemporary UDB-ists, have failed to break decisively with the domination of their ideas by nineteenth-century concepts of Celticism.

PART II

Ruling Brittany

4

The Politics of Faith: Chouannerie, Religion and the Making of a White Landscape

In the previous chapters we examined the slow, awkward process of transforming Brittany's status: from its seventeenth-century position as the most backward of backward provinces, to the more challenging nineteenth-century debate over its status and ethnic identity. The Revolution of 1789 was a vital factor in this cycle of interaction. As has been shown, the revolutionary authorities recast the stereotype of the 'backward west' in a new shape. A clumsy amalgam was formed from images of monarchist aristocrats, Counter-Revolutionary conspirators, rebellious clerics, rioting peasants, blood-thirsty brigands and cultural illiterates. This cliché obviously hindered communication between the region and the government, for it immediately suggested an underestimation of the Republican presence within Brittany.[1] More seriously still, it may have persuaded Republicans and liberals to anticipate opposition in areas where there was the potential for active cooperation. In this manner, the cliché of the backward west could become self-fulfilling.

In this chapter we will examine non-modernist forms of Breton political culture, based on the older values of faith rather than newer concepts of rationality. These not only survived into the nineteenth century, but often underwent substantial adaptation to changing circumstances. It has to be stressed from the beginning that these forms are not necessarily compatible and do not form a coherent whole. The faith which motivated the Chouan brigand was not the same that motivated a pilgrim to walk for miles to a *pardon*: in turn this second faith was not the same as that which inspired the Catholic political militant of the early twentieth century. Nonetheless, all three forms represented, in some manner, a challenge to the rationalist, modernist values propounded by successive Paris-based governments. All three forms contributed to a religious culture which became so rooted in Brittany that it almost seemed natural and organic to the land of the region: a 'white' landscape.[2]

Chouannerie in the nineteenth century

In 1829 Balzac published his first full-length novel under his own name with the title *The Last Chouan*. It examined the rebellion of 1799. Three years later, Chouannerie re-erupted. In 1832 a state of siege was declared in the departments of La Vendée, Deux-Sèvres, Maine-et-Loire, Loire-Inférieure and in the arrondissement of Vitré in the Ille-et-Vilaine. Balzac swiftly re-entitled his novel *The Chouans*: he had been too quick to assume this movement had ended in 1799. In the first section of this chapter, we will consider the history of Chouannerie in the nineteenth century.

'Blues' in Nantes enthusiastically participated in the July 1830 revolution, but this movement produced little reaction elsewhere in Brittany. The new government certainly expected trouble from 'the backward west' and therefore known legitimists and Chouan families were carefully watched. The local administration was purged: most of the Prefects and Sub-Prefects in the following decades were strangers to the region.[3] However, the autumn and winter of 1830 seemed calm. The general elections of July 1831 proved surprisingly successful for the new regime: of the thirty-two new Breton deputies, only one was an avowed opponent of the July Monarchy.[4] But while there was no open subversion, there were some indications of an underlying political tension. For example, there were more arguments between priests and schoolteachers in villages, and more clashes between priests and mayors over practices such as the ringing of church bells for old celebrations which had been abolished in the 1801 Concordat.[5] There were also some problems with conscripts. Some young men were either refusing to attend the meetings at which conscripts were chosen, by lot, from their ranks, or were deserting after being chosen. Rumours circulated concerning the methods by which these young men were encouraged to rebel. For example, it was said that the priest in Maumasson (Loire-Inférieure) told families that if their son was conscripted, both he and they would be damned.[6] In 1831 there were 194 such rebels in the Morbihan, and 119 in the Ille-et-Vilaine, but only 13 in the Côtes-du-Nord and 8 in Finistère.[7] In 1833, there were forty-four such conscription outlaws in the Loire-Inférieure.[8]

Such groups were not new: for example, there had been bands of conscription rebels in Châteaubriant arrondissement (Loire-Inférieure) since 1816.[9] But conscription rebels after 1830 did not simply hide from the authorities with others on the run. They also contacted the old Chouan underground. Guns which had been distributed by the British to the Chouans in 1815 were still held.[10] Sometimes they also spoke with the aged leaders of past rebellions, more often they met a new generation of anti-Orleanist militants, inspired by the illegal presence on French soil of the Duchesse de Berry, daughter-in-law of the last Bourbon monarch (Charles X) and mother of the new legitimist pretender (Henri V).[11] The Duchess was a rare creature: a Bourbon with a knack for publicity and the ability to motivate crowds. She promised honour, liberty, a legitimate ruler . . . and lower taxes.[12] One proclamation by her declared:

> I was separated from you by the misfortunes from which we have all suffered. [But] I know of your woes, I heard your wishes. The mother of Henri V, I have come in his name to grant [your wishes]. The regent of the kingdom, I am now with you, called by the wishes of a loyal population: I have not forgotten the duties that this double title imposes on me.[13]

In part, she was inspired by hostile liberal and Republican accounts. Where they had seen La Vendée and Brittany as the backward west, she believed that this unique region of France would become the unshakeable bastion of the legitimate monarchy.

The Chouan movement of 1832, however, was quite different in character from the movement implied by her idealistic pronouncements. The duchess was a figurehead rather than a leader, for this was not a well-organized, disciplined party. Chouannerie's strength lay in its ability to mark the landscape, to galvanize and mobilize those who resented the new Blue administration and, above all, to terrify the Blues.

After 1830 there had been a noticeable rise in the number of conscript rebels. In 1831 there were other visible signs of tension. In Morlaix (Finistère), the peasants were terrified by rumours of the Chouans' return.[14] In Quintin (Côtes-du-Nord), one Guillaume le Boulanger was arrested for shouting 'Long live the Chouans!' and for flying a white flag from his window.[15] Two deserters were caught in Etrille (Ille-et-Vilaine). As they were being escorted by the police to Vitré, about eighty to a hundred unarmed peasants attacked the patrol and freed the prisoners.[16] Such apparently minor incidents were indications of a growing political crisis.

The Chouans seized the white flag of the Bourbon monarchy and made it the symbol of their movement. Easily manufactured, its presence evoked memories of earlier battles against the Blues' tricolour flag. It was left, prominently displayed, around the centres of administration: outside town halls, opposite barracks, in central squares, on trees and windmills. It often inspired fear, sometimes real terror, among the Blues, and was effective in intimidating municipal officials. And yet it was clearly a substitute for a movement: the white flag was no more than an anonymous claim concerning a community's political commitment. The ideological content of the movement can be summarized in three letters: VHV, meaning 'Vive Henri V' (long live Henri V), the Duchess of Berry's son and increasingly the focus for legitimist hopes. These three letters appeared on anonymous placards, or at the end of threatening letters. In an analogous manner, coins were issued, marked with the head of Henry V. These circulated at markets and fairs; some were still to be found as late as 1843.[17] With the white flag, these simple symbols represented the movement's culture: non-political or pre-political, loyal to a personal monarch, and above all contemptuous of Louis-Philippe's liberal monarchy. The conscription rebels who attacked a police patrol in Parigné (Ille-et-Vilaine) told the police that they had been conscripted to serve by Charles X and therefore they were not bound to serve Louis-Philippe.[18]

There were few attempts at outright insurrection. The turning-point to the Duchess of Berry's revolt occurred in the last weeks of May and the first weeks of June 1832. During this period she issued an order for the mobilization of her supporters, and in some Breton departments there were isolated attempts to enlist, even to 'press', men into service. The Prefect of Ille-et-Vilaine issued a poster concerning this, warning that such actions would be severely repressed by the National Guard.[19]

The most representative activity of these last Chouans, however, was not the waving of a flag nor outright rebellion, but a pattern of violence. In Brittany, there was a long tradition of armed or threatening gangs of beggars terrorizing isolated hamlets and farmhouses at night, demanding food and drink from farmers: a tradition which certainly seems to date back to the eighteenth century, if not earlier.[20] Such older forms of aggression fed into Chouannerie. For example, in the Loire-Inférieure in January 1832 six thieves forced a mother alone in a farmhouse to give them bread, meat, and spirits. Was this simply robbery? Perhaps. But the six told the terrified woman that they had picked on her household because her family were liberals.[21]

Elsewhere, Chouan gang violence was more politically explicit. Liberal mayors, officials and others connected with them were seen by the Chouans as representatives of Blue culture and therefore as legitimate targets. On 4 October 1832 the mayor of Moisdon (Loire-Inférieure) was assassinated by a Chouan gang.[22] In July 1832 two women were seized at La Taillau (Loire-Inférieure). As one of them had served as a cook for soldiers stationed in a nearby canton, it was feared that she would be a particular target for their violence.[23] Brisson, a landowner in Vieillevigne (Loire-Inférieure), was hit, stabbed with a bayonet, and then dragged through the fields.[24] Gouthier, a sharecropper, was attacked by eight Chouans in the evening; they broke his arm, but nobody came to help him, despite his cries. He was left to drag himself back to his home; it was uncertain whether he would survive.[25] A Chouan band beat the mayor of Treffieux (Loire-Inférieure) with sticks on one Sunday in October 1832. Most alarming for the authorities, this attack took place in broad daylight in the centre of the town, while the townspeople, gathered there for mass, did nothing to aid him. Understandably, the mayor then resigned.[26] Beyond the physical violence of these attacks, each incident also pushed back the influence of the Blues over rural communities. Officials themselves made such observations in their reports. For example, when the mayors of Langolen and Scaër (Finistère) were threatened, a police officer commented: 'the local people say that the government is scared of [the Chouans], and that the Chouans are stronger than the liberals.'[27] Without winning any outright political or military victory, the Chouans subverted and denied the Blues' bureaucratic power. Their power is neatly illustrated by the disappearance of Saint-Julien mayor's manservant in February 1832: it was widely assumed that he had left to join the Chouans.[28] If a mayor could not trust his own servant, then who could he rely on?

This intangible, psychological dimension of Chouannerie often took on a life of its own. Stories, rumours, exaggerations and outright fantasies circulated among villagers, local officials and even normally sober-minded Prefects. A report by the Sub-Prefect of Ancenis (Loire-Inférieure) demonstrates the Chouans' success in demoralizing local blue officials:

> [I want] to tell you the whole truth. Secret meetings have been held in several places. The mayors are too demoralized to give information which will serve no purpose, and so they stay silent: in this way they will not suffer any recriminations. Several of them have told me that it would be pointless to ask them for confidential reports. The priests and the *desservants* are mainsprings of this network which stretches from steeple to steeple. Several of these clerics have been warned.[29]

In a later letter, the same Sub-Prefect warned that, of the eighty-eight National Guards at Varuades, one could only count on a quarter of them.[30] The mayor of Nort (Loire-Inférieure) reported 'alarming rumours' that Chouan bands were gathering in the nearby hamlets of Petit-Mars, Saint-Mars and Cellier: 'Everyone knows that they will show themselves soon, they proclaim this openly to anyone who wants to hear. [The groups constitute] a well-organized Counter-Revolution . . . Their orders come daily from the chateaux and presbyteries, the central committee of the Counter-Revolution.'[31] The magnifying effect of these rumours is easy to demonstrate: where the mayor of Juigné (Loire-Inférieure) reported eight hundred Chouans, the police only found between sixty and one hundred and fifty.[32]

112   *The Politics of Faith*

One finds some calmer observers. A police report from Châteaubriant (Loire-Inférieure) attempted to deflate some of these rumours and exaggerations which surrounded the movement:

> Nearly all these young men are just looking for a reason to leave [the gangs] without attracting suspicion.
> They have no discipline, they are poorly armed and – as yet – they have no prestigious leaders. 100 National Guards or soldiers would have nothing to fear when attacking [these gangs]. The individuals who they are recruiting are above all those who have been found guilty *in absentia*. It is the height of stupidity to issue such condemnations, for then these wretches have nothing to hope for, they have nothing to lose, and so become the most valuable recruits for our enemies.[33]

This is probably as accurate an assessment of the Chouans' military capacity as one could expect. It is significant, however, that few other officials were able to take so measured a view of the Chouan movement.

Finding exact data on this shifting, secretive force is difficult, but some points can be drawn from police records of suspects. An undated list of fifty-three 'compromised' individuals in the arrondissement of Châteaubriant (Loire-Inférieure) notes the trades of forty-seven; to this we have added the details of seven conscription rebels from the whole of the Loire-Inférieure. (See Table 4.1.) The single largest category, 'labourer', seems misleading, particularly in the absence of any other agricultural categories. It seems likely that here the category is being used as a catch-all term for all who worked the land, including tenant farmers, independent peasants, share-croppers and landless labourers. This inexactitude is unfortunate, as it makes it difficult to ascertain the movement's social composition. What can be noted, however, is the near-perfect representation of rural society: those who worked on the land are in the majority, but the spectrum of rural artisanal trades is also represented. Furthermore, the micro-elites of the rural society are present: the merchants, cabaret-owners, even the teachers and officials.

Two further lists dated March 1833, also from the Loire-Inférieure, provide information on the ages of 'presumed Chouans' and deserters. (See Table 4.2.) Predictably, the largest single contingent (60.97 per cent) of these suspects were in their twenties – the age at which they would have been conscripted. However, as with the previous table, we can also get an impression of how closely this movement reflected rural society, drawing support from those over sixty as well as those under twenty. While these lists do not give

Table 4.1 Professions of political suspects and conscription rebels in the Loire-Inférieure[34]

Trade	Number of suspects
Woodturner	1
Woodcutter	1
Cobbler	1
Labourer	36
Cabaret-owner	1
Worker	1
Joiner	2
Merchant	2
Ex-customs officer	2
Tanner	1
Carpenter	1
Painter	1
Ex-teacher	1
Ex-tax-official	1
Servant	2
Total:	54

details of professions in most cases, they do add a few comments. These eighty-five suspects included three men with a *particule* – an indication of their aristocratic status, or pretensions to that status – plus one priest, and two aged Chouan chiefs.

Table 4.2 Age of suspected Chouans and deserters in the Loire-Inférieure, March 1833[35]

Age	Number of suspects
10–19	2
20–29	50
30–39	13
40–49	5
50–59	5
60–69	7
Total	82

While the sociological evidence presented here is sketchy, one possible hypothesis does emerge: rather than simply seeing this movement as representing a cross-section of rural society, we should consider the absence of the very poor. There are very few servants. No one is listed as a beggar (while according to Villeneuve-Bargemont's estimates, one in fifty-four Bretons were beggars).[36] Nearly all of them have a status, some of which are fairly prestigious: teachers, tax officials, customs men, even aristocrats. Some further evidence emerges when we consider the geography of the revolt. In a sense, the whole of Brittany was affected, for the *fear* of Chouannerie could be found in almost any Breton town, and the white flag was flown in communes across the five departments. But, significantly, the Chouan strongholds in western cantons of the Loire-Inférieure and the Ille-et-Vilaine were also areas in which the countryside was dominated by wealthy Legitimist landowners. Re-examining this fragmentary evidence, one wonders whether the Chouannerie of 1832 was more representative of a frustrated, conservative sub-elite which contested the Blues' hegemony, and – in part – commanded wider loyalty through terror and intimidation, rather than acting as the voice of the totality of Breton rural society.

One last point can be made about the political culture of Chouannerie. The 1830s and 1840s saw many disturbances around the issue of the price of grain (see chapter 5). One might have imagined that a conservative, anti-modernist movement, seeking to provoke anger against the administration, would have considered this an ideal issue to exploit. It is therefore significant that the Chouans almost never took up this issue. The rioters who attacked the Prefect of Finistère in April 1840 during a grain riot did cry 'Long Live Henri V!', but this appears to be the sole example of grain rioters making use of the vocabulary of Chouannerie. Significantly, the incident took place in an area without a strong Chouan tradition.[37] One is driven to conclude that, instead, Chouannerie may have drawn support from the big, grain-producing farmers who could benefit from the high price of grain.

In a curious manner, the Chouans' greatest political achievement was to affirm and even to strengthen the Blues' political identity. They were, according to one assistant mayor, 'our eternal enemies'.[38] The rebel movement provided a clear target for a politicized sense of conflict, which connected the local context to national politics. This sense of deepening politicization is made clearer in a report by the mayor of Vieillevigne, following a Chouan attack:

> This must stop, as the good patriots are suffering. The Chouans can find secure shelter among the masses. The armed forces can do nothing; the mobile units

which cross the countryside do not have clear enough information to work with success. The government must act to rid us of this plague which demoralizes the isolated good patriots. We have been waiting for this since 1830. It is time that we, like the people of France, enjoyed the benefits of peace.[39]

In this report, the sense of 'us and them' is stark and obvious. The Chouannerie of the 1830s did not simply revive memories of earlier Counter-Revolutionary violence: it enforced a historical interpretation, a sense of historical continuity, connecting discontent with the Orleanist regime with the older Vendéen rebellion. This memory of the Chouans would once again be mobilized against the Second Republic of 1848.

The Chouannerie of the 1830s left behind a divided society, more sharply separated than ever into the camps of Blues and Whites. But, above all, this desperate, violent, primitive movement reveals to us how shallowly the Orleanist administration was rooted in Brittany. The Orleanists faced massive problems in trying to develop their cultural and political presence in Brittany from a few, selected urban outposts into a hegemony over the entire region. In other areas of France, their tricolour flag might be positively welcomed or received with indifference. In Brittany, it often aroused sustained opposition. For example, in the arrondissement of Brest (Finistère), three mayors, including the mayor of Brest, immediately resigned in mid-1830 when forced to fly this flag over their town halls.[40] Further resistance came in the Ille-et-Vilaine, also in 1830. Thirty-six communes refused to fly the tricolour, of which thirty were in the arrondissement of Vitré, later to be the site of Chouan rebellions.[41] In other words, the establishment of the Orleanist regime at local level was *more* politicized in Brittany than elsewhere in France.

Looking at this situation, one might have thought that the wisest course would have been to drop requirements concerning political and religious symbols where they met hostility. But the Minister of the Interior was insistent: all communes were to fly the tricolour.[42] The Ille-et-Vilaine Prefect enlarged on the Minister's remarks:

> Each commune has a centre-point, some public building on which the flag may be placed. Some have placed it in front of their town hall, if it is used, on some high point. Elsewhere, in the countryside, it flies over the church-tower or the steeple, which is also a building belonging to the commune. This is the best spot, as it is the highest, the most visible – that is what has been done in the rest of France.[43]

To make matters worse, the new administration wanted to go further: it aimed to sweep the countryside clean of the provocative mission crosses, which the revivalist 'missions' of the Restoration had planted opposite the homes of landowners who had bought church property during the 1790s.[44] This measure was difficult to apply. One Sub-Prefect explained 'if this measure is implemented thoroughly it will have a bad effect in the countryside. It will allow the priests to tell the faithful that we are opposed to the Christian religion, that this is a time of persecution.'[45] The administration was even opposed to the fleur-de-lys which could be found in decorative work in many churches. In the eyes of the Orleanists, these were dangerous symbols, for they had been used by the previous Bourbon regimes as royal symbols. There is a deep irony here: the fleur-de-lys in many churches dated from the sixteenth century, when they had been adopted as a sign of the rallying of the formerly autonomous duchy to the French kingdom.[46] This old symbol of national allegiance was interpreted by the Orleanists as a sign of political subversion.

To a Prefect, a church steeple might appear the ideal site for a tricolour: to the priest, to Chouan sympathizers and perhaps to most of the inhabitants, the tricolour appeared an aberrant intrusion. As one mayor reported, the priest 'argues that I have no right to fly this flag from the temple of the Catholic religion'. In order to obey the Prefect's ruling, the mayor had to use a locksmith to force the lock on the church door, and then climb to the steeple. While this was taking place, someone shot at him – but missed.[47]

The drive to institute a Blue political culture clashed with the imagined geography of rural Brittany. The calvaries, crosses, magic springs and steeples wove the referents of the countryside into a certain pattern: Blue political culture could not be integrated into this arrangement. Without seeking a quarrel with the church, without being consciously provocative, let alone revolutionary, deep-seated animosity was created by the July Monarchy's innovations. One should be careful about assuming this apolitical, traditionalistic, local, Catholic patriotism was expressed through Chouannerie: indeed, it is significant that in the most highly clerical cantons of Léon (in the northwest of Finistère), which showed the highest rates of church attendance, there was no Chouan violence in 1832. But this ingrained, rooted Catholic culture of cross and steeple was nonetheless a pervasive force which resisted Orleanist innovation. One Sub-Prefect's observations drew some useful general conclusions: 'It is certain that in many small communes [the priests] are always the masters, whoever is in the municipal administration.'[48] The evidence surveyed so far certainly suggests that Orleanism had a hard battle to fight in the early nineteenth century.

In 1832, Balzac found that he had been too quick in his attempt to turn Chouannerie into a Walter Scott-style historical fable. Two decades later, however, Catholic writers were starting to idealize the Chouans of the 1790s. According to Charles Barthélemy, there were two sides in 1792:

> On the one hand, there were poor people, forced from their homes, defending with their scythes and their sticks Christ's old cross, the one which had freed the world. On the other hand, there were the fanatics of the new religion, who imposed their symbols at gunshot, and who were convinced that they would save France.[49]

Such narratives idealized the rebel areas, depicting them as zones of simple, patriarchal communities, without inns or beggars, based on face-to-face contact, in which commercial agreements would be made and honoured without the interventions of lawyers. Such images clearly distorted the reality of Breton rural society, but they were politically important in creating a type of utopia to inspire opposition to Republican France.[50]

A White landscape: the pardons

Alongside the regular, rational, Blue hierarchy of communes, cantons, arrondissements, departments and nation established by the French Revolution, there was another sense of space which structured the lives of many Breton people. This alternative culture can be termed 'white', the colour adopted by the Counter-Revolutionaries during the 1790s, and previously associated with the Bourbon monarchy. At times, it seemed that this 'other' force was best represented by local aristocrats, Chouans and monarchist networks. Closer investigation, however, suggests the greater importance of the church and associated, semi-autonomous, popular cultures.

Many of our travellers and Celticists note the particular religious quality of Brittany. What is fascinating about their comments is that alongside their vague references to the mystical Celtic soul, there are also clearer, more concrete observations about the landscape. Souvestre's notes neatly illustrate how these two types of observation could go hand-in-hand. He writes of the Léon region: 'Everything in this land is possessed by some enchanting and peaceful fertility. It is as if this land, which is covered by churches, crosses and chapels, has been impregnated by so many sacred objects.'[51] Mérimée commented, more dryly, that there was a wooden or stone calvary at each crossroads: a point echoed by both Richer and Serbois.[52] Brousmiche addressed this theme when he considered the difficulties experienced by the confused traveller. There were no accurate maps available of the numerous tracks, alleys and side routes which criss-crossed the countryside. If there was no local person present to give directions, then how was the traveller to find the right route?

> As he walks along, the lonely traveller, above all the traveller who does not know Breton, would get lost if – from stage to stage – he could not see the lofty spires of our churches, which are always placed at the centre of each commune, and which act like a staff by which he can recognize the path he wants to follow.[53]

Guérand, travelling along the south coast of the Morbihan, noted a different aspect of this religious presence: 'Sainte Anne: the greatest, the most generous, the best of saints, the beloved protectress of Brittany. She is everywhere, in the churches, in the chapels, in the roads and on the houses.'[54] Serbois's notes on this same theme concentrated on crosses: 'Crosses dominate the whole of Brittany. You find them on the top of the churches and on the doors of humble cottages; they are fixed onto *dolmen* and stuck beside the menacing cliffs.'[55] Examining Finistère, Sylvette Denefle calculates that there were probably about four or five fountains with a religious significance in every commune. About half of them were named after a saint or the Virgin Mary.[56] While this culture is often referred to in an unthinking and simplistic manner as 'traditional', it is important to note that it was growing and adapting in the nineteenth century. For example, the experience of the Revolution led to a host of new tombs and shrines to commemorate and therefore to interpret the victims of those years.[57]

The key symbol for this semi-underground semi-religious culture was the *pardon*: a local, annual pilgrimage to a particular site to commemorate the patron saint of a church or a chapel. The importance of the *pardon*, as Anatole Le Braz perceptively noted, was that it made visible the opaque historical traces hidden in the landscape. A tiny chapel, half-buried and barely visible, would momentarily become the site of a *pardon* and therefore a centre of remembrance and popular culture.[58] Such *pardons* were common practices in early modern France. In Brittany, however, they developed with particular intensity. In part, this is due to an economic and cultural conjuncture. In the seventeenth century, the themes of the Catholic Reformation were being elaborated with great force in the region, thanks to committed, energetic and well-trained clerical personnel.[59] Brittany was still undergoing the slow process of integration into French administrative and political structures, and the Breton economy was booming, with its weavers supplying linen and canvas to buyers across the world. This meant that more money was available to finance the churches and religious monuments built during this period and that – arguably – greater religious fervour accompanied their construction, resulting in a unique blend of vernacular styles and religious themes: in many cases, there are no named sculptors for these *calvaires* and statues.[60] The finest example of such work is probably the enormous *calvaire* at the church of Saint-Jean-Trolimon (Finistère). This enormous granite slab, more than four metres long and three metres high, depicts over a hundred religious figures.[61]

The religious authorities of the Catholic Reformation, however, were often suspicious of the *pardons*. In theory a *pardon* was like a pilgrimage: through the experience of privation in walking to a faraway place, the pilgrim was supposed to feel a sense of identity with the suffering Christ. The vows taken during the *pardon* were to sustain the believer for the rest of the year. But it was clear to seventeenth-century priests that other aspects of the *pardon* were more prominent. Each *pardon* was organized around a particular saint; such appeals often seemed to degenerate into particularistic, locally-based cults at the expense of any more general, universal religious perspective. Moreover, the pilgrims' habit of stopping at taverns along the way and the dancing that celebrated the end of the event all had the potential for encouraging immoral rather than moral behaviour.

As is often the case with so-called 'traditional' practices, the *pardon* reached its apogee in the nineteenth century.[62] Indeed, it is only in this century that the term becomes the standard one to describe such events. Their function was now subtly different from that of previous ages. In place of celebrating the new and prestigious seventeenth-century church, the *pardons* now took pilgrims to half-forgotten spots, ignored for most of the year. The Post-revolutionary Catholic church was generally less censorious than the church of the Catholic Reformation, and priests were more willing to cooperate. Certainly, *pardons* had a capacity to draw in people who would not normally attend church. Ellen Badone cites the example of La Feuillée in Finistère in the early twentieth century, when fifteen or twenty of the commune's six hundred inhabitants would attend Sunday mass, but over two hundred would join the annual *pardon* on 24 June.[63] *Pardons* could fulfil a number of religious functions: the Audierne clergy would bless the sea at Saint-Julien-de-Poulgroazec (Finistère). At the *pardon* for the chapel of Saint-Jean (Plougastel-Daoulas), birds would be sold, and in Ploneour-Lanvern girls would dance round a noticeably phallic *menhir* which was topped with a tiny cross. In the mid-nineteenth century, the pardon of Saint Loup at Guingamp (Côtes-du-Nord) had grown to include two days of public dancing.[64] Moreover, this was still a developing tradition: following the curing of a very sick child at Saint-Brieuc on 31 May 1848, a new annual pardon was initiated.

For the ceremony of the crowning of Sainte Anne in 1868, about a thousand priests attended: alongside representatives of the army, the law, the administration and even some deputies: 'The roads were packed with vehicles of all sorts, from luxurious carriages of the bourgeois to the humble carts of the peasants.'[65] The attendance of some two hundred thousand people at the *pardon* of Sainte-Anne-d'Auray on 25 July 1920 was perhaps the high-water mark of this movement.[66] (Today, this annual pardon attracts between twenty and thirty thousand people.) Such events were veritable counter-institutions, and allowed churchmen to speak as if they represented the region; they were 'national festivals', remarked Nicol.[67] In 1868 abbé Freppel told the crowd at Sainte-Anne-d'Auray: 'now, more than ever, you need to remain what you are . . . protected by the triple walls of your faith, your language and your traditions . . . keep your strong convictions, your simple customs and your manly, austere traditions.'[68]

Often the churches were too small for the crowds which gathered, and pilgrims would kneel outside during the commemorative services.[69] From postcards and paintings one often gets the impression that these festivals were better attended by women than men; certainly the women's white *coiffes* make them more visible than their black-suited brothers. Nineteenth-century *pardons* grew into what Georges Provost has usefully termed 'total festivals', incorporating 'devotion and meeting old family friends, solemn masses and punch-ups'.[70] While not exactly big business, their economic dimension had expanded: transport companies could offer to carry people; wine- and cider-sellers certainly expected increased sales; and stall-holders of religious knick-knacks would set up their stalls as close as possible to the site of the *pardon*. Beggars would crowd round the processions, often making it difficult to move. Bagpipe players and drummers would entertain the pilgrims and dances would follow the church service. Legend has it that, of course, brothels would also find many customers among the pilgrims. Aspects of courtship had also been institutionalized within *pardon* rituals. Young men would fight for the privilege of carrying the flags, banner, statues and relics of the church to the central point. In some cases these had lead weights attached to them, so that all might appreciate the strength of the carrier. Usually *pardons* were identified with particular villages or hamlets: attending other villages' *pardons* could be a means by which to cement inter-village solidarities. Equally, rivalries could come to a head, and there were few *pardons* without scuffles between young men of rival villages.

The number of pilgrims could become a problem in themselves: overcrowding, competition to seize the best places and contests to carry statues and relics could lead to injuries and even, on occasion, deaths. Many *pardons* would last several days. By the late nineteenth century crowds would travel by specially-organized trains, and then sleep outdoors beside the temporary cities of stall-holders' tents who sold religious objects, food and, often, alcoholic drinks.[71] Le Goffic was to note, cynically, that three-quarters of the day was spent in worship, and one-quarter on spirits.[72] The people who come to worship a saint, wrote Le Braz, end the day in the cult of alcohol.[73]

The sight of crowds walking across fields carrying crosses, relics and flags – the women often dressed in white and carrying long candles, the men dressed largely in black – rapidly became a sight 'which tourists eagerly sought', according to the popular nineteenth-century novelist Jeanne Schultz.[74] Nineteenth-century tourist guides to Brittany usually listed the dates of the most colourful *pardons*: 'It is at these ceremonies that you will get the best impression of Breton customs and be able to admire their colourful clothes that they wear almost everywhere' noted the *Guide Bleu* of 1920.[75] It then listed the best and the most 'Breton' *pardons*. Here, *pardons* are functioning as a type of cultural exchange, as the presence of tourists encourages a demand for *bretonnitude*: the now-obvious stereotypes of black velvet waistcoats for men and starched white lace *coiffes* for the women.

The most thought-provoking commentary on this engrained, rooted religious culture comes from a more recent work: Pierre-Jakez Hélias's autobiography *Le Cheval d'orgueil*, which describes his childhood in the early twentieth century in the south-west of Finistère. Hélias's work must be treated with caution: its distinctive mixture of nostalgia, Breton-language militancy and Republican commitment often make it difficult to analyse with precision. One passage, however, seems to give us a glimpse into the manner in which a Breton child might have made sense of the landscape around him:

> There were many magic springs across the canton. There were so many of them, that not all of them were visited. Some of them were hidden in distant parts of the countryside, hard to get to, but old tales said that they did the poor people a lot of good. The women spoke of them among themselves, taught each other about them, and checked with each other the properties of one spring or another . . . We also knew that the big-heads in the towns, people who were as rich as the sea, would travel very far, at great expense, to drink from such springs. They would even put their waters in bottles, to sell them to weak people who could not get used to cider or wine. Vichy, Vittel, that was the name they called them. They came out of earth like ours, but ours tasted better to us, and it did not cost pounds! As for the saints' springs, there was no reason to doubt their power as those very same saints were

exhibited in our churches and chapels. The Virgin, Lady Mary, belonged to everybody, as was right. So, she was everywhere. It seemed that there was a place which she particularly liked. This was in the south, beyond the Dordogne, in a sort of Holy Land that was called Lourdes. It would be good to go there, particularly if you had something: you came back with the water from that land [pays]. For the moment, Notre-Dame of Pehnors, next to the sea which bathed our parish, was quite enough for us. She would not leave her chapel. She knew us. We could ask her for all the favours we needed, above all to protect the fishermen, our brothers, who went out on the bay.[76]

As we read these words, we can almost feel the child struggling to make sense of the bigger world. Like Brousmiche's traveller, he tries to find landmarks by which to orientate himself. The physical layout of his countryside is marked by points of significance: firstly the magic springs, identified by the local women, which can be both pagan and Christian in nature. Thinking of these springs, this child is able to conceptualize ideas of a bigger area, taking in Vichy and Lourdes. But in thinking on this bigger scale, Hélias's child narrator then needs to refer back to Catholic culture: the images of Mary and Lourdes are necessary for him to frame the picture.

Hélias appears to be writing of some unspecified moment in the early twentieth century. A second point which can be drawn from his text is the simple absence of the French state's administrative presence in his mental geography. The mayors' Blue political geography based on communes and cantons seems quite irrelevant. Most Bretons, particularly in the countryside, lived with what Lagrée has termed the 'topographical and psychological omnipresence of the sacred'.[77]

Catholic politics

The Republicans saw the rural church as inherently backward. This cliché often made little sense to Catholics and peasants: it ignores a basic truth about the work of the Church which, from the seventeenth century, was attempting to modernize the region. It was no coincidence that the first grammars and dictionaries of the Breton language were written by clerics, signifying their commitment to education. The counter-reformation Church launched the cultural modernization of Brittany, combating what it saw as superstition, acting against riotous and crude behaviour, and presenting a 'more systematic and organized teaching in the Breton countryside through preaching, Masses, greater use of sacraments and schools'.[78] It was this commitment to education which inspired independent Catholic scholars like abbé

Joseph Mahé, an unauthorized priest in the 1790s, a member of the Académie Celtique and one of the first collectors of folk lyrics in the Morbihan in the 1820s.[79] Ernest Renan's account of his childhood gives a glimpse of this educated milieu in its declining years in the early nineteenth century. Renan recalled Tréguier (Côtes-du-Nord): 'a completely ecclesiastical town, foreign to all commerce and industry: a great monastery in which no outside noise penetrated, where one called the occupations of other men "vanity", and in which what the secular people called an illusion was the only reality.'[80] In 1876, the bishop of Côtes-du-Nord proclaimed his commitment to faith and science, and welcomed the victory of enlightenment over ignorance.[81] In Brittany, the Catholic church was rightly seen as a promoter of learning, not ignorance.

A socio-economic dimension to this clerical cultural modernization was often added by the big landowners in eastern Brittany. Here, many landowners pushed their tenants to modernize production, taught their farmers and encouraged emulation. 'The Republic brought nothing. It was a regime from outside; it was a threat.'[82] To the West, it was conservative elites who encouraged a slow process of agrarian development, first via the institution of the *comices agricoles*, which organized annual prizes for the most productive farmers. By 1858, such *comices* were held in seventeen of Brittany's forty cantons.[83] Later, in Finistère, such elites sponsored a cooperative movement, encouraging small land-owning peasants to group together to share expensive machinery.[84] In general, the aristocracy appreciated the need for economic modernization: its political priority was to ensure that such developments took place without a loss of their political control.[85] Such considerations help explain why, in areas of efficient aristocratic social management, the Republican state seemed to many a dangerous enemy of an established social harmony.[86]

In other words, the problem for the Republican state was not so much that Brittany was backward, as that it had already been partially modernized by existing elites, usually either clerics themselves, or those linked to the Church. In most cases, such elites did not initially need to build powerful mass organizations to counter Republican politics. Instead, they relied on the natural groupings of rural society. For example, like the Republicans, conservatives organized temporary local committees to fight elections. In 1876 the Loudéac (Côtes-du-Nord) committee, with fifty-four members, met to consider their candidate for the next elections. The committee consisted of ten priests, twelve mayors or adjuncts, four lawyers, and eleven big landowners.[87] Predictably, many of them were also nobles: their committee provided a near-perfect representation of these natural, unelected groupings which sustained conservative organizations into the twentieth century. Such social forces proved surprisingly resilient. From 1879 to 1914 approximately one third of all Breton deputies were nobles.[88] Even in 1909, some 216 of the one and a half thousand Breton mayors were nobles.[89] This political culture sustained 'a political and moral counter-society' to rival the Republicans' political project.[90] 'Administrative and government action thus has almost no hold over them', noted one Sub-Prefect – a point to be explored further in the following chapters.[91]

The centenary of 14 July 1789 provided many telling examples of the strength of this conservative culture.[92] The Breton Catholic press cheerfully announced that, yes, 1889 was an anniversary year and then invited their readers to celebrate the bicentenary of the vision of Saint Margaret-Marie of the Sacred Heart. With little explicit polemic, Catholic writers simply suggested the contrast between the two commemorations. Again, in 1893, Catholics were invited to celebrate the re-establishment of the Catholic religion on the island of Jersey, and to consider the past one hundred years as 'a century of restoration', devoted to repairing the damage created by the Revolution. At other moments, figures such as Joan of Arc were popularized to counter the Republic festivals.[93]

In some areas of Brittany, particularly the Léon region of Finistère, such measures were more than effective. Here, the church 'educated, organized, and helped: it truly federated Léonard society.'[94] Elsewhere, imaginative clerics would attempt to adapt Catholic themes to the needs of particular local audiences. In Paimpol, on the northern coast, a succession of priests worked with the fishermen who sailed out to Iceland each year. Their 'Icelandic Pardon' was challenged by the anticlerical municipal council, which proposed its own 'Icelandic Festival' in 1904. Significantly, one of the church's local leaders, the abbé Millon, began to identify the *Breton* nature of his parishioners as an important constituent of this local Catholic faith.[95] This union of faith and Brittany, of *Feiz ha Breiz*, could be the basis for a specific type of Catholic regionalism (to be discussed in chapter 7), but was more commonly asserted as a simple, apolitical source of pride for the mainstream church. Max Nicol felt confident in 'the bright, firm faith which forms the foundation of the Breton race.'[96]

In other areas, where the alliance of Catholics, priests and conservatives was less solid, more aggressive means were sometimes needed to repel the Republican influence. In such cases, the landowners' economically based powers of patronage were vital: they could, for example, force their tenants to send their children to the Catholic private school.[97] In other localities, Catholic and conservative groups would organize the boycott of shops run by anticlericals and Republicans, and would even attempt to enforce the surveillance of newspaper reading.[98]

Such elites also realized the importance of a partial adaptation of their political culture to the necessities of modern political life. Despite the stereotype of a bluntly reactionary political culture, Breton conservative organizations showed gradual signs of innovation in the early twentieth century. For example, a vibrant, mass-circulation Catholic and conservative press developed. In the early twentieth century, the most successful Catholic daily was *Ouest-Éclair* (created in 1899) which 'has reached all the countryside and all situations, above all because it is first and foremost a current affairs paper'.[99] This difficult, almost painful, process of mass politicization was often initiated by protest groups such as the League of Patriotic Frenchwomen (or LFFP), which had as one of its slogans: 'Peace with the Republic, war on Freemasons, make room for freedom!' A public LFFP meeting at Dinan (Côtes-du-Nord) in 1908 attracted about one hundred and twenty people, including some ladies, their maids and about twenty workers: a telling indication of the type of audience which this group could mobilize.[100] A similar function was played by the anti-Dreyfusard Ligue de la Patrie française (LPF), which gained some real popularity in Ille-et-Vilaine. By 1911 this organization was claiming sixteen thousand members in this department, organized in 120 committees.[101] While such organizations were politically active, they never attempted to form permanent parties with political programmes: in other words, while constituting an offensive force to prevent the development of Republicanism, their existence never challenged or replaced the 'natural' hegemony of aristocrats and clergy.

A more radical step on the path of political modernization was Action Libérale populaire (ALP), which was established in 1901 with the aim of creating a conservative party which would defend religious interests, but which was not clerical in character.[102] In the 1902 elections, fourteen ALP deputies were elected: five of them were from Breton constituencies, including Comte Albert de Mun, one of the party's two leaders.[103] Significantly, in its public declarations, the ALP presented an extremely innovative conservative stand: 'There are no more chouans and no more blues', proclaimed one ALP poster, 'there are only two great parties: that of Liberty, and that of Sectarianism'.[104] However, while claiming to transcend this age-old division of Breton politics, the ALP was clear about what its commitment to 'liberty' implied: it meant, first and foremost fighting against the influence of the Republic's 'atheist' schools. The ALP redefined the nature of right-wing political culture, drawing its inspiration from the contemporary difficulties experienced by village clergy and ordinary Catholics, rather than re-fighting the battles of the past.

The most significant step, however, towards the creation of a modern, independent Catholic voice was the establishment of Christian–Democratic forms of politics. This can be dated to a by-election in 1894, when the social–Catholic, Comte Albert de Mun, successfully contested the election of a rival monarchist candidate in Finistère, thus demonstrating the willingness of some Catholics to cut the political ties which linked the church to the right, and even to contest the social domination of the aristocracy.[105] Following De Mun's breakthrough, there were two further significant political-religious projects which attempted to redefine the nature of Catholic culture. Neither of these was specifically based in Brittany but in both cases Bretons were prominent in their formation and development.

The first of these was Marc Sangnier's Sillon grouping (1902–10). This group can arguably be seen as the first left-wing Catholic organization in France. Sangnier's lyrical 'Appeal to youth' gives a good indication of this current's idealism: robustly, stubbornly orientated toward the future, Sangnier appealed to young people to join him in a fight against egotism. He spoke the language of empowerment, calling on young people to form circles within which Sillon-ists would act 'as advisors and friends, not as masters'. The movement's aim was to encourage cooperation, to build a sense of confidence among the young, to accept diverse cultures, in a great movement to fight for 'justice and love'.[106] How this must appeal must have resonated among young Breton Catholics! In December 1900, some two hundred workers came to listen to Sangnier in Brest; in April 1903, some two thousand people, grouped in thirty-eight different associations, attended the Sillon's first Breton congress at Brest.[107] While never a mass movement, the Sillon did gather significant and growing support in Brittany, before its early Papal banning in 1910. Above all, it was able to appeal to the urban working class.[108] Predictably, the reality of the movement was often different from its idealistic rhetoric: in practice, Sangnier was jealously protective of his hold on the movement.[109]

The second significantly innovative Catholic organization was the Parti Démocratique Populaire (PDP), created in 1924 partly as a reaction against a perceived Sillon-ist leftism.[110] Fourteen of its candidates were elected in the general elections of 1924: five of them in Brittany. In 1928, the region supplied six of its seventeen deputies.[111] These election results, however, are misleading. PDP deputies were only successfully elected if they were members of broader, right-wing coalitions: this situation led to an awkward dilemma for the PDP. At a local level it appealed to young people, and it initiated the intensely difficult and long overdue debate on the relation of the Church to the Republic. In some places it became relatively popular: in April 1925, some four hundred people marched in a PDP demonstration in Guingamp, and some eight hundred gathered for the subsequent banquet.[112] In developing its political and social activities, it frequently annoyed clerical authorities.[113] Its political stance was difficult to define. Sometimes it proved to be surprisingly bold in unexpected ways. For example, when one reads the electoral declaration of Auguste Bastianelli, who contested the right-wing constituency of Vitré (Ille-et-Vilaine) in 1928, one finds references to poverty, the need to re-establish the Republic, to strengthen the government, to introduce proportional representation, to establish means of economic coordination, to reduce unemployment, to encourage larger families and to create a spirit of union. But . . . not a word about the defence of Catholic schools.[114] (Predictably, he was not elected.)

The entrenched hostility of all Republican groups presented this would-be independent group with a recurring problem at elections. Throughout the Third Republic, small groups could only succeed at elections if they were part of a larger coalition. Given the Republicans' permanent refusal to cooperate, the PDP was more or less forced to work with conservative and clerical groups at elections, inevitably re-fuelling the Republicans' suspicions. Worse still, it was even possible for its conservative partners to manipulate its presence, using its cross-party appeal as a means to break down the resistance of 'blue' constituencies. In this awkward environment, it was difficult for the PDP to develop into a genuinely critical and autonomous voice. Its pronouncements often reverted to a simplistic type of 'neither-right-nor-left' sloganizing: thus in 1934 one PDP speaker in Rennes declared that 'liberalism has collapsed, but Statism cannot replace it.'[115] But what was the PDP's perspective? In 1935, with formation of the left-wing Popular Front coalition, it found itself, once more, forced to work in partnership with the old conservative right.[116] In the more heated and polarized political atmosphere of the 1930s, its solutions increasingly sounded like simple, pious hopes, and the number of its deputies and members declined.

The Sillon, the PDP and, to a much lesser extent, the ALP all sketch out a potential new identity for Catholics in the Third Republic: a critical, independent, campaigning, ethical voice. None of these groups were specifically Breton, but all of them gained a significant degree of support in the region from young people, from some parish priests and sometimes also from peasants and workers.[117] This independence concerned the Catholic hierarchy.

The difference between the Catholic political initiatives noted above, and the more clerical projects sponsored directly by the Church is clear. The Church was concerned by the secularizing legislation of the Republican state. The anticlerical legislation of the early 1900s led to the closure of many Catholic schools: while this was opposed by most priests and bishops, they were reluctant to lead active resistance. In Brittany, instead, opposition was based on small, local groups of activists. This grew into 'nothing less than an armed insurrection' as both Catholic and anti clerical communes rose in defence of 'their' Catholic schools.[118] This militant stance was then revived, under somewhat different circumstances, in 1924.

In March 1919, the first post-war election was won by a conservative coalition, the Bloc National, which made use of wartime themes such as patriotism and unity to sustain a series of governments. No new anticlerical legislation was proposed: in some cases, existing legislation was moderated to the advantage of Catholic organizations. A French Embassy was re-established in the Vatican. In the May 1924 elections, the 'Cartel', a loose electoral arrangement between the left-of-centre Radicals and the socialist SFIO (Section Française de l'Internationale Ouvrière), transformed the political scene. While the absolute number of votes changed little, the Cartel won an absolute majority of seats (327 out of 610). Almost sixty years later, Julien Gracq could still remember the shock that this result created in his Nantes boarding school; it was the first – and only – political event to be widely discussed by its teachers and pupils.[119]

The SFIO refused to join a Radical government, so the cabinet was formed from small centre and left-of-centre groups. The Radicals reinitiated an anticlerical programme. In order to resist these changes, the Fédération Nationale Catholique (FNC), headed by General de Castelnau, was created.[120] The centrepiece of the FNC's campaign were massive demonstrations against the Radical legislation, organized by locally based parish committees. Significantly, some of the biggest meetings of this campaign were held in Brittany. (See Table 4.3.)

Abbé Jean Desgranges wrote a memorable description of the massive mobilizations of Catholics at Quimper and Folgoët:

> Who would not join us in contemplating these seventy thousand men chanting the *Credo*, their eyes wet with tears? They marched for hours without a single harsh shout, without a single misplaced gesture, and they listened, with an impressive silence, to the speeches which were made to them. You would feel in your heart that united enthusiasm that they felt when one spoke of the heroes of the war or of the country's higher interests. Can anyone cite another

Table 4.3 The five biggest FNC meetings, October 1924–January 1925[121]

Town	Estimated numbers
Landernau	60,000–100,000
Folgoët	50,000
Saint-Brieuc	30,000
Bayonne	21,000
Quimper	20,000

popular demonstration which has marched with a more perfect order or a more impeccable dignity?

A secular counter-demonstration was organized on Sunday at Quimper. Even if you count the women and children, the crowd barely reached a thousand. Mr Le Bail marched at its head. He is a radical who is very proud of his patriotism and his love of order. Among those who followed him, some looked as if they were carrying out a sad duty, while the keenest struck up the *Internationale*. This revolutionary hymn created a bit of agitation in the peaceful Breton city, and Le Bail and his friends went pale. The Catholic march, however, praised France, flew the tricolour and sung the national hymn.'[122]

Such dramatic descriptions successfully evoke a sharp, politicized polarization. While the FNC certainly exploited the region's native, engrained Catholic identity, it did much more that simply affirm a Catholic presence. Rather than engaging Catholics as a voice within the Republic, these post-war Catholic mobilizations positioned Catholics as a voice against the Republican government, separated from Republican political culture by their morality and their faith.

The postwar context of this movement was revealed clearly in another leaflet: 'Catholics are and will always be the best patriots. They constitute the immense majority of French people . . . We were front-line soldiers, who knew the war and its muddy trenches: we never met those who oppose us and who try to enslave us [in those trenches].'[123] Here, a second source of legitimacy is spelt out: this is a movement of the majority of male adults, authorized through their suffering in the war to rebuke and condemn governmental actions.

As its name suggests, the FNC was intended to be a movement which promoted a sense of French nationhood. It is therefore noteworthy that, at times, these angry Catholics took up the regionalist language of *bretonnitude*:

'We refuse to allow southern Freemasons to impose their will on Breton Catholics.'[124] They were not, of course, separatists or Breton nationalists, although often their militants shared a fascination about the older, pre-revolutionary provinces with previous right-wing thinkers. Like Villemarqué, they asserted a specific positive, spiritual quality for their region.

Did these angry Catholics fear a Republican counter-attack? In terms of simple numbers, it is unlikely that the tiny Republican groups could have organized demonstrations of a similar size. But there was another medium through which Republicans could respond. Significantly, this was identified by the Finistère bishop, who claimed that worried parishioners had come to him to tell of the pressures which had been placed on them *not* to march on the demonstrations: 'Watch out, if you join, you'll lose your pension!'[125] There is good reason to think that the bishop's story is untrue: nonetheless, the story is telling. To these protesting Breton Catholics, the Republican state was not a progressive, equitable body which provided social security to those in need; instead it was a twisted, malign body, ever-ready to take back what it had given in a partisan manner.

Such movements did nothing to aid the region's cultural liberation: they locked Catholics into an oppositional stand, based on an alleged moral superiority, preventing dialogue with secular groups. Instructions from the Côtes-du-Nord bishop in 1925 illustrate this point neatly: 'When the bishop has given an order, all Catholics *must* obey. Whoever refuses to march is a bad Catholic, whatever he says. During the war, what did we call a soldier who refused to obey and who encouraged others to forget their duty?'[126] This movement promised to win back the status which Catholics had lost in the Republic: but it did so by attempting to organize them in a militaristic and authoritarian manner. The Radical government, concerned by the protests, had second thoughts about pushing through its anticlerical legislation. The protest movement had successfully voiced anger and even feelings of exclusion: following the government's change of heart, the FNC lost its dynamism. It did not form a permanent mass organization.

Conclusion

These faith-based groups certainly produced some of the most eloquent, inspiring and resonant images of Brittany. While clearly separate, the weaving together of Chouan violence, religious awe and social hierarchy by local communities could produce a tough, informal political culture, rooted in daily practice, which was able to resist the governmental initiatives of the

Blues. This white landscape was certainly compatible with the Celticism of Villemarqué, but its clerical leaders and spokesmen were usually careful to avoid accepting or promoting the non-Catholic values of such movements. The one weakness of this political culture was its informal, even its non-verbal, nature. The modern state, with its rational–bureaucratic values, required literate, educated, organized citizens: any Breton with ambition, looking to make his or her fortune, would eventually realize how constrained were the borders of this white landscape.

5

The Politics of the State (1)
People and Protests, 1830–52

This chapter analyses two issues: the state's programmes for Brittany in the early nineteenth century, and some popular reactions to those initiatives. It will be argued that authoritarian structures of rule developed in this period, and that these stayed almost constant for the succeeding century and a half. The one significant exception to this observation is the utopian moment of Revolution in 1848: a missed opportunity which permanently warped political culture in Brittany.

These issues will be discussed through reference to the occasions for mediation between power structures and popular culture. In the last chapter, we considered the *pardon*; here, we will turn – first – to its secular equivalent, the political festival and, secondly, to an unplanned gesture of rebellion, the food riot.

The National Guard

The concept of 'the Breton people' is a difficult one. The previous chapter, and the material to be presented here, give some reasons for this: as a result of the Bretons' distance from the dominant cultural forms of the nineteenth century, it was difficult to assess, to study and even sometimes simply to *see* this people. The July Monarchy devised a distinctive solution for this problem: it used the National Guard as a symbol to disguise the real absence of the mass of the population from political processes.

The National Guard was created in 1789 as a volunteer urban militia. The guard had a proud legacy of liberal opposition to the Bourbon regime (it was actually banned from 1827 to 1830), but guardsmen also played a conservative role in policing and sometimes repressing popular protests: they put down grain riots, rebellions and disorder. They played a vital role in the re-creation of French revolutionary political culture by the July Monarchy (1830–48), for they symbolized a patriotism which was both orderly and active, and their quick public acceptance of the regime in July 1830 functioned as a substitute for a referendum or any other more formal consultation with the population.[1] Whilst they were constantly referred to by the Orleanist authorities as 'the citizens in arms', covert devices such as the cost of uniforms and hours of service worked to ensure that, in practice, this was a middle-class militia. A. Besnier has perceptively studied the guard's minute social base in the Côtes-du-Nord: in the 1840s, only rich town-dwellers were voters. They in turn formed the backbone of the National Guard, and they then stood for election as municipal, arrondissement or departmental councillors. From this small group of elected officials, the regime then chose its mayors.[2] By the 1840s the National Guard often featured as an easy target for anti-Orleanist satire. Daumier, the greatest of French nineteenth-century cartoonists, produced a striking series of images mocking the pseudo-militaristic patriotism of these pot-bellied Napoleons, admiring their blue uniforms before the mirror.[3]

In Brittany, however, things were different. For a moment, in 1832 and 1833, service in the National Guard meant the real possibility of service under fire. Guard units were ordered to work with the police in sweeping through forests, patrolling villages and escorting prisoners. Membership of the guard usually meant a real, personal allegiance to Blue political culture (although there were always fears of subversion of the National Guard by legitimists). The importance of these small groups of Blue patriots was widely recognized. In Vitré (Ille-et-Vilaine) these 'patriots' were 'one against ten':[4] a tiny minority, faced with the constant, amorphous threat of Chouan violence which could be manifested through a pounding on the door at night, or merely evoked, anonymously, by a white flag flapping from a nearby tree. 'If the citizen militia falls, then all is lost' wrote one Sub-Prefect in 1832.[5] In the absence of any visible sign of popular support for the regime, the National Guard's presence at the regime's political festivals was vital.

The festivals of the July Monarchy

While political power was concentrated in Paris, its presence needed to be re-enacted in each locality, in order to create an effective national polity. Nineteenth-century regimes used public festivals to bring political power into the localities. We can define such events as: 'A ceremony or ritual, usually centred on the activities of local officials, which claims to represent the government regime (or the *spirit* of the government) in a specific locality, to the inhabitants of that locality.' It is important to stress the difference between the festival and the political meeting: the first claimed to be unitary, and to present citizens with a consensual image of the dominant political structures; the second was militant, challenging and potentially divisive.

Such events were not new: even the *ancien régime* monarchy had its calendar of public ceremonies and rituals.[6] The church also instituted a parallel religious calendar of events: thus René Cavaro de Kergorre led his flock at ten annual processions in Le Croisic in the decades before 1789.[7] The *ancien régime* festivals had instituted the political principles of its monarchy. They required the presence of the people as an audience, to witness an event. At times such principles could lead to some bizarre situations. This is dramatically illustrated by an unusual incident in December 1820. The Duchess of Berry, Louis XVIII's sister-in-law, unexpectedly gave birth while the official witnesses were absent. Showing remarkable presence of mind, she refused to allow her newly born son's umbilical cord to be cut until the birth was witnessed by six National Guardsmen.[8] This episode demonstrates the importance of the role of the people as witness to the ceremonies and rituals of monarchical festive culture. Such activities, however, do not suggest that this older culture encouraged any meaningful political initiative by popular audiences, let alone instituted popular sovereignty.

Ancien régime principles were radically challenged by the Revolution of 1789 and the regimes it inspired. Article 3 of the Constitution of 1791 noted that sovereignty was based in the nation: a term which became central to Republicanism, as Claude Nicolet observes.[9] This radical transformation of political doctrine demanded a corresponding shift in the nature of festivals. Mona Ozouf, in her ground-breaking study of Republican festivals after 1789, notes some distinctive features in the principles which Republicans set for their festivals:[10]

a. they should be spontaneous, unplanned events, distinct from the regimented ceremonies of the *ancien regime*;
b. they should unite a confident, peaceful, self-assured crowd, with no hint of the madness that sometimes erupted in the *ancien regime* celebrations;
c. festivals should implement or establish a type of federation across the whole of the national territory: the isolated commune should be integrated into the wider nation. During the *ancien regime*, festivals had, instead, often appeared to celebrate the individual distinctiveness of personalities, localities or institutions;

d. festivals should bridge social divisions: rich and poor, noble and commoner should participate equally. This was in sharp distinction to the *ancien regime* celebrations which were often intended to mark out and clarify a social hierarchy;
e. women and children should participate, for they too were part of the nation. This reflects the 'femininization' of political symbolism initiated by the Republicans: just as the masculine symbol of the king was replaced by the female Marianne, so women, often represented as mothers, were to participate in these politicized ceremonies.

Predictably, these demanding ideals were rarely met in practice. In Brittany, where the revolutionary process often revealed or provoked social divisions, Republican festivals were more likely to split communities than to create national or social harmony. However, as ideals, the list of points presented above is still significant in that it indicates a radically new approach to the representation of political power. The monarchs and princes of the restoration (1814–30), while certainly refusing these new Republican forms of festive culture, were reluctant to consider a realistic replacement. The revolutionary experience had left permanent scars on them: appealing to the people, even in the form of a happy, festive, conservative crowd, was a step too far for most members of the Restored royal family.[11]

The July Monarchy (1830–48) was more innovative, but – in the last analysis – it still failed to devise a successful approach to political festivals. Created by a popular revolution in July 1830, and originally sustained by a wave of references back to the revolutionary tradition initiated in 1789, the July Monarchy's governments then spent much time and effort denying this first source of legitimacy. In place of popular sovereignty, Guizot elaborated the tortuous argument of government by rationality: a difficult concept to place at the centre of a popular festival.[12] The July Monarchy's festivals lacked both the grandeur of those presented by the *ancien régime*, and the excitement of the revolutionary *fêtes*. As is now generally recognized, these Orleanist festivals demonstrate one of the most telling failures of the July Monarchy: its inability to devise a public face.[13]

The Orleanists' wretched pastiches and their farcical imitations of the great revolutionary festivals of the 1790s, assumed a profound political significance in Brittany. Initially the new regime sponsored three annual political festivals: a commemoration for the 504 victims who died in the three days of fighting in Paris in July 1830; the celebration of the king's birthday (and therefore of the new Orleanist dynasty) on 17 April; and the anniversary of the royal oath of 9 August 1830, which marked the constitutional beginning of the new regime. This third celebration was quickly dropped. As was the case with the flying of the tricolour (see chapter 4), the regime appealed to local mayors, who were ordered to organize local celebrations for these anniversaries.

Let us look at one of these Orleanist festivals in more detail. We will take as our model the commemoration of the July revolution organized at Sarzeau (Morbihan) on 27, 28 and 29 July 1835.[14] There was a church service on 27 July, to which the commune's 'civil and military authorities' paraded. The church bells were rung on the evening of 28 July to announce the next day's celebration, and rung again on the dawn of 29 July. Houses flew the tricolour, and at 5 p.m. the 'civil and military authorities' met for a 'patriotic banquet' at the town hall. They ate in a specially decorated room, with flowers and eighteen tricolour flags. At the end of the banquet they drank toasts to the king of the French (Louis-Philippe's official title) and to the Prefect. Afterwards there was a dance on the main square, and at 9 p.m. a bonfire and fireworks. 'The festival ended as the authorities wanted, with shouts of "long live Louis-Philippe!".'

As elsewhere in France, the National Guard acted as a substitute for the people: their presence marked the Orleanists' festivals as celebrations of a particular form of Blue culture. A ritual which was intended to integrate a locality's inhabitants was immediately perceived by many as one-sided, particularistic and divisive. One wonders what effect the Prefects' instructions had. Significantly, a report from Pénestin (Morbihan) in 1835 noted that this was the first time that the commemoration of the July revolution had been celebrated.[15] How many other mayors may have quietly decided to ignore Orleanist anniversaries? As one examines these events more closely, the true fragility of the Blue administration becomes clear. The question of popular participation in festivals was a permanent dilemma for their organizers. Significantly, very few official accounts contain any estimate of the numbers involved: partly because such statistics might have starkly revealed the more than marginal nature of the festival but, more importantly, because these festivals were rarely expected to rally entire populations. Instead, they functioned in a quite different manner.

One key feature of many Orleanist festivals was the march by a small group of officials in their localities. For example, in March 1835, in Saint-Servan (Ille-et-Vilaine) the 'civil authorities', naval officers, local officials and National Guard officers were joined by a hundred National Guardsmen.[16] Elsewhere army officers, customs officials, firemen or even schoolboys might march in these groupings. The mayor of Plounevez-Moëdec (Côtes-du-Nord) explained to the Prefect how he had chosen people for such a procession in 1834: he looked for those 'suitable to carry arms'.[17] Having met, usually early in the morning, the group would march 'in procession' from the *mairie* (the town hall) to, normally, the church, but sometimes the main square, for the formal ceremony. What was the purpose of this ritual? A comment from an infantry captain stationed at Pontivy (Morbihan) allows us to understand it more fully: 'I can assure you, my General, that we were in our finest uniforms, and I am sure that, although there were few of us, everyone could see that the 13th light infantry unit had not neglected anything.'[18] An article in a Nantes-based review made a similar point: this 'great national festival' was open to 'enlightened men' who knew not to abuse politics.[19] First, these marches clearly identified the leading representatives of the Blues in any particular locality. Secondly, they were a small example of group bonding and affirmation: to gather together for this event, and to march, often in uniform, in a compact group suggested a moral and even a political unity. But, thirdly, this ritual also had a quasi-military role. It warned the inhabitants of a locality who were the masters; it demonstrated who was armed, and who had access to military power; it presented the people with an image of political domination and direction.

If the people were not invited to join these processions, and were usually absent from the banquets that marked the end of the formal festival, then how might they participate in these events? One possibility was by responding to the official invitations to inhabitants to illuminate their houses in the evening – in other words, to place rows of candles on window ledges and other surfaces. Often this practice almost functioned like an opinion poll, allowing a zealous mayor to gauge the commune's sympathy or hostility for the regime. Occasionally the crowd might chant slogans: 'Long live the King of the French! Long live France! Long live the Nation!' festival participants shouted 'with an enthusiasm which is difficult to describe', according to the Saint-Servan mayor.[20] The Trébeurden (Côtes-du-Nord) mayor reported that 'we all shouted, with one voice, "Long live Louis-Philippe, the king of the French, long live his illustrious family, long live peace, unity and tranquillity"' – an unlikely slogan, which hardly seems to trip off the tongue.[21] Elsewhere the evening could end with dances, which proved to be one of the few elements of these festivals which were genuinely popular. As the Auray police chief wrote, 'many of the lower people attended' a free dance held at the end of the festival in May 1843, while in Plounevez-Moëdec (Côtes-du-Nord) 'joy and gaiety' continued into the evening in 1834.[22] Elsewhere races, shooting contests, fireworks and bonfires were arranged. The dilemma here, of course, was that such dances and celebrations often had little political content: was a good Orleanist official to value popularity more than principle?

Of course not. Instead of creating a new secular centre for the development of political symbolism the Orleanists, inevitably and perhaps unwillingly, were drawn back to the Church. These reports of Breton rituals remind us of the Church's domination of the political landscape. These festivals were often announced by the ringing of church bells the evening before. In their accounts, mayors, police officers and Sub-Prefects stress that the formal ceremony in the church, attended by a small group of officials and notables, was the festival's focal point. The singing in church of a *Te Deum* ('We praise thee'), to celebrate the creation of the July Monarchy, or the chanting of a *Domine Salvum* ('God save the king'), substituted for any more spontaneous or popular form of political expression.

This choice by the regime led to further problems. Priests were sometimes reluctant to participate in this Blue regime, or – more often – reluctant to participate wholeheartedly. It is significant that the most commonly discussed issues in official reports are quite minute details of church services, as officials concentrate their attention and their criticisms on this purely religious event. The Sub-Prefect of Saint-Malo (Ille-et-Vilaine) was disturbed to report in August 1835 that the priest had sung a *Te Deum*, but had *deliberately* omitted to chant the *Domine Salvum*.[23] The Saint-Servan priest made the same mistake that year, but his mayor was more charitable in his report, remarking that the priest has perhaps forgotten it.[24] The absence of this vital part of the ritual was significant: it could well imply that the priest in question did not consider that Louis-Philippe was the legitimate king of France. The Sub-Prefect of Ancenis (Loire-Inférieure) complained that while the religious ritual had been correctly observed, it had been performed by the youngest priest, and it had lacked dignity.[25] In Auray, the clergy had remained seated during the ceremony.[26] In Vitré arrondissement, the priests in the main town usually celebrated the ceremony properly, but it was often neglected in the surrounding rural communes.[27] There are even some indications of a growing disaffection toward the regime among the clergy. One priest in Pluméliau (Morbihan) refused to present a *Domine salvum* on the grounds that it 'disturbed people'.[28] In 1847 it was reported that seventeen of the fifty-one ceremonies conducted in the arrondissement of Pontivy (Morbihan) had omitted the *Domine Salvum*.[29]

This concentration on the religious ceremony therefore often irritated church officials without successfully winning any popular support for the

July Monarchy. Were there no other options available to the government? One possible substitute in garrison towns and naval ports was to make use of military resources to replace or reinforce the church bells. Barracks could be decorated and illuminated.³⁰ Cannon salvoes could be fired to announce the day of the ceremony, and to mark its end. Soldiers or marines could be used to swell the ranks of National Guardsmen and officials marching back and forth. Such expedients could make festivals more visible and audible to townspeople. But their use in ports and garrison towns shows us, once more, the July Monarchy's real weakness. This is neatly revealed in the comments by the Vannes mayor, justifying his decision to cut the cannon from the 1838 festival. 'The solemnity of a public festival lies more in the co operation and participation of the citizens than in artillery fire.'³¹ But which of the Orleanists' festivals won the citizens' 'co-operation and participation'? As we turn to examine some of the clearly less successful festivals, we can see how shallow the regime's presence was.

A police official in Ploërmel (Morbihan) was required to write a general report on festivals in the four neighbouring cantons in 1843.

> The festival of the King took place in all the cantons of my section in the most perfect calm. A mass was celebrated in the head-town of each canton: all the civil and military authorities were present. The ceremonies were restricted to that: in the evening only the civil servants' houses were illuminated.³²

Still more revealing is the 1845 report from the Nivillac (Morbihan) mayor. These few words constitute the whole of the document: 'We gave the poor fifteen francs from our budget, and we attended the religious ceremony.'³³ Such reports, from the 1840s, show how little the mass of the population were involved in these events: not necessarily through apathy or opposition, but simply because the festivals were arranged so as to exclude them. Among all reports relating to public festivals held in Brittany during the July Monarchy, it would be hard to find a single one which convincingly records any real popular enthusiasm for their political content.

The records suggest that these early nineteenth-century Blue festivals had little success in Brittany. They may have helped suggest some stronger sense of group identity among Blue officials – but, arguably, this task had already been achieved by the Chouan attacks in the early 1830s. They failed to replace the older monarchist and religious public rituals with a new language of political symbolism; they failed to communicate the regime's priorities and programmes to the popular classes; and they therefore failed to win any significant popular support for the regime.

The politics of bread

The Bourbons and the Orleanists were both, for different reasons, reluctant to appeal to the Breton population as a whole, and correspondingly neither regime won significant popular success. Chouannerie certainly mobilized a vocal minority, and probably terrified a broader majority among the Breton population, but this movement can hardly be described as 'representative'. There was, however, one protest movement which seemed able to unite the rural labourers and urban working class, and to win the sympathy of many notables and aristocrats. This was the cycle of protests, riots and near rebellions provoked by the price of bread and other essential food: an issue which acquired great importance during the early 1830s and late 1840s, particularly from 1845 to 1847. These developments are part of a Europe-wide evolution: across the continent, harvest failures, a particularly virulent potato disease and the resulting financial and commercial crises meant that most populations were faced with the threat of starvation, and that many protested.

This type of protest was part of an ancient, almost venerable, tradition in France, even in Europe.[34] Once again, the July Monarchy marked a sharp break with previous regimes with its distinctive approach to such protests: a change that became obvious as early as 1832. In the last days of January of that year, a crowd of about one hundred and fifty women and fifty men gathered on the dockside at Lannion (Côtes-du-Nord).[35] They intended to prevent a shipment of potatoes leaving, on the grounds that food was already too scarce and too expensive, and that if this shipment left, then it would be still harder for the poor to feed their families. The captain of the ship, either terrified at the sight of so many angry people, or – perhaps – feeling some genuine concern for their condition, stopped the loading, and sold the potatoes at a price below the current market rate. Following this incident, a minority of the crowd then gathered outside the house of Le Bail, whom they accused of being a hoarder. Some threw stones. They were easily dispersed by the municipal police.

Given the political context, the local authorities were terrified that this might be the start of some Chouan machination. The mayor attempted to reassure the Sub-Prefect. 'I do not think that politics had anything to do with this brief outbreak of disorder. It is unemployment, and the resulting poverty, which are the direct causes.'[36] Such incidents, while frightening, were not unexpected. Indeed, while reading reports concerning food riots, one often gets the impression that those involved were acting according to a mutually agreed script, and that rioters, food-dealers and police forces all knew how to play their part. This basic plot had been repeated thousands of times over the past centuries. The following response from the Ministry of the Interior, however, marked a dramatic innovation:

> Freedom of commerce was obstructed, and property rights violated: in a word, this was anarchy . . .
> The absence of means of repression may explain, up to a certain point, the concessions which the authorities judged necessary to preserve the peace. But these factors do not excuse [the concessions] . . . If there were not enough soldiers or policemen present, then the National Guard should have been called, even if it seemed possible that they might refuse this duty, or that they might join in the disorder, for sooner or later justice would have had effect.[37]

Such a dogmatic defence of commercial liberty was radically new: it indicated a head-on collision between the political culture of the July Monarchy and the traditional culture of the towns and villages. Fortunately, the economic crisis of the early 1830s was quickly over, but the stage was set for more serious clashes in the late 1840s. In this section we will draw together evidence from the cycles of protest that stretched from 1832 to 1847, beginning with some observations concerning the crisis of the late 1840s.

By 1845, the situation had grown so serious in parts of Brittany that local officials were required to write daily reports concerning the price of food – and, above all, grain – in their areas. From their reports we can gauge how prices soared. At Moncontour (Côtes-du-Nord), grain prices rose from 9.5 francs per hectolitre on 1 November 1845, to 12.5 francs on 21 November.[38] At the Saint-Brieuc market, wheat prices escalated from 30 francs per hectolitre on 26 December 1846 to 37 francs on 16 January 1847. Prices then fell to 27 francs by 17 February, but steadily rose in the following weeks, to 45 francs by 6 March 1847.[39] The Finistère Prefect attempted to estimate some average prices for his department in the years 1846–7. This steep rise in prices was the result of two linked catastrophes: the disease which wiped out the potato harvest in 1845, and the sudden and unexpected failure of sardine-fishing. Writing in 1905, Jean-Marie Déguignet could still recall the severity of conditions in that year.

> What a disaster! What dreadful famine the sudden death of the potato caused among the Irish and among us, the Bas-Bretons, who lived on potatoes and black bread. Oh! What stories, what tales, what legends were created by that black disease which, with one blow, wiped out a whole type of potato.[40]

Table 5.1 Average prices for grains in Finistère (in francs per hectolitre)[41]

	1846	1847
Wheat	19.98	26.80
Rye	14.47	20.50
Barley	12.32	16.94
Oats	7.79	9.09
Buckwheat	10.75	15.66

The Finistère Prefect warned the Minister of the Interior about the fate of the Douarnenez sardine-fishers: the collapse of their trade had meant that they were reduced to 'the most terrifying misery, with no means of existence, and in danger of dying from starvation'.[42] A police official noted the same desperate condition among sardine-fishers at Concarneau (Finistère). 'It is very difficult to estimate their misery ... they have such a sense of honour that they would prefer to shiver than to make known their unhappy condition.'[43]

Aside from attempts to gather statistical evidence of a crisis, officials had other means through which they registered the extent of poverty. One traditional method was simply to count the beggars and destitute. There were forty-seven people registered as destitute in Plozévet (Finistère) in 1846, and over five hundred by March 1847.[44] A Sub-Prefect reported five hundred beggars in Pont-Croix (Finistère) in November 1846.[45] Some officials remained cool enough in the face of this growing poverty to dabble in sociological speculations. Why was it, wondered the Morlaix (Finistère) Sub-Prefect, that the richest cantons always seemed to have the most beggars? He noted that many peasants could only provide for themselves during the good years, and were therefore thrown into vagabondage in crisis years. Furthermore, 'a rich and charitable clergy' almost encouraged such behaviour.[46] Characteristically, Déguignet reduced statistics to a more brutal truth. 'How were we to live? . . . Those looking for bread doubled,' he remembered, 'while the numbers of those who could give it had shrunk.'[47] The Morlaix Sub-Prefect also shows us that there was a more macabre way through which the administration learnt of crisis. In a later letter he noted the number of recent deaths in Plouzévédé: 'It cannot be said that they died of hunger,' he hurried to tell the Prefect: their deaths were due mainly to illness. But – in truth – the inhabitants of this commune had certainly grown weaker due to the long-term effects of the grain crisis. For months, many had survived on a diet of carrots, turnips and parsnips.[48]

Officials also noted the changing behaviour of people at markets. During periods of crisis, grain-dealers, termed *blatiers*, could swoop down on markets and buy up stock: at Moncontour (Côtes-du-Nord) in January 1839 they bought up almost the entire stock on grain in a single hour. 'How much do you want for your grain?' they would ask. On hearing the seller's response, they would respond: 'close your sack, that's sold'. Such practices threatened the town's workers with starvation.[49] In Gournin (Morbihan), the established market rules allowed strangers to buy grain after midday: two hours earlier than most of the surrounding markets. As the bell rang, 'a frenetic contest would begin, sacks would be taken away in seconds, and the bakers and inhabitants of Gournin found it very difficult to buy grain'.[50]

Alongside the simple, physical shortage of grain and the consequent rise in prices, crises were made worse by panic-buying by a nervous population.[51] Rumours were vitally important in creating local perceptions of the state of the market, and they also reveal how peasants and workers might attempt to calculate their prospects.[52] As E. P. Thompson noted, with reference to eighteenth-century England, the poor had their own sources of information: 'they often know the local facts better than the gentry'.[53] The Quimperlé Sub-Prefect (Finistère) made some precise distinctions. Following the export of grain to Britain, there was no famine, he argued, but there was some shortage, which was made worse by fear and exploited by disorder and greed.[54] In 1845, the inhabitants of the coastal plain in the north of the Côtes-du-Nord were anticipating a famine if the export of grain continued.[55] Rumours, however, also carried a more critical dimension. They suggested who was to blame: they named grain-hoarders and, ultimately, they questioned the legitimacy of a government which could not – or would not? – provide its population with enough food to survive.

The administration understood the current of political criticism provoked by grain crises in a quite different manner. Orleanist officials were always suspicious of local legitimists: during times of economic crisis, they suspected such notables of deliberately encouraging agitation and direct action. The Morlaix Sub-Prefect (Finistère) observed: 'almost all the local landowners are legitimists. They unceasingly criticize the traders, claiming that they are starving the land, and [they criticize] the government for not taking measures to prevent famine. Unfortunately, local officials often ally themselves to these gentlemen.'[56] In other words, as was the case with Chouannerie, grain crises were also an opportunity to battle for the hearts and minds of the Breton people: a battle for political hegemony. Once again, the Orleanists were not successful in this political contest. In a later letter concerning the effects of the grain crisis, the Morlaix Sub-Prefect remarked that 'at Saint-Pol, there is not a single man on who we can rely'.[57]

The Orleanist government's first response to a grain crisis was to demand that local officials defend the freedom of commerce. Such arguments failed to convince a frightened, sometimes starving, population, who reacted by demanding food at a fair price, and preparing to fight to get it. The beggars that officials saw on the roads could turn into robbers. With each crisis, there were new cases of these simple, desperate acts. Around Morlaix (Finistère), a band of seven or eight criminals terrorized isolated farmhouses in 1847.[58] In the commune of Baud (Morbihan), a rather more polite band approached an isolated hamlet. They demanded bread and promised to go away once they had been given a loaf. The farmer in question was willing to give them one of his two loaves, but he was too frightened to open his door while the seven strangers stood outside. They agreed to step ten metres away while he placed a loaf outside his door. 'God bless you!' they cried to him as they walked away with his bread.[59]

Frequently, local officials were blamed for the crises. 'Down with the mayor! Down with the police!' cried rioters at Dinan (Côtes-du-Nord) in November 1845. They besieged the mayor's house for three hours.[60] In Quimper the mayor received a threatening letter, telling him that he would be killed if he allowed grain exports to continue, and the Brest mayor was warned that if he did not act, rioters would tear his head from his body and parade it around the town.[61] Elsewhere, crowds mobilized to strike out at grain-dealers and hoarders. At Plancoët (Côtes-du-Nord), crowds threatened to kill grain transporters, and screamed insults at the stall-holders in the market.[62] At Saint-Jacut (Côtes-du-Nord), the fishwives learnt that wheat was being exported. They armed themselves with sticks and stopped the wagon, telling the driver that if they allowed this wheat to be exported, then the price would rise by half in six months, and they would be reduced to the most absolute misery.[63] At Callac (Finistère), urban customs posts were attacked.[64]

On occasion, hand-made posters proclaimed the protestors' aims:

People of Lamballe, fathers!
Do you have no blood in your veins? Because you have failed to support your fellow citizens, you are permitting food to be taken away from you and your children, without considering that if next year, the harvest fails, then where will you get food? Act together so that those who want your families to grow hungry will be crushed. Act without fear, with your fellow citizens. Show them true Breton courage, throw out these grain-hoarders, punish them for their deeds, buy grain instead of stealing it, and all will see that you are honest citizens.[65]

Let's go to these grain-dealers who take the bread from our children's hands. Every day we work and we die from starvation. Let's take, let's steal from their stores if the mayor doesn't help us. My hands are trembling and my children are dying.

As nobody gives us anything, let's kill, let's massacre, let's take as they've taken everything from us.[66]

Despite this incendiary rhetoric, most actions by 'rioters' were often surprisingly peaceful. For example, port-workers at Dinan (Finistère) stopped a cart which was taking grain to a ship. They unloaded it 'without violence, and showing a truly surprising respect for property'.[67] At Coray (Finistère) rioters stopped two wagons charged with grain, distributed the produce among themselves, and then paid the drivers what they considered to be the fair price.[68]

Crowd behaviour during these crises reveals some of the Bretons' economic attitudes. Market-places had rules and ethics, which were usually respected and enforced by local authorities before 1830, and to which many still deferred after 1830. A key regulation was the division of the market day: in the morning, only local people were allowed to buy. Then a bell would be rung, and outside dealers would enter. In normal times, such arrangements worked well enough, as stall-holders would usually be reluctant to wait the entire morning without selling. In crises, however, the stall-holders acted with greater confidence: secure in the knowledge that outside dealers would offer higher prices, they would simply refuse to sell during the morning.[69] In 1832, a woman selling grain at Uzel market (Côtes-du-Nord) spoke of raising her prices. The women shoppers were so furious that they turned on her: she ran out of the market-place and took refuge in a house. Eventually soldiers rescued her.[70] In times of crisis, local people also became suspicious of any strangers who appeared at markets, and were worried by any secrecy, or any whispered deals between sellers and *blatiers*.[71]

Occasionally these market ethics were projected onto a bigger scale, suggestive of patriotic feeling. Some argued that the reason why grain was being exported to Britain from the Breton ports was because the government wanted peace at any price with its northern neighbour.[72] There were also some isolated examples of other forms of xenophobia: French-speaking Bretons sometimes feared that their Breton-speaking cousins would take mass direct action in their markets.[73] Another example of this wider, semi-politicized, projection of market ethics can be seen in the frequent acts of charity for which Brittany became famous.[74] Agitation over grain prices could also stimulate greater sympathy and more active aid for conscription rebels.[75]

Such feelings of sympathy significantly often extended beyond the immediate circles of the poor and hungry up into the ranks of the well-to-do and the landowners.[76] In Tréguier (Côtes-du-Nord), the local notables organized a petition which was sent to the Ministry of Commerce, demanding that the authorities take action to provide affordable bread for the mass of the population.[77] The conservative and liberal press in Rennes condemned the decision by the city's bakers to end the tradition of a free distribution of bread at Christmas: this ritual had been a worthy moral example.[78] Following several days of riots in Dinan (Côtes-du-Nord) the mayor had to acknowledge that, in general, public opinion 'in all classes' was with the rioters and against the export of wheat.[79] The Finistère Prefect was amazed to realize that many wealthy landowners sympathized with the rioters.[80] (Obviously, in such cases, authorities could comfort themselves by blaming support for oppositional ideas on legitimist sympathies, but it seems unlikely that this provides the complete explanation for this significant divergence of opinion.) The evidence gained from these scattered sources is clear: peasants, workers, bourgeois and aristocrats were not convinced by the July Monarchy's economic liberalism. All groups in Breton society instead tended to remain loyal to older ideas of a moral economy and a fair price: arguments which seemed all the more convincing during a grain crisis.

During these crises, local authorities were in an extremely difficult position. Often, their isolation from local cultures became obvious. The Saint-Brandon (Côtes-du-Nord) mayor explained to the Prefect that it was difficult for mayors to act, as 'the peoples' tended to blame the mayors for the crisis.[81] Another recognition of political isolation came from the Dinan mayor (Côtes-du-Nord), who predicted that as the crisis worsened, rural mayors would refuse to act, and prosecutors would be overwhelmed. The mayors' duty was to 'die in their posts', he remarked gloomily.[82] In Quimperlé (Finistère), a handful of policemen faced an angry crowd who threw stones at a trader's house. As the evening grew darker, the crowd grew more angry. The mayor wondered whether he should call out the National Guard. 'One can only count on their officers', he noted despairingly: the ordinary, urban middle-class men, who formed the backbone of the Orleanist regime, were no longer reliable.[83]

More seriously for the government, it is also obvious that many mayors sympathized with the rioters.[84] In their letters to the Prefects, they frequently echo the rioters' demands to place immediate restrictions on the freedom to trade and to export grain and other foods. Anticipating a crisis, the Paimpol (Côtes-du-Nord) mayor wrote to the Prefect to demand 'prevention or repression', and voiced his frustration that it was still legal to export potatoes during a time of famine.[85] The Gournin mayor (Morbihan) noted that while grain exportation continued, prices would continue to rise.[86] A baker told this mayor not to interfere in matters which did not concern him. 'I replied to him', recorded the mayor, 'that it was my duty to listen to complaints from the unfortunate who were literally dying of hunger, and to respond to their fair demands. [I told him] that we did not want to be the victims of his poor organization.'[87] A later letter from the same mayor was addressed to the Prefect. 'Act so that the government's paternal intentions are enforced', he begged. 'May the workers live from their work, and [may they not be] at the mercy of dealers, proud, heartless men, who speculate on the hunger of the poor.'[88] In Brest, the Sub-Prefect complained, the bakers sold bread as they wanted, motivated by their greed.[89] The Morlaix Sub-Prefect (Finistère) explained that the recent rise of prices was mainly due to the greed of farmers, who could not be persuaded to sell their produce.[90] Even municipal councillors and landowners were in favour of distribution of grain at a fixed price: a policy which was implemented in some communes.[91] In Landerneau (Finistère), bakers ignored an agreement with the mayor to stick to an agreed price for their bread: this resulted in 'some agitation' among the workers.[92] In Quimperlé (Finistère), the Sub-Prefect attempted to encourage municipal charity in his arrondissement.[93] But the Prefects and the government consistently refused to act on such observations and suggestions.

Even when mayors made practical points about the difficulties in enforcing government policy, they were still ignored. For example, as the security forces were clearly overstretched at moments of crisis, some mayors proposed that the smaller ports should simply be closed, and that grain and food exports should only continue from the bigger, better-policed resorts. The Minister of the Interior bluntly refused this suggestion.[94] However, in many localities, it was clear that the demands of the crowd were stronger than the government's regulations. Grain-dealers took to driving their carts at night in order to avoid angry crowds.[95] Even when troops and mounted policemen were posted in Paimpol (Côtes-du-Nord), farmers still felt too scared to approach the town to load their supplies onto a ship bound for Britain. The mayor commented that 'this loading must take place, to prove to this misled mass that they have neither the right nor the power to prevent what the law allows'.[96]

The Orleanist regime was inflexible. Even at the worst moments of the 1847 crisis, the government stuck to its implacable defence of the liberty of commerce. While an *ancien régime* monarch would have accepted the role of 'father-to-his-people', and with this the responsibility to see that his people were fed, the July Monarchy preferred to defend the rights of the dealer and the hoarder.[97] This point was revealed clearly in a circular from the Interior Ministry.

> In many areas of the west and the centre, grain circulation has been violently obstructed. We have seen wilful crowds seize the grain taken to markets and sell it according to the rioters' demands. Citizens' homes have been violated, some houses have been ransacked: murder has followed theft. These criminal acts will be vigorously repressed . . .
> There cannot be commerce without security: sedition will bring about the disappearance of [commercial] confidence . . . It is therefore an absolute duty to protect the safety of the roads and the freedom of trade. No concession will be tolerated. Enlighten the people about their real interests: make them understand that disorder will immediately and necessarily cause a rise in prices . . . [Authorities must be] firm and unwavering.[98]

Curiously enough, one bold mayor attempted to follow the Minister's instruction to the letter. The Quimperlé mayor drafted a poster for the local people.

> Who in the world could stop a rise in prices after the shortage of grain last year?
> These disorders, which trouble us deeply, are quite contrary to your honest and peaceful customs. They must be the work of young men, who had been misled by some anarchic trouble-makers, who oppose our institutions and our town's commercial prosperity.[99]

The Finistère Prefect's report for 1847 echoed such inflexible thoughts: begging was mainly the result of laziness; he criticized the willingness of the wealthy to give to those in need, but he hoped that the poor would recognize their effort and feel gratitude.[100]
On 24 January 1847 even the Côtes-du-Nord Prefect finally instituted a partial ban on food exports: no further exportation of potatoes or dried beans was to be allowed.[101] The standard official response, however, was to understand the crises purely in police and security terms. Sub-Prefects and mayors watched markets carefully.[102] After the arrival of troops at Dinan (Côtes-du-Nord), 'even the most turbulent of the protestors do not dare move'.[103] The presence of troops at Landerneau market (Finistère) kept 'the agitators in fear'.[104] If troops were withdrawn, considered the Finistère Prefect, then there

would be renewed disorder.[105] Thirty-nine were arrested for offences connected with the grain crisis in the Côtes-du-Nord in January 1847.[106]

Food was an issue of vital importance to this impoverished population, yet the Orleanist government remained deaf to their fears and concerns. Whether offering local people the chance to participate in a new political culture, or attempting to impose the hegemony of a ferociously strict market discipline, the July Monarchy did not seek the cooperation of the mass of the population. Instead, it understood Brittany as a region to be conquered or tamed through administrative action.[107]

Celebrating the Second Republic (1848–52)

The Second Republic came as a surprise to Brittany: 'it burst out, suddenly, without any of us hearing a word about it before' wrote Déguignet, our peasant autobiographer.[108] By the late 1840s the July Monarchy was losing whatever support it had once commanded in Brittany. Peasants and workers were infuriated by its dogmatic defence of commercial freedom during a protracted and severe grain crisis. Legitimists, and even some Republicans, had begun to voice criticisms of its political principles. But such disparate oppositions failed to affect the region's tiny electorate. The last elections of the July Monarchy took place in August 1846. The region's thirty-two deputies were evenly split between the centre-right and centre-left.[109] Their obvious failure to represent the protests and opposition that circulated in the region is a sure indication of the dislocation of the established political process from the region's actual political experience. Brittany was also absent from the protest campaigns which marked the last years of the July Monarchy. The reform banquet campaign of the late 1840s, which could be seen as the precursor of the revolution of February 1848, barely touched the region: a police list of forty-seven prominent banquets only lists two banquets in Brittany – one in the Ille-et-Vilaine, one in the Loire-Inférieure.[110]

After an initial shock caused by the revolution, there was a widespread, significant and largely spontaneous drive to 'rally' to the regime.[111] In places, this may have been assisted by a Legitimist desire to see the definitive end to the Orleanist July Monarchy, but elsewhere it represented something more substantial. The swiftly appointed Republican 'Commissaires' (who briefly replaced prefects in March and April 1848) worked hard to stress the

Republic's *moral* force in order to attract as much broadly-based support as possible.¹¹²

The first article of the Republican constitution, which was finally promulgated in November 1848, stated that 'sovereignty resides in the French people'.¹¹³ After the monarch-centred political culture of the *ancien régime*, and the July Monarchy's compromise ideology of rationalism and free trade, this declaration amounted to a genuinely revolutionary transformation of political principles. What effect did this shift have in Brittany?

We will discuss this question by, once more, examining the public face which the regime presented through its festivals. The collection of documents describing Republican festivals in Brittany is certainly irregular: patchy in its representation of the five departments, and with more than two-thirds of the accounts concentrated on the revolutionary year of 1848, in particular on the 'promulgation of the constitution' in November 1848. In most cases, festivals were quite carefully planned, nationally coordinated events. However, occasionally, one finds specific, one-off celebrations. For example, a festival welcomed De Saint-Georges's return to his home commune of Pluvignier (Côtes-du-Nord) in October 1848. He had been wounded while participating in the repression of the workers' revolt in Paris in June 1848, and was celebrated as a hero by his compatriots.¹¹⁴ There were also some genuinely spontaneous celebrations to greet the declaration of the Republic in the last days of February 1848 and the first days of March. In Le Faouët (Morbihan) the mayor reported that 'all the inhabitants have spontaneously illuminated their houses' on 29 February.¹¹⁵

Let us consider one ceremony in more detail. This report was written by Soret, a delegate from the Paris-based 'Club de Clubs' which tried desperately – and unsuccessfully – to coordinate Republican electoral lists for the election of April 1848. He watched the ceremony of the planting of a Liberty Tree at Guérande (Loire-Inférieure) early in April 1848. Soret's account begins with a familiar list: prominent at the festival were unarmed National Guards and the local authorities, led by the clergy.

> The tree was carried by twelve young girls, dressed in white, with scarves in the national colours around their waists. They made a magnificent sight. All the nobles were in the National Guard, and all wore tricolour cocades. The Commissaire [of the Republic] gave a perfect speech. The priest responded less warmly, but in a manner which was compatible with the solemnity of the occasion. The religious ceremony ended with a *Te Deum*, led by the priest. In the evening, the town was lit up, and there were some patriotic banquets: few in number, it is true, but still cordial and fraternal. Poems and speeches were read.¹¹⁶

Guérande is a small town near the salt marshes of the Loire-Inférieure. It was the setting for Balzac's novel *Béatrix* (1839–44), in which it functions as a symbol of a patriarchal, medieval, unchanging Brittany, resisting the innovations of the nineteenth century. It seems no coincidence that Soret's account echoes some of these conservative themes, through his references to the nobles and the church.

We can draw a number of points from his account. First, as was the case with the previous Orleanist accounts, Soret is more than vague about the numbers attending. Very few accounts from the Second Republic provide more detailed information on this point. As in the case of the older Orleanist festivals, the National Guard still plays a central role. While Soret notes the relatively prominent presence of women at the Guérande festival, this was actually rather unusual in 1848. Most Republican festivals were clearly centred on important men; it seems probable that, in many cases, the audience was only composed of men.

So far, we have noted the continuity of practices from the July Monarchy to the Second Republic. There were, however, some important differences. An innovation from the earlier Orleanist festivals is the variety of social groups represented: the festival is a meeting of civil and religious authorities, and of old and new elites. The Liberty Tree creates a new space for their interaction. Significantly, Soret suggests some rivalry between the participants: an observation which reminds us of the relationship between priests and mayors during the July Monarchy. Looking at his remarks concerning the presence of the nobility, it could be inferred that Soret is noting the threat that they represent to the Republic. However, a second interpretation is also possible: Soret is more probably proposing that the Republic is a space in which secular, progressive elites and the established clerical and aristocratic elites can meet, peacefully. In other words, he considers that the Second Republic has the power to transcend the conflicts and arguments of previous regimes. George Sand, the celebrated proto-feminist novelist, was briefly employed by the Provisional Government as a Republican propagandist. She wrote an ecstatic, utopian description of a Republican ceremony in Paris at almost the same time that Soret was considering the festival in Guérande. Significantly, she too noted the presence of priests, who carried 'crucifixes that float over the heads of the crowd, next to the flag of the Republic: a natural and perfectly logical alliance'.[117] Soret is less affirmative than Sand, but his observations suggest similar forms of thinking: for example, the presence of the twelve young girls with their sashes is reminiscent of older Catholic ceremonies, and the ceremony as a whole suggests a synthesis of Catholic and Republican practices.

Soret's notes, however, leave one question hanging: what of 'the people'? If the Republic is a regime based on *popular* sovereignty, then how should this political value be represented in local ceremonies and rituals? The Second Republic's failure to provide a coherent response to this issue demonstrates its central political failure. As George Fasel identified over thirty years ago, the Republicans were fighting 'the wrong revolution'. Their debates and proposals concentrated on the relief of urban poverty; they ignored the plight of the rural poor, tending to confuse all rural labourers and peasants with landowners. Above all, 'they tended to regard *le peuple* as "a great child", too readily tempted by socialist demagogues and their easy utopias'.[118]

Instead, the key value stressed by these early, enthusiastic observers of Republican festivals is unity: unity of civil and religious authorities, military and civilian forces, of people and regime, perhaps also of men and women, and of region and nation. Their assumption is that a regime which implemented such political, social and even spiritual unity has by this gesture alone abolished the barriers which divided French society, and therefore established popular sovereignty. Sous-Commissaire Herman spoke of the joy he witnessed in Morlaix on 30 April 1848 as an immense crowd gathered round a Liberty Tree to shout 'long live the Republic!'. They included regular soldiers, National Guardsmen and ordinary citizens, all mixed 'fraternally': many people could not believe their eyes.[119]

Curiously, the role of 'the people' in these new Republic festivals resembles their function as witnesses in the *ancien régime* ceremonies. This can be seen most clearly when we consider the importance of speeches. In this still semi-literate society, speeches were a vital part of Republican political culture: a point which made Republican festivals significantly different from the more visual ceremonies of the *ancien régime*. However, a speech's success was judged by the warmth, the *hwyl* as is said in Welsh, it roused in the audience, not by any more sophisticated ideological or rationalist criteria.[120] 'The people', or the audience, were not passive at this point, but neither were they active. The ideal ceremony was always described as 'calm', even 'orderly'. 'Not for one second was the most perfect order interrupted' the police-lieutenant of Locminé proudly reported to the Morbihan Prefect in September 1848.[121] However, this crowd was still supposed to demonstrate enthusiasm. 'There was no pleasure [réjouissance]' noted the same police official, more sadly, two years later.[122] The audience played the role of a sounding-board for the speaker's presentation, to amplify and to register the sentiment of the speech. Indeed, it could be argued that this communion of speaker and audience, nation and people, was the Republicans' equivalent to the *Te Deum* and *Domine Salvum* of the Orleanists' ceremonies.

What other activities were undertaken by the audience in these Republican festivals? They might shout slogans: 'Vive La République! Vive la Nation! Vive la Liberté!' even, occasionally, 'Vivent les ouvriers!' They could sing songs: an activity which normally took place after the formal ceremony. Predictably, the most common song was the *Marseillaise*, but early in 1848 audiences also sung the fiery Republican anthem the *Chant du Départ*, and the less well-known *Girondins*. In the more formally organized ceremonies of late 1848, 'citizens' were also invited to 'illuminate' their houses, or to decorate them with flags and ribbons. As had been the case in the July Monarchy, such activities were monitored by officials and used as a rough-and-ready check on the degree to which the festival's message had been accepted by audiences. Elsewhere audiences might watch fireworks or bonfires.

In some festivals in early 1848 audiences might arrive in groups formed by workers' corporations or political clubs. Following the repressive legislation of the summer of 1848, it became impossible for clubs to operate so openly, and – whether legal or not – workers' corporations no longer played an active public role: although there were still some in Brittany who attempted to publicize the ideas of a social Republic to the peasants.[123] These changes meant that the identity of 'the audience' was increasingly dictated by the festival organizers. An important change was introduced in November 1848, when it became increasingly common to include distributions of charity to the poor as part of a festival. In November 1848, even the smallest commune was given 9 francs for this purpose. While this sum may have aided the poor, it cannot be seen as empowering them. Sometimes Republican ceremonies might dissolve into village *fêtes*, as inventive mayors include shooting contests and races as part of the festivities, and dances continue into the evening.

These reports outline a Breton political geography. They mention *mairies*, Sub-Prefectures, and squares; they also often evoke that new symbol of political power, the Liberty Tree. But, without doubt, the centre of symbolic power at local level remained the Church. The first Republican festivals of 1848 were usually based on the working assumption of a cooperation between the Republic and the Church: Sand's utopian rhetoric about the crucifix and tricolour captures an important aspect of these first ambitious weeks of the Republic. In Brittany, this point was of vital importance. F. Guérin, commissaire in the Morbihan, reminded the clergy that in 1789, the deputies of the first estate had joined those of the third estate. 'Liberty needs religion, and religion needs liberty', he argued.[124] Significantly, there was some basis for this appeal to the region's religious culture. The Finistère bishop even produced instructions on how to bless a Liberty Tree and, as was seen in the report from Guérande, many priests did perform this task. The bishop's blessing ended:

> Bless this tree ... May Christian liberty and the legal equality of citizens grow and flourish in its protective shadow, may charity and fraternity reign! May it be a living reminder of that tree on which your son shed his blood to win liberty and fraternity for us, and to give each of us the right to eternal happiness.[125]

The Revolution of 1848 revealed pockets of 'Blue Catholicism' around – for example – Châteaubriant (Loire-Inférieure) and in the Trégor-Cornouaille area along the border of the departments of Finistère and Côtes-du-Nord.[126] Significantly, in December 1848, the Breton departments of Morbihan and Finistère registered two of the highest, Republican, pro-Cavaignac votes in France.[127] Michel Lagrée's meticulous work on the Vannes diocese stresses that these priests' sympathy for Cavaignac's candidature was, in part, a sincere expression of their commitment to a Republican form of government.[128] In contrast, the relatively high votes for Louis-Napoleon in the other three departments can probably be explained as a consequence of legitimist patronage or direction.[129]

One small detail in these reports on Republican festivals demonstrates this important shift in perception by local administrations of the Church. During the July Monarchy, festival reports almost consistently made use of the set phrase 'civil and military authorities' when describing the presence of local authorities. In 1848, almost overnight, this phrase is replaced by the term 'civil and religious authorities'. One could even say that there was a demand for this type of cooperation. Significantly, the critical report written by the Republican militant, Charles Elgasse, concerning the festival for the planting of a Liberty Tree at Brest in April 1848, complained that only one *curé* was present.[130]

However, this utopian spirit of cross-cultural cooperation was not to last. The preparations for the parliamentary elections of April 1848 revived the old political and religious networks. Almost despite their best instincts, Blues and Whites found themselves once again on opposing sides. This certainly posed difficulties for both clans. While there were loose networks of friends, clients, patrons and notables among legitimist, Catholic and Orleanist circles, none of these groups were really prepared for the shock of shifting from a situation where less than 0.5 per cent of the population were enfranchised to the new challenge of male democracy. The Blues probably faced a harder struggle: in most areas there was no Republican organization. During the period of Provisional Government (March–April 1848), Commissaires like Guépin or Hamon were reluctant to purge municipal, arrondissement and departmental administrations of known monarchists for the simple reason that there were no trustworthy Republicans to replace them. Guépin appears to have dismissed nobody from the local administrations in Morbihan, while Hamon dismissed 25 of the Ille-et-Vilaine's 346 mayors.[131] Elsewhere in France, some primary and secondary school teachers responded to these Commissaires' appeals for assistance in preparing for the elections: in Brittany, they ignored such requests.[132]

The reports from Parisian club delegates like Soret consistently voice deep despair about the lack of preparation, the naivety, opportunism and sheer amateurishness of local Breton Republican initiatives. In most cases, however, the solutions proposed by these radical club delegates would merely have exacerbated the Republicans' isolation. Their fervent anticlericalism and immediate suspicions of all forms of compromise were clearly unsuited to the Breton terrain.

The lack of formal party structures and the tendency for many conservative candidates to describe themselves as Republicans make it difficult to calculate the results of the April 1848 elections. Pascal suggests that somewhat fewer than thirty of the seventy Breton deputies were genuinely Republicans, and somewhat more than forty were right-wing and probably monarchist in their outlook.[133] The Côtes-du-Nord was the only department to return a Republican majority: elsewhere, conservative deputies clearly outnumbered Republicans.

After these elections, the spirit of utopian unity which had animated the first Republican initiatives faded away. Officials' reports analysing the failure of the Republican vote stressed the role of the clergy: they prevented Republican propaganda and organization from reaching the rural people, they prepared villagers to vote for monarchist candidates, some even abused their sermons to deliver political messages, they distributed completed ballot forms to voters, and – finally – they marched their parishioners to the ballot box in well-policed ranks.[134] A familiar story, which is no doubt to some extent true. One must, however, question how much it was propagated in order to explain away the evident failure of the Republicans to reach the people.

This widening political polarization between Blues and Whites was worsened by the shock of the June 1848 revolt by the Parisian working class. Fears of a return to the terror gripped the region's notables. Travellers, strangers and tramps became objects of suspicion;[135] even travelling singers became suspect in this flood of hostility towards the outside world. In the Ille-et-Vilaine they were insulted as 'Jews, Parisians, Chouans and thieves':

a telling summary of the fears felt by rural people in this period.¹³⁶ Following the vigorous repression of the workers' revolt, directed by General Cavaignac, conservative notables might then rally to the Republic. However, this move to 'rally' to the Republic was quite different from the utopian cross-cultural cooperation evoked by Sand and Soret. These notables wanted a tough, authoritarian regime, with no respect for popular sovereignty: a Republic without Republicanism.

The growing alienation between the Church and the regime was expressed at local level through tensions concerning the Republic's festivals. Firstly, there were a number of petty, genuinely localized conflicts about the boundaries of power: could a priest be required to participate in a festival? Was the church the correct place for the reading of the Constitution? By 1850, however, there is clearer evidence of a real political disengagement. Yet, paradoxically, it was at this moment that the conservative Republican authorities began to recentre their ceremonies ever-more firmly on the church. By the time of the third anniversary of the February Revolution in 1851, the Morbihan Prefect could instruct the department's mayors that 'the commemorative ceremony will, as in previous years, only be composed of a memorial service followed by a *Te Deum*.'¹³⁷

A telling illustration of the regime's increasing reliance on the Church can be seen in the ceremony to commemorate the second anniversary of the establishment of the Republic in May 1850 at Muzillac (Morbihan). National Guard officers, police and the mayor met at the church, expecting to hear a *Te Deum*. Instead, they were kept waiting for thirty minutes. Then, finally, the *Te Deum* was sung quietly in a side-chapel. The National Guard officers considered that they had been 'robbed'. According to the police report, the priest's actions were discussed by the whole town: even Legitimists thought that he had gone too far. But most significant of all was the mayor's reaction: the shock of this slight to his authority made him feel so ill that he immediately went to bed!¹³⁸

Looking at the ceremonies held in Brittany after the spring of 1848, it is clear that they did not meaningfully represent popular sovereignty. Instead, as was the case during the July Monarchy, their main function was to attempt to group together elites, drawing in the 'authorities, officials, clergy, the entire National Guard, and a lot of the people', as one mayor wrote.¹³⁹ Given these conservative political imperatives, it is not surprising that many Republican festivals seemed to exclude all popular presence. This was clearly illustrated in the ceremonies to celebrate the drafting of the Constitution, in November

1848, which seem to have been expressly designed to repress all popular enthusiasm and joy. Mayors were instructed to read out the 116 articles of the Constitution to their fellow citizens. Did anyone seriously imagine that this would be met by spontaneous joy? Moreover, this programme was doubly problematic in Brittany, where the first language of approximately half the inhabitants was Breton. Significantly, two reports do refer to translation problems, as local officials desperately attempted to convert the abstract language of the Constitution into peasant Breton. One wonders what happened elsewhere: did other officials mechanically recite the Constitution in French to their Breton-speaking listeners? One could certainly sympathize with the telling reaction by Moustoir-ac mayor (Morbihan) to these instructions. He refused to obey the instructions to read out the Constitution, on the grounds that 'it wasn't worth the effort, that it was too long to read out and, anyway, he was sick.'[140]

Particularly after 1850, festivals were increasingly strictly policed, with a clear stress on the rigorous surveillance of popular participation, and a censorious sensitivity to the implications of the smallest gestures and symbols.[141] Often it appears that the political field open to the conservative Republic was shrinking: while not able to exploit the older symbolism of monarchy and the Church, administrators were equally hostile to the possible radical implications of the newer Republican imagery. One illustration of this comes from Ploërmel in 1850, on the second anniversary of the February revolution. The Sub-Prefect reported that, as in previous years, young people had walked about the town after the festival proper, singing the *Marseillaise*. This was tolerated. In 1850, however, they were accompanied by a drummer: this innovation was promptly stopped by the police.[142] In Châteaubriant (Loire-Inférieure), the Sub-Prefect was concerned by the activities of what appears to be a group of radical, even proto-socialist, workers during the ceremony for the second anniversary of the election of the Constitutional Assembly. They constructed some kind of structure to place on top of the Liberty Tree, which was illustrated by designs representing the 14 July 1789, the 25 February 1848 and universal suffrage. For all the suspicion which the Sub-Prefect felt concerning this dissident group, there was nothing to which he could object in this design. However, commenting on their use of a tricolour colour scheme, the Sub-Prefect noted 'these are fine and noble colours, as long as they are not permitted to become provocative colours.'[143]

The logical consequence of such cautious, conservative thinking was to produce the effective abolition of any meaningful Republican ceremony, whether popular or not. The Morbihan Prefect's report on the ceremonies of May 1851 in his department was eloquent. 'No cry was shouted, no hostile demonstration was started. Every measure was taken to repress promptly and decisively all attempts at disorder.'[144] Rather than mobilizing people, festivals increasingly aimed to stop all attempts at political expression. The administration could insist that flags were flown and – above all – that cannons were fired: 101 cannon rounds were heard at Brest in November 1848 to celebrate the promulgation of the Constitution.[145] When one puts together the stress on cannons, on National Guards and on military units, and considers the memories of Chouannerie in Brittany, then it becomes clear that these festivals were far from opportunities for popular expression.

Conclusion

One obvious point to draw from this chapter is the relative unimportance of the Celticist discourse to power politics in mid-nineteenth-century Brittany. Those with power, and those who organized to oppose them, whether food rioters or clerics, were not interested in Villemarqué's speculations about Breton folk culture.

Instead, the evidence surveyed here demonstrates the failure of Blue political culture and the Republican regime to develop a language of populism in Brittany. Both the Orleanists and the Republicans of 1848 were small minorities in the region. Two possibilities were available to these administrations: first to develop an accommodation with the Catholic Church (one Republican commissaire even proposed increasing priests' pay), and therefore to appeal directly to the Catholic masses. Secondly, the Republicans could have worked with the embryonic working-class groupings, and offered a practical programme of social reform, as the left-wing Démoc-Socs were later to do elsewhere in France. Neither governments nor local Breton administrations during the Second Republic followed either the policy of Catholic or radical populism. Hence their festivals resounded to the booming of the cannon, rather than the mass singing of the *Marseillaise*.

Liberty Trees were planted across Brittany early in 1848. This symbol, with its ability to bring together crucifix, tricolour and workers' corporation, is an indication of, firstly, another potential relationship between the region and the Republic but also – more importantly – another political identity for Brittany. The apparently fixed divisions of Whites and Blues could have been overcome. This lesson was ignored by later generations of Parisian governments.

6

The Politics of the State (2)
The Management of Democracy, 1852–1940

When did France become a democracy? The first occasion when all men were, in principle, given the vote was in September 1792, as the newly declared Republic rushed to demonstrate its popularity through a consultation with the people. Immediate circumstances stopped any meaningful implementation of democratic principles: fear of war in the east of France, shock at the sudden creation of the Republic, incomprehension about the meaning of the vote, and a growing sense of horror inspired by political violence were sufficient to persuade many citizens to stay away from the polls. Probably less than 15 per cent of the adult male population participated.[1] Aside from these immediate problems, there were also significant limitations to the Jacobins' understanding of 'democracy'. Concern about the ability of bosses, masters and landowners to manipulate, respectively, their workers, servants and tenants, meant that the Jacobins considered that all 'dependants' should be excluded from the consultation: only 'independent' men would be allowed to vote. (Given the political confusion of autumn 1792, it is hard to know how strictly this ruling was enforced.) Similar thinking also persuaded these early Republicans to exclude women from the political process: girls were seen as represented by their fathers, wives by their husbands.

There are some deeper qualifications to be made concerning this first male-democratic experiment. The Jacobins' concept of democracy was inspired by Rousseau's idea of the 'General Will'. This held that if petty, self-seeking considerations could be removed from political processes, voting and other forms of popular expression would reveal a unified consensus, a single voice of the nation and people. Mass consultations with the electorate were not supposed to demonstrate a plurality of opinions: on the contrary, their purpose was to unite the nation politically. Such ideas still influenced Republican circles in 1848: arguably they remained important into the early twentieth century.[2] One consequence of this Rousseau-ian legacy was the extremely slow development of organized political parties in France. The first modern French party was the Radical Party, created in 1901.[3]

'When did France become a democracy?' is therefore a complex question. One could cite September 1792 as a first limited experiment in democracy. The principle of manhood suffrage was established in February 1848, then implemented in the April 1848 elections, and has never been denied by any of the succeeding regimes. But if one considers that an open, fair recognition of different political opinions is a key component of any democratic system, then the first decades of the twentieth century might appear as a more accurate date for the real birth of French democracy. Lastly, the principle of female suffrage was not recognized until 1944, and women first participated in elections in 1945.

A more substantial consideration concerns the *quality* of French democracy. Anthony Arblaster suggests the following, tentative, characterization of democracy: 'the idea of popular power, of a situation in which power, and perhaps authority too, rests with the people'.[4] Has this ever been the case in France? The material to be considered in this chapter suggests a quite different impression of 'democratic' political processes. Instead of a system which empowers a people, the consultations of the Second Empire (1852–70) and the Third Republic (1870–1940) seem to be exercises in which governmental elites attempt to teach, to guide and – occasionally – to intimidate a population. Brittany provides a unique vantage point from which to see these features of French political culture.

Elections and politics, 1850–1940

An electoral stereotype of Breton politics developed during the second half of the nineteenth century: a political equivalent to the idea of the 'backward west' discussed in chapters 4 and 5. Breton votes during the Second Republic (1848–52) were unremarkable. The region returned conservative candidates: some more Catholic than monarchist, some willing to accept a form of Republican rule, but all united in their fear and rejection of a 'red' Republic. However, the Presidential elections of December 1848 suggested a more distinctive Breton political profile.

The first two candidates' scores demonstrate Brittany's distinctive voting patterns: while across France, three out of four voters chose Louis-Napoleon, in Brittany, only two out of four made the same choice. And while only one in five French voters chose Cavaignac, in Brittany more than two in five chose him. We discussed some reasons for this disparity in the last chapter;

Table 6.1 Voting in the presidential elections of December 1848 in France and Brittany[5]

Candidate	Votes in France (%)	Votes in Brittany (%)
Louis-Napoleon Bonaparte	74.2	53.4
General Cavaignac	19.4	43.06
Ledru-Rollin	4.9	2.09
Raspail	0.49	0.02
Lamartine	0.24	0.16

it is probably explained by the clergy's influence, although it is still hotly debated whether these priests were motivated by anti-Republicanism or conservative Republicanism.

Louis-Napoleon was elected President in December 1848. The coup d'état in December 1851 established a long-term base for his power; he then became the permanent President of the Second Empire in December 1852. On 20 and 21 December 1851, a referendum was held to approve his coup: across France, over three-quarters of voters accepted his actions. In Brittany, majorities appeared still higher.

These statistics must be qualified: Breton abstention rates were significantly higher than in the rest of France. Only 68.7 per cent participated in the Côtes-du-Nord, only 51.6 per cent in Finistère: figures which are probably significantly lower than participation elsewhere in France.[6] This evidence suggests a pattern which became common during the Second Empire: while the regime was able to dominate the political process and to stifle forms of dissent, it was not able to command mass loyalty.

Table 6.2 Votes approving Louis-Napoleon's rule, 20–1 December 1851[7]

Department	Yes vote (%)
Côtes-du-Nord	97
Finistère	94.5
Ille-et-Vilaine	94.6
Loire-Inférieure	91.8
Morbihan	93.2

Table 6.3 Referendum results, 1851–70

Referendum	Yes votes in Brittany (%)	Yes votes in France (%)
1851	51.4	75.2
1852	66.2	76.0
1870	69.8	68.0

Note: voting figures are given as a percentage of total number of registered voters, not as a percentage of total number of participants.[8]

In February 1852 the Second Empire held its first parliamentary elections. In principle, it still recognized manhood suffrage. But the 900 national representatives were cut to 261, and the Breton contingent shrank from 70 to 26. Moreover, basic freedoms were denied to voters: there was strict censorship of press and political meetings; and pressure was placed on voters to choose particular candidates. The regime did not create its own party, but it adopted a system of 'official' candidates, under which Prefects would back likely collaborators. Their choices were eclectic: moderate Republicans, resigned Orleanists, compliant legitimists and opportunist Catholics were all chosen alongside some genuine Bonapartists. In the February 1852 elections, 260 of the 261 official candidates were elected. The one exception was Audren de Kerdrel, a legitimist representing the Ille-et-Vilaine. His surprise election contributed to the image of Brittany as a land ruled by legitimist aristocrats.

In the 1860s some further opposition to the Second Empire emerged in Brittany: two successful opposition candidates were elected in 1863, five in 1869. However, the majority of the Breton population voted loyally for the regime in the three referendums called – respectively – to approve the coup d'état of December 1851, the creation of the Second Empire in 1852, and, in 1870, the new Imperial policies designed to create a liberal Empire.

The Second Empire fell in September 1870, as a result of a disastrous military campaign led by Louis-Napoleon against Prussia. The Third Republic was created during the Franco-Prussian war (1870–1). The first elections took place in February 1871, in order to elect a government which could negotiate peace terms with Prussia. Censorship was lessened, but still remained significant until the late 1870s. Under the new regime, Brittany elected sixty deputies of whom fifty-four were monarchists, mainly legitimists, who were particularly strong in the Morbihan.[9] There were few other areas of France in which monarchists won such convincing majorities.

The numbers of Republicans increased across France in the important elections of 1876 and 1877, and Brittany began to appear out of step with majority French opinion. While the Third Republic was 'republicanized', Brittany seemed to remain monarchist. For example, in 1881, across France Republican candidates won 457 seats while the various oppositions (royalist, bonapartist and others) won 100 seats. In Brittany, the Republicans won 23 seats, the anti-Republican oppositions 26: the Loire-Inférieure and Morbihan emerged as strongholds of the right, Finistère and Ille-et-Vilaine as departments where Republicans were more secure.[10]

In the following decades, simple generalizations about Republicans and conservatives become more difficult. This neat split was already muddied by bonapartist deputies, who often – but not always – sided with the monarchists. In the 1880s, distinct strands of moderate and radical Republicanism emerged. On the right there were a series of ambitious and imaginative initiatives; first to create a form of right-wing political culture which could co-exist with the Republic, and secondly, to develop independent forms of Catholic political culture, freed from any alliance with the legitimists. This last strand of thinking was of particular importance in Brittany (see chapter 4). Finally, the development of parliamentary socialism in the 1890s makes simple generalizations about a single Republican camp yet more difficult.

The Dreyfus Affair (1896–1904) recreated a stark, clear political polarization. A French-Jewish army officer was unjustly accused of spying for Germany: his case became headline news, and reawakened first Republican fears of a clerical conspiracy to subvert France, and secondly Catholic fears that believers were treated as second-class citizens within the secular Republic. Moderate and radical Republicans were joined by socialist deputies in voting through anticlerical legislation to push back the Catholic presence in schools, to reaffirm municipal control over church buildings and, finally, to enact the separation of church and state in 1905. In the 1906 elections, Brittany returned twenty-nine deputies who were hostile to the government's anticlerical legislation, and thirteen who supported it.[11] Despite the vigorous mobilization of the Catholic electorate, the anticlerical vote actually increased in Brittany during these elections. None of these anticlerical deputies were socialists, as these were not successful in Brittany until after the First World War.

One must insist, however, on the permanent presence of left-leaning, radical Republican deputies in Breton politics. From 1906 to 1932 such deputies formed the single biggest party among the Breton deputies. About 6 per cent of the Breton electorate voted for them in 1889; this proportion tended to increase in the following decades, reaching 11 per cent in 1936.

Through this period Bretons regularly elected approximately sixteen or seventeen radical Republican deputies.[12]

The important point to draw from this rapid survey is the variety of political opinions in Brittany.[13] Certainly, one can find some areas dominated by conservatives: the area around Vitré, in the east of the Ille-et-Vilaine, and the larger area around Redon, in the south-west of the Ille-et-Vilaine, and stretching into the Côtes-du-Nord and the Morbihan, were two zones in which conservative candidates consistently won high votes, and in which monarchist sentiment survived well into the twentieth century. To the west of Brittany, in the Léon area of Finistère, was another zone which vigorously refused anticlericalism, and which was seen by anticlericals as right-wing. This area, instead, gives us an important indication of Brittany's political character. It was principally Catholic, and from this region a number of innovative Catholic initiatives began: agrarian syndicates, youth groups, Christian-Democracy and even a distinctively left-wing interpretation of Catholicism (see chapter 4). Socialism began to appeal to voters in the western and southern ports, particularly in Brest. Elsewhere, a variety of centrist groups, and in particular the Radicals, thrived.

The sections which follow will examine two forms of political direction in turn: the Second Empire and Third Republic. Once again, we will begin our discussions of these regimes by considering their attitudes to festivals.

The Empire

Following the coup d'état of December 1851, festivals became simple, naked expressions of militarism. A ceremony in Brest in January 1852 can be cited as typical. It started with a salvo of cannon fire and the ringing of church bells. During the day, public buildings were decorated and many also flew the tricolour flag. Bread was distributed to the poor. At 11.30 a.m. the authorities, including officers from the National Guard, infantry, marines, and artillery, marched to the church, where they heard a *Te Deum*. At the end of the ceremony there was another round of cannon fire and military music. As the weather was bad, there was no review of the soldiers. At dusk, there was a third salvo of cannon fire, and public buildings were illuminated. One thousand people then attended a ball at the Maritime Prefecture. Significantly, throughout the whole day, there was not one opportunity for any form of expressive or active popular participation in the event. Not surprisingly, the Sub-Prefect reported that the crowd was 'calm and silent' – the ideal crowd for the Bonapartist regime.[14]

The political culture of the Republic was slowly dismantled. The last remaining Liberty Trees were chopped down: by July 1852 there was only one left in the sixty communes of Loudéac arrondissement (Côtes-du-Nord).[15] Public political expression was reduced to tiresome, empty recitations of praise for the Emperor by officials. For example, the Morlaix Sub-Prefect wrote the following circular to his mayors after Louis-Napoleon's victory in the December 1851 referendum: 'Who does not admire this strong, devoted man who, blessed by this extraordinary mandate, now undertakes that immense task of restoring to France the principle of authority which has been so stupidly forgotten for so long?'[16] Mayors, he instructed, must organize the chanting of the *Te Deum* 'to thank God' for protecting France from anarchy.

Voting became a sham. Without clear information, without any proper access to debate or discussion, in the absence of opposition voices, in the face of a regime which openly celebrated militaristic values, imprisoned and exiled dissidents and used the resources of the administration to promote particular candidates, can it be said that the regulated political procedures of the Second Empire (1852–70) were exercises in democracy? Not surprisingly, the *Juge de Paix* of Loroux-Bottereau (Loire-Inférieure) reported that the rural people 'did not understand either the aim or the purpose' of elections.[17] Official electoral discourse was marked by a clear hypocrisy. On the one hand, the mechanical process of placing a ticket in a ballot box was preserved. In December 1851 the Loire-Inférieure Prefect even reminded his department's mayors that voting 'was to be a spontaneous expression of the country's will'.[18] On the other hand, the statement by the Paimboeuf Sub-Prefect (Loire-Inférieure), preparing his mayors for the regime's second referendum in December 1852, reveals the real nature of the regime's political culture:

> You will understand, *monsieur le maire*, the importance of this vote. You realize that to vote YES is to end the revolutions: it guarantees us calm and well-being, in the present and the future. I request that you remind your officials of this truth.
>
> What man would not come to the centre of his commune for the well-being of his father, mother, wife or child? Proclaim it everywhere, *monsieur le maire*, that in participating in this consultation, each voter is doing himself and his nearest and dearest a great service: he is contributing to the establishment of a government which will protect religion, the family, and the most important civil rights.[19]

A poster written by the Morbihan Prefect proclaimed a similar message to voters. It exhorted support for Louis-Napoleon, and warned against abstention: 'Society must know how many enemies she has, and how many defenders are prepared to rise for her.'[20]

The public sphere of debate and mobilization, which had briefly developed in March and April 1848, was now being strangled. The Morbihan Prefect explained the reasons for this. Why should the press be allowed to keep their monopoly over the direction of public opinion? Such procedures were clearly not fair: they disadvantaged those without access to means of publicity. Henceforth, Sub-Prefects must act to ensure that the press did not mislead voters. The first step in this process was to ban all hostile press comments concerning official candidates.[21] The new government and its associated local administrations took an active role in the construction and direction of a now-submissive body of political opinion.

All the Second Republic's political ceremonies were abolished early in 1852, and were replaced by two ceremonies. The first was the festival of 15 August, Napoleon I's birthday, which revived a ritual of the First Empire (1804–14).[22] A second annual ceremony was to be held on the second Sunday in December, to celebrate the battle of Austerlitz in 1805, one of Napoleon's greatest military victories.

How was the regime received in Brittany? As has been seen from the voting results from December 1851, there was some resistance to Louis-Napoleon. For example, in March 1852, the priest of Saint-Molf (Loire-Inférieure) was accused of preventing a rural policeman from distributing electoral propaganda in favour of the official candidate in a forthcoming by-election – a conflict which neatly illustrates the potential political difference between the state administration and the Church.[23] But opposition did not take the form of the demonstrations and virtual peasant rebellions that broke out in other areas of France in December 1851.[24] Instead, some Breton clerics, legitimists and aristocrats would simply withhold their full support for the regime. Prefects quickly became aware of the potential danger in such attitudes, and demanded that Sub-Prefects and mayors try harder to fight such 'apathy'. 'Voters' indifference is the only enemy we have to fight', the Loire-Inférieure Prefect warned the department's mayors in 1857.[25]

In general, the majority of these obstinate conservative elites 'rallied' to the regime. Some considered that they were learning from history: just as France had moved through the cycle of constitutional monarchy, Republic, Empire from 1789 to 1814, to finish with the Restoration of the monarchy in 1814, so – they considered – a second such cycle was unwinding in the mid-nineteenth century. Following the Second Republic, the Second Empire would end with the third restoration of the monarchy. For other conservatives, immediate political factors were of greater importance. During the Second Republic they had seen the alarming workers' revolt in Paris in June 1848, the partial electoral successes of the 'red' démoc-socs in 1850 and 1851, and widespread revolts against the coup d'état in December 1851. Scared by this 'red' menace, many Breton Whites preferred to rally to the Empire rather than allow social and political radicalism to spread. Moreover, more subtle political considerations could persuade some conservatives to 'rally'. For example, the dynamic archbishop of Rennes, Brossays-Saint-Marc, calculated that leading the Church to support the regime would be a means by which he could free Catholics from dependence on legitimist–aristocratic patrons.[26]

The Empire was prepared to play to such Catholic sensibilities. The Morbihan Prefect reminded voters that one of Louis-Napoleon's first acts had been to end the use of the Parisian church of Sainte-Geneviève as the secular Panthéon (a type of temple for Republican heroes) and to return it to its proper religious use.[27] The Falloux Law on schooling, passed in 1850, was then implemented by the Second Empire to ensure a dramatic growth in the number of schools run by Catholic teaching congregations in Brittany.[28] In the 1850s and early 1860s the Church actively supported the regime. Priests such as the village *curé* of Saint-Julien-de-Corcelles (Loire-Inférieure) were commended when they issued instructions to their parishioners to vote for the official candidate from their pulpits, while the isolated legitimist complaints at such behaviour were brushed aside.[29]

The alliance between the Empire and the region was sealed by the triumphant Imperial tour of the west in 1858, which was energetically supported by both Prefects and the Church. Large crowds gathered along the route, and triumphal arches greeted the official procession at each town. The tour's high point was the visit to Rennes, at which approximately a hundred thousand people crowded into the city to cheer the imperial couple. On 15 August 1858, the couple were at Sainte-Anne-d'Auray, and so were present for both the anniversary of the Assumption of the Virgin and the official Imperial festival.[30]

On occasion, the Empire also seems to have been markedly more successful than either the Second Republic or the July Monarchy in motivating local administrations. Its combination of political authoritarianism and economic development certainly suited many civil servants: it was a 'golden age' for Prefects, comments Ménager.[31] Some local officials clearly identified with its rule. 'I am just a humble official in this canton', explained one *Juge de Paix*, 'I think of myself as the advance guard, in the middle of these rural people among who I live. My duty is to bring to the higher administration's attention all that passes in the countryside.'[32] In a speech at a rural banquet in Finistère, one mayor explained that, in Breton, the relationship of the Prefect to the department was like that of Louis-Napoleon to France. The Emperor had stifled the revolution of 1848; he had restored French honour; and it was to him – and his Prefect – that the Bretons therefore owed their prosperity.[33]

There were two principal forms of mass support for the Second Empire. During its first decade we see another coalition of Catholic and secular forces. This was not the idealistic coalition of the crucifix and the tricolour proclaimed by Sand and Soret (see chapter 5), but a more pragmatic, law-and-order partnership, whose principal aim was to repress expressions of popular opinion, and which was marked by its permanent suspicion of all dissidence, all questioning, and even of any obvious signs of non-support. 'Don't let public opinion get lost', warned the Morbihan Prefect.[34]

Alongside this clerical-Bonapartist alliance, there was another, less prominent popular movement. Rural voters in particular could understand Bonapartism as an anti-noble force; the Empire was the regime that challenged, even abolished, the power of the conservative aristocracy.[35] This explains the underlying pattern of the continuing rise in support for the regime, as seen in Table 6.3. As the 1850s saw a slow but steady rise in prices and the expansion of the railway system, many farmers were content with the Imperial leadership. In 1873, a monarchist Sub-Prefect noted how peasants still respected the regime which had given them 'twenty years of prosperity'.[36] Bonapartism would remain a distinct political tradition in areas such as Ancenis and Châteaubriant (both Loire-Inférieure) into the 1880s, before merging with the reconstituted parliamentary right-wing traditions of the early twentieth century.[37]

The happy alliance of Church and State was suddenly ended on 9 October 1860 when Brossays-Saint-Marc, the Breton archbishop, held a funeral service in Rennes cathedral for the Papal soldiers killed at the battle of Castelfidardo. Imperial policy and Papal policy had collided in Italy: while the Empire supported Italian nationalist movements, the Pope opposed them. Partly as a result of clerical propaganda, some eight hundred and fifty Bretons volunteered to fight for the Papal armies.[38]

Following this break, political conditions changed radically in Brittany. Official election reports from 1863 sound similar to reports following the April 1848 elections. This was 'an electoral crisis'.[39] The clergy 'had forgotten everything that they owed to the Empire'.[40] They were motivated by 'a blind, savage, incomprehensible hatred'.[41] Their churches had become 'political arenas'.[42] Priests and other clerical officials travelled through the countryside, even from house to house, spreading libel against the Empire. The Church would collapse in two months, they declared, if voters returned official candidates. Priests tore up the voting forms of official candidates, and handed out those of the opposition.[43] Rural mayors were intimidated by this force.[44] 'We have to fight against a large, determined party,' explained one mayor, 'priests, congregations, believers and many legitimists are on the march.'[45] Even Republicans had joined forces with the clergy.[46] Aristocrats met parishioners as they emerged from Sunday mass, and stood drinks for those who would vote for the opposition.[47] Priests were even to be found in the election booths, influencing voters.[48]

A police report from 1863 commented succinctly on the opposition's forces:

> [Such landowners] have a crowd of people dependent on them: . . . tenants, servants, day labourers, etc. They have all abstained. We are therefore facing the toughest elements of the legitimist party: the clergy and the nobility . . . For the nobles, this is a matter of principle. But, for the clergy, the cause of their behaviour is the Italian question . . . If the elections are better for us in the small rural communes than in the cantonal towns, this is because fewer rich legitimist landowners are there.[49]

The 'Italian question' was certainly prominent in the leaflets issued by the opposition: it was 'France that obeyed Piedmont!' declared one candidate, neatly linking Catholicism and national pride against the regime and its Italian policy.[50]

Perhaps the fears of Prefects and mayors were exaggerated. Only two of the twenty-two Breton deputies elected in 1863 represented the opposition (one for the Loire-Inférieure, one for the Côtes-du-Nord). Only one was a convinced Catholic; the other, Glaiz-Bizoin, was a veteran anti-Bonapartist. The administration's reactions are, however, significant. Throughout the campaign, mayors, policemen and Prefects stressed the ignorance and naivety of the Breton electorate. Voters' willingness to listen to clerical propaganda was offered as proof of their foolishness, and therefore as a further argument for firmer political direction. Small meetings in the countryside should be banned, the Morbihan Prefect declared: the notables exploited them to spread criticisms of the government.[51]

By the mid and late 1860s, it was harder to find open enthusiasm for the Second Empire, although it must be stressed that the Breton electorate returned a substantial majority of official candidates in 1869 (sixteen out of twenty-one), and voted decisively in favour of the liberal Empire in the 1870 referendum (see Table 6.3). Thus, rather than seeing this process as a simple rise of the opposition, the situation was more complex: an increasingly open fight for hegemony between local elites (divided between legitimist, Catholic, liberal and Republican strands) and a national government.

The public representations of the regime suffered accordingly. In 1858 Louis-Napoleon and his wife had seemed able to combine their commemoration of the regime with the religious festival of the Assumption, but by the early 1860s it was no longer possible to work this synthesis so easily. Serbois, a French tourist, visited Lorient on 15 August 1863 and considered that 'bells and cannon' rivalled each other for the attention of the crowds: one either attended the religious ceremony or the secular festival, but not both.[52] Luzel, visiting the same port two years later, left a still more dispiriting impression of the secular festival:

> It was 15 August, the Emperor's festival. The town really did not seem to be making an effort. There were only a few sad illuminations: some candle-ends lined up on window ledges. There were also a few free public dances, under the trees by the quay. What else? I saw nothing.[53]

The Second Empire's legacy is mixed. At first sight, when one considers the clerical-Bonapartist coalition of the 1850s, it appears as if the Empire was the revenge of the Whites on the Blue regimes of 1830 and 1848. But, in the long term, a different profile emerges. For all its compromises with the power of the Church, the Second Empire remained a secular regime: it was therefore Blue. And, when one compares the relative performances of the July Monarchy, the Second Republic and the Second Empire, it becomes clear that through devices such as the referendum and the official candidate, this latter regime was the most successful of the mid-nineteenth-century Blue regimes in acquiring substantial popular legitimacy in Brittany. Indeed, Robert Tombs notes that 'the most popular regime of the nineteenth century was not a Republic but the Second Empire ... neither "Red" nor "White", it guaranteed both the Revolution and order.' It was dynamic, led a programme of economic modernization, and contributed to the emancipation of the masses. Tombs is generous with his praise for the Bonapartist tradition, calling it 'the most convincing' solution to the problems initiated by the 1789 revolution and claiming that it ended 'the long post-revolutionary trauma'.[54]

This is substantial acclaim indeed, and one is entitled to ask whether it is justified. Tombs' work expresses a type of pragmatic, half-hearted appreciation of democracy: authors who follow such arguments seem to consider that mass participation in political processes is all very well, as long as it does not lead to excesses.[55] The Revolution of 1848 is considered as dangerously destabilizing, and in this way Bonapartist dictatorship is justified. The problem with these 'moderate' political perspectives is that they ignore the long-term effects of rule by such administrations. Instead of opening up popular culture, the Second Empire closed down the public sphere. The successive votes in favour of official candidates and Imperial policies have only limited validity, for they cannot be considered as meaningful expressions of freely given support. More seriously still, the Second Empire set a dangerous precedent: its eighteen-year rule offered a model for all who wished to ignore public opinion. This was the long-term legacy of the Second Empire: an apparently convincing justification for administrative arrogance.

The Republicans

Given Brittany's fearsome reputation as a stronghold of legitimism and conservative Catholicism, it is perhaps worth stating, once more, that there were Republicans in the region. As was seen in chapter 2, some Bretons participated enthusiastically in the revolutionary process initiated in 1789. After the Restorations of 1814 and 1815, Republicanism had no organized movement, but it did not disappear from Brittany. It became a secretive, underground movement, which would briefly burst into the open through actions such as the shouts of students and youths in Rennes in the 1830s, who annoyed their compatriots by shouting 'long live the Republic!' in the evenings and winding coloured ribbons round their hats to indicate their political commitments.[56] Crowds in Nantes sometimes behaved similarly: during a period of international tension, they sung the *Marseillaise* outside the town's main theatre. A crowd of a hundred went on to protest outside the British consul.[57] In the same town, tailors leaving a craft banquet clashed with police and shouted 'Long live the Republic!' during their scuffles.[58]

Was Republican culture limited to shouts and scuffles? Some notes from the Interior Ministry suggest otherwise: police chiefs talked of an attempt to form a Republican Association in Brest in 1833, and of an all-Brittany

Republican organization, headed in Rennes, and with branches in Quimper and Brest.[59] How significant these organizations were – and, indeed, whether they really existed – is uncertain. Brittany's one notable early nineteenth-century Republican intellectual, Doctor Ange Guépin (1805–73), lived in Nantes. Influenced by the utopian socialists of the early nineteenth century, he was the co-author of a pioneering social study, *Nantes au XIXe siècle,* which categorized the city's inhabitants into eight social classes, from the rich to the extremely poor.[60] He served as a Commissaire in the Loire-Inférieure and Morbihan in early 1848.

The evidence surveyed above certainly demonstrates the existence of a Republican presence in early nineteenth-century Brittany; but it also reveals the Republicans' weaknesses. There were only a handful of small rural towns which decisively moved to Blue positions during the 1790s; Siegfried cites the example of Loudéac (Ille-et-Vilaine), which in 1789, 1793, 1848 and even 1851 was 'a centre of independence and Republican resistance'.[61] But Republicanism was largely limited to the big cities – Rennes and Nantes – and to the rapidly growing port towns of the western and southern coasts. Even in these sites, Republicanism usually only attracted a minority of young men, essentially students. There is only some sketchy evidence of Republican participation in the early workers' movement. Such small, isolated groups did not grow during the early months of the Second Republic: they were unable to meet the challenge of mass suffrage, ineffective in their appeal to crowds, and often suspicious of rural people.

During the Second Empire, Republican circles were repressed by police action. The most prominent forms of opposition to the regime were Catholic, legitimist or, sometimes, liberal-Catholic. The creation of the Third Republic in September 1870 came as a surprise to the small groups of Breton Republicans, just as the Second Republic had in February 1848. The rushed elections of February 1871, held in the aftermath of the French defeat in the Franco–Prussian war, gave these isolated militants little chance to organize. Of the sixty Breton deputies, only seven were Republicans – and six of these were elected in by-elections conducted in July 1871.[62]

The first years of the Third Republic did little to assist these small groups. It was a period of monarchist domination, and many commentators expected the monarchist majority of the new National Assembly to produce the Third Restoration of the monarchy in France. Open, public celebrations of Republican values could be dangerous; even commemorations of 14 July were often held in secret.[63] Outside these circles, the majority of the Breton population expressed little interest in politics. Following disagreements between the monarchist groupings in the Assembly, and indications from by-elections in the years after 1871 that Republican and perhaps also Bonapartist feeling was growing in France, some liberal and Orleanist deputies left the monarchist majority and voted through the Constitution of the Third Republic in February and July 1875. To the amazement of many monarchist officials, the Bretons seemed uninterested. One Sub-Prefect noted that the announcement of the Constitution: 'has certainly not caused the emotion that many papers seemed to expect. In Saint-Malo, one flag was raised . . . The population was as calm as ever. One could perhaps see a little more animation in the *cabarets*, where political life is concentrated in the countryside.'[64]

Two extremely hard-fought general elections, in February–March 1876 and October 1877, formed a climax to this contest between monarchists and Republicans. In 1876, twelve of Brittany's forty-four deputies were Republicans, in 1877 fourteen out of fifty-five deputies.[65] Following the decisive Republican victory in this second election, the new government judged that seventy-six deputies had been elected by 'invalid means': a phrase normally meaning that voters had been subjected to undue pressure. Eight of these invalidated elections were in Brittany.

While these figures show that the conservative elites could still dominate the electoral process in Brittany, the ability of Republican groups to win about a quarter of the Breton constituencies suggests something of the struggle which was taking place. Déguignet – our peasant autobiographer – wrote a vivid description of the February 1876 election in Ergué-Armel, near Quimper (Finistère). For him, the central issue concerned power: 'The nobles and Jesuits wanted to take us back about four centuries: to the good old days when peasants and workers were judged to be seventeen degrees below the status of beasts of burden and dogs.'[66] The favourite candidate was a millionaire industrialist, who was a monarchist and clerical. His opponent was a poor Republican lawyer. The monarchists issued leaflets in Breton and French. They employed full-time agents to spread their message across the countryside, handing out papers, cigars and spirits. The landowners, whom Déguignet refers to as 'châtelains' [that is as squires, or lords of the manor], indicated to their tenants and labourers how they should vote. Déguignet's local landowner even decided to organize them on the day of the elections: he took them first to a pub, then to the voting booth. Déguignet, however, had thought of a way to counter such influences: he distributed Republican voting cards, but told his fellow voters to hide them in their waistcoats. (As Seigfried notes, even in 1913 the secret ballot had not yet been established in many Breton villages.[67]) After they had drunk the *châtelain's* health, they were led along the road and, as predicted, given voting cards for the monarchist candidate. Each voter held these openly in his hand. The *châtelain* walked behind them, and as they approached the booths they saw other groups of fifty or sixty peasants and labourers, each guided by their landowners. Some of Déguignet's friends began to get restless with the excitement of the trick they were going to play. 'Don't speak so loud', he warned them, 'we'll see what happens this evening.'

The mayor, an ex-Bonapartist and now employed by the 'clerical–monarchists', stood at the entrance to the election booths. He confidently told each of the *châtelains* that electors would vote as one man for the right candidate, and shook their hand. However, Déguignet noted how voters grinned as they left the booths to go back to the pub to eat and drink at the landowners' expense. Déguignet records that of the commune's five hundred voters, four hundred and fifty voted for the Republican candidate.[68] The *châtelains* and their agents simply could not believe their eyes: they shouted; they stamped their feet; they even burst into tears. More surprising still, the Republican candidate, Louis Hémon, won enough votes to be elected in the Quimper I constituency.

Déguignet records the reaction of a local aristocratic lady. At first she doubted the reports concerning the election result. When they were confirmed, she was 'like an enraged hyena'. She rushed into her grounds, screaming at her estate workers words which stuck in her throat: they were scoundrels, thieves, bastards, cowards and worse still. She hit the terrified workers: if they protested, she grew still angrier. She dismissed them all – but had to re-employ them a few days later. Déguignet's account cannot be taken at face value: one wonders, for example, exactly how important his role was in persuading the others to vote Republican. Yet, if we move away from the precise details, this account reveals much about authority relations in rural Brittany. Déguignet's sense of the distance between the ordinary voters and the elite of landowners is corroborated by other evidence: the *châtelains* exercised a type of 'natural' hegemony over these peasants, labourers and workers, sustained by the very real threat of dismissal. Under these circumstances, it was difficult, almost impossible, for the rural people to speak out. A public sphere of information, debate and discussion simply did not exist. Voting against the *châtelain* took a type of courage that many lacked, and even required information which was often unavailable to ordinary voters. However, underneath this apparent easy domination, there was a diffuse but deep sense of resentment: more of a brooding feeling that this society was not arranged fairly than an articulate sense of class consciousness. At times Republicanism could appeal to such resentful rural folk, but often its language was too abstract, its attraction too weak, or its proposals too apparently far-fetched to encourage tenants and peasants to break from their subordination.

At first sight, Déguignet's story sounds like a happy one. However, like all good stories, there is a twist in the tale. He notes the Republicans' decisive electoral victory in 1877, but comments on the resulting government:

> Unfortunately, among all these Republican representatives, there was not a single democrat. Democracy means government of the people by the people ... and, in our Republic, the people, the real people, has no true representative. Among these representatives, however, there are fine speakers, sophists and phrase-mongers who know how to send the people to sleep.

Was Déguignet's final judgement correct?

In the years following 1876–7 there are indications that Brittany was republicanized. One of the most eloquent symbols of this new political culture could be heard after 1880; priests were asked to ring the church bells to celebrate the newly established festival of 14 July. Where they granted this request, it was often understood as a sign of the victory of the mayor over the priest.[69] For once, the national legislation concerning this new festival was quite subtle: the celebration of 14 July was not compulsory. Prefects were supplied with a relatively small budget – enough to pay for celebrations in the main departmental towns – and instructed to encourage celebrations elsewhere in their departments. Mayors could raise local taxes to finance their commune's celebrations, but this was rarely popular. They would submit budgets to the Prefects, who would share out the available funds. In the 1890s this usually amounted to between fifteen and thirty-five francs per commune.[70]

Many mayors complained that they simply had not got sufficient resources to celebrate the anniversary. Even during the great centenary celebrations of 1889, mayors would signal that they had celebrated the anniversaries as well 'as their resources allowed' – a phrase which could well reduce the celebrations of the centenary of the meeting of the Estates-General on 5 May 1789 to a flag flying over a rural town hall.[71] On occasion, it seems likely that this avowed poverty was actually serving as a political excuse; it allowed a moderate mayor to avoid arranging a celebration without actually refusing the Prefect's invitation. In other words, even after the Republicans' establishment of a reasonably stable Republican regime, there was only a minimal Republican presence in many Breton communes.

Voting records demonstrate that the new Republic failed to replace the older White political culture. Republican officials were therefore faced with the task of working within the hostile context created by previous regimes, local traditions and established elites. The result was an intense and unusual politicization of even the most innocuous and banal ceremonies. Republican officials would approach minor events, such as school prize days and agricultural festivals, almost as if they were one of the great battles of the French Revolution. The Morlaix Sub-Prefect's notes demonstrate the degree of hostility that Republican officials faced. He reported to the Prefect that he had only visited thirty-one of the sixty communes in his arrondissement, and then explained why:

> I cannot see the point of official visits to regions dominated by aristocracies or theocracies which are hostile to the Republic, unless [such visits] are arranged with such splendour [éclat] that they give the peasants the feeling that the national government is greater than the *châtelain* or the priest, than the landowners or masters. While bringing solutions and favours, one must be accompanied by an entourage like that which escorts the bishops and even the priests when they visit a parish, or like that that military leaders have when they take possession of their posts. Banquets and festivals have to be organized: taking care, of course, to pay for everything that will produce joy and recognition. A modest Sub-Prefect must do, in miniature, what the President of the Republic does on a grand scale.[72]

This shows the extent to which Brittany was understood as 'enemy territory' by Republican officials. The most revealing aspect of this memorandum, however, is the comparisons which are drawn: the Sub-Prefect must act like a bishop, a priest, a general or a President. He must impose his presence on the rural people through a combination of bribery and drama. None of these thoughts suggests a genuinely democratic spirit.

Schools were a particular site for conflict. Republican school legislation passed in the early 1880s gradually took effect in the following years, forcing even the most distant communes to accept the creation of secular, public and free boys' and girls' schools. The Church retaliated by creating new private, religious schools.[73] Schooling, rather than the more abstract issues of Republicanism or religion, became at once the most visible indicator of political loyalties and the site of the hardest fought battles.

A telling commentary on these petty, localized political battles came from the Fougères Sub-Prefect (Ille-et-Vilaine) in 1909. He noted the prestigious ceremony with which a private girls' school had been opened in the canton; the archbishop, and Comte de La Riboisière, who held the posts of mayor and senator, were present. The Republican riposte came on 18 July 1909. A banquet for 450 guests was organized to celebrate the opening of a public, secular girls' school. The Sub-Prefect and Le Hérissé – the Antrain mayor

Politics of the State: 1850–1940   177

and a Republican deputy – were present. The Comte de La Riboisière was also among the guests; he asked to speak. The Sub-Prefect invited him to speak from the high table of the banquet, but the Comte refused, provoking agitation within the hall. If he had joined the Sub-Prefect, this would have implied that he accepted the priorities of the regime, and therefore suggested a Republican victory. On the other hand, the fact that he was present at the ceremony suggested that it had been organized with such *éclat*, or splendour, that the Count simply could not ignore it. The Republican forces had engineered a 'win-win' situation, and the Sub-Prefect was clearly delighted:

> In fact, this was the first time in twenty-five years that . . . Republicans had the courage to demonstrate publicly their feelings on the Comte's home ground. It was also the first time that he'd had a setback. He had been considered almost as holy, above all partisan politics: it was the first time that his image had been cracked. It's the first blow which has hit the untouched and truly feudal authority which he wields here: it's the first step towards liberation for all those who suffer from the oppression of this powerful and most rich lord.[74]

Such comments also remind us of Déguignet's account: the hegemony of these conservative notables often created a type of 'total' environment which even a Sub-Prefect found difficult to challenge.

While the Fougères Sub-Prefect was certain that this action had been a success, elsewhere similar official interventions could backfire. Sometimes local Republicans asked officials to avoid giving the appearance of supporting them; such open patronage could be dangerous, as it could compromise them in the eyes of their anti-Republican neighbours.[75]

The evidence surveyed in the pages above demonstrates the Republican administration's willingness to challenge the conservative notables' hegemony. Was Déguignet therefore wrong to argue that the Republicans were not democrats? Not necessarily. The most obvious sign of a political-administrative continuity with the authoritarian political culture of the Second Empire can be seen in the manner in which civil servants were treated. Successive Republican governments saw them as soldiers to be mobilized to fight for the Republican cause. Their behaviour was surprisingly strictly monitored. For example, the Sub-Prefect checked that no civil servants were present at the mass for the Imperial (that is, Bonapartist) pretender at Morlaix in July 1889.[76] The Vitré Sub-Prefect (Ille-et-Vilaine) complained about the number of civil servants who sent their children to private schools: 'They are not giving the example which they should be giving: the effect on the local people is deplorable.'[77] In a revealing phrase, the Paimboeuf Sub-Prefect (Loire-Inférieure) spoke of some civil servants being 'too strictly neutral'.[78] Public officials would also intervene quite openly in local political struggles in an attempt to limit or counter the forces of the anti-Republican right. For example, following the 1906 elections, the Ille-et-Vilaine Prefect publicly rebuked Etienne Pinault, candidate for the modernizing conservative group the ALP (Action Libéral Populaire), for describing himself as a 'Republican'.[79] Jean-François Tanguy is clearly correct to conclude that, in the eyes of the government, political neutrality was not possible.[80]

While many of the bigger towns converted to the Republican cause, the Blues were unsuccessful in persuading the mass of rural people to accept their ideals. In other words, there was no strong, independent, *popular* Republican movement. This heavy-handed mobilization of administrative resources was, at best, a substitute for a popular movement that would liberate Breton society.

Compared with resources wielded by the administration, the local Breton Republican groups appear both weaker and less dynamic. We could consider, for example, the brave actions of the schoolteacher at Frossay (Loire-Inférieure), who in 1907 single-handedly mobilized a Republican committee to celebrate 14 July by a 'fraternal banquet' held in a tent. Reading between the lines, one understands that the mayor was obviously not willing to organize a celebration, nor to allow municipal buildings to be used. The banqueters 'toasted the Republic, and the extension of the Republican movement at Frossay – which is developing slowly but surely'.[81] The teacher's report ended by inviting the Sub-Prefect to attend their next celebration.

Early twentieth-century Republican political organizations seem primitive: little more than several competing, loose federations of committees, each with a few dozen members, grouped around a single prominent leader in the cantonal town. For much of the time these committees were inactive; they usually only showed signs of life immediately before elections, and officials regularly commented on such committees' failure to organize their political campaigns in time for voting.[82] It was also obvious how these committees' reliance on prominent, charismatic individuals led to frankly ridiculous feuds, as minor differences between personalities were translated into bitter schisms.[83] Officials often adopted a tone of patronizing superiority as they criticized these ineffective little groups.[84] Republicans themselves were aware of these weaknesses, and occasionally militants such as Georges Dottin worked to create more substantial organizations: in Dottin's case, an organization to campaign for the cause of secular schooling in the Ille-et-Vilaine in 1904.

This group did stage ninety-one lectures in the department's rural communes between December 1904 and March 1905, but like so many similar organizations it declined as its leader grew older, and was effectively broken by the First World War.[85]

Under these circumstances, Breton Republican political culture assumed a distinctive form. Rather than the rationally considered programme of a bureaucratically organized party, Republicanism was closer to a faith, sustained by personal loyalty to a local charismatic leader.[86] In 1937, over ten thousand people attended the funeral service for Georges Le Bail, a master-Republican from Finistère.[87] These Republicans were best at vigorous polemic against their opponents, exploiting vague, sonorous phrases such as 'the struggle against reaction' to develop their criticisms.[88] Picking one example out of hundreds, we could consider the following election leaflet of Léon Thebault, who stood in the constituency of Rennes II for the 'Left Union', as a representative sample of Breton-Republican verbiage:

> I consider that, in the great social battle, there are two forces: the Republic and reaction. The Republic is the future, justice, liberty, equality and fraternity; it is progress, reform of workers' lives, well-being and happiness for the benefit of all. Reaction is the past, the preservation of errors, prejudices, and inequality, it is the conservation of privilege for the benefit of a few. I stand firmly against those reactionaries who try to fool the electorate, who falsely call themselves Republicans, who will do anything to get power and who, with this aim, have even withdrawn their capital from France in order to provoke a crisis, and yet have the astonishing audacity to blame the Republicans. I stand firmly for a strictly secular, democratic and social Republic.[89]

Obviously there are some points in this text which are specific to the 1920s: for example, the references to the flight of capital refers to the French financial problems of that decade. In a broader sense, Thebault's denunciation of 'false' Republicans could also locate the text as having been written after 1890: it was in that year that Pope Leo XIII called to Catholics to 'rally' to the Republic. The papal appeal did influence some right-wing groups: a few moderated their denunciations, or shifted from refusing the Republic to refusing this Republican government. However, the most striking feature of Thebault's text is its near-timelessness. Despite his references to the future and the past, Republicans such as Thebault saw the world in terms of an unchanging conflict between fixed moral entities. Indeed, they resisted or criticized all innovations which might blur or soften this sharp, stark differentiation between the two.

Christian–Democracy, socialism and, later, communism all posed problems for those who understood political culture in such simple terms. Surprisingly, the most frequent target for these Republican polemicists were the post-Ralliement attempts by some Catholic groups to bridge the gap between Church and Republic. *Ouest-Éclair*, the successful and quite startlingly new Breton-based Social–Catholic daily created in 1899, was regularly referred to in official reports as 'so-called Republican' or dismissed as standing 'for a Republic without Republicans'.[90] 'All this land's politics are distorted' by the Catholic press, wrote one critical Sub-Prefect, 'the people kept in complete ignorance about what's happening.'[91] Of course, one can debate exactly what 'Republicanism' signified to this first generation of 'rallied' Catholics, and one can note their continuing reticence about some aspects of the government's programme. In the last analysis, however, what is striking is the determination with which *all* Republicans, moderate, radical, socialist and administrative, refused *all* dialogue with this new political presence.

Such peculiar political perspectives led Republicans to adopt a curious approach to the development of political democracy in Brittany. Breton Republicans constructed their entire belief system around a rejection of a corporate, hierarchical, backward-looking, superstitious rural society: a model of rural Brittany which was, at best, a simplification and, at worst, a politicized stereotype. At times, this stance certainly led them to note aspects of oppression within rural political culture. It is clear that Déguignet's account of the *châtelain's* rural political hegemony was not mere fantasy: landowners did use their economic power over their tenants for political ends. Republicans noted this power relationship, and, on occasion, vigorously protested against it. The libertarian socialist Emile Masson noted the Republicans' shortcomings, and spoke with passionate intensity about their failure to develop a radical social reform programme to appeal to the Breton peasants, who were 'hoping and waiting for a social revolution as a lover waits for his fiancée' (see chapter 7).[92] But the Republicans' polemical critique developed instead into a means by which to explain the Republicans' own grave political failings. The rural population was 'kept in ignorance' by priests and *hobereaux* (an insulting term for conservative petty aristocrats).[93] Such populations were therefore incapable of understanding the Republican message, for they were 'so steeped in their crude faith that they [were] unable to reason'.[94] The Breton-speaking clergy preached 'the hatred of foreigners.'[95] The peasants were consequently 'fatalists'; they could not be persuaded to question tradition or imagine a better future.[96]

For Republican observers with a taste for the deterministic sociology of a Zola or a Taine, the Bretons' mental weaknesses could be 'explained' by reference to alcoholism which – like dirt in the early nineteenth century – was used by outside observers almost as a symbol of Breton identity. 'For them, everything is an excuse for drunkenness', whether baptism, marriage, funeral or fair, noted Kano.[97] Left-wing satirists would equate religious faith with alcoholism, and point to the brisk sales of drinks following mass.[98] Similar themes were found in early twentieth-century novels such as Le Goffic's *Le Crucifié de Keraliès* and, more stridently, in Yves Le Febvre's blistering anticlerical polemic, *La Terre des Prêtres* in which a raped, pregnant peasant girl is forcibly married to an alcoholic farm labourer.[99] Here, the most appropriate response to these stereotypes is not to consider comparative studies of rates of alcoholism in Brittany and France, but to note how they so easily reinforced the earlier clichés of 'Oriental passivity'. Such simple stereotypes were still being used by Republican officials after the First World War: 'the rural people are still under the clergy's influence, and this situation will continue while they are told that a communist revolution is imminent'.[100]

Any initiatives or actions by Breton rural people themselves were understood through reference to this rich stock of Republican myths and stereotypes. Thus, protests concerning the implementation of the anticlerical legislation of the early 1900s was quickly dismissed as mere 'Chouannerie'.[101] Furthermore, Breton folk culture or popular religious rituals were often understood by Republicans as practices which were designed merely to serve the priests and aristocrats. Such critical attitudes effectively isolated the bulk of Breton Republicans from rural popular culture.

These limited political attitudes also explain the importance of charismatic local leaders to Breton Republicans. Without a substantial mass movement, without a clear body of critical theory, there was no other focus available to these Republican groups other than these individual loyalties. One Sub-Prefect commented that 'the Republican party' in Fougères was nothing more than a 'sketch . . . because there are no striking personalities to lead it'. His argument is valid for all Breton Republican political culture in this period.[102] Republicans believed that it was impossible to bring democracy to the countryside, so they attempted to create a kind of counter-aristocracy. Like the Morlaix Sub-Prefect cited above, Republican groups wished to bribe or stun the rural masses, sometimes to educate them, but never to empower them. Instead of acting to generalize their political culture, their critical attitudes usually isolated Republicanism to the pockets of Blue political culture. Siegfried's description of Republicanism in Vitré and Fougères (Ille-et-Vilaine) neatly captured this point: 'once you have passed through the urban toll posts, a few hundred metres after the last houses, then rural feudalism resumes its powers'.[103]

To conclude this section: Brittany should have been the ideal region for Republicanism. Its rural people were undoubtedly oppressed and exploited by local elites. While as good historians we must refuse the Republicans' clumsy polemical use of the concept of 'feudalism', as many of these nobles were acting to implement a particular version of capitalist modernity in Brittany, there can be no doubt that the Republicans' criticisms of rural inequity were substantially accurate. The Republicans' failure to initiate a widespread, popular Republican movement in the region was clearly, in part, a result of their own misguided political perspectives.

Conclusion

Brittany was a region which was ruled by the three thieves. First the Empire, in the name of the Counter-Revolution and order, ended debate, discussion and fair voting. Secondly the Republic, in the name of progress, modernization and unification, intimidated and manipulated administrative resources in attempts to deny the political identity of the Breton peoples. And thirdly the Church, seeking to defend its schools and associations, counter-attacked, ordering Catholics to protest against the Republic. None of these three brought the substance of democracy to the region. While none of these problems were unique to the region, studying Brittany in particular reveals these issues acutely. In chapters 4, 5 and 6, we have avoided both the current paradigms of Breton studies; that is, we have refused to see Brittany as a separate nation, oppressed by the French Republic, but have equally refused the French–national perspective which considers Brittany merely as a backward region, slow to follow the normal course of events. Instead, these chapters have shown that Brittany reveals the contradictions of French political culture in their most acute form.

If we centre our investigations on Brittany, we can also question the standard historiographical reading of the mid-nineteenth century, which usually identifies three different, conflicting traditions: Republicanism, monarchism and Bonapartism. Instead, in Brittany, one can legitimately argue that all governments from 1830 onwards were *different* variants of 'Blue' administrations, representing different aspects of the revolutionary legacy, and contesting the apparently 'natural' domination of the region by aristocrats and priests.

What part did the Celticists play in this? Once again, we can note their near-irrelevance. To some extent, Blue administrators understood the Bretons as representing a different racial or cultural group. To some extent, the Church played on notions of Breton peculiarity, particularly the idea of a specific Breton faith, as it mobilized people to defend its privileges. But neither the Church nor the Republic were genuinely concerned about questions of Celtic identity.

7

The Politics of Brittany
Regionalism and Nationalism

Breton nationalism has been largely absent from the preceding three chapters. The eighteenth- and nineteenth-century debates on the ethnic identity of France and Brittany were formulated in ways which side-stepped the issue of Brittany as a nation. The power politics of the nineteenth century were constructed along the lines of the Republic clashing with the Church, or the national competing with the local; Villemarqué's fanciful musings on the validity of Breton folk art seemed of little relevance. And yet, there was a third discourse, which gradually grew both clearer and more radical from the mid-nineteenth century to the mid-twentieth century. This has been summed up with the approximate title of the *emsav*: a loose network of Breton language militants, cultural activists and political nationalists which never developed into a well-organized party. It must be remembered that such groupings, despite their rhetoric, could never accurately claim to speak for the majority of the Breton population. As will be seen, on the few occasions that they stood for election they attracted only a tiny minority. So, why study them? First, one has to add a qualification concerning their minority status: in a situation in which neither the Blues nor the Whites were genuinely committed to democratic norms, it is possible that this third current of Breton militants may have some valid claim, on occasion, to voice the repressed protests and projects of the majority. Secondly, even if one can be reasonably certain about their minority status, it remains true that they form a revealing and interesting political current, one which can be seen as uniquely Breton, and for that reason alone they are worth considering.

In the first sections of this chapter we will consider some particular examples of regionalist and proto-nationalist activity, before turning to consider the group which achieved the greatest notoriety, *Breiz Atao*.

The precursors

A disinterested, humanitarian observer examining the condition of Brittany in the late nineteenth century might have noted a number of pressing social and economic issues. The Breton economy was contracting; the process of deindustrialization stimulated an ever-growing emigration from its villages.[1] While tourism was becoming more popular, this was a poor replacement for the textile industries and maritime commerce which had thrived in the region during the sixteenth, seventeenth and eighteenth centuries. Breton agriculture was poorly served by a communications infrastructure that had been designed principally to facilitate travel between the naval bases of Brest and Lorient and Paris. Linked to these issues were some worrying social issues such as high levels of alcoholism and high suicide rates. Lastly, one should not forget the disastrous state of Breton political culture, as discussed in the previous chapters. Regionalists, however, tended to focus on other aspects of Brittany. While Villemarqué's extraordinary ideas were never fully accepted by any strand of Breton politics, something of the tone of his thinking became commonplace in late nineteenth-century debates.

The end of the Second Empire (1870) was an important political turning point. A key word among the anti-Bonapartist forces was 'decentralization'. This could mean something akin to the democratization of society, or a revived interest in local cultures, or merely the restoration of the old, conservative, local elites to their positions of privilege. A petition signed by some Breton aristocrats during the last days of the Second Empire illustrates some of the ambiguities of this term. The petition argued for the necessity of vigorous provincial societies at the 'extremities' of France, constructed around local languages, which would help stop the drift of the rural people to the towns. The Breton language, argued the petitioners, was of particular importance: 'It is the most national language in France, in a way more national than French itself, for it is a dialect of the language of our Gaulish ancestors before the Roman conquest.'[2] There are clear links here with the earlier ideas voiced by Villemarqué, with the proviso that these petitioners are not so forceful in their aim – that Brittany should be at the centre of France – and were moving to a lesser aim, that of a limited, conservative autonomy for the region. During the Franco–Prussian war (1870–1), such ideas were debated anew: ephemeral regional leagues were formed to coordinate the war effort.[3]

The years immediately after the fall of the Second Empire constituted the Indian summer of French monarchist Legitimism. In the February 1871 general elections they had won the majority of seats. The Third Republic, stained by the shame of the French defeat in the Franco–Prussian war and the blood of the massacres at the end of the Paris Commune (1871), seemed a doomed regime. For a few brief years legitimists could believe that history was, once again, on their side, and that Henri V would soon be restored to the throne. During these years, they reassessed Brittany's status within France. They could, for example, note the contribution that the region had made to the war effort in 1870–1. The response of the Breton conscripts proved that the province was 'the most French' of all the French provinces.[4] A procession on 8 December 1872 commemorated Brittany's contribution to the French war effort; it gathered in Sainte-Anne-d'Auray, and some twenty thousand pilgrims carried two hundred flags and banners in 'an explosion of faith'.[5] These points suggest a complex vision of nationhood; while French national unity was desirable, this should not be enforced through the annihilation of provincial identities. 'France only has one heart', noted one writer on decentralization, 'but she has several languages.'[6] Decentralization would permit a strengthening of the provinces, which would in turn benefit France as a whole.

At the centre of these debates was the revival of the noble-dominated Association Bretonne (AB) in 1873. The first version of the AB was formed at a meeting of twenty-two people in Vannes in March 1843.[7] It was primarily a discussion group, with three sections: statistics and the economy; agriculture and cattle; and archaeology. The first two sections considered practical issues of economic development. In its early years, the local agricultural sections often appeared the most active within the AB. These often sponsored the annual *Comices Agricoles,* in particular cantons – a type of ceremonial prize day in which awards would be distributed to particularly successful farmers.[8] It was the archaeological section which was open to the more controversial speculations of the Celticists, but even here the most prestigious contribution was that made by Arthur de La Borderie (1827–1901), a committed Catholic and a painstaking historian. He was always concerned by Villemarqué's Celticism, and refused to accept Druidism as a true religion.[9] For La Borderie, historical writing was a science; it depended on meticulous attention to detail. Documents, data and facts were carefully verified before their integration into a wider analysis.[10] While La Borderie made use of the term 'nation' to describe an ancient Brittany, he saw this status as existing in the past, never in the future. As new scientific knowledge of the 1850s and 1860s established with ever greater confidence that Brittany's prehistoric monuments were not 'Celtic' in nature, there was something of a crisis of confidence among Celticists. For some, Villemarqué's *Barzaz Breiz* was seen almost as

Table 7.1   Geographic origins of members of the AB in 1887[11]

Place	Membership	(%)
Côtes-du-Nord	150	34.7
Finistère	70	15.9
Ille-et-Vilaine	84	19.1
Loire-Inférieure	48	10.9
Morbihan	69	15.7
Paris	8	1.8
Elsewhere	10	2.3
Total	439	

an alternative historical monument, providing another route to an ancient historic legitimacy. La Borderie had been prepared to accept the *Barzaz Breiz* as a collection of historical documents revealing aspects of the Breton past, but in the 1870s he led the revived AB into the study of the early Breton saints.[12] He argued that it was the immigrants from the British Isles who had brought a fully-fledged Christian culture to Brittany.[13] La Borderie achieved some official recognition as a historian; from 1890–3 he taught a course in Breton history at the University of Rennes.[14]

The AB was suspended briefly in 1854, and then closed in 1859 before being reinstituted in 1873. The new AB showed incredible confidence in the 1870s. It was never intended to be a mass organization, but it was still noticeable that its numbers were growing: three hundred attended the revival congress in Quimper in 1873, and more than nine hundred were present at its meeting at Guingamp in 1875.[15] In 1887 it had 439 members. Almost a quarter (23.7 per cent) of its members were nobles. It also included two bishops, twenty-five other men with religious positions (priests, abbés and cathedral officials), seven senators and only two women. Its strength in the Côtes-du-Nord, where over a third of its membership lived, is unusual; this department was not noted for its contribution to Breton regionalism. This profile perhaps reflects the manner in which this organization was structured; it had successfully exploited familial links and networks among particular groups of the Breton nobility. These figures also suggest that the AB did have some limited success in drawing such groups, the 'natural rulers' of the countryside, into a regionalist stance.

The AB was not a political organization, and thus never attempted to articulate a coherent ideology – indeed, its members rehearsed the old arguments that they were enemies of all forms of politics.[16] Nonetheless, there was something of an intellectual and political renovation in its ranks. In particular, it began to construct a specific vision of Brittany, based on a renewal of the old conservative visions of the west as a patriarchal, rural utopia. Louis de Kerjégu spoke lyrically of the peasant family, headed by its active chief, who was involved in all its work, surrounded by his many children, his servants and his workers, and motivated by conservative common sense. This formed a fine model of stability, threatened only by 'magic lantern' empires and 'false, unhealthy' education.[17] The Baron de Jouvenel was pleased that there were no great factories in Brittany; it was a land of 'labourers and soldiers.'[18] The Marquis de l'Estourbeillon applauded the work of the AB in encouraging the Breton just to 'live his life, free from the countless transformations and travesties that so-called Modern Progress attempts to impose on him'.[19]

Decentralization was the means to prevent unwelcome change corrupting such idylls, and to preserve Brittany's unique contribution to French national life. As one speaker suggested, the role of the association was to teach Brittany's children 'to love and respect their mother's white hairs, to console her and prolong her noble old age'.[20] But this sentimental conservatism could, paradoxically, include a progressive dimension. To save the province, economic development was also needed.[21] AB speakers could even complain about the conservatism of the Breton peasant, who merely followed the ways of his father. The organization sponsored the technical innovation of Breton agriculture.[22] The proviso to such programmes was that, of course, they should be implemented within the traditional structures of social domination. While the AB was generally somewhat guarded about Villemarqué's Celticism, it did eventually encourage some research into Breton folk culture, and after 1900 it ran Breton-language poetry competitions.[23]

Despite its relatively small membership and the rather poor quality of its research, the AB was still an important organization. The first generation of Breton Celticists – people like Cambry, Brizeux and Souvestre – tended to be left-of-centre in their thinking and sympathetic to Republicanism.[24] While Villemarqué later emerged as the most significant thinker within their ranks, even his idiosyncratic Celtic Catholicism cannot be easily labelled 'right-wing' (see chapter 1). It is the AB which seized the opportunity presented by the Indian summer of monarchism to develop an assertion of Breton particularism as a clearly conservative creed. Significantly, it neither stressed the cultural importance of the Breton language, nor the Celtic characteristics of the Breton race, but instead based its arguments on a perception of Brittany as a conservative social model.

Faith and Brittany

A more original organization developed among Catholics in the Léon region of Finistère. From 1865 to 1884 a parish paper was printed in Breton, entitled *Feiz ha Breiz*, or 'Faith and Brittany'.[25] In May 1899 the journal was revived as a thirty-two page bi-monthly; by 1900 it had four hundred subscribers, and by 1912 a circulation of some seven thousand. After 1907, it was printed almost entirely in Breton.[26] In 1919 its circulation reached the figure of ten thousand – probably its peak. It then declined in the succeeding years, falling to fifteen hundred in 1939.[27] While nobles contributed to the journal's finance, it was the parish clergy who directed it.

While avoiding explicit political comments, *Feiz ha Breiz* warned about the dangers of emigration to the town, publicized the consequences of alcoholism, criticized immoral papers and books, and applauded the virtues of patience and restraint. It also encouraged modern hygienic practices. Under the editorship of abbé J.-M. Perrot, which began in 1907, *Feiz ha Breiz* began to move to a more clearly Breton-nationalist position, and created the Bleun-Brug [Flower of the Heather] organization. At its annual festivals, there were competitions in Breton-language singing and storytelling. Perrot called for: 'a Catholic, Breton, peasant and social Republic' – a stance which attracted the hostility of Monseigneur Dubillard, the bishop of Quimper.[28] The tension between the Church hierarchy and this radical initiative came to a head in the 1920s. In 1926 the new Quimper bishop, Monseigneur Duparc, demanded the right to censor the columns of *Feiz ha Breiz*. In 1927, he publicly condemned Bleun-Brug. Perrot backed down, accepting the bishop's criticisms, and *Feiz ha Breiz* turned away from nationalism.

This incident illustrates the uneasy relationship between the Catholic Church, the Breton language and *bretonnitude*. On the one hand, Catholics seemed to dominate Breton-language publishing: in 1912–13 there were only twelve Breton-language periodicals, all of which were either directly controlled by the Church or run by committed Catholics.[29] Many Catholics were concerned by the Republic's anticlerical record; they were therefore a ready audience for ideas concerning decentralization, and even for more radical, right-wing forms of opposition to the Republic. As Michel Lagrée notes, the Breton language could be seen as an instrument to protect the region from modernity: 'the language added, in an almost miraculous manner, a sort of cultural barrier, a *cordon sanitaire* against the successive assaults of modernity.'[30] On occasion, this could mean a defence of *bretonnitude* against the Republic. For example, at a public meeting in 1935, the abbé and deputy Jean-Marie Desgranges bitterly criticized those civil servants who came to

Brittany as if they were colonizers, and who considered Bretons as backward people.[31] But such moves were often marked by a deep political ambiguity. Was the region being defended because it was Breton or because it was Catholic? The official attitude of the Church hierarchy was essentially pragmatic: where the defence of Breton culture and Breton language could strengthen Catholic culture, then the Church would campaign on these issues. Where, however, such issues appeared to be lost causes, the Church was more likely to revert to its traditional role as a force of cultural modernity, and therefore of the 'Frenchification' of the region.[32]

The Union Régionaliste Bretonne

The Union Régionaliste Bretonne (URB) resembles the earlier Association bretonne. Constituted in 1899, it had 150 members in 1901, and 689 by 1911. Its social profile is revealing. Aristocrats dominated the URB's leadership. Some of its leading members realized the political problem set by this social composition: in a region where vague but increasingly strong anti-aristocratic sentiments were voiced, an aristocratic 'tone' could well discourage potential sympathizers. For example, Déguignet was swift to dismiss the URB as 'all nobles and priests'.[33] One solution was to ignore or deny political debate, and merely to claim that they campaigned for 'the reconstitution of Breton life, in all its forms'.[34] After all, argued the leading URB member Charles Le Goffic, one could be a regionalist and a conservative, a French nationalist, a progressive, a radical, a socialist or a libertarian. Regionalism was an 'open house', available to Bretons of all political persuasions.[35] More significant still, URB members would also repeat the old arguments that, worthy as they were, the Breton people were incapable of organizing themselves, because they were 'neurotics, a race of women, with no grasp on

Table 7.2 Social composition of the URB[36]

Social category	Percentage of members
Professions	20
Aristocracy	17
Clerics	11
Non-industrial middle class	8
Businessmen	2

reality'.³⁷ Such beliefs allowed URB members to sidestep any questions concerning any substantial appeal to the Breton people.

URB leaders attempted to resolve these contradictions by asking the prominent Breton Republican writer, Anatole Le Braz, to head the organization. His political position was ambiguous. In his previous works he had admired Brittany's Celtic religiosity, and applauded attempts to rediscover 'the old France' in the heart of the countryside: such research was worth more than the modernity represented by the Eiffel Tower.³⁸ On the other hand, he had sided with the plebeian Republican Luzel when Luzel criticized the aristocratic Villemarqué in the tempestuous arguments concerning the authenticity of the *Barzaz Breiz*,³⁹ and in 1903 he expressed his sympathy for the unemployed and the starving who marched in the streets of Brest and Nantes.⁴⁰ His speech at its inaugural congress in August 1899 spoke of the need to 'resist the invasion' of centralization, a 'Roman' tradition, but explained that this proposal was not anti-French in character. After all, what real benefit was there to France in 'de-Bretonizing' Brittany? Le Braz ended his short speech by proclaiming that the URB was not a 'retrograde' enterprise; its goal was to awaken the soul of Brittany from its sleep, and to lead it to its resurrection.⁴¹

Le Braz's words briefly gave the conservative URB a progressive image. The contradiction between Le Braz's brand of patriotic–Republican Breton regionalism and the more backward-looking creed of the URB nobles, however, was too great for it to survive. Le Braz resigned in 1902, and was replaced by the thoroughly conservative Marquis de l'Estourbeillon de la Garnache, who remained president of the URB until its final collapse in 1946. From 1906 onwards the annual URB congresses began with a Catholic mass: a gesture which was sufficient to stop any further involvement by Breton Republicans. The organization worked in the same manner as the older AB: it avoided mass politics and mass mobilizations, and instead attempted to build a network of similarly-minded elites. Its annual congresses provided its principal public presence: each was centred on the formal parade of the URB leaders and local notables through the town hosting the congress, often dressed in allegedly 'traditional' dress which, with each year, came to resemble more and more an upper-class fancy dress competition.

Nonetheless, some interesting voices emerged from within the URB, which was never as solidly conservative and simply backward-looking as the AB had been. It was instrumental in linking *bretonnitude* with neo-druidism, a practice imported from Wales. A URB delegation attended the Eisteddfod at Cardiff in 1899, although the cause then became more divisive in the increasingly Catholic URB after 1908.⁴² In particular, the URB had some real contacts with modernizing artists. A new generation was attempting to reformulate and transform the traditions of folk art into a more modernist, developed cultural practice.[43] Thus Batillat spoke at its 1928 congress about regional architecture, arguing that 'Brittany can no longer be the land of the Past: its creed must be the Future.'[44] Through this channel, new images of Brittany began to circulate across France. Fred Orton and Griselda Pollock make some interesting comments on this rapid transformation of artists' paintings into tourists' clichés: 'It is probable that part of the appeal of Brittany for tourists was precisely that there was a leisured, wealthy, socially acceptable peasantry which was not too strange, not too other.'[45] The Breton delegation to the Regional Centre at the 1937 Exposition in Paris owed something to this inspiration, for the wave of 1930s regionalism, with its anti-Americanism, anti-industrial and artisanal values, was clearly compatible with the URB's version of Breton values.[46]

However, alongside these interesting initiatives and links, the dominant tone of the URB was clearly conservative. L'Estourbeillon invoked the need to defend fifteen centuries of history, and called for an 'unceasing struggle' to conserve the identity, traditions and language of Brittany.[47] Even in the 1920s, the URB still repeated the older arguments that a stronger Breton-regional culture would strengthen, not weaken, the French nation.[48]

The AB, *Feiz ha Breiz* and the URB are perhaps best seen as political experiments. They show that alongside the militant Catholicism of the FNC (see chapter 4), there was the potential for local resentments and protests to be expressed through the language of *bretonnitude*. But in all three cases, the limitations of such initiatives are also obvious: the AB and URB were tiny groups of regionalist nobles could not extend their hegemony among forward-looking, Republican Bretons, while *Feiz ha Breiz* was constrained by the need *not* to confront or contradict the official guidance given by Church leaders.

Other voices: Republicanism and socialism in Brittany: Emile Masson

Outside of the ranks of monarchist aristocrats and Catholic peasants, another Brittany was emerging. As was seen in chapter 5, there was a network of Republicans, social reformists and utopians in early nineteenth-century Brittany. However, none of these was able to lead a real social movement. Significantly, the revolt of the Paris Commune (1871) barely caused a flicker of sympathy in Brittany.[49] But, despite the vigour with which conservative and

Catholic structures attempted to limit or to direct modernization, there were areas which escaped their control. For some conservatives this was merely a cause for regret. In 1897 *De toute son âme* (With all her Soul) was published by the noted conservative novelist, René Bazin. The novel concerned the fate of young, innocent Bretons from Auray or Quimper who suffer 'the corruption of the factories' in the urban, industrial context of Nantes.[50] Any working-class interest in ideas of socialism or Republicanism was seen by Bazin as simply proof of the corruption of these gullible, rural people. Nevertheless, left-wing political cultures began to gain some significant local support in early twentieth-century Brittany. Michel Lagrée notes how working-class protests prevented Catholic processions from marching through the new industrial towns of Saint-Nazaire and Brest in 1901.[51] Socialist groups were formed in Rennes in 1876, in Nantes in 1880 and in Brest in 1883; between 1900 and 1909 they were followed by the creation of seven Bourses de Travail (Trades Councils: centres for trade union organization).[52] In 1909, the newly formed working-class suburb of Caudan, near Lorient in the Morbihan, voted in Brittany's first socialist town council.[53] The elections of May and June 1936 suggested some substantial growth in Breton socialism: eight of the region's forty-four deputies were socialists and six were Radicals who, at that moment, were allied to the socialists in the coalition of the Popular Front.[54] Few Breton workers joined the massive strike wave of June 1936, but some in the sardine processing factories went on strike in September 1936.[55]

Louis Guilloux wrote a touching, observant, semi-autobiographical novella concerning the first, idealistic working-class socialists in Saint-Brieuc in the early twentieth century. The town was dominated by 'businessmen and nobles' who were linked by their families, forming a vast 'feudal clan'.[56] When the socialists attempt to constitute a branch of the new socialist party, one comments that the party seems too Parisian: 'it will never do anything in a land like ours, in which it is so difficult to be a socialist'.[57]

This, then, was the problem for the Breton left in the early twentieth century: to assert a Breton culture or identity seemed to imply resistance to modernity, but to accept modernity seemed to mean reducing Breton culture to a mere folklore.

For some left-wing militants, the solution was to accept French modernity as the best manner in which to eradicate conservative and clerical attitudes from the region. The short-lived 'Bleus de Bretagne' organization was the clearest expression of this tendency. For its leader, Yves Le Febvre, the Breton cause was simply reactionary: leftists should join with Republicans of all varieties in opposing the rule of the clergy and the nobles. His *La Pensée bretonne* monthly, while fully situated in Brittany, propagated anticlerical and anti-separatist themes in the years before the First World War.[58] On the other hand, there were other Breton leftists who found it difficult to follow Le Febvre. The most articulate of these was Emile Masson (1869–1923), truly one of the lost intellectuals of Breton political culture.[59] We will now turn to consider his thought in more details.

Masson's espousal of the Breton cause was not clear-cut. Following a severe medical and psychological crisis in 1909–11, Masson committed himself to Brittany. However, in the years which followed he was a member of both the left-of-centre, regionalist Fédédération Régionaliste de Bretagne (FRB – a small split from the URB), and the tiny nationalist Parti Nationaliste Breton (PNB). At the same time he contributed articles to the left-wing, anti-regionalist *La Pensée bretonne*. Masson's thinking is certainly a 'moving target': he was influenced and motivated by a variety of currents during his lifetime. Rather than attempting to force the political views of this pronounced pragmatist into coherence, it may make more sense to accept his pragmatism and attempt to understand him through his political tactics.

Masson was suspicious of all forms of political organization. His most pointed comment about this appears in a private letter during the First World War, in which he declares that 'love alone: love, love, love! That is the supreme organization.'[60] Such comments suggest the manner in which Masson interpreted Tolstoy's teaching. This letter is not some chance reference; even in his previously published work in Grave's anarcho-syndicalist periodical *Temps nouveaux*, Masson writes of his contempt for 'the herd', and uses such sub-Nietzscheian themes as a justification for his reluctance to take up syndicalism.[61] Moreover, Masson was fiercely idealistic. In 1913 he defined revolution as 'becoming aware of beauty' – hardly an orthodox position among the tough-minded anarcho-syndicalists of the early 1900s.[62] Masson argued that socialism was more than an economic doctrine, it was something to be felt in the heart.[63] While Masson could follow the anarcho-syndicalist CGT into anti-militarism, he was less inspired by their concentration on the economic, and frankly alienated by their contempt for the spiritual.

The great cause which Masson eventually championed was that of the Breton language. Significantly, he produced at least three different arguments to attempt to persuade the readers of Grave's *Temps nouveaux* and wider leftist circles in Brittany of the validity of this campaign in general, and the publication of left-leaning Breton-language periodical – *Brug* – aimed at the Breton peasantry.

(a) the first was a simple pragmatic argument. The rural proletariat speaks Breton. The church and the priests speak to them in Breton and write for them in Breton. If socialists fail to do the same, they will never reach the rural masses;
(b) when addressing Breton regionalist and nationalist circles, Masson rehearses a more principled argument, based on the idea that the Breton language was some sort of repository of wisdom; that it was the backbone of a tradition or 'the soul of the people'.[64] This led Masson to take a position directly in contradiction with the centralizing 'Jacobin' tendencies of the Third Republic;
(c) there was also a third argument. Masson was an individualist, in the true sense of the word, not in the Thatcherite sense of each person assessing their life as if it were a small business and applying concepts of profit and loss to their daily interactions. He was an individualist in the Tolstoyean and, perhaps, the Stirnerite sense: he believed that at the heart of any significant political movement was the full development of each individual personality. This explains his antipathy to 'the herd'. Applying this logic to the Brittany of the Third Republic, Masson argued that the Breton language and culture were integral parts of the personality of the Breton peasant. He saw in these practices elements of 'autogestion': 'Every Breton is a poet and a musician.'[65] It was through the flowering of this culture that Brittany could become internationalist and even universal. In other words, Masson's 'socialism' was applied firstly to the cultural sphere. From this insight, there then flowed his ideas about cooperatives, leagues and free schools – institutions which certainly sketch out the foundations of a cooperative economy.

The apparent contradictions in Masson's thinking can be explained by reference to his political values. His first priority was that of a leftist: he therefore supported Le Febvre and *la Pensée bretonne* in their Republican campaigns to break the aristocratic domination of the region. On the other hand, his ideal of a liberated Brittany was based on his faith in the native abilities of the Bretons themselves – hence his defence of the Breton language and culture.[66]

After the war: the formation of Breiz Atao

During August 1914, normal political life ended in Brittany. Catholic, Republican and socialist organizations closed, one by one, as their best militants were drafted to fight at the front.[67] For those who remained in Brittany, the war brought massive social disruption.[68] Masson was horrified by the arrival of the first convoy of wounded soldiers at the end of August 1914. His secondary school was converted into a temporary hospital. Throughout the rest of the war, he served as a volunteer nurse. The ever-growing number of casualties caused him to become deeply depressed: his only relief was in the reading of Tolstoy. After the war, he was a broken man.

The number of Bretons killed in the conflict remains a subject of intense debate: Roger Dupuy suggests that there may have been as many as one hundred and twenty thousand deaths.[69] It seems quite possible that the men of rural Brittany suffered more severely than other groups in French society. Among some Breton conscripts there was growing awareness that this conflict marked the end of an era, and that the relationship between France and Brittany would permanently change.[70]

The long-term socio-cultural effects of the war are registered with a lyrical intensity, almost as folk legends, in the pages of Hélias's *Cheval d'Orgueil*. His thoughts on this important matter are well worth quoting at length.

> There was another reason why our parents wanted so strongly that we should learn the [French] language of the bourgeois ... This was that they themselves were humiliated by their ignorance of French. Each time they had to deal with an official, each time they went into the city, they were picked on. They were called hay-pickers, for example ... Or worse still, they had to put up with a patronizing charity. Sometimes people just told them to go to the Devil if they couldn't learn to speak like Christians. During their military service they were insulted. The illiterate amongst them had to give a few pennies to some minor officer who would agree to write their news to their families. God knows how this public letter-writer interpreted the feelings of these poor fellows: usually all he bothered to do was to write out the same phrases for each one. When some of them dared to form, with difficulty, a few words in French they were greeted with roars of laughter from the 'Parisians'. Because of this linguistic imperialism, the Breton-speakers were seen as stupid ... What could they do? After four years of war and after having mixed with comrades who could more or less speak French, they learnt to act. From the colonel's orders they took a few phrases that sounded as if they came from the [fashionable, Parisian] quarter of Saint-Germain: 'I beg you to do me the honour of accepting my greetings' they would say to the tax-collector, who could hardly believe his ears. Others were infected by the Parisian accent, and took to mixing their Breton phrases with words like *chic alors* [that's nice] or *épatant* [splendid], following the time-honoured tradition by which a speaker who mixed French words into Breton phrases gained more respect for himself. For the Breton-speakers, the 'Parisian' was

someone who was at once admired and feared: admired for his confidence, his easy speech and quick wits, but feared for his cheekiness, and his jokes which left their jaws hanging ... The Breton-speakers were miserly and slow with their words ... They seemed stupid in the eyes of the city-dwellers, which didn't really matter, but they also seemed stupid in their own eyes, which was more important. To make things worse, the children of our land [pays] who went to Paris to earn their bread during the war of 1914 soon came to hate their own language, which seemed a symbol of poverty and ignorance, and which seemed to invite insults. They even came to curse their own parents for bequeathing them an inheritance which seemed worse than a physical deformity.[71]

Hélias's evocation of the effects of war-time military service is a powerful and thought-provoking passage, neatly capturing the sense of cultural inferiority which Bretons often felt when they met Parisians and other French speakers.[72] He suggests that the war functioned almost as a compulsory crash-course in French civilization. It drew previously marginalized Catholics and conservatives into the French nationalist-inspired war-time coalition of the Union Sacrée, and forced Breton peasants and artisans to begin to think of themselves as French.

A second, compelling account of the effects of war is provided in a more indirect, allusive form by *La Brière*, a novel published in 1923 by Alphonse de Chateaubriant (1877–1951). This work makes no direct comment about the war: it appears to be set at some point in the late nineteenth century. But its themes show all the signs of a post-war narrative.[73] It is a grim story, punctuated by violence, set in the Brière marshlands to the west of Nantes. The book joins two parallel narratives, concerning Aoustin, a forest guard and peat-cutter. Aoustin's life is threatened by two forces: first a big agricultural enterprise wants to buy up the Brière marshes with the government's support. To stop this venture, Aoustin is required to find a copy of the original contract giving the local inhabitants the right to exploit their land, granted by Louis XVI in 1784. Secondly, following his condemnation of his son's marriage, Aoustin is now challenged by his daughter, who has also chosen a partner he finds unacceptable. The post-war context of the text becomes more evident when, following an attack, Aoustin's left hand is amputated, and he is forced to confront the hostility of his old friends and neighbours. The key theme in the text is of a legitimate, traditional authority threatened by betrayal from above and rebellion from below. Much of the novel concerns Aoustin's boat journeys through the narrow rivulets of the maze-like marsh landscape: a metaphor for the complexity and confusion of the quests which face him.

La Brière is an important work as it suggests a different interpretation of the 'authenticity' evoked in previous works on Brittany. In contrast to the images of a harmonious, peaceful society, *La Brière* locates the region's authenticity in a tough, marginalized individual, fighting a losing battle.[74]

It was in this new, strange, post-war context, with its evident tensions and challenges, that *Breiz Atao* was born. Like the other new movements of the post-war world – fascism, communism – it was 'produced in the trenches', inspired by the Dublin Easter Rising and 'a new spirit'.[75] One later publication included the revealing line that the organization was intended to form a 'Union sacrée' of all Bretons: an indication of the lasting importance of the war-time experience on these nationalists.[76]

Breiz Atao's origins lie in a small group of young students (all under 20) who created the Groupe Régionaliste Breton in Rennes in September 1918.[77] Most of them came from right-wing families; many had a connection with Maurras's proto-fascist Action française. The first edition of their journal, *Breiz Atao*, was published in January 1919. From their initial praise for nineteenth-century Breton novelists and writers, the group moved on to adopt a characteristically violent, radical tone, unsparing in its criticisms of the URB and of the secular, centrist split from the URB, the Fédération Régionaliste Bretonne. In 1920 it declared its support for autonomy, and from August 1921 the journal carried the subheading 'The Breton Nation'. From its origins, one can note a mismatch between the region's problems and *Breiz Atao's* concerns. The economic problems associated with reconstruction soon resulted in a relative decline of wages and prices in Brittany, which in turn provoked the emigration of more than a fifth of a million people from the region during the 1920s. Meanwhile, *Breiz Atao* published articles on Breton history, language and literature, and engaged in debates on the region's Celtic identity.

Breiz Atao first came to public notice through the political crisis concerning the eastern French provinces of Alsace-Lorraine. Seized by the victorious Germans in 1871, this area had been returned to France in 1918. Integration into the French polity, however, was not an easy process. One obvious sticking point was that the territory of Alsace-Lorraine had not been covered by the important legislation of 1905, establishing the separation of the church and state in France. A small but lively autonomist current developed in the east, demanding an exemption from the 1905 law, and also raising other questions about the nature of the French state's centralizing political culture. *Breiz Atao* was one of the few public supporters of the autonomists' campaigns during 1927. Inspired by the example of the Alsatian militants, the *Breiz Atao* team sponsored the formation of the Parti Autonomiste Breton (PAB) in 1927. A political and financial crisis shook this organization in 1930–1. The PAB was then reformed as the Parti National Breton (PNB) in 1931; it gradually became obvious that this formation was moving toward the right. A left-leaning rival, the Ligue Fédéraliste Breton (LFB) competed with the PNB from 1931 to 1935, but failed to gain sufficient members to form a significant political force. In the late 1930s the PNB became marked by an ever-increasing fascination with fascist rituals and politics.

Keeping track of the totality of currents, schisms and movements within the broader context of Breton autonomist and nationalist politics in the inter-war years is a complex task. Rather than exhausting readers with the details of these often tiny groups, this chapter aims to identify a few broad themes. For this reason, I follow contemporary observers in using the term *Breiz Atao* to identify the whole constellation of inter-war autonomist, proto-nationalist and nationalist movements.[78]

Breiz Atao: a nationalist ideology

Contemporary observers were shocked by *Breiz Atao's* verbal violence, which certainly made a dramatic contrast with the romantic nostalgia of older groups such as the URB. *Breiz Atao's* rhetoric marked a real shift in identity politics in Brittany. In their early pamphlets one could read phrases such as: 'All our trials have one cause: a malign, foreign domination', or that France had reduced Breton men to stone-breakers and Breton women to prostitutes.[79] For the French, Brittany was merely a military–strategic zone or a colony to exploit.[80] French schools worked to kill all Breton-national character in young Bretons,[81] and France was blind and deaf to the Bretons' legitimate demands.[82] Another typical *Breiz Atao* publication declared that French domination would create a nation of degenerates in Brittany, people who had no true knowledge of where they were born or where they lived: 'You are just idiots, fools, traitors and you will decay!' Instead, Bretons had to wake up to the truth: they needed to choose between 'on the one hand, a rotten Brittany ... and on the other, regenerated Brittany! ... Will you be one of those who stay strong and healthy, [who form] the superior race?'[83] Within such phrases there was a powerful sense of disgust with a false Breton identity that had been foisted on the Bretons. Such feelings were eloquently captured in a manifesto for *Gwalarn*, a Breton-language literary and cultural review linked to *Breiz Atao*. This described *Breiz Atao* as 'the rational, violent reaction by educated youth against the outdated fashions and the fake ruralism celebrated by the regionalists: a reaction against the tawdry, the clichéd, against twaddle, against flat and naïve propaganda'.[84]

Breiz Atao attempted to replace the older nostalgic stereotypes. These young nationalists saw Brittany as 'a spiritual community',[85] or as 'a homogenous human family, a traditional economic organism and a natural country'. Their aim was to draw out 'an exclusive Breton national feeling' from this land:

> In this age when the world has been invaded by a brutalizing mechanization, ruined by the unleashing of egotistical appetites and conquered by money, and [yet] aspires to a moral redressment, how wrong it would be to deny one of the last sources of spirituality in Europe. [86]

Perhaps, predictably, identifying the exact characteristics of this Breton identity proved difficult. *Breiz Atao's* inflammatory anti-French rhetoric served to differentiate the Breton from the French, but it still left open the question of what constituted *bretonnitude*. At times, *Breiz Atao* answered this point by following Villemarqué's arguments, defining Brittany as essentially Celtic: the Bretons were a race faithful to their roots while France had denied its Gallic past.[87] Elsewhere, one finds a type of humanism: 'Against anonymous, heartless, gutless organizations, we represent *the living people*.'[88] A PNB manifesto from 1938 struck a similar tone: 'We do not want to disappear by fusion with the undifferentiated mass of French people. We want to stay ourselves: we want to become more Breton and better Bretons than those before us.'[89] *Bretonnitude* is frequently defined as the living, organic, or natural, against the bureaucratic, artificial and mechanical political culture imposed by the French.

Placing *Breiz Atao's* political culture into the more orthodox categories of right and left is a difficult task. Many contemporaries, particularly Republican officials, almost automatically assumed that the group was right-wing and conservative. While there is some justification for such analyses, it must be noted that the voice of *Breiz Atao* was distinctively different from previous nostalgic conservatisms. This new team felt no 'regret for the past';[90] they were an organization of 'new men',[91] disappointed that there was nothing modern in Brittany.[92] One PAB declaration stated 'The old Brittany of our kings and dukes is gone forever ... We do not look towards the past, but towards the future. We are modern Bretons.'[93] The same declaration called for a Breton artistic and cultural renaissance. Another PNB text stressed the theme of youth in a revealing manner. The peace established in 1919 had been an opportunity to create a new order, but European leaders had not proved capable of seizing their chance. Therefore, 'it is we young people who will take charge.'[94] We can read in these words some indication of the continuing importance of the legacy of the First World War into the 1930s.

Shifting the terms of our analysis slightly, one can find a striking illustration of the political values of Olier Mordrel, an architect and a leading militant in *Breiz Atao*, in his architectural work. While the inter-war years saw the burgeoning of neo-rural styles, referring back to some traditional features of Breton design, Mordrel's most prestigious project was the dramatic 'Ty Kodaks', a camera and photography shop, in Quimper. This was an austere, streamlined neo-classical building, free of ornamentation, very different from any traditional Breton design, and resembling the contemporary 'International Style' of architecture.[95]

Breiz Atao's publications tended to evade direct questions concerning their preference for right-wing or left-wing political philosophies. The official line was often: 'na ruz, na gwenn, Breizhad hepken' – neither red, nor white: Breton above all.[96] Such themes were obviously used to encourage a sense of political unity within the organization, which, on occasion, could proudly point out how its support stretched from the old Action française families to the Communist dissidents, led by Maurice Duhamel.[97] Morvan Marchal's description of those attending the PAB's founding congress in 1927 is revealing:

> Most extraordinary of all is the absolute unity of opinions, the real spiritual communion of all these men. Divided by their education, their social condition, even by their language, we saw them fraternally united by the same thoughts, the same doctrine.[98]

At the congress, they were 'nothing but Bretons'. Through an ethic of unity, the 'Breton people would be cemented into a single fighting bloc'.[99] G. Mazéas, who stood as the PAB's one parliamentary candidate in 1930, made use of a similar formula: he told voters that he was 'a Breton candidate, and nothing but a Breton'.[100] In the same vein, the later PNB refused to choose between democracy, dictatorship, Republic or monarchy.[101]

With the deepening economic crisis of the 1930s, however, the PAB was almost forced to address issues of economic policy. In many respects, their solutions were unoriginal. Like a wide range of independent political commentators in the 1930s, they were critical of market-orientated capitalism, and fascinated by corporative schemas.[102] An article written in 1930 by Debauvais proposed a form of corporatism as a means to encourage Breton producers to cooperate, and therefore to modernize and rationalize production.[103] The controversial 'Saga' programme (1933), which never became official PNB policy, clearly drew inspiration from Italian fascist and German Nazi programmes. Its concept of corporatism included the abolition of 'usury' and the slavery of interest, and proposed the transformation of private property into a social function.[104]

It was clear, however, that even these brief discussions of socio-economic themes were often merely vehicles for the political issues which *Breiz Atao* took more seriously. Thus discussions of corporatist projects were linked to the older accusation that the French state favoured 'the southern vine-growers' over Breton producers.[105] Mazéas's electoral manifesto echoed this theme: 'Brittany is in danger of being ruined by party politics, which profits this regime's favourites: the parasitic peoples of the south, and the big industrialists of the North-East.'[106] Such phrases suggested a type of return to old-style regional lobbying – with the important qualification that *Breiz Atao's* solution was some form of regional autonomy.

During the 1930s, a distinctly racist tone began to develop in *Breiz Atao's* writing which, while it was never official or explicit party policy, certainly reveals something of the group's mentality. Firstly, one can find ambiguous phrases such as: 'We're fed up with being treated worse than blacks.'[107] It is possible to read this as a misphrased expression of sympathy for black people, and – in line with this thought – it should be stressed that *Breiz Atao* often supported anticolonial struggles. An eloquent article from 1936 denounced the French record in Algeria, and implored Bretons not to visit the colony: 'You also belong to an oppressed people: do not help France to oppress another.'[108]

Breiz Atao's most substantial treatment of racism, however, came in its discussions of Breton ethnic identity. In the first place, this could take the form of a simple assertion of Celtic identity: 'The Celtic spirit [génie] will be reborn, freed from French lies, and revived through direct contacts with other peoples.'[109] Such phrases are, in themselves, relatively innocent and may well have been deliberately constructed in such a way to leave unclear whether a racist meaning was intended. In some texts, they were joined to a pronounced 'anti-Latin' rhetoric. Such themes revived older ideas about the enmity between Celts and Romans: what is telling is that they were not presented as a clash between two separate political traditions, but that they were often seen in moralistic terms. A PAB declaration from 1929 stated that its aims were:

> to encourage the renaissance of our traditional arts and the development of a healthy national literature, as close as possible to our nordic, western tradition, and as distant as possible from Latin smut, which is exemplified in the poison of the novel, the song, the theatre and the Parisian paper.[110]

The controversial 'Saga' programme was brutally clear on this point: in an independent Brittany, 'Latins' and coloured people would be excluded, Nordic people accepted.[111]

Such thinking also clearly influenced *Breiz Atao*'s treatment of foreign policy. Having previously celebrated the rise of small, vigorous nations, such as Catalonia, in September 1938 *Breiz Atao* announced that it accepted the German invasion of Czechoslovakia. Indeed, it admired Germany's patience, for 'the Czech people do not exist'. Those who felt any sympathy for Czechs had been fooled by French lies: 'France has lied to us with its talk of its "Democratic Front", uniting Wall Street capitalists with Moscow's butchers, whose only link is the desire for revenge felt by those Jews who have been expelled from Germany.'[112]

Turning from the issue of racism and ethnic identity to the question of the relationship of the party to the mass of the people it claimed to represent, we can find a similar evolution in *Breiz Atao*'s political culture. In 1932, the newly formed PNB still spoke in terms of a 'mass politics' for the whole of the Breton people.[113] The left-leaning FLB was even more forthright, issuing a leftist appeal to Breton peasants to fight against the big farmers.[114] But, through force of circumstance, the PNB was led to produce ever less convincing justifications for the guidance of this putative nation by 'an audacious minority'.[115] Mordrel discussed this issue in his memoirs. How was the Breton nation to be represented? 'The guardians of nationhood are those who are conscious of it. They alone count. The others are excluded from the debate. It was for the patriots, and for them alone, to decide how Brittany should face the events which called her existence into question.' He defended the right of an elite, 'the best', to represent 'the inert mass'.[116] His rival, the sinister Célestin Lainé, issued an appeal for a warrior ethic to guide *Breiz Atao* militants.[117] While Lainé's influence within *Breiz Atao* circles was minimal in the 1930s, it appears that his solution to the organization's failure to recruit a larger proportion of the Breton masses was to adopt a militaristic, even a terrorist strategy, inspired by his romanticized image of the Easter rising in Dublin.[118] Bomb attacks on public buildings and monuments in 1932, 1938 and 1939 were probably organized by Lainé.

The issues which have just been raised – the fascination with fascist corporatism, the use of racist concepts, the justifications of guidance by an elite – suggest that, like many other fringe political groups in France, *Breiz Atao* was loosely inspired by the model of fascism.[119] Before reaching a conclusion, however, we should note one further development in *Breiz Atao*'s evolution. Alongside *Breiz Atao*'s cult of youth, alongside the uncompromising radicalism apparently offered by fascism, another influence can be detected. The 'Saga' programme condemned the evil influences of books, papers, theatre, art and cinema.[120] In 1938, the PNB criticized the 'great modern forces of propaganda' available to the French state.[121] Such a statement suggests a type of 'return to source'. *Breiz Atao* was targeting the classic hate-figures of the old conservative right: the mass culture of modernity.

Breiz Atao: in search of a nationalist practice

The ideas put forward by *Breiz Atao* certainly mark a turning-point in Breton political culture. Evidence of the shock-wave their publications caused is plentiful; for example, the veteran Republican anticlerical Yves Le Febvre spoke of his shame in having to write of the 'violent outrages' of these 'young polemicists', and his friend Léon Dubreuil noted their 'cynical audacity'.[122] When the small groups of *Breiz Atao* paper-sellers arrived at *pardons* and festivals, they often found that even the word 'autonomy' terrified people.[123] Similar doubts came from older, Catholic, regionalist circles. *Feiz ha Breiz's* discussion of the 1920 manifesto of *Kornog* [West], a cultural review loosely linked to *Breiz Atao,* is a telling indication of conservative worries. *Kornog's* manifesto, in characteristic *Breiz Atao* style, promised readers that it would defend 'furiously modern' artistic concepts. This drew the following response from *Feiz ha Breiz*: 'This phrase has worried us ... One must be modern, but why "furiously"? Why not reasonably? The company of a reasonable man is always more pleasant than that of a furious man, and this is also true for reviews!'[124]

There is, however, a far more significant point to make about *Breiz Atao's* influence: beyond the raised eyebrows of a few Republican and conservative dignitaries, very few people ever noticed its existence. Hélias's memoirs are revealing on this point. At the moment of the 1932 *attentat*, Hélias was living in Rennes, and was a young Breton-speaking student almost consciously looking for a political cause to follow. He felt almost no connection with the nationalist movement; it was 'old hat'. He never read either *Breiz Atao* or the Breton language review, *Gwalarn*; neither seemed relevant to what he considered 'the real situation'.[125] More provocatively still, Hélias records that, in 1932, the big political issue which gripped his circle of students was the shock caused by a theatrical version of Le Febvre's anticlerical novel, *La Terre des prêtres*.

The records of the prefectoral administration reinforce this impression of *Breiz Atao*'s marginality. At several points during the interwar period, officials were asked to estimate the group's potential political influence. Throughout the two decades their replies were quite consistent:

'"Separatism" does not exist in the Morbihan, and *Breiz Atao* does not have the slightest influence.'[126]

[*Breiz Atao* is a] 'bad joke'.[127]

'*Breiz Atao* is more or less without importance or influence.'[128]

'In Rennes, the separatist movement has no influence, and is unnoticed. The group shows no signs of life: it does not organize public meetings or demonstrations.'[129]

'Properly speaking, there is no autonomist movement in the Ille-et-Vilaine ... There are a handful of fanatics and agitators in Rennes.'[130]

Still more telling is *Breiz Atao*'s frequent *absence* from the many lists of the political suspects and dangerous agitators identified by police officials during the 1930s. The conclusion is obvious: while the French administration certainly disapproved of the new nationalist movement, they never saw them as a serious political threat.

Given this situation, it is not surprising that officials spent little time in trying to analyse the movement. Their comments are usually dismissive, merely characterizing the protestors as Chouans or *hobereaux*. Some officials linked these observations to vague generalizations about the closed, taciturn, Celtic character of the Breton.[131] One isolated comment notes the movement's ability to draw in some communists, but does not explore the implications of this observation in any depth.[132] In 1935, in an attempt to gauge the movement's strengths, a Rennes police official drew up the following estimates of *Breiz Atao*'s circulation (see Table 7.4).

These figures show that the single biggest market for this Breton nationalist movement was actually in Paris, usually among migrants from the region. The centre of the movement remained Rennes, where it was supported principally among students. It is, however, significant that *Breiz Atao* had won some support in Finistère, usually from lower middle-class Breton speakers. These three strands can be seen as making up *Breiz Atao*'s core support: with the heavy qualification that in none of these three areas had the journal acquired anything like the adhesion of the majority. The movement grew further in the late 1930s, possibly as part of a right-wing reaction to the election of the

Table 7.4 Estimates of sales of *Breiz Atao* in 1935[133]

Area	Subscribers	Sales	Unsold	Circulation
Abroad	94			94
Ille-et-Vilaine	70	480	240	550
Côtes-du-Nord	50	150	75	200
Finistère	200	450	225	650
Morbihan	60	200	100	260
Loire-Inférieure	40	150	70	190
Paris	73	700	250	773
Seine-et-Oise	20			20
France		250		250
Totals	607	2,380	960	2,987

left-reformist Popular Front government of 1936. Déniel cites estimates that there may have been some six thousand PNB members and twenty thousand *Breiz Atao* readers in 1938, but acknowledges that these figures should be treated as generous 'maximum' estimates.[134]

Breiz Atao's electoral record confirms our impression that this was a small group with little influence. Mazéas stood as a 'Republican Federalist' candidate in a by-election in Guingamp (Côtes-du-Nord) in April 1930. Ten thousand francs were spent in support of his campaign, and twenty thousand free copies of *Breiz Atao* distributed: this expenditure contributed significantly to the bankruptcy of the PAB in the succeeding year.[135] Mazéas only won 349 votes out of a possible 13,872. Two further candidatures – in 1931 and 1932 – won higher proportions of the votes, but without achieving the elections of the candidates.[136]

Another protest: Dorgères and the Greenshirts

Before reaching any conclusion concerning *Breiz Atao*'s minimal political influence, let us briefly consider another radical protest movement which developed in Brittany, which presents us with a contrasting perspective on Breton political cultures.

During the late 1920s and early 1930s the price of basic agricultural produce dropped alarmingly. From a post-war peak of 198 francs per quintal in 1926, wheat was selling at 147 francs by 1930.[137] The most evident sign of the consequent economic crisis in peasant society was the spread of forced sales, as bailiffs seized peasant-farmers' goods and possessions, and put them on auction. These common tragedies marked rural politics with a new sense of urgency, to which the established conservative corporative structures were not able to respond. After all, what could conservatives propose as a solution to declining prices? Subsidies by the state would have given the secular Republic too much power within rural societies, and price-fixing suggested communism. The established organizations searched for policies which would allow state assistance to rural families without permitting state interference.[138] Meanwhile, agrarian political culture was marked by an angry populism which sought an easy enemy to blame for the plight of rural society. One flashpoint was the 1930 extension of the 1928 Loucheur law, which provided social security for workers. Having been applied in an industrial context, it was now extended to agriculture, producing immediate fury among small farmers – following years of declining prices, they were now being asked to contribute to a social security scheme from which they were unlikely to benefit. Hatred of the urban worker, who was cocooned and cushioned by a distant, alien state, marked a series of demonstrations. Some twelve thousand farmers gathered for a protest meeting in Vannes in December 1928, at which they were addressed by a fiery new journalist: Henry Dorgères.[139]

In 1933 he created a network of Comités de Défense paysanne, whose main public presence was in aggressive, sometimes violent, protests against forced sales of peasant property. These organizations attracted approximately thirty thousand members in 1934 across France, and maybe half a million members by 1938.[140] By 1935, their militants began to adopt green as a distinguishing colour. The two strongholds of these committees were among the big 'industrial' farmers of northern France, and among the independent, family farmers of the west. Their patterns of militancy form a clear contrast with those of *Breiz Atao*. Greenshirt militancy was never centred on the written word, but on provocative, angry speeches and clashes with the police.

Dorgères warned about the sinister rise of rural socialism, based on an evil coalition of the officials of the state-run Wheat Office, the secular schoolteacher and the socialist agitator.[141] Instead of arguing among themselves, rural people should unite to fight their true enemies; landowners should help tenants, for they had the same interests, and thus a vast Rural Front could be created.[142] The old men were without ideals: the young should rally to the energetic Greenshirts, in which they would learn to 'believe, obey and serve'.[143] Predictably, Dorgères always denied that he was a fascist, but the close similarities between his movement and the new movements of the far right are obvious.[144]

How does this movement compare with *Breiz Atao*? Perhaps the most significant difference is in their numbers: even allowing for Dorgères's inevitable over-estimation of the support gained by his organization, it is clear that the themes which he articulated had a real resonance in many Breton villages. Why did the Greenshirts gain this mass support, while *Breiz Atao* was left with a few thousand subscribers? The simple answer must be that Dorgères's rhetoric was addressed to what many felt were the most vital issues of their day, while even Breton speakers were sceptical about the analyses offered in the columns of *Breiz Atao*. There is a bizarre paradox here: both groups proposed forms of non-statist corporatism as panaceas for all economic problems. Yet the Greenshirts managed to articulate this myth in a form with which Breton farmers could identify, while *Breiz Atao's* pronouncements appeared offbeat and obscure.

Some of *Breiz Atao's* intuitions, however, were correct. There was a common Breton resentment of Parisian rule, and – in the context of a widespread rural economic crisis – this cannot be dismissed as the expression of some arcane, irrational prejudice. Indeed, it is possible to compare the ideals of Breton nationalism with the cultural struggles associated with the processes of de-colonization and the establishment of a 'post-colonial' culture.[145] But the political concepts on which *Breiz Atao's* political culture was based – the priority which it gave to the language issue, its proud assertions of Celtic identity, its stress on culture, literature and art – all served to obstruct its contact with the mass of the population. A more pragmatic group might have considered adapting or reforming their thinking. *Breiz Atao*, however, never discovered the virtues of pragmatism: proud of their thinking, they preferred to rationalize their minority status as evidence of their position as an elite in Breton society.

Conclusion

Françoise Morvan, in her autobiographical confessional concerning her disillusion with Breton nationalism, is scathing about these groups. They were, she argues, sad fantasists, doomed to adopt fascist values, from Villemarqué onwards.[146] *Breiz Atao* was merely a development of Maurras's Action française; the modernistic and innovative Seiz Breur artistic group were just totalitarians: 'nothing escaped their aim to saturate space, to make every object into an expression of the race.'[147]

These are harsh judgements. Morvan is too quick to place *Breiz Atao* at the centre of Breton nationalism, and too eager to define *Breiz Atao* by its wartime collaborationism (see chapter 8). Even by 1939, Breton nationalism was still the 'open house' celebrated by Charles Le Goffic, with the tragic Emile Masson as its lost prophet – a Breton Tolstoy or Kropotkin, psychologically destroyed by the blood of the First World War. Rather than stressing fascist connections, we should first note the variety of expressions of the Breton nationalism, from the URB's aristocratic fancy-dress competitions, through the Seiz Breur's work in ceramics, music and graphic art, to Masson's project of a peasant socialism. Despite Morvan's scorn, there is an eloquence and innovation here which deserves some degree of respect.

This was first and foremost an inchoate political culture which nonetheless inspired the durable images of Brittany which have worked to attract both tourists and historians for decades. Within this set of images, we can note a particular set of political values: despite the left-wing strands, from Emile Masson, through the FRB and the LFB, these movements are dominated by conservative values, celebrating the closed, hierarchic community of the rural world. Significantly, even *Breiz Atao*, despite all its fascistic modernization, finally argues that the class conflict of big capitalism is alien to little Brittany. And here, at last, Morvan does have a point. 'The heritage of Breiz Atao is not only accepted by the far right, but first and foremost by the left of the Breton movement, who take on the task of making it appear acceptable.'[148] One can reformulate this more accurately: while there are many clearly left-wing Breton nationalist movements, they have failed to produce a clean break with the rural, conservative values which dominate the politics of *bretonnitude*. Masson's importance is that he began just that process: to date, his project remains incomplete.

8

The End of the Road? Breton Nationalism and Vichy France, 1940–5

This chapter discusses one of the most controversial and tragic episodes in the history of Brittany. In the nineteenth and early twentieth centuries, this land had been imagined and reconstituted in different ways. For French-nationalist historians such as Michelet it represented the Celtic origins of French identity; for innovative and original conservative thinkers such as Villemarqué it was a type of alternative centre – a social, Christian counterpart to the secular individualism of Paris; while for more orthodox conservatives such as the Marquis de l'Estourbeillon, Brittany represented a social model of a closed, hierarchic community formed by honest Catholic peasants grateful for the dedicated leadership provided for them by honourable aristocrats. In 1940, such dreams and representations took an alarming turn: a small group of Breton nationalists saw Brittany as a territory in which fascism could grow.

This chapter does not aim to provide a full, social history of the experience of the Breton population during this tragic episode, but to trace the itinerary of one particular strand of Breton nationalism, putting it into a wider historic context and considering some of its consequences.[1] In raising such topics, one immediately has to face the issue of how to define fascism accurately: an issue which has led to many complex and often inconclusive debates.[2] For our purposes, fascism can be characterized as an open admiration for the government, techniques and political culture of Nazi Germany and – more loosely – as a desire to invigorate, reform or radicalize existing political cultures in a manner inspired by Nazi methods.

Brittany and fascism

The simple presence of fascism within the various currents of Breton nationalism is unmistakeable. It had begun with the rightward turn of *Breiz*

Atao in the early 1930s, its growing racism and its proud self-definition as an elite. These tendencies grew more pronounced as its contacts with Nazi Germany developed in the mid-1930s. Noting these points, however, is not equivalent to closing an argument. Important questions and qualifications remain. First, a wider political context needs to be noted: it can reasonably be argued that all French political tendencies were affected, to a greater or lesser degree, by fascist ideas and practices in the 1930s. For example, the agrarian protests of the Greenshirts (discussed in the previous chapter) show how commonly something of the rhetoric and style of fascism was spreading within rural France. Pushing this argument a little further one could even cite an example from within the socialist SFIO. Marcel Pivert sponsored the development of an aggressive hyper-militancy among socialists in 1934–6. Alarmed by the spread of fascism across Europe, he proposed a type of 'fighting fire with fire' strategy. He met with an enthusiastic response from branches of the Socialist Youth in Paris, who marched, wearing uniforms, in military-style formations, carrying giant portraits of the revered leaders of French socialism.[3] Further indications of fascist-inspired radicalism can be found across the political spectrum, particularly as the notoriously amorphous political culture of fascism can be expressed as much through attitudes and style as through any coherent political stance.

Secondly, it must be stressed that the Occupation of France by the Nazis from 1940 to 1944 was a highly effective stimulus to a frightening spectrum of far-right tendencies across the whole of French society. It is important to be realistic about this point: very, very few French people seriously considered active resistance to the German occupier in the summer of 1940, for the obvious reason that Hitler's armies seemed unbeatable. Instead, the vast majority of the population considered forms of 'accommodation' with their new rulers: practices which might be as simple as realizing that contacts with the German occupation authorities were momentarily unavoidable, and therefore had to be accepted by anyone wanting – for example – work.[4] Thus, for example, Odette Jolly, a midwife working in the Loire-Inférieure, found that she had to learn the German term *Hebamme*, meaning midwife, in order to get the identification papers she needed for her profession.[5] On the other hand, some French people went further. Rather than merely devising means by which to deal with the new German authorities, they developed a more politicized attitude, leading to forms of collaboration which might, for example, aim to secure France's position as an equal partner in a future fascist New Europe. Once again, it must be stressed that such pressures operated upon and within *all* political tendencies: only a tiny minority emerge from the Occupation years with genuinely clean consciences.

These two important qualifications suggest that we should see the fascistic evolution within *Breiz Atao* in a different light. This shift was not something unusual in French political culture in the late 1930s and early 1940s; it does not imply that Breton political culture, or Breton nationalism, was uniquely cursed by some form of politicized Original Sin. Indeed, as will be seen, it seems legitimate to argue that popular support for the Occupation and for collaboration with Nazi Germany was probably weaker in Brittany than in the rest of France. But equally, the fascist development within *Breiz Atao* cannot be ignored or side-stepped. Breton nationalists have not served their cause well by attempting to minimize this episode. The weakest passages in Morvan Lebesque's otherwise magnificent essay, *Comment peut-on être Breton?*, are those in which he attempts to downplay this moment, arguing that a notorious pro-Nazi formation (to be discussed below) consisted merely of a handful of hated and hopeless youngsters.[6] No matter how small, marginal or atypical such formations were, they still serve as a warning of what Breton nationalism was capable of producing, and it is legitimate to insist that contemporary Breton groups clarify their relationship to this repellent past – as should all political groups in France. 1944 was the end of the road for a certain variant of Breton nationalism, but not for the *Emsav* as a whole.

The pages below will address the question of the presence of such fascistic elements within the ranks of Breton nationalism, and will evaluate their influence and significance. A more important question to discuss, however, is that posed by Michel Denis. 'Why and how', he asks, 'could such a deep misunderstanding have developed between a militant minority and the majority of the population?'[7] We will return to this question in the conclusion.

As the examples of Pivert's Socialist Youth groups and Dorgères's Greenshirts demonstrate, there was a widespread, 'soft' fascistization of French political cultures in the 1930s. Brittany was not immune to such developments: the various far-right 'leagues' were certainly present across the region. In particular, the old, far-right group Action française, with its unique blend of monarchism, regionalism, anti-semitism and proto-fascism, certainly gained some real influence in the region. In 1923 the Morbihan prefect could dismiss it with the withering comment that the Lorient branch merely contained 'a few old ladies, a few old men with their medals, and some young people'.[8] But the group's influence grew over the succeeding years. Even local officials were impressed by it. The Sub-Prefect of Dinan (Côtes-du-Nord) considered them to be: 'a humanitarian party, with some great ideas, opposing all wars and supporting religion'.[9] Their Camelots du Roi, a group of street-sellers organized to distribute their paper, rapidly acquired a reputation for rowdy violence elsewhere in France, but actually gained the admiration of police authorities in Saint-Brieuc. They appeared 'full of bravery, well-disciplined and resolute: these are sure signs of their future success.'[10] In 1928, the Prefect of the Loire-Inférieure noted Action française's success among the *hobereaux*, the priests and even with the bishop.[11] The Lannion (Côtes-du-Nord) Sub-Prefect also found them to be 'permanent and discreet' in 1935: they successfully gained the aristocracy's support in his arrondissement.[12] An Action française militant controlled the Brittany-based *La Province* paper. It popularized xenophobic causes: for example, it called on the shoe-workers of Fougères (Ille-et-Vilaine) to defend their jobs against foreign competition, and it denounced the activities of socialist and communist schoolteachers.[13] Its print-run reached about thirty-two thousand and eight hundred in 1938.[14] It seems more than likely that the intangible, discreet influences of this group among aristocrats and notables prepared the ground for the collaborationist tendencies which emerged in the 1940s.

Other representatives of the troublesome, noisy, far-right 'leagues' of the 1920s and 1930s were also active in Brittany. The Jeunesses patriotes had about eight hundred members in Rennes in 1929, about seven hundred in Nantes in 1934, and about two hundred in Redon in 1935.[15] The Croix de Feu successfully recruited shopkeepers, officials and veterans in Saint-Brieuc; some two hundred and fifty joined this group in 1936.[16] Such groups contributed to the eruption of street-fighting in Rennes, Saint-Brieuc and Nantes in the mid-1930s. Following the victory of the left-wing Popular Front coalition in the May–June 1936 General Election, disappointed right-wing parliamentary parties and the fascist-leaning 'leagues' cooperated in organizing a protest meeting at Saint-Marc-la-Jaille, near Nantes, on 30 August 1936. It attracted between twenty-five thousand and forty-five thousand people.[17] Alongside these largely urban groups, Dorgères's Comités de défense paysanne won some real popularity in villages along the northern Breton coast in the late 1930s.[18]

As the 'leagues' did not stand candidates for elections, it is not possible to give a precisely calculated evaluation of their influence in Brittany. In general, however, these aggressive far-right groups, with their ever-present threat of street violence, only attracted a small, if significant, minority. 'In general', noted the Dinan Sub-Prefect (Côtes-du-Nord), 'the population is hostile to parties who want to disturb public order' – a comment which could be applied to the whole of Brittany in the 1930s.[19] The real test of their popularity would have come in 1940. The Croix de Feu league was converted into the Parti Social Français, a legal political party, in 1936;

it planned to stand candidates in the 1940 General Election. Its growing presence in the region led to alarming rumours concerning secret arms dumps and military training.[20]

Another factor disturbed conservative opinion in Brittany still further. Following the successful advance of Francoist forces into Barcelona in February 1939, a massive wave of refugees, probably numbering about half a million, crossed from Spain, across the Pyrenees, into France. Official policy was to disperse them as much as possible in order to prevent their concentration along the Franco-Spanish border. In the last week of February 1939, contingents began to arrive in Brittany. Earlier in the war, the arrival of small groups of Spanish refugees had aroused some sympathy; in 1937 the Loire-Inférieure Prefect even instructed his Sub-Prefects and officials to co operate with a 'Socialist Committee to Aid Republican Spain', which attempted to provide resources for the first refugees.[21] By 1939, the public mood seemed to have changed. In Dinan (Côtes-du-Nord), the refugees were sent to small towns across the arrondissement. Their arrival aroused much anxiety: they were unexpected; they arrived in far greater numbers than predicted; and, inevitably, hostile rumours quickly began to circulate concerning the contagious diseases that they brought with them.[22] A wonderful semi-autobiographical novella by Louis Guilloux records the shock and alarm that the arrival of three hundred Spanish refugees made in Saint-Brieuc. Among their ranks were sixty-three men who needed hospital treatment.[23]

The real significance of the presence of these refugees was, however, not so much political as diplomatic. They demonstrated that Brittany could not be isolated from events happening elsewhere in the world. The Breton population had been relieved by the apparent settlement of international tensions which the Munich agreement of autumn 1938 had seemed to represent; the presence of a new wave of refugees in 1939 showed that the world outside was still unstable. 'We want to stay ourselves', proclaimed *Breiz Atao's Manifeste de Guingamp*, issued in August 1938.[24] This was looking to be an increasingly untenable proposition in 1939.

Brittany and the war

There was little or no resistance in Brittany to the call-up notices which were sent out in September 1939. To many, the war was not even a surprise: Père Amand Boulé, who taught in a Catholic college in Brittany, had warned his class in July 1939 not to expect him to return in September.[25] The two most prominent leaders of the PNB, Debauvais and Mordrel, were also prepared: they left on 29 August, secretly, for Germany. From there, they issued a defiant manifesto, warning that France wanted to make Brittany disappear, and calling for Breton neutrality in the forthcoming conflict.[26] Their party had been outlawed and *Breiz Atao* banned by the French state on 28 August 1939; officials judged that it constituted an 'intolerable challenge' to the authorities.[27] Arrests of PNB militants followed in October 1939 in Paris and in all the Breton departments except the Côtes-du-Nord: 2 were arrested in Morbihan, 12 in Ille-et-Vilaine, 18 in Finistère, 13 in Loire-Inférieure and 17 in the department of the Seine.[28] Other political groups were abolished or repressed. The PCF was particularly harshly hit. In Finistère and Côtes-du-Nord, five Communist mayors and forty councillors were dismissed from their posts.[29] Prominent Communist leaders were interned, and their party structure collapsed as their militants were mobilized as soldiers. In mid-1939, there had been approximately a thousand members of the PCF in the Loire-Inférieure; by July 1940 only forty remained.[30] But the experience of PNB and PCF members is clearly not typical of Bretons as a whole. The great majority accepted the rule of the French government in September 1939. After that date, however, there was a general slowdown or even closure of political and trade union activity.

The last months of 1939 and the first months of 1940 were an awkward, tense period. The strain was made worse by the fact that many had thought that they knew what to expect: memories of the First World War were strong in the region. 'I was only ten', recalled Georges Gendreau in his autobiography, 'but I already knew about war for the good reason that I had heard people talk about it every day since I was born.'[31] The First World War formed the automatic point of comparison: Boulé immediately contrasted the 'resignation' of the conscripts of 1939 with what he remembered as the 'enthusiasm' of 1914.[32] But instead of savage trench-fighting, conscripts and civilians experienced the long, empty months of the *drôle de guerre*, the strange sort of war. The old Breton towns looked and felt different; Saint-Brieuc was at once strangely animated and sad, transformed by the 'posters, thousands of posters, plastered over the walls: stupid posters, pretentious posters'.[33] They warned of dangers such as German parachutists landing in the region, disguised as nuns.

New migrants arrived in Brittany. Firstly, children were evacuated from the north and east of France, and from the Parisian area.[34] Some three hundred Parisian children arrived in the little peninsula of Le Croisic (Loire-Inférieure) in September 1939.[35] Then another, more frightening wave of refugees arrived in May and June 1940; this time they came from Belgium. They brought with them alarming stories of French soldiers and officers who fled from the battlefields quicker than the civilian refugees. Such tales contributed to an apocalyptic mood.[36] They were soon joined by new waves of refugees from Holland, Luxemburg and north-east France. Gendreau could remember what a curious sight they made, driving old cars with mattresses tied to their roofs to protect them from attacks by the German dive-bombers.[37] By 23 July, about ten thousand had arrived in the Loire-Inférieure.[38] In June and July 1940 there were approximately one hundred and thirty-nine thousand refugees in Ille-et-Vilaine. For a few weeks, the population of Rennes was double its normal size. Most of these refugees returned to their homes later in the summer, but in November 1940 almost eight thousand internal refugees remained in the department.[39]

Alongside the evacuees and refugees, there were other groups sent to Brittany. In the first week on June 1940, just before the collapse of the French army, some six hundred prisoners were transported from an internment camp near Paris to a camp in Audierne (Finistère). They were mainly Austrian and German; many of them were Jews. Soma Morgenstern has written a poignant record of their reception as they were transferred from the station to a coach in Quimper. At first the local people stared. The rumour quickly spread that these internees were subversives or German agents, saboteurs or parachutists, and a near-riot started: the people shouted, screamed and spat at the coach.[40] This public demonstration of xenophobia and stigmatization could be seen as an expression of identity similar to the *pardons* and festivals discussed in chapters 4, 5 and 6. It suggests that by 1940 an intolerant, aggressive sense of *bretonnitude* was developing, even before the German Occupation.

News of the defeat of French forces followed. This formed part of a dreadful experience, the collapse of a world. Gendreau records that on hearing the news, he ran up to his room, seized his plaster bust of Marianne, his little tricolour flag and his pictures of Gamelin, Darlan and Pétain, and threw them all in the bin.[41] On the other hand, there were some more resilient responses. Marie-Paule Salonne, a female resister, recalls a 'spirit of 1940', a type of stubbornness which insisted: 'No! No! Not beaten! Not subjects! Never conquered!'[42] The actions of the men on the island of Sein are the clearest expression of this spirit. Almost the entire adult male population, 133 men, sailed from the island between 24 and 26 June 1940, and joined General de Gaulle in London.[43] He later reviewed his tiny force of some four hundred soldiers, and was amazed at the proportion who came from the island. At the end of the review, according to legend, he remarked: 'the island of Sein now forms a quarter of France'.

On 17 June 1940 the advancing German forces caught up with the ill-disciplined remnants of the French army at Fougères (Ille-et-Vilaine). Following some machine-gun fire, the French forces scattered, and the route was open to Rennes. On 18 June 1940, German soldiers entered Rennes without a shot being fired.[44] A few days later, three tired German motor-cyclists, with muddy helmets and filthy bikes, arrived in Saint-Brieuc. Units of the *Wehrmacht* followed later in the evening.[45] In Vannes, they paraded through the town with tanks, machine-guns and lorries.[46] The occupation had begun: under the armistice agreement, the whole of Brittany formed part of the zone directly occupied by the German army, not part of the zone with a nominal – and increasingly fictitious – autonomy in the south of France, which was controlled directly by the Vichy government. Most of the Breton coastline was also subject to special military regulations, which hampered the movements of fishers and sailors. Confusingly, however, Vichy was still the seat of the French government, and its laws still applied in the occupied northern zone.

It seems probable that the Occupation was first met with a long period of silence, as ordinary people attempted to come to terms with this extraordinary event. Bretons had been told, by governments and military experts, that there would be no war, that the Maginot Line would hold, and that France would not be defeated. Instead of the stability they had expected, an avalanche of frightening events overwhelmed them. As was the case with most French people, their immediate concern was finding food: prices soared, particularly in the cities, and the rationing system was unjust and inefficient. The black market started almost immediately. 'We went short of everything', recalled Gendreau, 'not enough milk, not enough coffee, fish, vegetables or fruit. We went hungry.'[47] Under these exceptional circumstances, rural people could find that they were living better than the townsfolk. Roland de Kermadec was demobilized in the summer of 1941, and went to live with his wife's family in Trégourez (Finistère). He found it a paradise: on their farm there was milk, eggs, butter, vegetables, rabbit and chickens.[48]

Most of the Breton press stopped publishing in the last two weeks in June, most political parties were not functioning and very few Bretons would have heard de Gaulle's now-famous BBC radio broadcast from London on 18 June 1940. A few newspapers reappeared over the summer of 1940 but, for the moment, Brittany was 'hors de combat' as Pierre Jakez Hélias recalled.[49] One hundred and thirty-seven thousand Breton prisoners of war were sent to Germany.[50] Very few of those who remained immediately chose to join the Resistance. Under these circumstances, Marshal Pétain appeared more persuasive than General de Gaulle. Pétain offered some sort of return to normality, and even the promise of a peace with honour. 'The Marshal knows what must be done', commented Michel Chaillou's uncle.[51] In the schools, Pétain's picture replaced the busts of Marianne.

> In all the homes, the photo of him wearing his *képi* with its oak leaves was placed between the photo of the conscript and the wedding pictures. However low we had fallen, however beaten we were, we did not lose heart as we looked at this noble old man, loyal to the quasi-divine mission of which he was the guardian.[52]

It was difficult for Bretons to make sense of this new universe.

There was confusion about who was really Brittany's enemy. Sixty-seven people, including thirty-nine children, were killed by an RAF air-raid in January 1943 on the town of Morlaix (Côtes-du-Nord).[53] Similar raids, usually causing fewer casualties, took place along the coastline in 1942 and 1943. Predictably, the Breton collaborationist press exploited these events, reminding Bretons of the long legacy of maritime antagonism between Brittany and Britain, and appealing for cooperation with Germany.[54]

The first political and social initiatives taken by Bretons after the armistice reveal their confusion. For example, in Le Croisic, the pioneering explorer and geographer, Odette du Puigaudeau threw herself into the creation of a type of female volunteer social service, the Service feminine français (SFF). She began without any funds, with no building and no institutional support. But quickly she adopted the rhetoric of the time: the aim of the SFF was 'to serve the nation'. The SFF collected goods for French POWs, organized cultural events and raised money. Du Puigaudeau wrote enthusiastically of the efforts of these 'resolute, well-trained women, inspired by religious faith and patriotic values'.[55] Unfortunately, she seemed unaware of the wider political context. The hard-line collaborationist daily, *La Gerbe*, publicized her initiatives, and her SFF developed links with the German National Sozialistische Volkswohlfahrt. Was she therefore a collaborator? A fascist? A few years later she was to join the Communist Party. Her initiatives are probably best seen as an indication of the confusion of the period. While simply wishing to help the population at a crisis moment, the only means she could find led her to cooperate with the Occupation authorities.

Such political innocence was common, even typical of the first months of the Vichy regime. Vichy's projects often met with general acceptance, if not positive enthusiasm. On 2 December 1940 the Vichy government announced the creation of a Corporation Paysanne. To many in Brittany this seemed a welcome development of the previous corporatist associations of farmers which had been organized in the 1920s and 1930s.[56] Regular radio broadcasts in Breton were instituted.[57] There was an even more positive reception to the proposal to create a third, regional, level of government, between the eighty-five French departments and the central state. In April 1941, Rennes became the centre of a regional prefecture for Brittany. Many were then deeply disappointed that this new region would be based on only four departments. The area formed by the Loire-Inférieure, considered a part of Brittany since the tenth century, was now reclassified as part of the new region of the Pays-de-la-Loire.[58] It seems likely that the Vichy government had made some sort of policy decision on this issue; their aim was not to revive the old provinces, but to create forward-looking administrative entities, guided by technocratic considerations rather than traditionalism.

It was genuinely difficult to be sure what Pétain and Vichy stood for. The themes of stability, order and honour were probably popular. For many, there was even a certain continuity in their political attitudes. So, for example, the right-wing Protestants of Nantes, attracted by the PSF in the late 1930s, easily transformed themselves into keen Pétainists in the early 1940s.[59] The dismissal of left-wing mayors continued: but this had been started by the Daladier government in 1939, and could not be seen as a distinctive policy of the Vichy regime. But by 1942 there were growing signs of discontent. Local officials began to talk of an epidemic of 'resignation-itis' as mayors and councillors left.[60]

Clarifying collaboration

In Le Croisic, du Puigaudeau had believed in 1940 that it was the right moment to create a female social service section, and accepted that this meant cooperating with the Vichy and even German authorities. Other authorities considered that the political situation represented a real opportunity. Yvon Tranvouez's typology of Catholic reactions is one of the best guides to Breton public opinion in this period.[61] He suggests four principal strands of opinion. Clearly, there were some active resisters, often drawn from the young Catholic groups of the 1920s and 1930s, and from the PDP. (We will discuss this strand in more detail below.) Secondly, for many conservative, Catholic authorities, Vichy France was an acceptable regime: its anti-communism and anti-masonic programmes were simply a continuation of the political values that a conservative weekly such as the *Courrier du Finistère* had promoted before 1939. Such conservative opinion was led by bishops such as Duparc, the bishop of Finistère, a convinced Pétainist and a promoter of the Breton language. However, Duparc kept his distance from too close a collaboration with Nazi Germany. He had even gently chided the pilgrims at a *pardon* in

Folgoët: 'France, finished? Finished? Come on now.' More significantly, his ideal Brittany was clearly Catholic in its values: he was sceptical about the new ideas which sprung up in 1940 and 1941. Thirdly, there were those who could be classified as Celtic conservatives, symbolized by the abbé Perrot. They were cautious about propagating their political values too loudly, but they were active in their cultural sphere. The children's weekly, *O Lo Lê*, published from November 1940 to May 1944 and widely circulating among Brittany's private, Catholic schools, is the most prominent expression of their ideas. Like the previous strand, these tendencies were anti-communist, Pétainist and Catholic, but they linked this to an implicit Breton nationalism. For such people, the French defeat of 1940 represented an opportunity to be seized. Some members of the PNB were active in such initiatives. Lastly, and most notoriously, there were those who openly put their trust in the programmes of Nazi Germany, seeing the Third Reich as the best ally of a future independent Brittany. Here, there was impatience and open criticism of Pétain's programmes.

Much of the debate concerning Breton politics during the Occupation has centred on the fourth strand, and has therefore ignored or minimized the impact of the more typical Pétainism of Breton conservatives. Perhaps there is good reason for this: there is certainly something shocking about the public declarations of the post-1940 PNB. One of the most astonishing summaries of their politics can be found in Olier Mordrel's *Breiz Atao*, published in 1973. In one often-cited passage, he distinguishes between different reactions to the Occupation:

> As soon as the soldiers of the Reich appeared on our roads, some – to which one can add the Party [PNB] – saw them as objective allies who would not require any ideological compromises. Others, largely the majority, saw them as the 'Huns' that propaganda had prepared them to see. A handful of the initiated saw these soldiers as our soldiers, this army as our army, and their flag as our flag.[62]

In the sections that follow, we will first consider the activities of this small strand of explicitly pro-Nazi collaborators, then set their activities into the wider context of Breton political cultures.

L'Heure bretonne: the collaborationists of the new PNB

Since the mid-1920s, far-right German nationalists had been interested in Brittany. For example, Hans-Otto Wagner was in contact with the PAB in the late 1920s. German Nazis were therefore familiar with these militants before 1940: however, they were shocked to realize the extent to which the evolving Breton nationalist movement expected the newly victorious Nazi government to act on its behalf.[63] The status of Brittany in Occupied France was debated by the Reich government. Himmler and Ribbentrop argued strongly against the creation of a separate Breton nation: they feared that a new Brittany would swiftly build up contacts with Ireland, Wales and Britain, and would therefore present a possible point of weakness within the Europe of the New Order.[64] Once again, Brittany's geographic position determined its political fate: with its major ports of Saint-Malo, Brest, Lorient and Saint-Nazaire, it was out of the question that the Nazi authorities would loosen their control of the region. The Germans were, however, prepared to tolerate a revived PNB in the same manner that they tolerated the activities of the diverse hard-line collaborationist groups in Paris. (For the sake of clarity, we will henceforth refer to this group as the 'new PNB'.) This point is important, because it means that, in the absence of obvious competitors, the new PNB was eventually seen as 'representative of the whole of the movement' for the period of the Occupation.[65]

Mordrel and Debauvais were met by Wagner as they got off the train in Cologne late in August 1940.[66] The two had some further direct contact with the Nazi authorities in late 1939 and early 1940. They were inspired by what they understood as the Irish nationalist stance in 1914: the enemies of their enemies would be their friends.[67] In general, they were disappointed. The Nazis refused to treat them as equal partners, and retained a respect for France. Nonetheless, Mordrel considered in May 1940 that it was 'now or never'.[68] Debauvais dreamt of the creation of a new network of local committees to replace the old PNB. Mordrel was less optimistic:

> French domination had prevented our influence from reaching beyond an elite: people who could think for themselves and who had the courage to do so. But the day when we acquired a state and all its machinery, we would have the same influence on the masses as that which Paris currently enjoyed. French nationalist culture would disappear from our land with the last officials and last pensioners of the Third Republic.[69]

The important point here is that Mordrel openly acknowledges the minority position of the PNB, and clearly states his reliance on Nazi power to impose a form of Breton nationalism on the Breton population.

While German officials were not prepared to accept either Mordrel's or Debauvais's proposals, they did authorize a project to recruit Bretons from POWs held in German camps. The long-term aim seems to have been the creation of some form of military unit. For most of the Breton POWs, this was a depressing and alienating experience. Boulé, held in a German camp, recalled suffering a year of intensive propaganda.[70] True, there were some advantages to the Germans' new interest in them: Boulé asked for, and obtained, the right to hold a weekly mass for Bretons. But, in general, few were receptive to the touring Breton nationalist speakers: 'Among [this minority], some were sincere, while others believed that this could be a useful way of getting their liberation. But it must be said that the vast majority of their comrades considered them to be traitors.'[71] Boulé perceptively noted that the first time a team of Breton nationalist speakers visited, they arrived alone. The second time, they came with a team of German soldiers. Clearly, they no longer felt able to address Breton prisoners without protection.

A new camp, especially for Bretons, was set up in Luckenwalde. Lectures and Breton-language courses were organized. For Mordrel, this would become the sacred centre of 'the Breton national revival'.[72] Towards the end of June, a contingent of some hundred and thirty men was sent back to Brittany, under Debauvais's leadership. In reality, they dispersed as soon as they reached France, and Debauvais was left almost alone when he arrived in Rennes. The new German authorities would not even allow him to demonstrate publicly in the city.

Lainé and Debauvais seized the *château* of Rohan, near Pontivy (Morbihan), and made this the headquarters of a new National Breton Committee (CNB). A new bilingual, weekly paper was published here, *l'Heure Bretonne*, 'the Breton moment': a suggestion of the importance of the opportunity the small group of activists felt that they had. Early in August 1940 this new title had a print run of some thirty-seven thousand.[73] This was the largest circulation figure of any periodical produced by the *Emsav* since 1918. However, in later months the team would constantly complain of distribution problems and falling sales. By 1941, its print run may have been as low as eight thousand.[74] The title grew progressively less ideological in tone. There was one brief moment of hope: a mysterious German radio broadcast on 27 July 1940 seemed to announce the creation of a Breton state. It proved to be fallacious.

Even the fanatics of the new team could see that their efforts met with little public enthusiasm. New strategies emerged. Mordrel organized the new PNB in October 1940, while Célestin Lainé pressed for a separate military formation. Debauvais grew more cautious, and his efforts in the succeeding years aimed to renew contacts with the more orthodox, conservative supporters of Pétain. Delaporte, appointed as a more conciliatory leader of the PNB, clashed with the militaristic ambitions of Lainé. The movement lacked coherence, lost confidence and grew more splintered. As early as October 1940 a report from the CNB stated that its members were exhausted. The strategy of the movement, however, remained to rely on German aid. The report's author assured the German authorities that *Breiz Atao* leaders held ideas which were 'very similar' to those of National Socialism, and that only Breton nationalism had the force to chase out the 'Jewish–French' from Brittany.[75] Mordrel's approach to the issue of Breton nationalism was horrific, but telling of his frame of mind.

> In reality, the Breton people are like a child who has fallen to the ground and is then crushed by the ruins of his own house. You cannot expect him to pick himself up. You have to pull him clear of the rubble, and then haul him up into a standing position. Then, and only then, he will say thank you and embrace his liberators.[76]

These reports also demonstrate the isolation of these new Breton nationalists from the majority of Breton society. The new team was dismayed by Bishop Duparc's public condemnation of their activities on 14 July 1940.[77] In June 1941, Mordrel reported to the German authorities that Breton elites were eighty to ninety per cent in favour of de Gaulle. The Freemasons and the 'jew-ified' [enjuivés] retained their influence in Brittany. The Breton nationalist movement was seen as an anachronism, and no one saw Germany as an ally. 'What have the Germans done to gain the Bretons' friendship?' he asked. 'Nothing.'[78]

It is difficult to estimate accurately the size of the membership of the wartime PNB, for its archives were destroyed in 1944. However, some indications of their support can be given. A PNB congress in Rennes in October 1941 was attended by three hundred people.[79] A German report identified two Breton-nationalist groups in the Loire-Inférieure in May 1942. The new PNB had between three hundred and three hundred and fifty members, while the less prominent *Brezona* had about sixty members.[80] Hamon points out that estimates of total new PNB membership range from under three thousand to over fifteen thousand: he calculates that the hard core of activists may only have numbered about eighty.[81] What is clear is that even under the conditions of the Occupation, when PNB membership seemed to offer privileges such as exemption from labour service in Germany, the total number of people attracted to the PNB remained stubbornly low. It mainly recruited in the big towns, and along the smaller coastal centres. The established 'red' towns of central Brittany – Carhaix, Guingamp and Morlaix – tended to resist its advances.⁸² The PNB's first main activity was to distribute *l'Heure bretonne* and other pamphlets. In 1942 and 1943 its militants took on a more sinister task: identifying Jews and Freemasons.⁸³

As it became more obvious that the new PNB had backed the wrong camp, the situation grew sombre. Increased resistance activity meant that the members of the new formation were in some real physical danger. The murder of abbé Perrot in December 1943, probably by a Communist resistance group, was a sign of the manner in which Breton politics were developing. From 1943 to 1945 the Resistance killed 581 people in the new, four-department Brittany.⁸⁴ Moreover, the German authorities were still attempting to mobilize all possible forces against both the Resistance and a future Allied attack. Groups of white Russians, popularly identified as 'Georgians', were transferred to Brittany: they quickly acquired a horrific reputation for savage violence, theft and rape. Groups such as the hard-line and clearly fascistic Parti Populaire Français were allowed to form their own militia: a small unit of twenty-six men was formed in the Ille-et-Vilaine in May 1944.⁸⁵

In November 1943, Lainé created his own mini-army, which was later incorporated into the SS: the Bezen Perrot (BP – the Perrot Brigade). This was named after the murdered *abbé* who, in reality, had strongly disapproved of Lainé's methods. Estimates concerning the numbers of its members vary: writers seeking to criticize the legacy of the force talk of eighty or more, while contemporary Breton nationalists suggest fewer than sixty.⁸⁶ The most recent study, by Kristian Hamon, suggests that thirty-three joined the force in December 1943, and that there were sixty-seven members in January 1944.⁸⁷ It attracted young, desperate men – their average age was twenty-two – joining either to escape compulsory labour in Germany or out of a genuine acceptance of Nazi ideals.⁸⁸ Delaporte, the then-leader of the PNB, finally made his choice: he expelled BP members from the PNB.⁸⁹ In March 1944 BP members were supplied with SS uniforms. First, the force was made responsible for guarding prisoners. Then in mid-1944, it was involved in the armed repression of Resistance activities. It withdrew eastwards, with the retreating German forces, in August 1944. Thirty-three of the formation arrived at Strasbourg, and then withdrew to Tübingen with other hard-line French collaborationists.⁹⁰

Other collaborations

Many other strange initiatives began after 1940: a wide, disparate range of curious Celtic, mystical and cultural activities. Before concluding this review of forms of collaboration, it is worth noting some of the more memorable initiatives of this period, in order to be able to understand more fully the context within which the new PNB was operating.

There was a real development in what one might term 'Celtic Studies' in Brittany: initiatives ranged from the semi-lunatic to serious linguistic research. In the first category, one can find a most curious publication, *Kad*, which stated that it was printed in Year 11,502 of the post-Atlantic era and which appears to date from 1941. It welcomed the end of the Roman dictatorship in Brittany, and heralded the revival of the Druids.[91] The Nazi occupation also stimulated interest in Brittany's pre historic past. German archaeologists arrived to study Brittany's megaliths, in search of evidence to prove their own racial theories.[92] More seriously, in July 1941, Roparz Hemon, a new PNB member, successfully devised a 'unified' form of the Breton language: he believed that such linguistic initiatives were essential for the creation of Brittany as an independent nation. He also sponsored the publication of a number of new Breton-language publications.[93]

An old regionalist, Georges Toudouze published a strange children's novel in 1942, a type of illegitimate fusion of Enid Blyton and Pétain. His *Anne et le mystère Breton* dramatizes a type of rediscovery or reconceptualizing of Breton identity, in which a new Brittany is created within a revived France.[94] A group of six teenagers, four from Paris and two from Brittany, travel across this new Brittany. They are met by a succession of austere, historically-minded rustic folk, who recite sonorous phrases to evoke the eternal mysteries of their beloved land. 'Whoever says Brittany, says authority', remarks one.[95] 'Where does our language come from?', another asks. 'But everyone knows: from the depths of time.' A third notes that 'there are times when legends are more valuable than histories, and when poems are worth more than documents.' The work ends with a fervent prayer to Sainte Anne, the venerated saint of Brittany.

In the absence of any reliable expressions of public opinion, it is extremely difficult to judge whether these initiatives were typical or representative of Breton political culture. However, while leftists and federalist–nationalists had no access to the mass media, these publications certainly gave the impression that Pétainist, collaborationist politics dominated a new Brittany, in which the older themes and images of Celticism functioned as part of a fascist reordering of Europe. Significantly, the most notable Breton novel from these years is probably Henri Queffélec's *Un recteur de l'île de Sein* [A priest on the Island of Sein], written in 1944. Set in the eighteenth century, the novel recounts the story of a fisher who takes on the role of priest when the island's regular priest resigns. Like Pétain (or like de Gaulle?) he is then accepted by the majority of the islanders as a legitimate authority, although he is eventually refused by the Church. The novel memorably evokes the harsh, primitive life led by the islanders, and the permanent threat of hunger that they suffered – a context which would have sounded more than familiar to Bretons in 1944. One is given a troubling depiction of this strange, uncomfortable search for a legitimate authority in tough conditions, but ultimately the novel fails to 'cast its vote', and could be read as either a Pétainist or a Gaullist fable. Perhaps this type of cultural ambiguity could be seen as the most typical expression of Breton political culture from this period.

Brittany was neither a great centre for hard-line collaborationists (despite the best efforts of the new PNB) nor a base of magnificent resistance struggles. The most important consequence of the efforts of the new PNB was to further confuse an already muddled situation, to the point where it becomes almost impossible to categorize and conceptualize the range of Breton reactions to the German Occupation.

Breton resistance

One point, however, emerges clearly. The new authorities spoke Celtic. The German Occupation forces outlawed the public singing the *Marseillaise*, but permitted the Breton-language anthem *Bro gozh ma zadoù* [Land of my fathers].[96] New radio programmes and new periodicals used the Breton language more frequently than ever before. The masthead of *O Lo Lê* sported a Celtic cross.[97] Vichy adopted the old Celtic hero Vercingétorix and his axe as their icons, and its Légion organized meetings at Alésia. In reaction to this, the Resistance spoke the language of French cultural nationalism. Significantly, no Resistance unit or fighter in Brittany adopted a Celtic pseudonym.[98] Angèle Jacq's two volume series, *Les hommes libres*, is a cliché-ridden account of lovable, plucky Asterix-style stereotypes playing a game of cops and robbers with a poorly-depicted Occupation force. However, one detail in this meandering prose rings true: Jacq's Breton-speaking Resistance units celebrate the Liberation of Brittany in 1944 by singing the *Marseillaise*. 'Their hearts beat, as did the space around them, for the long-awaited moment had arrived.'[99] It is easy to depict this moment in 1944 as a type of French-nationalist victory over Breton separatism. However, the truth seems more complex.

A few brave Bretons began to act against the German Occupation almost as soon as it began. In Nantes, on 7 August and 13 September 1940, someone cut the telephone lines used by the German authorities.[100] Such early acts of Resistance were usually carried by isolated individuals, without any contacts with wider networks. A Resistance *movement* took longer to emerge. As elsewhere in France, the resisters were a tiny minority: young, activist and fervent. In their improvised, clandestine structures, a curious synthesis took place. As Salonne notes, they included Bretons, Parisians and southerners, acting together as approximate equals.[101] There is something almost comic about Salonne's constant referral back to her previous experiences in the scouts as a training for her resistance work, but these observations do make sense: scouting – and the allied Catholic youth groups of the interwar years – were fine preparatory instruments for this new sense of youthful idealism and confidence.

Gendreau records a similar type of discovery of a different Brittany during the Occupation. He grew up in a left-leaning, anticlerical family. At his secondary school in Saint-Brieuc he found fellow pupils who shared his Resistance sympathy, and began to organize pilfering of German stores and forces for the Resistance. In December 1943 twenty schoolboys from his school were arrested. He was identified as the ringleader but, thankfully, only considered to be a common thief. He was released early in 1944, and was then sent by his parents to a small Catholic seminary near Guingamp. Gendreau dreaded this:

> I expected a sad school, and to my surprise I discovered a non-conformist seminary, with a happy, even amusing, atmosphere, with forward-looking priests and *abbés*, who were friendly with their pupils and also willing to listen to the farmers who were their neighbours . . . What devotion, what generosity they showed! And how they refused to judge or to condemn others: yes, their attitudes reconciled me with the church.[102]

Gendreau continued to be active in the Resistance. In 1945, while still a convinced atheist, he was chosen by his former classmates as their representative in Jeunesse Etudiante Chrétienne, the Student Christian Youth. It was a gesture which touched him, and he retained an affection for this form of youthful, idealistic Catholic activism for years after.

Other, organized, forms of Resistance emerged. In Nantes, the old Communist networks were not simply rebuilt; they were transformed into an effective urban guerrilla force. Their assassination of a German colonel in Nantes in October 1941 had tragic consequences. Hitler personally ordered the shooting of over a hundred hostages in retribution. In fact, forty-eight were shot.[103] The Communist resistance group in Nantes continued to grow:

it was launching five attacks per month in the city in 1942.[104] A small group of young members of the old PNB of the 1930s built up contacts in the Saint-Nazaire docks, and organized Resistance activities among the fifteen thousand workers at the submarine base.[105] Most of the tiny groups of Breton Protestants remembered the legacy of their southern, *camisard*, rebel ancestors, and identified with the Resistance. They often had a sentimental affection for Britain, and they could easily feel a sense of solidarity with the persecuted Jews. However, for many Protestants, their participation in these Resistance networks was the first time that they had worked closely with Catholics. No specifically Protestant Resistance grouping was founded. Instead, between Catholics and Protestants, the Resistance formed a structure for a unique process of 'mutual discovery'.[106] Salonne observes, probably accurately, that the armed, underground resistance network of the *maquis*: 'was a crossroads. So many different routes met there!'[107]

This cultural framework was radically new in Brittany: the new ideal of the Resistance seemed to possess a capacity to dissolve the region's internal barriers. Protestants and Catholics, workers and peasants, Breton-speakers and Francophones, Christians and anticlericals, conservatives and socialists, outlaws and solid citizens could all meet as approximate equals in this movement. Perhaps the ultimate taboo which the Resistance appeared to shatter was the oldest prejudice of all: the idea that Bretons could not stand on an equal footing with French people. In other words, the culture of the Resistance allowed a type of rediscovery of Brittany, a recasting of the old region as youthful, modernizing, idealistic, and a refusal to allow its White landscape to become the base for the racial fantasies of fascist fanatics.

As was the case elsewhere in France, the active resisters probably only constituted a tiny minority. Estimates of their numbers vary: contemporary British authorities estimated that there were about fifteen thousand in the Resistance at the beginning of August 1944, grouped mainly to the north of Vannes and to the west of Pontivy.[108] By the end of August 1944 there may have been as many as thirty-five thousand enrolled in the Resistance-organized FFI (Forces françaises de l'intérieur) in Brittany: approximately 1.5 per cent of the total population.[109] But their political and social importance far outweighed their demographic size. For every one resister, there was a support network to supply identity cards, food, information and medical assistance. It was only with this informal aid that the Breton Resistance grew into an organization that was capable of carrying out 348 armed attacks in March 1944 in the four departments of the new region, and causing between fifteen hundred and two thousand German casualties in August 1944.[110]

August 1944: the Marseillaise in Brittany

There was no civil war in Brittany in the summer of 1944. But the population had to choose between Vichy and the Allies, Pétain and de Gaulle, Occupation and Liberation. This was a difficult and sometimes extremely dangerous moment. Nervous German soldiers and hard-line, militarized collaborationist groups now had nothing to lose – they would often act with extreme violence. For example, when the German authorities withdrew from Cancale (Ille-et-Vilaine), the population thought they were safe, and then rushed out to applaud a column of marching Allied soldiers. They had made a tragic mistake: the infantry column was German. Forty people were immediately killed by machine-gun fire and hand-grenades.[111]

Resistance authorities took control of Rennes on 3 August 1944, of Saint-Brieuc on 5 August and of Vannes between 4 and 5 August.[112] Quimper was more difficult to take: some two thousand German soldiers fought to the end between 4 and 9 August.[113] De Gaulle himself visited Rennes on 20 August 1944. Pockets of German military forces remained in Brittany, around Brest and Saint-Nazaire, into 1945. Often the Liberation brought with it a strong sense of political continuity: of the 5,033 municipal councillors in position in the Côtes-du-Nord in December 1944, 3,358 (58 per cent) had been elected in the last local elections – those held in 1935.[114] Above all, the new respect accorded to de Gaulle was the symbol of this new political legitimacy: 'not to respect him was to cut oneself off from the patriotic nation.'[115]

The new, mass identity which emerged from these processes was based less on the left-leaning activism of the Resistance than on a sense of common suffering. The evidence was clear to see. In the Côtes-du-Nord, 40 of the 378 communes suffered Allied bombing.[116] On 4 August 1944 the Germans ordered the evacuation of Brest's civilian population. Six weeks of fighting followed, during which eighteen thousand homes were destroyed.[117] In the Ille-et-Vilaine, 28 per cent of the department's buildings were totally destroyed in 1944, and 48 per cent were partially damaged. One third of the department's Jews had been deported; very few of them returned in 1945.[118] Images and episodes from the Occupation, such as the forty-eight hostages from Nantes who were shot by the Occupation authorities between 20 and 22 October 1941, and the sixty-seven deaths caused by the RAF air raid on Morlaix in January 1943, were drawn together into a single memory of common anguish after August 1944.[119] This sense of shared suffering was the basis for a new political consensus, constructed by de Gaulle, across France: it was therefore a means by which Brittany could be integrated into France.[120]

Interpretations of the Occupation developed quickly. As established by Capdevila's research, it was soon remembered as a moment of humiliation, expressed through common feelings of having been dishonoured, even of having been made to feel dirty.[121] For this reason, Liberation was often expressed through cleansing rituals, which in practice meant the scapegoating of particular targets. Very quickly, it became impossible to remember the various collaborationist groups, including *Breiz Atao*, with anything but shame. At an Allied investigation of atrocities committed during the Occupation, one witness commented that the collaborationists were just 'self-interested brutes, they worked for money'.[122] Another target was young women who were accused of sexual or romantic relations with German authorities. In Breton towns, as in the rest of France, their heads were publicly shaved, and they were paraded through the streets. Guilloux records what may well have been a typical scene in August 1944. Six or seven young lads draw up in a car outside a bar. Instead of going inside, they slip down the alley alongside. Guilloux recalls hearing plaintive cries, like those of a rabbit. Everyone left the bar to see: the six were holding the girl, and forcibly cutting her hair with a large pair of scissors. One tells her not to be afraid: he is not here to hurt her, but to make her feel shame. She is then forced to shout 'Long live France!' and 'Down with the Huns!'.[123] These were, by any measure, ugly scenes. They suggest another image of the Resisters who were often, in Capdevila's words, young, armed and drunk.[124] Salonne condemned these forced humiliations: 'This practice, which attacked defenceless women, was neither brave nor clever: so it was not French. It was not even intelligent, because many felt more sorrow than mistrust for the victims.'[125] In some cases there was an explicit reaction against such attacks. Hanna Diamond records that after two women were humiliated in this fashion in Châteaulin (Finistère), the entire female population of the town wore headscarves as a gesture of solidarity with the victims.[126] There were other victims. Capdevila notes that fourteen Algerians were arrested in Brittany (B4) in the second half of 1944: about one quarter of all the Algerians present in the region.[127] It seems more than likely that some form of racism was operating here, in which the desire to explain the humiliation of the Occupation was rationalized and expressed through blaming obvious outsiders.

It was in this context that a swift evaluation was made of the activities of the Celtic collaborationists. The new PNB were, above all, remembered as a source of shame.[128] But, more importantly, many of the less obviously politicized initiatives of nationalists during the Occupation years were also rejected. Hélias records that, after 1944, 'it was hardly possible to defend the ancestral language or even their descendants' civilization without being seen as a Nazi infiltrator'.¹²⁹ His own autobiographical work provides some evidence of this: the Occupation years are swiftly passed over in seven pages. Such attitudes may well have had important long-term cultural consequences. Fañch Broudic suggests that these years were crucial in the serious acceleration of the long-term decline in the use of Breton as a normal language of daily speech. He has argued that among the young, French quickly became seen as the language which gave access to knowledge, which allowed an easy participation in the school or army, which carried social prestige and which liberated the individual from conservative traditions.¹³⁰ It has to be stressed that there was no organized French-national plot against the new PNB, its allies, its cultural initiatives or its work. But in the confused, often vindictive atmosphere of 1944 and 1945, in which many scores were settled in a violent, rushed manner, association with the new PNB was something of which to be ashamed. In November 1944 there was a substantial police round-up of suspected new PNB militants, which may have arrested as many as two thousand eight hundred people – although there is good reason to believe that the number actually charged with an offence was substantially lower. The legal processes dragged on into 1947 when twenty were condemned to death.¹³¹

Echoes and legacies

Many issues, however, remain unresolved. There has been some excellent scholarly research on this episode: the works by Capdevila, Déniel and Hamon (see references) each demonstrate a strong commitment by Breton scholars to uncover and come to terms with this past. In such works, one finds a careful respect for the evidence; there is no attempt to minimize or to apologize for the fascistic tendencies within the new PNB but, equally, no attempt to exaggerate their importance or to stigmatize the whole of the *Emsav*. On the other hand, there are some more worrying elements of continuity. Morvan Lebesque's reluctance to speak about this period was noted in the first section of this chapter. One obvious reason for this may well be his own involvement: Lebesque was actually on the editorial team of *L'Heure bretonne* in the autumn of 1940.¹³² The recent polemical work by Françoise Morvan was at least in part inspired by the disgust she felt with the praise expressed by Per Denez, an elder statesman of today's *Emsav*, for the activities of the new PNB during the Occupation years.¹³³

Such debates are still politically charged: indeed, it could be argued that they are actually growing in importance. For example, in May 2000 there was an angry exchange of articles in the French and Breton press concerning 'Roparz Hémon' secondary school, run since 1988 by the Breton-language alternative school movement, *Diwan*. *Libération* demanded the end of the 'law of silence' which, it claimed, covered all considerations of the activities of Breton nationalists during the Occupation.[134] The *Diwan* leaders' reactions were more nuanced. Some argued that it was possible to respect the linguistic and cultural work of Hémon without sharing his political views. The then president of *Diwan*, Andrew Lincoln, commented: 'this is not a black and white issue. Roparz Hémon was neither a nazi nor an anti-semite, but he cannot be presented as an innocent figure.'[135] The school was eventually 'de-baptized' in June 2000.[136]

In these debates one can see three attitudes within the post-1945 *Emsav*. First, the continuators of the attitudes of the 1940s: people such as Olier Mordrel who were proud of their collaborationist attitudes, plus others who still occupy positions of some authority, and who have never clearly renounced their collaborationist past. Secondly, there is another current which could be termed 'Celtic amoralism', which refuses to make moral or political judgements concerning the period, but which applauds any apparent advance for the causes of the Breton language and Celtic culture. The group which chose the name 'Roparz Hémon' for their school could be cited as an example of this attitude: not, in any meaningful sense of the words, fascist or anti-semitic, but unwilling to confront such political issues seriously. Lastly, a point often ignored by the French–national writers, there has also been substantial critical research from within the Breton nationalist movements concerning this episode. To argue that there is a 'law of silence' is clearly inaccurate. What remains, however, is a deep sense of shame which has short-circuited some important and necessary debates.

The *Emsav* did not end in 1944. There were some swift developments almost immediately: a growth in Celtic dance groups, a revival of Celtic music, and a new interest in Breton folk costumes and customs. The discussion in the parish of Locronan in 1950 is a nice way of summing up some of these moves. In 1949, a priest had allowed the traditional *pardon* to be accompanied by a parallel festival of Breton-language poetry and dance. In 1950, a similar festival was proposed at Saint-Pol-de-Léon. The organizers were Bleun-Brug, the Breton Catholic group that had been created by abbé Perrot in 1905, and which was best remembered for its festivals. Its popularity had declined in the years before 1940, but now it seemed to be reviving. The mayor of Saint-Pol was sceptical; weren't these the same people who had collaborated in 1940? In Quimper, in 1948, a similar festival had been disrupted by stone-throwing protestors who shouted 'collaborators!' at the participants.[137] The

Finistère bishop's public approval of the event ended his confusion: he was persuaded to accept the event.[138]

The first manifestations of Breton cultural particularism after 1945 tended to follow these patterns. They were not political; often, they were not even orientated around words, but more around instrumental music, dance and visual culture. In fact, the late twentieth-century development of Breton folk music can be dated to this moment.[139]

The Liberation brought other changes to Brittany. The first elections of 1945 revealed a substantial swing to the left, with the Communist Party (PCF) winning its first seats, the socialist SFIO winning more seats than ever before, and the new, left-leaning Catholic party, the MRP (Popular Republican Movement), becoming the single most successful party in the region. (See Table 8.1.) These new deputies carried with them a new faith in their region. Typical of this spirit was the initiative of the PCF deputy Pierre Hervé (representing Finistère), who in 1947 proposed a bill favouring the teaching of Breton in Breton-language areas.[140] There was even a brief wave of secular female political activism, as Resistance-inspired women's committees campaigned against the Cold War and for better rations. Unfortunately, they won few converts in the rural areas, and their PCF connections often began to split these organizations by the early 1950s. Their numbers then contracted rapidly.[141]

Such movements represented a new mood in the region. Of course, the youthful idealism of young Resisters soon faded into the monochrome world of party rivalries in the Fourth Republic, but there remained a commitment to building a better place for Brittany within a reformed France. This was led by René Pleven, a close associate of de Gaulle during the Occupation,

Table 8.1 Left-wing deputies elected in Brittany in October 1945[142]

	PCF	SFIO	MRP	Total number of deputies
Côtes-du-Nord	2	1	3	7
Finistère	2	2	4	9
Ille-et-Vilaine	0	1	4	7
Loire-Inférieure	1	2	1	8
Morbihan	1	1	0	7
Totals	6	7	12	38

and a left-of-centre deputy during the Fourth Republic. He sponsored the creation of the CELIB: the Comité d'Etudes et de Liaison des Intérêts Bretons (the Breton Research and Liaison Committee) in 1951. This developed into a powerful cross-party lobby group, which rejected the separatism of *Breiz Atao* and the fascistic posturing of the new PNB, and campaigned for institutional and administrative reform to aid economic and social development in the region.

Conclusion

In autumn 1944, Odette du Puigaudeau watched a *pardon* at Douarnenez:

> You can see faces like those carved in stone at Plogoff or Penmarc'h, or like those carved in oak at Menez: they looked solemn, as suited for a pilgrimage. Others were red-faced, lit up with a naïve magic; lads excited by their own joy; boys, labourers, fishers, sailors all out for booze and love; girls half-strangled by their velvet bodices, well-rounded, as ripe as fruit, and decked out in lace and tricolour aprons.
>
> Everyone milled about: they sung, with their mouths full and their hearts overflowing with joy, gathered round the sparkling boats, as the fumes of alcohol and the fairground din swirled round them ... Each of them was looking for joy.[143]

Her work is another example of the new, post-Liberation fascination with Brittany's liminal spaces: its islands and its coastal towns. These isolated cultures seemed to hold a secret message about the region. For some, they revealed a culture that had not changed over the centuries; for others, on the contrary, they showed a civilization which was adapting, modernizing almost before one's eyes.

Such places did not suddenly become fascist in 1940. Brittany supplied more than its fair share of fascists, collaborationists, Pétainists and opportunists, and the role of the new PNB in encouraging such developments is shameful and reprehensible. But, just as elsewhere in France, such activists were a tiny minority. There was no creation of a mass fascist movement in Brittany, no mass support for this ugly combination of collaboration and Celticism, and not even any substantial appreciation of the Vichy-sponsored programme to revive the Breton language. The Nazi pseudo-scientists who visited Carnac to research the continent's racial origins understood less about the region than the Third Republic's bureaucrats and administrators. The mass of the population remained silent: they were unwilling to follow the collaborationists and were then scared by the ready violence and vindictiveness of the Resistance. Many voted for left-wing parties in 1945 and 1946, but these groups were unable to act cohesively: the MRP slid to the right in the late 1940s, the Communist Party was soon locked into a Cold War ghetto, and the socialists remembered their old anticlericalism. The later activities of the Celib certainly represented a substantial improvement for the region's farmers and fishers, but it left unresolved the question which was later to torment Morvan Lebesque: how to be Breton.

Conclusion:
Mordrel's Children

Michel Denis pinpoints the most important question to be drawn from the Breton experience of the Occupation: how could such a gulf have developed between a group which claimed to be inspired by Breton nationalism and the political culture of the majority of the Breton population?[1] And Mordrel leads us to an answer with his sickening picture of the Breton population, 'like a child who has fallen to the ground'.[2] Breton nationalism in the 1940s was divorced from the Breton population. Rather than seeing the tragic end of *Breiz Atao* as exceptional in the history of Brittany, it makes more sense to see it as typical of a strand of Breton political culture, and, more generally, of the manner in which the idea of Brittany has been presented over the past two and a half centuries.

The idea of Brittany is overdetermined, for the region has suffered multiple occupations since the eighteenth century. Each occupying group has, in turn, manufactured its own ideologically constructed images of the region's people, whether as loyal defenders of the King, as sober, patriarchal families, or as poor, alcoholic, superstitious peasants. Linked to these multiple Brittanies, one can also note the frequency with which political militants in Brittany have appealed for external intervention: from Pontcallec's appeal to the Spanish monarchy in the 1720s, through the Vendéens' appeal to the British in the 1790s, Villemarqué's infatuation with the Welsh in the 1830s, the Breton Blues' repeated calls to Paris, ending with Mordrel's final appeal to Nazi Germany to liberate Brittany from the French Jews. In each case, the appeal is not the result of some peculiar conjuncture of political circumstances, but the product of the deep structure of Breton politics: a persistent mistrust of, and distance from, the Breton people. The final result can be seen in *Breiz Atao*, perhaps the least nationalist of any European nationalist grouping and probably also the least Breton. For such militants, the faith in

Conclusion: Mordrel's Children   237

an ideal Brittany, constructed according to the criteria of race, language and tradition, stifled any true contact with the living reality of Breton society.

An important aspect of this political culture has been the effective exclusion of women from political life. Whether one considers the White discourse of the Church, the Blue discourse of the Republic or the Bretonist discourse of the nationalists, one finds their near-complete domination by men. This is curious; certainly women were prominent participants in *pardons* (chapter 4) and food riots (chapter 5). However, each of these discourses was based on the rallying of existing social elites – none sought to empower women or female cultures. This point still applies today; it is noticeable that women are consistently less sympathetic to Breton nationalism or regionalism, and this is usually interpreted as evidence of a female conservatism.[3] The evidence surveyed here suggests otherwise; Breton women correctly understood that Breton regionalism and nationalism were both designed as movements for men. Lastly, this point might also explain the prominence of women in the 'antagonistic' camp identified in section 3 of the Introduction.

Have these multiple occupations created a colonial situation in Brittany? Certainly, there are many similarities. When reading the administrative reports by Prefects and Sub-Prefects, which evoke such a strong sense of alienation and distance from the people who inhabit this land, one could almost believe that they were colonialists in North Africa. The similarity between the Celticist romanticization of Brittany and the Orientalist love for the 'true' Arab adds to this illusion. There were, however, some important differences. Colonialism was the violent annihilation of an indigenous society's ability to govern itself, and a reduction of the mass of the population to the status of legal minors, incapable of political or civic activity. In Brittany, something else was occurring: not so much a denial of political capacity as the forced redirection and exploitation of that capacity for other purposes. A colonial situation does not produce figures such as Chateaubriand and Renan – writers and politicians of absolutely central significance within French political culture. A colonial situation does not produce institutions such as the French missionary societies, often led by Breton clerics, nor the important centres of French–Catholic bodies in Brittany.

Thus, while there are certainly similarities between the Breton situation and the colonial situation, they are clearly not the same. Unlike Algeria, Brittany was and is part of France. A more productive comparison might be to compare Brittany and Scotland, where in each case regional development has taken place through a forced alliance with a larger exploitative partner, and in which the final result has been the production of plausible (if paradoxical) examples of the regional identity as the quintessence of the larger national identity. One thinks of Prince Charles in his kilt; just as the British royal family occasionally like to pretend that they are Scottish, so occasionally Brittany is presented as central to France – as the beginning of a French–Celtic identity, as a refuge, as a conservative force – but rarely as an opponent.

However, unlike Scotland, Brittany has never been the home for a viable or politically significant regional–nationalist movement. In part, this is because the iconic images of Brittany are already partly French. Vercingétorix was accepted by French leaders as an ancestor for their own rule, not as a symbol of a foreign power. Chouannerie was romanticized by French conservatives as well as Breton regionalists. Villemarqué presented his *Barzaz Breiz* as the original source of French literature, not as an example of separate and distinct regional literature.

Alongside this French cultural exploitation of images of Brittany, there are severe and deep socio-cultural divisions within Brittany itself. Bretons can be divided many times over into countless camps: they are Chouan or Republican; White or Blue; Catholic or anticlerical; rural or urban; Breton-speaking or French-speaking; land-dwelling or seafaring; collaborators or resisters . . . even members of B4 (the post-1940, four-department Brittany) or of B5 (the original five-department region). These divisions make it extremely difficult to produce positive, unifying images for the construction of an 'imagined community'. In place of this, each occupying culture has produced its own particular images, which are refused and negated by other Bretons. One cannot even appeal to Breton history to provide safe images of an imagined past: there are still major arguments concerning the role of Celtic culture in the construction of Brittany, the place of migrants from the British Isles, the contribution of the Church and the role of the Republic. These intense political and historical debates have certainly made Brittany tough ground for French nationalism, and for this reason they make Brittany a perfect observation post from which to observe both the strengths and weaknesses in the construction of French nationhood. Equally, however, the same features have also prevented the growth of a viable sense of Breton nationalism.

One last obstacle to the development of Breton nationalism is the performance of Breton nationalists. We have already noted their failure to develop viable forms of populism. To this should be added the record of wartime collaboration, a lasting stain on this political tradition, and one which cannot be explained away as a propaganda image manipulated by French national parties for their own ends. The Breton population is right to be sceptical of a political tradition which firstly produced figures such as Mordrel and,

Conclusion: Mordrel's Children 239

secondly, is still experiencing some significant difficulties in coming to terms with that legacy. The major challenge for the Breton left is to create a rupture with that past: this is an extremely difficult task and, not surprisingly, left-Breton groups have often preferred to attempt to recycle the older political legacy rather than to break with it.

The last two and a half centuries successfully produced a palate of *bretonnitude*. The visual clichés are now readily available and easily understandable: the white-coiffed women, the men in their black velvet waistcoats, the bagpipes, the crowds at the *pardons*, the striking, contrasting, horizontal lines of sea and land, the blue and the white horizontal stripes on the Breton T-shirts, the casual references to the Celtic spirit . . . perhaps, lastly, that intangible sense of human community that can still operate its magic to turn a commercially successful rock concert like the Vieilles Charrues into some sort of spiritual experience. These themes are, above all, non-verbal and apolitical. This is not a nationalism in the normal sense of the word; it has no institutions, no passports, no manifesto, no nationality test and precious little in the form of organization. The sceptical political scientist looking for empirical evidence and the cynical anthropologist looking for congruity between dedicated militants and the mass of the population will both find that this state of mind appears contradictory, delusionary, even suspicious. Yet it is still a nationalism, an effective form of imagined community, a means by which to create the banal solidarities and alliances on which any human association must depend. Mordrel's children have, by and large, rejected his blood and soil determinism to create something more playful, more fitting to a human scale: they live in an invisible nation.

Notes

Introduction: The Rocks of Brittany

1. Emile Souvestre, *Les Derniers Bretons* (Rennes: Terre de Brume, 1997 [1836]), p. 25. All translations from French-language works are my own, except where otherwise noted.
2. Anatole Le Braz, *Il était une voix... discours et conférences* (Rennes: Apogée, 1995), p. 37.
3. Charles Le Quintrec, *Une enfance bretonne* (Paris: Albin Michel, 2000), p.25.
4. Cited in Jean-Pierre Mohen, *Standing Stones: Stonehenge, Carnac and the World of Megaliths*, trans. by Harry N. Abrams (London: Thames and Hudson, 1998), p. 31.
5. On the recent regional successes of the UDB and similar groups, see Michel Nicolas, 'Les Bretons et la politique: entre suivisme et particularisme', *Ar Men*, 150 (January 2006), 54–61.
6. Niccolò Machiavelli, *The Prince* trans. G. Ball (Harmondsworth: Penguin, 1999) pp. 7–8.
7. J. S. Mill, *Considerations on Representative Government* (London: Dent, 1972) pp. 363–5.
8. Jules Michelet, *Tableau de la France* (Paris: Société des Belles Lettres, 1934), p. 18.
9. Fañch Broudic, *Qui parle Breton aujourd'hui?* (Brest: Brud Nevez, 1999), pp. 15 and 24.
10. Stefan Moal, 'Breton: Construire un avenir', *Ar Men*, 150 (January 2006), 44–53.
11. On the history of the Breton language, see Fañch Broudic, *La pratique du breton de l'Ancien Régime à nos jours* (Rennes: Presses Universitaires de Rennes, 1995).
12. See my 'The politics of language: debates and identities in contemporary Brittany', *French Cultural Studies*, 13:2 (2002), 145–64.
13. This point is a complex one: there are means through which many *Diwan* schools do benefit from some indirect funding from local and regional bodies. On the *Diwan* schools, see Jean-Charles Perazzi, *Diwan: vingt ans d'enthousiasme, de doute et d'espoir* (Spézet: Coop Breizh, 1998) for a sympathetic study, and see my interview with Andrew Lincoln, the ex-President of the *Diwan* movement: 'The seed thrower's story', *Planet: the Welsh Internationalist*, 161 (October 2003), 52–64.

14 Broudic, *Qui parle breton?*, p. 101
15 For a useful historical survey of this issue, see Paul Cohen, 'Of linguistic Jacobinism and cultural Balkanization: contemporary French linguistic politics in historical context', *French Politics, Culture and Society*, 18:2 (2000), 21–48. Marie Landick, 'French courts and language legislation', *French Cultural Studies*, 11 (2000), 131–48, and Lynne Wilcox, '*Coup de langue*: the amendment to Article 2 of the constitution: an equivocal interpretation of linguistic pluralism', *Modern and Contemporary France*, 2:3 (1994), 269–78 address more contemporary issues.
16 See my 'Roots, rock, Breizh: music and the politics of nationhood in contemporary Brittany', *Nations and Nationalism*, 11:1 (2005), 103–20.
17 *Libération*, 12 August 1999.
18 For a provocatively sceptical reaction, see Meic Stephens, 'An empty chair in Lorient: the thirtieth Interceltic Festival', *Planet*, 143 (October 2000), 86–91.
19 Jean-Michel Le Boulanger, 'Réflexions sur l'identité de la Bretagne', *Hopala*, 3 (1999), 8–15.
20 *Ouest-France*, 11 January 2001; *Le Monde*, 20 October 1999.
21 *Télégramme*, 19 November 1999.
22 Ibid., 29 May 2001.
23 Ibid., 19 January 2000.
24 Yvon Rochard, 'Lannion et la Trégor Valley', *Ar Men*, 124 (September 2001), 2–13.
25 *Télégramme*, 5 January 2000.
26 *Le Monde*, 19 October 2001, *Ouest-France* 8 January 2003.
27 *Télégramme*, 18 May 2001.
28 Ibid., 30 June 2000.
29 For a short survey of such shifts, see Michel Nicolas, 'Les Bretons et la politique: entre suivisme et particularisme', *Ar Men*, 150 (January 2006), pp. 54–61.
30 Gustave Flaubert, 'Par les champs et par les grèves: voyage en Bretagne, 1847', *Œuvres complètes II*' ed. B. Masson (Paris: Seuil, 1964), pp. 472–548.
31 Fortuné de Boisgobey, *Voyage en Bretagne, 1839* (Rennes: Ouest–France, 2001).
32 See Manuel Jover, 'Gauguin, la découverte', *L'œil*, hors-série (2003), pp. 18–31.
33 Honoré de Balzac, *Les Chouans, ou la Bretagne en 1799* (Paris: Gallimard, 1972 [1829]), p. 40.
34 Michelet, *Tableau*, p. 8.
35 *The Complete Wild Body*, ed. Bernard Lafoucade (Santa Barbara: Black Sparrow Press, 1982).
36 Katie Trumpener, *Bardic Nationalism: the Romantic Novel and the British Empire* (Princeton: Princeton UP, 1997), p. xi.
37 See Patrick Galliou and Michael Jones, *The Bretons* (Oxford: Blackwell, 1991), p. 133.
38 Louis Guilloux, *Ma Bretagne* (Bédée: Flolle Avoine, 1998 [1973]), p. 35.
39 Maryon McDonald, *We are not French! Language, Culture and Identity in Brittany* (London: Routledge, 1989), p. 77.
40 Ibid., p. 88.
41 Ibid., p. 217.
42 Ibid., p. 111.
43 Ibid., p. 116.

44 *We are not French*, p. 276 n.
45 Françoise Morvan, *Le Monde comme si: nationalisme et dérive identitaire en Bretagne* (Arles: Actes Sud, 2002), pp. 38, 57.
46 *Le Monde*, p. 174.
47 Ibid., p. 77.
48 See, for example, her *L'Ille-et-Vilaine, 1918–1958: vie politique et sociale* (Rennes: PUR, 1996).
49 Jean-Jacques Monnier, 'Des militants bretons dans la Résistance', in C. Bougeard (ed.), *Bretagne et Identités régionales* (Brest: CRBC, 2001), pp. 103–19 (p. 103).
50 Michel Denis, 'Le mouvement Breton pendant la guerre: un bilan', in Bougeard (ed.), *Bretagne et Identités régionales*, pp. 151–66 (p. 153).
51 On the theme of a declining French nationalism, see my 'An extremism of the center: Jean-Pierre Chevènement, French presidential candidate, 2002', *French Politics, Culture and Society*, 22:1 (2004), 76–97.
52 E. P. Thompson, *The Making of the English Working Class* (Harmondsworth: Penguin, 1993), p. 12.
53 Caroline Ford, *Creating the Nation in Provincial France: Religion and Political Identity in Brittany* (Princeton: Princeton UP, 1993), p. 5.
54 In this respect, there is some similarity between the methodology adopted here, and that used by Ronan Le Coadic. See his *L'identité bretonne* (Rennes: PUR and Terre de Brume, 1998), p. 18.
55 Example cited in Charles Le Goffic, *L'Ame bretonne* (Paris: Honoré Chapman, 1908), vol. III, p. 56.
56 The paragraphs which follow are largely drawn from Galliou and Jones, *Bretons*.
57 Myles Dillon and Nora Chadwick, *The Celtic Realms* (London: Phoenix, 2000), p. 57.
58 Henri Hubert, *The Rise of the Celts*, (London: Constable, 1987 [1934]), p. 167.
59 See Jean-Paul Bihan, 'L'urbanisme de Quimper au Moyen-Age', *Ar Men*, 125 (November 2001), 2–13 for a recent survey of some new ideas on this topic.
60 Nora Chadwick, *Early Brittany* (Cardiff: University of Wales Press, 1969), p. 197.
61 Galliou and Jones, *Bretons*, p. 151. See also Wendy Davies, *Small Worlds: the Village Community in Early Medieval Brittany* (London: Duckworth, 1988), p. 20.
62 Davies, *Small Worlds*, p. 10.
63 Galliou and Jones, *Bretons*, p. 182.
64 Michael Jones, *Ducal Brittany, 1364–99: Relations with England and France During the Reign of Duke John IV* (Oxford: Oxford University Press, 1970), p. 2, and Michael Jones, *The Creation of Brittany: a Late Medieval State* (London: Hambledon Press, 1988), p. 287.
65 Jones, *The Creation*, p. 305.
66 Galliou and Jones, *Bretons*, p. 206.
67 Ibid., *Bretons*, p. 210.
68 Ibid., p. 253.
69 James B. Collins, *Classes, Estates and Order in Early Modern Brittany* (Cambridge: Cambridge University Press, 1994), p. 33.
70 Davies, *Small Worlds*, p. 211.

1 The Question of French Nationhood: Celts, Romans and Bretons

1. 'La Bretagne à pied', *Nouvel Observateur*, 20 July 2000.
2. Rabindranath Tagore, *Nationalism* (London: Macmillan, 1991 [1917]), pp. 50–5.
3. Frantz Fanon, *Les damnés de la terre* (Paris: Maspero, 1968), pp. 138–9.
4. Michael Billig, *Banal Nationalism* (London: Sage, 1995), p. 14.
5. The literature on nationalism is immense. Good starting-points can be found in the edited reader by John Hutchinson and Anthony D. Smith, *Nationalism* (Oxford: Oxford University Press, 1994), and the essays edited by Stuart Woolf, *Nationalism in Europe, 1815 to the Present* (London: Routledge, 1996).
6. This chronology has been contested by Anthony D. Smith, who has produced some challenging arguments to suggest that nationalism is a far older phenomenon. See, for example, his *Nationalism: Theory, Ideology, History* (Cambridge: Polity, 2001). For reasons which will become clearer in the course of this chapter, I cannot accept his arguments.
7. Benedict Anderson, *Imagined Communities: Reflections on the Origin and Spread of Nationalism*, revised edition (London: Verso, 1994), chapter 4.
8. John Breuilly, *Nationalism and the State* (Manchester: Manchester University Press, 1985).
9. Stuart Woolf, 'Introduction' to his *Nationalism in Europe*, pp. 1–40.
10. See the useful observations by George L. Mosse in chapter 4 of his *Nationalism and Sexuality: Middle-Class Morality and Sexual Norms in Modern Europe* (Madison: University of Wisconsin Press, 1985).
11. Billig, *Banal Nationalism*, p. 94.
12. On the case of female teachers, see my *Women and Schooling: Gender, Authority and Identity in the Female Schooling Sector, France, 1815–1914* (Keele University Press, 1995). On patriotic women's groups, see Roger Chickering, '"Casting their gaze more broadly": women's patriotic activism in imperial Germany', *Past and Present*, 118 (1988), 156–86.
13. This point is made particularly forcefully by Ernest Gellner in his *Nationalism* (London: Weidenfeld and Nicolson, 1997).
14. 'The new programme of the PNF [National Fascist Party], November 1921' in Charles F. Delzell, *Mediterranean Fascism, 1919–45* (London: Walker, 1971), pp. 26–37, p. 94.
15. See his *The Break-up of Britain: Crisis and Neo-Nationalism*, 2nd edn (London: Verso, 1981).
16. Erwan Vallerie, *Nous barbares locaux: théorie de la nation et autres textes de 'Sav Breizh'* (Le Relecq-Kerhoun: An Here, 1997), pp. 50–5.
17. Montserrat Guibernau, *Nations without States: Political Communities in a Global Age* (Cambridge: Polity, 1999), p. 31.
18. See, for example, the debates in Jane Aaron and Chris Williams (eds), *Postcolonial Wales* (Cardiff: University of Wales Press, 2005).
19. Peter Burke, 'Did Europe exist before 1700?', *History of European Ideas*, 1 (1980), pp. 21–9 (p. 21).
20. Smith, *Nationalism*, p. 54.
21. George Schöpflin, *Nations, Identity, Power: the New Politics of Europe* (London: Hurst, 2000), p. 29.

22 Fanon, *Les damnés*, p. 137.
23 William Bloom, *Personal Identity, National Identity and International Relations* (Cambridge: Cambridge University Press, 1990), pp. 38–40. See also Cornelius Castoriadis, 'La crise du processus identificatoire', in his *La Montée de l'insignifiance* (Paris: Seuil, 1996), pp. 125–39 for a fascinating analysis of failures of identification mechanisms in contemporary Western society.
24 Jean Bethke Elshtain, 'Sovereignty, identity and sacrifice', in *Real Politics: at the Centre of Everyday Life* (Baltimore: Johns Hopkins University Press, 1997) pp. 126–44.
25 Anderson, *Imagined Communities*, p. 5.
26 David McCrone, *The Sociology of Nationalism: Tomorrow's Ancestors* (London and New York: Routledge, 1998), p. 25.
27 On this nineteenth-century development, see Matthew Jefferies, 'The age of historicism', in S. Berger (ed.), *A Companion to Nineteenth-century Europe* (Oxford: Blackwell, 2006), pp. 316–32.
28 Schöpflin, *Nations, Identity, Power*, p. 74.
29 See my 'France, orientalism and Algeria: fifty-four articles from the *Revue des Deux Mondes*, 1846–1852', *Journal of Algerian Studies*, 3 (1998), 48–70.
30 Stuart Woolf, *Napoleon's Integration of Europe* (London: Routledge, 1991), pp. 8–9.
31 See Bernard Guenée, *States and Rulers in Later Medieval Europe* (Oxford: Oxford University Press, 1985), trans. J. Vale and Geary, *Myth of Nations*.
32 Josep Fontana, *The Distorted Past: A Reinterpretation of Europe*, trans. Colin Smith (Oxford: Blackwell, 1995), p. 38. On the continuing prestige of Latin, see Peter Burke, '*Hen domine, adsunt Turcae*: a sketch for a social history of post-medieval Latin', in P. Burke and R. Porter (eds), *Language, Self and Society* (Cambridge: Polity, 1994), pp. 23–50.
33 See Bernard Guenée, 'Les "Grandes Chroniques de France": le Roman aux roys, 1274–1518', in P. Nora (ed.), *Les Lieux de Mémoire* I (Paris: Quarto/Gallimard, 1997), pp. 739–58.
34 See, for example, the analysis of the works of the Maurist order in Jean Quéniart, 'Les mauristes et l'historiographie bretonne', in N.-Y. Tonnerre (ed.), *Chroniques et historiens de la Bretagne* (Rennes: PUR, 2001), pp. 111–23.
35 See Pierre Goubert, *The Ancien Regime: French Society, 1600–1750*, trans. S. Cox (London: Weidenfeld and Nicolson, 1976), p. 160.
36 Jean-Yves Guiomar, *La Nation entre l'histoire et la raison* (Paris: La Découverte, 1990), p. 89.
37 Guiomar, *La Nation*, p. 91.
38 Joseph Rio, *Mythes fondateurs de la Bretagne: aux origines de la celtomanie* (Rennes: Editions Ouest-France, 2000), pp. 240–1.
39 See Krystof Pomian, 'Franks et Gauls', in P. Nora (ed.), *Les Lieux de Mémoire*, II (Paris: Quarto/Gallimard, 1997), pp. 2245–300.
40 John Collis, 'Celtic myths', *Antiquity*, 71 (1997), 195–210.
41 See Clare O'Halloran, 'Irish re-creations of the Gaelic past: the challenge of MacPherson's *Ossian*', *Past and Present*, 124 (1989), 69–95.
42 For a useful introduction to recent research on Celtic history, see Miranda Green (ed.), *The Celtic World* (London: Routledge, 1995).

43 Timothy Chapman, 'The Celt in archaeology', in Terence Brown (ed.), *Celticism* (Amsterdam: Rodopi, 1996), pp. 61–78.
44 Maurice Duhamel, *Histoire du peuple breton des origines à 1532* (Kergleuz: An Here, 2000 [1939]), p. 109.
45 David Rankin, 'The Celts through classical eyes', in M. Green, *The Celtic World* (London: Routledge, 1995), pp. 21–33.
46 Andrew P. Fitzpatrick, '"Celtic" iron age Europe: the theoretical basis', in P. Graves-Brown, S. James and C. Gamble (eds), *Cultural Identity and Archaeology* (London: Routledge, 1996), pp. 238–55 (p. 244). See also Burke, 'Did Europe exist before 1700?'.
47 Rankin, 'Celts through classical eyes', p. 21.
48 Fontana, *The Distorted Past*, p. 15.
49 Rankin, 'Celts through classical eyes', pp. 21–7.
50 Olivier Buchsenschutz and Alain Schnapp, 'Alésia', in P. Nora (ed.), *Les Lieux de Mémoire*, III (Paris: Quarto/Gallimard, 1997), pp. 4103–40 (p. 4104).
51 Caesar, *The Gallic War*, trans. H. J. Edwards (Cambridge, Massachusetts: Harvard UP, 1994), p. 187.
52 See, for example, Henri Poisson and Jean-Pierre Le Mat, *Histoire de Bretagne* (Spézet: Coop Briezh, 2000), pp. 14, 35; Maurice Duhamel, *Histoire du peuple breton*, p. 30.
53 See Fontana, *The Distorted Past*, pp. 12–13.
54 This is the argument taken by, for example, Poisson and Le Mat, *Histoire de Bretagne*, p. 14.
55 Henri Hubert, *The Rise of the Celts*, trans. M. R. Dobie (London: Constable, 1987 [1934]), pp. 13–14.
56 For some interesting considerations on the differences between written and oral cultures, see Walter J. Ong, *Orality and Literacy: the Technologizing of the Word* (London: Routledge, 1982).
57 Nora K. Chadwick, *Early Brittany* (Cardiff: University of Wales Press, 1969), p. 198.
58 See, for example, the considered views of Galliou and Jones, *Bretons*, pp. 128–29.
59 Myles Dillon and Nora Chadwick, *The Celtic Realms* (London: Phoenix, 2000 [1967]), preface.
60 Miranda Green, *Celtic Art: Reading the Messages* (London: Weidenfeld and Nicolson, 1996), p. 11. Since writing this essay, Green has revised her ideas, and now prefers the term 'Iron Age' to Celtic.
61 Peter Beresford Ellis, *The Celtic Dawn: a History of Pan-Celticism* (London: Constable, 1993), p. 21.
62 Patrick Galliou and Michael Jones, *The Bretons* (Oxford: Blackwell, 1991), p. 1. On such images of the Celts, see also Moya Kneafsey, 'Tourism images and the construction of Celticity in Ireland and Brittany', in D. C. Harvey, R. Jones, N. McInroy and C. Milligan (eds), *Celtic Geographies: Old Cultures, New Times* (London: Routledge, 2002), pp. 123–38.
63 Michael Dietler, '"Our ancestors the Gauls": archaeology, ethnic nationalism, and the manipulation of Celtic identity in modern Europe', *American Anthropologist*, 96:3 (1994), 584–605 (p. 586).
64 Fitzpatrick, 'Celtic Iron Age Europe', pp. 244–5.

65 Colin Renfrew, 'Prehistory and the identity of Europe', in Siân Jones and Paul Graves-Brown (eds), *Cultural Identity and Archaeology* (London: Routledge, 1996), pp. 125–37.
66 Simon James, *The Atlantic Celts: Ancient People or Modern Invention?* (London: British Museum Press, 1999), p. 137.
67 See Siân Jones and Paul Graves-Brown, 'Introduction: archaeology and cultural identity in Europe', in their *Cultural Identity and Archaeology* (London: Routledge, 1996), pp. 1–24.
68 Patrick Sims-Williams, 'Celtomania and Celtoscepticism', *Cambrian Medieval Celtic Studies*, 36 (1998), 1–35.
69 Dietler, 'Our Ancestors the Gauls', p. 586.
70 Lynn Hunt, *Politics, Culture and Class in the French Revolution* (London: Methuen, 1984), p. 28.
71 See Annie Jourdan, 'The image of Gaul during the French Revolution', in Terence Brown (ed.), *Celticism* (Amsterdam: Rodopi, 1996), pp. 183–206 and the useful article by Mona Ozouf, 'L'invention de l'ethnographie française: le questionnaire de l'Académie celtique', *Annales ESC*, 36 (1981), 210–30.
72 See Guiomar, *La Nation*, chapter 5.
73 The argument presented here owes much to the perceptive study by Nicole Belmont, 'L'Académie celtique et George Sand', *Romantisme*, 9 (1975), 29–38.
74 Buchsenschutz and Schnapp, 'Alésia', p. 4121.
75 On early modern studies of popular culture, see Natalie Z. Davis, 'Proverbial wisdom and popular errors', in her *Society and Culture in Early Modern France* (Cambridge: Polity, 1987), pp. 227–70.
76 Emile Souvestre, 'Les récits de la muse populaire: le sorcier du Petit-Haule', *Revue des Deux Mondes*, 15 February 1849, pp. 608–39.
77 Jacques Cambry, *Voyage dans le Finistère* (Paris: Layeur, 2000 [1794–95]), 150–1, p. 266.
78 Prosper Mérimée, *Notes d'un Voyage dans l'Ouest de la France* (Paris: Adam Biro, 1989), p. 95.
79 Emile Souvestre, 'Les récits de la muse populaire: la fileuse', *Revue de Deux Mondes*, 1 April 1849, pp. 102–33.
80 See Martyn Lyons, 'The Audience for Romantism: Walter Scott in France', *European History Quarterly*, 14 (1984), 21–46.
81 Katie Trumpener, *Bardic Nationalism: the Romantic Novel and the British Empire* (Princeton: Princeton University Press, 1997), p. 152.
82 See Jean-Yves Guiomar, 'Le celtisme chez les intellectuels français/bretons de gauche au XIXe siècle', in A. Draguet (ed.), *Les bleus de Bretagne* (Saint-Brieuc: Fédération 'Côtes-du-Nord, 1789', 1991), pp. 283–92.
83 Dietler, 'Our ancestors the Gauls', p. 588.
84 On the importance of this excavation, see Michael Dietler, 'A tale of three sites', *World Archaeology*, 30:1 (1998), 72–89 and Buchsenschutz and Schnapp, 'Alésia'.
85 Jean-Yves Guiomar, *Le bretonisme: les historiens bretons au XIXe siècle* (NP: Société d'Histoire et d'Archéologie de Bretagne, 1987), 167–9.
86 Buchsenschutz and Schnapp, 'Alésia', p. 4124.
87 Caesar, *Gallic War*, p. 509.
88 Charles Le Goffic, *L'Ame bretonne* Vol I (Paris: Champion, 1908), p. 158.

Notes 247

89 See Dietler, 'Three sites'.
90 J.-F. Brousmiche, *Voyage dans le Finistère en 1829, 1830 et 1831* (Quimper: Morvan, 1977), p. 160.
91 Henri Hubert, *The Greatness and Decline of the Celts* (London: Constable, 1987 [1934]), trans. M. R. Dobie, p. 167.
92 Per Denez, 'Le Barzhaz Breizh et la Renaissance Bretonne' in his edition of the *Barzhaz Breizh* (Spézet: Coop Breizh, 1997), pp. 9–31 (p. 9).
93 Jean-Yves Guiomar, 'Le Barzaz Breiz de Théodore Hersart de La Villemarqué', in P. Nora (ed.), *Les Lieux de Mémoire*, Vol. III (Paris: Quarto-Gallimard, 1997), pp. 3479–514 (p. 3487). Mary-Ann Constantine, *Breton Ballads* (Aberystwyth: CMCS, 1996), p. 14. The analysis presented in these paragraphs owes much to Constantine's eloquent work.
94 On Lamennais see Bernard Reardon, *Religion in the Age of Romanticism: Studies in Early Nineteenth Century Thought* (Cambridge: Cambridge University Press, 1985).
95 Guiomar, *Bretonisme*, p. 66.
96 Théodore Hersart de La Villemarqué, 'Préface', *Barzaz Breiz* ed. Per Denez (Spézet: Coop Breizh, 1997), p. 53.
97 Fañch Postic and François de Beaulieu, 'Le nouvel essor de la littérature orale', *Ar Men*, 1998 (hors série), pp. 40–9.
98 On this point, see Bernard Tanguy, *Aux origines du nationalisme breton*, 2 vols (Paris: Union générale d'éditions, 1977), 1, 135–6.
99 Guiomar, *Le Bretonisme*, p. 74; Constantine, *Breton Ballads*, p. 9
100 Villemarqué, 'Préface', p. 36.
101 See Mosse, *Nationalism and Sexuality*, pp. 6–7, for some perceptive comments on the nature of this movement.
102 Brousmiche, *Voyage*, p. 23.
103 Patrick Galliou and Michael Jones, *The Bretons* (Oxford: Blackwell, 1991), p. 185.
104 Georges Minois, 'Anne de Bretagne: un portrait sans concessions', *Ar Men*, 106 (Sep 1999), 14–23.
105 Jean Kervhervé, 'Ecriture et récriture de l'histoire dans l'Histoire de Bretagne de Bertrand d'Argentré: l'exemple du Livre XII', in N.-Y. Tonnerre (ed.), *Chroniques et historiens de la Bretagne* (Rennes: PUR, 2001), pp. 77–109.
106 Heather Williams, 'Une sauvagerie très douce', in N. Harkness, P. Rowe, T. Unwin and J. Yee (eds), *Visions/Revisions* (Oxford: Peter Lang, 2003), pp. 99–106. On Brizeux, see also the same author's 'Le voyage transculturel de Brizeux', *Seuils et traverses*, III (2002), pp. 275–85.
107 Théophile Gautier, *Le salon de 1847* (Paris: Le Livre à la carte, 1997), p. 131.
108 Mérimée, *Notes d'un Voyage*, p. 13.
109 Daniel Leloup, 'Protection des monuments: les premiers classements en Bretagne', *Ar Men* 115 (October 2000), 12–19.
110 G. Bruno, *Le Tour de la France par deux enfants: devoir et patrie* (Paris: Eugène Blin: 1995 [1905?]), pp. 221–31. On this text, see Jacques Ozouf and Mona Ozouf, '*Le Tour de la France par deux enfants*: le petit livre rouge de la République', in P. Nora (ed.), *Les Lieux de Mémoire* I (Paris: Gallimard, 1997), pp. 277–302.
111 Mark Antliff, 'Cubism, Celtism and the body politic', *Art Bulletin*, 74:4 (1992), 655–68.

112 See Thierry Glon, 'Ecrivains de la Recouvrance (de 1960 à 1980)', *Plurial*, 5 (1995), 33–52. While this author is discussing a quite different time period, the use of 'Brittany' which he identifies is clearly consistent with that initiated by Villemarqué.
113 *www.asterix.tm.fr*, 20 December 2001.
114 See Béatrice Fleury-Ilett, 'The identity of France: archetypes in Iron Age studies', in P. Graves-Brown, S. James and C. Gamble (eds), *Cultural Identity and Archaeology* (London: Routledge, 1996), pp. 196–208.
115 See John Collis, 'Celts and Politics', in P. Graves-Brown, S. James and C. Gamble (eds), *Cultural Identity and Archaeology*, pp. 167–78.

2 Brittany and the French Revolution

1 Michel Denis, *Rennes, berceau de la liberté: revolution et démocratie, une ville à l'avant-garde* (Rennes: Ouest-France, 1989), pp. 10, 89, 114.
2 Loeiz Ar Beg, *Les Bretons et leurs libertés* (Brasparts: Beltan, 1989), p. 152. Emphasis in the original.
3 James B. Collins, *Classes, Estates and Order in Early Modern Brittany* (Cambridge: Cambridge University Press, 1994), p. 14.
4 See Jean Quéniart, *Le Grand Chapelletout: violence, normes et comportements en Bretagne rurale au 18e siècle* (Rennes: Apogée, 1993), pp. 31, 40 and 52.
5 For example, see Jacques-Louis Ménétra, *Journal of My Life* (New York: Columbia University Press, 1986), trans. A. Goldhammer, p. 61; Alain Corbin, 'Paris-Province', in P. Nora (ed.), *Les Lieux de Mémoire*, II (Paris: Quarto-Gallimard, 1997), pp. 2851–88.
6 Catherine Bertho, 'L'invention de la Bretagne: génèse sociale d'un stéréotype', *Actes de la recherche en sciences socials*, 35 (1980), 45–62.
7 Jean Markale, *Identité de Bretagne* (Paris: Entente, 1985), p. 87.
8 See Claude Nières, 'Rivalités France-Angleterre vue de Bretagne au XVIII siècle', in Robert Chaguy (ed.), *La Révolution française* (Grenoble: Presses Universitaire de Grenoble, 2002), pp. 21–34.
9 Collins, *Classes, Estates and Orders*, p. 36.
10 Jean Quéniart, *La Bretagne au XVIIIe siècle (1675–1789)* (Rennes: Ouest-France, 2004), 157–65.
11 Grégory Aupiais, 'L'urbanisme à Guérande au XVIIIe siècle', *Annales de Bretagne et des Pays de l'Ouest*, 106:4 (1999), 65–78 (p. 66).
12 T. J. A. Le Goff, *Vannes and Its Region: a Study of Town and Country in Eighteenth-century France* (Oxford: Clarendon, 1981), p. 43.
13 Dubuisson-Aubenay, *Itinéraire de Bretagne en 1636*, 2 vols (Paris: Layeur, 2000), I, pp. 58–9.
14 Louis Trenard, 'Images de Bretagne dans la presse du XVIIIe siècle', *Annales de Bretagne et des Pays de l'Ouest*, 54:4 (1976), 585–604.
15 Arthur Young, *Travels in France and Italy* (London: Dent, 1934), p. 101.
16 J. Gury, 'A la découverte de la Bretagne, dans la seconde moitié du XVIIIe siècle', in J. Balcou and Y. Le Gallo (eds), *Histoire culturelle et littéraire de la Bretagne*, 3 vols (Paris-Spezed: Champion – Coop Breizh, 1997), I, 391–8 (p. 391).
17 Nolwenn Juhel, 'La pastorale d'un prêtre breton dans la seconde moitié du XVIIIe siècle: les sermons de René Cavaro de Kergorre', *Annales de Bretagne et des Pays de l'Ouest*, 110:2 (2003), 77–109.

18 J. Meyer, 'L'environnement intellectuelle de la Bretagne au XVIIIe siècle', in J. Balcou and Y. Le Gallo, *Histoire littéraire et culturelle de la Bretagne*, I, 345–58.
19 Jacques Cambry, *Voyage dans le Finistère* (Paris: Layeur, 2000), p. 32.
20 Quéniart, *La Bretagne*, pp. 364–5; Yvon Rochard, 'Le bagne de Brest', *Ar Men*, 58 (April 1994), 12–25.
21 André Lespagnol, *Entre l'argent et la gloire: la course malouine au temps de Louis XIV* (Rennes: Apogée, 1995), pp. 12–13.
22 Lespagnol, *Entre l'argent et la gloire*, pp. 64 and 153.
23 Olivier Pétré-Grenouilleau, *Nantes au temps de la traite des Noirs* (Paris: Hachette, 1998), p. 32.
24 Pétré-Grenouilleau, *Nantes*, pp. 35–7.
25 Annick Le Douget, *Juges, Esclaves et Négriers en Basse-Bretagne, 1750–1850* (Spézet: Unesco, 2000), p. 38.
26 Pétré-Grenouilleau, *Nantes*, p. 109.
27 Alain Croix, *L'âge d'or de la Bretagne, 1532–1675* (Rennes: Ouest-France, 1993), p. 242.
28 Lespagnol, *Entre l'argent et la gloire*, pp. 39–40, 47–53.
29 Vincent Rogard, *Les Catholiques et la question sociale: Morlaix, 1840–1914* (Rennes: PUR, 1997), p. 16.
30 Denis, *Rennes*, pp. 23 and 31.
31 Christian Kermoal, *Les notables du Trégor: éveil à la culture politique et évolution dans les paroisses rurales (1770–1850)* (Rennes: PUR, 2002), pp. 25–9.
32 Bertho, 'L'invention de la Bretagne', p. 46.
33 See Sophie Duhem, 'XVe–XVIIe: le "costume" des Bretons', *Ar Men*, 117 (December 2000), pp. 28–39.
34 Paul Cohen, 'Of linguistic Jacobinism and cultural Balkanization: contemporary French linguistic politics in historical context', *French Politics, Culture and Society*, 18:2 (2000), 21–48 (p. 29).
35 J. Gury, 'A la découverte de la Bretagne', p. 391. On this point, see Dubuisson-Aubenay, *Itinéraire*. The first 256 pages of this work contain only three brief references to the existence of spoken Breton.
36 John Hurt, 'The Parlement of Brittany and the Crown: 1665–75', *French Historical Studies*, 4 (1965–6), 411–33; Quéniart, *Bretagne*, p. 17.
37 Collins, *Classes, Estates and Order*, p. 160.
38 Quéniart, *Bretagne*, p. 223.
39 Ibid., p. 16.
40 Ibid., p. 67; Roger Dupuy, *La Bretagne sous la Révolution et l'Empire (1789–1815)* (Rennes, Ouest-France, 2004), p. 19.
41 Jean Meyer, *La Noblesse bretonne au XVIIIe siècle* (Paris: Flammarion, 1972), p. 269.
42 François-René Chateaubriand, *Mémoires d'outre-tombe, Vol I* (Paris: Librairie Générale Française, 1973), p. 50.
43 Collins, *Classes, Estates and Order*, p. 45.
44 Quéniart, *Bretagne*, p. 36.
45 Marquis de Bellevue, 'La conjuration de Pontallec dans le pays de Ploërmel', *Association Bretonne: Comptes-Rendus, Procès-Verbaux, Mémoires*, 28 (1909), pp. 44–55; Quéniart, *Bretagne*, pp. 52–9.
46 Quéniart, *Bretagne*, p. 214.

47 Denis, *Rennes*, pp. 21–3.
48 Ibid., pp. 68–9.
49 Kermoal, *Les Notables*, p. 190.
50 De Botherel, *Protestations adressés au roi et au public*, ed. Loeiz Le Bec (Le Relecq-Kerhuon: An Here, 2000), pp. 63–4.
51 Ibid., p. 68.
52 Ibid., p. 79.
53 Ibid., p. 85.
54 Alain Croix, 'Blancs, Bleus et Doléances', in Alain Droguet (ed.), *Les Bleus de Bretagne* (Saint-Brieuc: Fédération 'Côtes-du-Nord 1989', 1991), pp. 23–43.
55 Kermoal, *Les Notables*, p. 221.
56 Dupuy, *La Bretagne*, pp. 27–9.
57 Kermoal, *Les Notables*, p. 234.
58 'Discours', *Moniteur Universelle*, 84 (5 November 1789), reproduced in Botherel, *Protestations*.
59 Claude Nières, 'Le pouvoir municipal en Bretagne en 1789 d'après les cahiers de doléances', in Droguet, *Les Bleus de Bretagne*, pp. 13–22.
60 Denis, *Rennes*, p. 128.
61 Jean Pascal, *Les députés bretons de 1789 à 1983* (Paris: Presses Universitaires de France, 1983), p. 38.
62 The best discussion of this controversial point is arguably provided by William H. Sewell, *A Rhetoric of Bourgeois Revolution: the Abbé Sieyes* (Durham: Duke University Press, 1994).
63 Quéniart, *La Bretagne*, p. 205.
64 Denis, *Rennes*, p. 135.
65 Ibid., p. 170.
66 Le Gendre, *Supplément à l'adresse au peuple breton par ses députés à l'Assemblée nationale* (no publisher, 1790), p. 9.
67 René Estienne, 'La correspondance de Joseph Delaville-Leroulx, député lorientais du Tiers aux Etats généraux', in Droguet, *Les Bleus de Bretagne*, pp. 137–48.
68 Le Marchand d'Epinay, *Seconde Adresse de la ville de Rennes aux habitans des campagnes* (Rennes: Vatar, 1790).
69 Dupuy, *La Bretagne*, p. 71.
70 *Lettres de P. de Clorivière, 1787–1814*, Vol I (Paris: Durassié, 1948), p. 42.
71 *Justification des prêtres qui refusent de faire le serment civique* (Rennes?: no publisher, no date 1790?).
72 Le Breton, *Lettre . . . à MM. les Ecclésiastiques du Département de Morbihan* (Paris: Imprimerie Nationale, 1791).
73 Dupuy, *La Bretagne*, pp. 81–3.
74 Ibid., p. 90.
75 Adolphe Orain (ed.), *La Chouannerie en Pays Gallo* (Bouhet: La Decouvrance, 2002), p. 42.
76 Watkin Tench, *Letters from Revolutionary France*, ed. Gavin Edwards (Cardiff: University of Wales Press, 2001), p. 124.
77 Dupuy, *La Bretagne*, pp. 101–3.
78 Denis, *Rennes*, p. 193.
79 AD I&V, L.449, 14 March 1793.

80 This revolt has stimulated volumes of historical writing. The best studies are arguably those by Jean-Clément Martin: see his *La Vendée et la France* (Paris: Seuil, 1978), and *La Vendée de la mémoire (1800–1980)*, (Paris: Seuil, 1989).
81 AD I&V, L.449, 15 March 1793.
82 Martin, *La Vendée et la France*, p. 44.
83 Joachim Darsel (ed.), *L'homme qui croyait en la République: livre de vie de Jean-Marie Jézéquel* (Morlaix: Le Bouquiniste, 2000), p. 31.
84 Donald Sutherland, *The Chouans: the Social Origins of Popular Counter-Revolution in Upper Brittany, 1790–6* (Oxford: Clarendon Press, 1982), p. 7.
85 Martin, *La Vendée et la France*, pp. 170–1.
86 'La marquise de La Rochejaquelein', *Mémoires* (Paris: Mercure de France, 2002), p. 119.
87 Souben, *Chouannerie*, pp. 33–5.
88 Souben, *Chouannerie*, pp. 45–6.
89 Ibid., p. 52.
90 Reports from the district of Vitré, reproduced in Orain, *Chouannerie*, p. 63.
91 Ibid., pp. 32 and 95.
92 Sutherland, *Chouans*, p. 12.
93 Souben, *Chouannerie*, pp. 95–8.
94 Sutherland, *Chouans*, p. 13.
95 Martin, *La Vendée*, pp. 54–6.
96 See Rouget de Lisle, *Historique et Souvenirs de Quiberon* (Rennes: La Découvrance, 1995 [1821]): a hostile but nonetheless informative account of the landing.
97 Emile Gabory, 'La Révolte des Cent-Jours en Loire-Inférieure', in G. Dottin (ed.), *Mélanges bretons et celtiques offerts à M. J. Loth* (Rennes and Paris: Plihon & Hommany, 1927), pp. 204–10.
98 Roger Dupuy, 'Les Bleus de Bretagne (1789–1801): essai de typologie sociopolitique', in Droguet, *Les Bleus de Bretagne*, pp. 189–95 (p. 194).
99 This argument is suggested by, for example, Bellevue, 'La conjuration de Pontallec', and is also present in Charles Barthélemy, *Histoire de la Bretagne ancienne et moderne* (Tours: Mame, 1853).
100 La Rochejaquelein, *Mémoires*, pp. 120–2.
101 Chateaubriand, *De La Vendée* (La Rochelle: Rumeur des Ages, 1990 [1819]), p. 3. On the later political exploitation of Chouannerie, see chapter 4 of my *French Revolutions, 1815–1914* (Edinburgh: Edinburgh University Press, 1999).
102 Alain Croix, 'Blancs, Bleus et Doléances'.
103 Barthélemy, *Histoire*, p. 266.
104 E. Bérest, 'Les voyageurs français en Bretagne', in J. Balcon and Y. Le Gallo, *Histoire littéraire et culturelle de la Bretagne* (Paris – Spezed: Champion – Coop Breizh, 1997), II 177–218 (179).
105 See, for example, Bérest, 'Voyageurs français', p. 190. See also the far later, but still revealing, text by Victor Hugo, *Quatrevingt-treize* (Paris: Gallimard, 1979 [1874]), p. 232.
106 Martin, *La Vendée et la France*, p. 133.
107 Darsel, *L'homme*, p. 11.
108 Dupuy, *La Bretagne*, p. 75.

109 P. Gervais, 'L'Autre Bretagne: les clubs révolutionnaires, 1789–1795', *Archives historiques de la Révolution Française*, 266 (1986), 422–47.
110 Barère, 'Rapport du comité de salut public sur les idiomes', www.languefrancaise.net, accessed 18 August 2005.
111 Orain, *Chouannerie*, p. 52.
112 Bertrand Frélaut, 'Les Bleus de Vannes (1791–95): naissance d'une classe politique', in Droguet, *Bleus de Bretagne*, pp. 167–76. Correct copies of figures as original by Frélaut. Figures do not total 100.
113 Orain, *Chouannerie*, p. 38.
114 AD I&V, L.449, 18 March 1793.
115 Conan, *Les aventures extraordinaires du citoyen Conan* (Morlaix: Skol Vreizh, 2001), p. 219.
116 Darsel, *L'homme*, p. 14.
117 Martin, *La Vendée et la France*, p. 158.
118 ADCdA, 1/M/263, letter dated 13 nivôse XII.
119 See R. S. Alexander, *Bonapartism and Revolutionary Tradition in France; the 'fédérés' of 1815* (Cambridge: Cambridge University Press, 1991).
120 Darsel, *L'homme*, p. 31.
121 Norman Hampson, 'From regeneration to terror: the ideology of the French Revolution', in Noel O'Sullivan (ed.), *Terrorism, Ideology and Revolution* (Brighton: Wheatsheaf, 1986), pp. 49–66.
122 Denis, *Rennes*, p. 230.
123 Quoted in Denis, *Rennes*, p. 243.
124 Dupuy, *Bretagne*, pp. 132–3.
125 Figures from Alain Pennec, 'La Bretagne pendant la Révolution', in Jean-Jacques Monnier and Jean-Christophe Cassed (eds), *Toute l'histoire de Bretagne* (Morlaix: Skol Vreizh, 1997), pp. 394–426. See also the map in Marc Bouloiseau, *La République jacobine* (Paris: Seuil, 1972), p. 234.
126 Anne Lebel, 'L'apprentissage de la citoyenneté à Saint-Brieuc de 1788 à 1795', in Droguet, *Bleus de Bretagne*, pp. 105–16.
127 Cambry, *Voyage*, p. 252.
128 Ernest Renan, *Souvenirs d'enfance et de jeunesse* (Paris: Nelson, n.d. [1883]), p. 116.
129 Anne de Mathan, 'Les insurrections girondistes de Bretagne en 1793: premiers résultats', *Annales de Bretagne et des Pays de l'Ouest*, 111:4 (2004), 29–42.
130 Orain, *Chouannerie*, p. 71.
131 Dupuy, *Bretagne*, p. 139.
132 AD CdA, 1/M/265, report dated 3 fructidor VIII.
133 Jean Ruellan, 'Moncontour dans la Révolution: une ville bleue au coeur d'un pays chouan', in Droguet, *Les Bleus de Bretagne*, pp. 79–92.
134 Tench, *Letters* p. 81; Cambry, *Voyage*, p. 24.
135 Orain, *Chouannerie*, pp. 55–6.
136 Ibid., p. 67.
137 *Adresse des citoyens de la ville de Brest à l'Assemblée Nationale sur les circonstances actuelles* (Paris: Patriote française, n.d. [1792–3?]), p. 3.
138 See M.-N. Bourget, 'Race et folklore; l'image officielle de la France en 1800', *Annales ESC*, 31 (1976), 802–33.

[139] This point is explored at greater length in Jean-Yves Guiomar, 'La Révolution Française et les origines celtiques de la France', *Annales historiques de la Révolution Française*, 1992, 63–84.

3 Oriental Brittany

[1] Tzvetan Todorov, *On Human Diversity: Nationalism, Racism and Exoticism in French Thought*, trans. C. Porter (Cambridge, MA: Harvard University Press, 1993), p. 322. Todorov's comments concern Loti's novel, *Le Roman d'un Spahi*.
[2] The key works by Said on this topic are *Orientalism* (Harmondsworth: Penguin, 1978) and *Culture and Imperialism* (London: Verso, 1994).
[3] Dubuission-Aubenay, *Itinéraire de Bretagne en 1636*, vol. I (Paris: Layeur, 2000), p. 33.
[4] Prosper Mérimée, *Notes d'un voyage dans l'Ouest de la France* (Paris: Adam Biro, 1989), p. 66.
[5] Stendhal, *Mémoires d'un touriste* (Paris: Maspero, 1981), vol. I, p. 320; vol. II, p. 5.
[6] Fortuné de Boisgobey, *Voyage en Bretagne* (Rennes: Ouest-France, 2001 [1839]), p. 24, p. 57.
[7] Hippolyte Taine, *Carnets de Voyage: Notes sur la province, 1863–65* (Paris: Hachette, 1897), p. 58.
[8] Taine, *Carnets*, p. 258.
[9] Ibid., p. 274.
[10] William Harbutt Dawson, *Across the Silver Streak: Holiday Rambles* (Plymouth: Latimer, 1884), pp. 14–16.
[11] Jean-Marie Déguignet, *Mémoires d'un paysan bas-breton* (Le Relecq-Kerhuon: An Here, 1998), p. 123.
[12] Jean-Yves Veillard, 'La Bretagne, cible des humoristes à la Belle Epoque', in M. Lagrée and Jacqueline Sainclivier (eds), *L'Ouest et la politique* (Rennes: PUR, 1996), pp. 141–7.
[13] Fañch Elegoët, 'L'identité bretonne: notes sur la production de l'identité négative', *Plurial*, 24 (1980), 43–67.
[14] J.-J. Baude, 'Les côtes de Bretagne: Saint-Malo et les malouins', *Revue des Deux Mondes*, 15 November 1851, pp. 651–90 (p. 679).
[15] Benoiston de Châteauneuf and Villermé, *Rapport d'un voyage fait dans les cinq départements de la Bretagne, pendant les années 1840 et 1841* (Rennes: Tud ha Bro, 1982), p. 20. Some readers will recognize similarities between this ritual and the contemporary *fest-noz*.
[16] J.-J. Baude, 'Les côtes de la Manche', *Revue des Deux Mondes*, 1 July 1851, pp. 5–46 (p. 38).
[17] Victor Hugo, *Quatrevingt-treize* (Paris: Gallimard, 1979 [1874]), p. 37.
[18] Jacques Cambry, *Voyage dans le Finistère* (Paris: Layeur, 2000 [1799]), pp. 36–7.
[19] Walter Scott, *Rob Roy* (London: Collins, ND [1818]), p. 28.
[20] Balzac, *Un drame au bord de la mer* (Rezé: Séquences, 1993), p. 24.
[21] Cambry, *Voyage*, p. 40.
[22] Emile Souvestre, *Le Foyer breton: contes et récits populaires* (Paris: Nelson, nd), p. 8.

23 Dawson, *Across the Streak*, p. 28; A. Guépin and E. Bonamy, *Nantes au XIXe siècle* (Ivry and Nantes: Phénix et Maison des sciences de l'homme Ange Guépin, 2000), p. 13.
24 Octave Mirbeau, 'Au pays de la fièvre', in Jean-François Nivet (ed.), *Croquis bretons* (Rezé: Séquences, 1993), pp. 83–94 (p. 84).
25 Boisgobey, *Voyage*, p. 241.
26 Honoré de Balzac, *Les Chouans, ou la Bretagne en 1799* (Paris: Gallimard, 1972 [1829]), p. 39.
27 André Cochut, 'L'Algérie et le budget', *Revue des Deux Mondes*, 15 March 1849, pp. 926–52 (p. 931). See my 'France, Orientalism and Algeria: fifty-four articles from the *Revue des Deux Mondes*, 1846–1852,' *Journal of Algerian Studies*, 3 (1998), 48–70 for further details.
28 On Loti, see my 'Loti, Orientalism and the French Colonial Experience', *Journal of European Area Studies*, 8:2 (2000), 149–66. Anatole Le Braz wrote a positive evaluation of Loti's work: see his 'Le roman de la terre basque', in *Impressions de Bretagne*, edited by Régis Louarn (Plougastell-Daoulaz: An Here, 2004), pp. 73–8.
29 Ann Rigney, 'Immemorial routines: the Celts and their resistance to history', in Terence Brown (ed.), *Celticism* (Amsterdam: Rodopi, 1996), pp. 159–81.
30 Edouard Richer, *Description du Croisic et d'une partie de la côte voisine* (Paris: Res Universis, 1993 [1823]), p. 91.
31 Théodore Hersart de La Villemarqué, 'Préface', *Barzaz Breizh*, pp. 55, 66–7.
32 E. Fleury, 'Excursion dans l'arrondissement de Brest', *Bulletin de la Société Académique de Brest*, 1 (1858–60), pp. 422–66 (p. 423).
33 Emile Souvestre, *Les derniers Bretons* (Rennes: Terre de Brume, 1997 [1836]), p. 108.
34 *Souvenirs d'enfance et de jeunesse* (Paris: Nelson, nd [1883?]), p. 78.
35 Monseigneur David, 'Discours', *Association bretonne: Comptes-Rendus, Procès-Verbaux, Mémoires* (1876), pp. xxxii–xxxviii (p. xxxiv).
36 François-Marie Luzel, *Journal de route et Lettres de mission* (Rennes: Presses Universitaires de Rennes/Terre de Brume, 1994 [1864]), p. 79.
37 Charles Le Goffic, *L'Ame Bretonne*, sixth edition (Paris: Honoré Champion, 1908), I, p. 1; Anatole Le Braz, *Il était une voix . . . discours et conférences*, ed. Yann-Ber Piriou (Rennes: Apogée, 1995), p. 93.
38 Nora Chadwick, *Early Brittany* (Cardiff: University of Wales Press, 1969), p. 4.
39 Villemarqué, p. 83
40 Charles de Keranflec'h, *Voyage dans les montagnes du centre Bretagne et de Vendée, 1857* (Spézet: Keltia, 1998), p. 47.
41 Luzel, *Journal de route*, p. 62.
42 A. Brizeux, *Les Bretons,* second edn. (Paris: Paul Masgana, 1848), p. vi.
43 Brizeux, *Les Bretons*, p. viii.
44 La Villemarqué, 'Préface', pp. 52–3
45 Mary-Ann Constantine, *Breton Ballads* (Aberystwyth: CMCS, 1996), p. 44.
46 Rana Kabbani, *Imperial Fictions: Europe's Myths of the Orient* (London: Pandora, 1994), pp. 6, 67. See also Malek Alloula, *The Colonial Harem*, trans. M. Godzich and W. Godzich (Chicago: University of Minnesota Press, 1986).
47 Linda Nochlin, 'The imaginary Orient', *The Politics of Vision* (London: Thames and Hudson, 1991), pp. 33–59.

48 On *Mon frère Yves*, see the thoughtful analysis by Philippe Carrer, in his *L'envers du décor: ethnopsychiatrie en Bretagne at autres terres celtes* (Spézet: Coop Breizh, 1999), pp. 15–40.
49 Examples of more sexualized depictions of Bretons include Emile Zola, *Les coquillages de M. Chabre* (Nantes: Joca Seria, 1994) and Anatole Le Braz, 'Le Gardien du feu', in *Gens de Bretagne* 2, ed. D. Besançon (Paris: Omnibus, 1998).
50 J.-F. Brousmiche, *Voyage dans le Finistère en 1829, 1830 et 1831* (Quimper: Morvan, 1977), pp. 84–5.
51 J.-J. Baude, 'Les côtes de Bretagne: la baie de Saint-Brieuc', p. 1054.
52 See, for example, Paul Leroy-Beaulieu, *La Question de la population* (Paris: Alcan, 1913). On the use of *bretonnitude* by the right, see Jean-Yves Guiomar, 'Le bretonisme, une expression de la droite française', in M. Lagrée and J. Sainclivier (eds), *L'Ouest et la politique* (Rennes: PUR, 1996), pp. 129–40.
53 Guy Haudebourg, *Mendiants et vagabonds en Bretagne au XIXe siècle* (Rennes: Presses universitaires de Rennes, 1998), p. 84.
54 Cambry, *Voyage*, p. 79; Stendhal, *Mémoires*, II, p. 51.
55 Alfred Gernoux (ed.), 'De Nantes à Brest en 1845: correspondance d'Armand Guérand, 1824–51', *Nouvelle revue de Bretagne*, January-February 1950, pp. 50–9 (p. 54).
56 Mérimée, *Voyage*, p. 59.
57 See, for example, Brousmiche, *Voyage*, p. 11 and p. 78.
58 Balzac, *Les Chouans* (Paris: Gallimard, 1972), p. 42.
59 Souvestre, *Derniers Bretons*, p. 119.
60 L. de Serbois, *Souvenirs de Voyages en Bretagne et en Grèce* (Paris: Le Clerc & Dillet, 1864), 179–81.
61 A. Thiers, *Histoire de la Révolution Française*, thirteenth edn vol. 6 (Paris: Furne, 1857), p. 321.
62 See Denise Delouche, 'Le peuple noir: à propos du numero de *l'Assiette au Beurre* du 3 octobre 1903', in A. Draguet (ed.), *Les Bleus de Bretagne* (Saint-Brieuc: Fédération "Côtes-du-Nord, 1789", 1991), pp. 223–47.
63 Octave Mirbeau, 'Le Nid de Frelons', *Contes Cruels II* ed. Pierre Michel and Jean-François Nivet (Paris, 1990), pp. 455–60.
64 David, 'Discours', p. xxxiv.
65 Balzac, 'Préface' to the first edition of *Les Chouans* (Paris: Gallimard, 1972), p. 504.
66 Châteauneuf and Villermé, *Rapport*, pp. 106–7.
67 J.-J. Baude, 'Les côtes de Bretagne: la baie de Saint-Brieuc', *Revue des Deux Mondes*, 15 Sep 1852, pp. 1053–79 (p. 1062). The Université was the semi-independent official body with responsibility for the administration of all forms of education, from nursery schools to University colleges.
68 F. de Saulcy, 'De l'étude des hiéroglyphes', *Revue des deux Mondes*, 14 June 1846, 603–21; J.-J. Ampère, 'Des castes dans l'ancienne Egypte', *Revue des deux Mondes*, 14 September 1848, pp. 645–52 (p. 652). See also my 'France, Orientalism and Algeria'.
69 Joseph Loth, 'Les langues romane et bretonne en Armorique', *Revue celtique*, 28 (1907), pp. 374–403 (p. 374).
70 Déguignet, *Mémoires*, p. 215.

71 Le Goffic, *L'âme bretonne*, III, p. vi.
72 Boisgobey, *Voyage*, p. 123.
73 Souvestre, *Derniers Bretons*, vol. I, p. 24–6.
74 Boisgobey, *Voyage*, p. 64.
75 Serbois, *Souvenirs*, p. 140.
76 Renan, 'La poésie des races celtiques', in *Oeuvres completes*, vol. II (Paris: Calmann-Lévy, 1948), p. 252.
77 Jules Michelet, *Tableau de la France* (Paris: Société les Belles Lettres, 1934 [1861]), p. 8.
78 Le Goffic, *L'âme Bretonne*, vol. I, p. 4; François-Marie Luzel, *Notes de voyage en Basse-Bretagne, du Trégor aux îles d'Ouessent et de Bréhat* (Rennes: Presses Universitaires de Rennes/Terre de Brume, 1997), p. 20.
79 Souvestre, *Derniers Bretons*, p. 43.
80 Michelet, *Tableau*, p. 8.
81 Henry Blackburn, 'De Saint Malo à Dinan en 1880', trans. P. Galliou, *Ar Men*, 62 (October 1994), pp. 26–40 (p. 32).
82 Yves Kano, *Les Populations bretonnes* (np: SEPEC, 2000 [1886]), p. 8.
83 Serbois, *Souvenirs*, pp. 136–7.
84 Ibid., pp. 154 and 224.
85 Gustave Flaubert, *Oeuvres complètes* II, ed. B. Masson (Paris: Seuil, 1964), p. 511.
86 Bernard Hue, 'Un Breton à la conquête des coeurs: Auguste Pavie face à l'identité Kmère et lao', *Plurial*, 8 (1999), pp. 23–30.
87 See the remarks in Said, *Orientalism*, p. 177, and *passim*.
88 Muriel Desfontaine, 'Odette du Puigaudeau: à la croisée des regards, entre Bretagne et Mauritanie', *Plurial*, 8 (1999), pp. 31–9. See also the comments by Gilbert Soubigou, 'Les auteurs bretons dans l'écriture exotique et coloniale', *Plurial*, 8 (1999), pp. 13–21.
89 See the useful and observant analysis by Josep Leerssen, 'Celticism', in Terence Brown (ed.), *Celticism* (Amsterdam: Rodopi, 1996), pp. 1–20.
90 See my 'What is a school?: defining and controlling primary schooling in early nineteenth century France', *History of Education*, 21:2 (1992), 129–47.
91 Tzvetan Todorov, *Nous et les autres: la réflexion française sur la diversité humaine* (Paris: Seuil, 1989), p. 299.
92 This argument is expressed most forcefully by Françoise Morvan in *Le Monde comme si: nationalisme et dérive identitaire en Bretagne* (Arles: Actes Sud, 2002).
93 Le Goffic's most recent biographer, Jean André Le Gall, in *Charles Le Goffic (1863–1932), ou: de la difficulté d'être breton* (Guingamp: La Planée, 2002), notes his frequent links with far-right thinkers such as Maurice Barrès and Charles Maurras.

4 The Politics of Faith: Chouannerie, Religion and the Making of a White Landscape

1 The best example of this type of thinking is Victor Hugo, *Quatrevingt-treize* (Paris: Gallimard, 1979 [1874]). See also Pascal Aumasson and André Cariou, 'La peinture d'histoire et les Bleus', in Alain Droguet (ed.), *Les Bleus de Bretagne* (Saint-Brieuc: Fédération "Côtes-du-Nord, 1789", 1991), pp. 207–21.

2   This chapter, and the three which follow, make frequent reference to the political regimes which governed nineteenth-century France. Readers who are unfamiliar with these regimes are advised to consult the list of regimes in the glossary.
3   See Jean Le Bihan and Yann Lagadec, 'Les sous-préfets de Bretagne sous la monarchie de Juillet (1830–1848): une génération d'administrateurs à part?', *Annales de Bretagne et des Pays de l'Ouest*, 111:4 (2004), pp. 47–70.
4   See Jean Pascal, *Les députés bretons de 1789 à 1983* (Paris: PUF, 1983), pp. 177–83.
5   On the schoolteachers, see Gilbert Nicolas, *Instituteurs entre politique et religion* (Rennes: Apogée, 1993), pp. 161–2. On the church bells see Alain Corbin, *Villages Bells: Sound and Meaning in the 19th Century French Countryside*, trans. M. Thom (London: Papermac, 1999), pp. 120 and 266; on the same point see also the ADF, 1/M/134, letter dated 6 April 1831.
6   ADLA, 1/M/509, report by the Sub-Prefect of Ancenis (Loire-Inférieure), dated 21 February 1832.
7   Michel Denis and Claude Geslin, *La Bretagne des Blancs et des Bleus, 1815–1880* (Rennes: Ouest-France, 2003), p. 73.
8   List dated 1833, ADLA, 1/M/150.
9   ADLA, 1/M/509, report dated 12 September 1832.
10 ADLA, 1/M/510, report dated 10 February 1832.
11 See notes by the Vitré Sub-Prefect, ADI&V, 1/M/113, dated 16 July 1831.
12 See the documents in my *French Revolutions, 1815–1914* (Edinburgh University Press, 1999), pp. 82–4.
13 ADI&V, 1/M/113, undated declaration.
14 ADF, 1/M/136, report dated 13 September 1831.
15 ADCdA, 1/M/325, report dated 11 March 1831.
16 AN, F/7/6780, report dated 12 February 1831.
17 ADI&V, 1/M/115, report dated 30 March 1843.
18 AN, F/7/6780, report dated 20 September 1831.
19 ADI&V, 1/M/112, poster dated 27 May 1832. See also ADLA, 1/M/509, report dated 31 January 1832.
20 ADI&V, 4/M/98bis, report dated 8 July 1823. See also Jean Quéniart, *Le Grand Chapelletout: violence, normes et comportements en Bretagne rurale au 18e siècle* (Rennes: Apogée, 1993).
21 ADLA, 1/M/509, report dated 17 January 1832.
22 Ibid., report dated 13 October 1832.
23 Ibid., report dated 14 July 1832.
24 ADLA, 1/M/511, report dated 16 January 1833.
25 Ibid., report dated 27 June 1833.
26 ADLA, 1/M/509, report dated 9 October 1832.
27 ADF, 1/M/177, report dated 9 September 1833.
28 ADLA, 1/M/509, report dated 23 February 1832.
29 Ibid., report dated 31 August 1832.
30 Ibid., report dated 13 September 1832.
31 Ibid., report dated 25 May 1832.
32 Ibid., report dated 6 June 1832.

33 ADLA, 1/M/509, report dated 5 June 1832.
34 Undated lists in ADLA, 1/M/510 and ADLA, 1/M/150.
35 Lists in ADLA, 1/M/510.
36 Guy Haudebourg, *Mendiants et vagabonds en Bretagne au XIXe siècle* (Rennes: PUR, 1998), p. 62.
37 ADF, 1/M/159, report dated 20 April 1831.
38 ADLA, 1/M/509, report dated 3 June 1832.
39 ADLA, 1/M/511, report dated 16 January 1833.
40 ADF, 1/M/134, report dated 9 August 1830.
41 ADI&V, 1/M/115, undated report [1830?].
42 Ibid., circular dated 16 December 1830.
43 Ibid., circular dated 30 December 1830.
44 On the missions, see Martyn Lyons, 'Fires of expiation: book-burnings and Catholic missions in restoration France', *French History*, 10:2 (1996), 240–66 for a vivid study.
45 ADF, 1/M/135, report dated 28 March 1831.
46 Yves-Pascal Castel, 'La fleur de lis aux fenestrages aux églises', *Ar Men*, 74 (February 1996), pp. 64–9.
47 ADI&V, 1/M/115, letter dated 27 November 1830, Bazouges-sur-Pérouse.
48 ADF, 1/M/134, report dated 6 November 1830.
49 Charles Barthélemy, *Histoire de la Bretagne ancienne et moderne* (Tours: Mame, 1853), p. 289.
50 Barthélemy, *Histoire*, pp. 290–300.
51 Emile Souvestre, *Les derniers Bretons* (Rennes: Terre de Brume, 1997 [1836]), p. 43
52 Prosper Mérimée, *Notes d'un voyage dans l'Ouest de la France* (Paris: Adam Biro, 1989), p. 59; L. de Serbois, *Souvenirs de voyages en Bretagne et en Grèce* (Paris: Le Clerc & Dillet, 1864), p. 3; Edouard Richer, *Description du Croisic et d'une partie de la côte voisine* (Paris: Res Universis, 1993 [1823]), p. 8.
53 J.-F. Brousmiche, *Voyage dans le Finistère en 1829, 1830 et 1831* (Quimper: Morvan, 1977), p. 159.
54 Alfred Gernoux (ed.), 'De Nantes à Brest en 1845: correspondance d'Armand Guérand, 1824–61', *Nouvelle Revue de Bretagne*, January–February 1950, pp. 50–9 (p. 55).
55 Serbois, *Souvenirs*, p. 153.
56 Sylvette Denefle, 'Croyances et pratiques aux fontaines en Cornouaille et Léon', in M. Lagrée (ed.), *Bretagne et Religion* (Rennes: Institut Culturel de Bretagne/ Skol-Uhel ar Vro, 1990), pp. 25–39.
57 See Lagrée and Roche, *Tombes de mémoire*.
58 Anatole Le Braz, *Au Pays des Pardons* (Rennes: Terre de Brume, 1998 [1894]), p. 25.
59 Alain Croix, *L'Âge d'or de la Bretagne, 1532–1675* (Rennes: Ouest-France, 1993), pp. 354–6. See also Elizabeth Musgrave, 'Momento Mori: the function and meaning of Breton ossuaries, 1450–1750', in P. C. Jupp and G. Howarth (eds), *The Changing Face of Death* (London: Macmillan, 1995), pp. 62–75.
60 This point is eloquently and convincingly analysed in Croix, *L'Âge d'or*, particularly in chapter 11.

61 Yves-Pascal Castel, 'La calvaire de Tronoën', *Ar Men*, 119 (March 2001), pp. 28–35.
62 Michel Lagrée, *Religion et cultures en Bretagne* (Paris: Fayard, 1992), p. 29.
63 Ellen Badone, 'Le folklore breton de l'anticléricalisme', *Annales de Bretagne*, 98 (1991), 423–45.
64 Erwan Chartier, 'La Saint Loup à Guingamp', *Ar Men*, 147 (July 2005), 20–7.
65 Max Nicol, *Sainte Anne d'Auray: histoire de pèlerinage* (Sainte-Anne-d'Auray: Librarie du Pèlerinage, 1877), p. 159.
66 Lagrée, *Religion et cultures*, p. 302.
67 Nicol, *Sainte Anne d'Auray*, p. 193.
68 Ibid., pp. 161–2.
69 Information drawn from the unpaginated work by Jacques Duchemin, *Pardons bretons du temps passé* (Brussels: Sodim, 1997).
70 Georges Provost, 'Entre cantiques et penn-baz: les pardons du Centre-Bretagne, XVIIe–XIXe siècle', *Kreiz Breizh*, 10 (2004), 13–20.
71 Nicol, *Sainte Anne d'Auray*, pp. 152–61.
72 Charles Le Goffic, *L'Ame bretonne*, Vol I (Paris: Honoré Champion, 1908), p. 26.
73 Anatole Le Braz, *Il était une voix*, ed. Yann-Ber Piriou (Rennes: Apogée, 1995), p. 66.
74 Jeanne Schultz, *Jean de Kerdren* (Paris: Nelson, 1933 [1890]), p. 104.
75 *Guide Bleu: Bretagne* (Paris: Hachette, 1920), p. xliii.
76 Pierre-Jakez Hélias, *Le cheval d'orgueil: mémoires d'un Breton du pays bigouden* (Paris: Plon, 1982) pp. 130–1.
77 Lagrée, *Religion et cultures*, p. 48.
78 Musgrave, 'Memento Mori', p. 72.
79 Jean Gourhand, 'L'abbé Joseph Mahé, premier érudit morbihannais', in N.-Y. Tonnerre (ed.), *Chroniques et historiens de la Bretagne* (Rennes: PUR, 2001), pp. 125–41.
80 Renan, *Souvenirs*, p. 26.
81 Monseigneur David, 'Discours', *Association bretonne: Comptes-Rendus, Procès-Verbaux, Mémoires* (1876), pp. xxxii–xxxviii.
82 Pierre, *Bretons*, p. 226.
83 Suzanne Berger, *Les Paysans contre la politique* (Paris: Seuil, 1975), p. 45.
84 Berger, *Paysans*, p. 37.
85 Pierre, *Bretons*, p. 215.
86 Berger, *Paysans*, p. 98.
87 Pierre, *Bretons*, p. 104.
88 Jack E. Reece, *The Bretons against France: Ethnic Minority Nationalism in Twentieth-century Brittany* (Chapel Hill: University of North Carolina Press, 1977), p. 44.
89 Pierre, *Bretons*, p. 243.
90 Ibid., p. 112.
91 ADF, 1/M/134, Brest Sub-Prefect, 26 Sep 1906.
92 The material cited in this paragraph is drawn largely from Michel Lagrée, 'Le clergé Breton et le premier centenaire de la Révolution française', *Annales de Bretagne*, 91 (1984), 249–67. I have found this article extremely useful.
93 ADF, 1/M/136, Morlaix Sub-Prefect, 1 June 1894.
94 Pierre, *Bretons*, p. 240.

95 See François Chappée, 'Les anticléricalismes "maritimes" à Paimpol, 1880–1914', in M. Lagrée (ed.), *Bretagne et Religion* (Rennes: Institut Culturel de Bretagne/Skol-Uhel ar Vro, 1990), pp. 39–55.
96 Nicol, *Sainte Anne d'Auray*, p. 13.
97 ADI&V, 1/M/142, Vitré Sub-Prefect, 27 September 1906.
98 Badone, 'Le folklore breton de l'anticléricalisme'; ADI&V, 1/M/143, Vitré Sub-Prefect, 9 April 1909.
99 AN, F/1/C1 (III)/1127, Côtes-du-Nord Prefect, 30 January 1924.
100 ADCdA, 1/M/352, police report of meeting, 10 January 1908.
101 See Patrick Gourlay, *Charles Daniélou, 1878–1953: Itinéraire politique d'un Finistérien* (Rennes: PUR, 1996), pp. 24–6; Lagrée, *Religion et Cultures*, p. 192.
102 Raymond Huard, *La Naissance du parti politique en France* (Paris: Presses de la fondation nationale des Sciences Politique, 1996), p. 257.
103 Ibid., p. 260; Pascal, *Députés*, p. 389.
104 ADCdA, 1/M/351, ALP, 6 March 1904.
105 Berger, *Paysans*, p. 72.
106 'Appel à la Jeunesse', 1899, on *www.cardijn.net*, accessed 22 August 2002.
107 Vincent Rocard, *Les Catholiques et la question sociale: Morlaix, 1840–1914: l'avènement des militants* (Rennes: PUR, 1997), pp. 201–3.
108 See Berger, *Paysans*, pp. 75–6; Rocard, *Catholiques*, p. 277.
109 See Paul Cohen, 'Heroes and Dilettantes: the Action française, Le Sillon and the generation of 1905–14', *French Historical Studies*, 15:4 (1988), 673–87.
110 Jean-Claude Delbreil, *Centrisme et Démocratie Chrétienne en France: le Parti Démocrate Populaire: des origines au MRP* (Paris: Publications de la Sorbonne, 1990).
111 Ford, *Nation*, p. 291, Pascal, *Députés*, pp. 459 and 473; Delbreil, *Centrisme*, p. 188.
112 ADCdA, 1/M/351 Guingamp Sub-Prefect, 27 April 1925.
113 AN, F/7/12.754, Loire-Inférieure Prefect's reports, dated 31 May and 1 July 1928.
114 ADI&V, 3/M/344.
115 'Une belle réunion du Parti Démocrate Populaire', *Ouest-Éclair*, 17 March 1935.
116 See Christian Bougeard, 'Bleus, Blancs et Rouges en Bretagne dans l'entre-deux-guerres', in A. Draguet (ed.), *Les Bleus de Bretagne*, pp. 403–17.
117 On the mid-twentieth-century formation of Catholic youth groups, see Sarah Whitney, 'Gender, class and generation in interwar French Catholicism: the case of the Jeunesse Ouvrière Chrétienne Féminine', *Journal of Family History*, 26:4 (2001), 480–507.
118 Ford, *Nation*, p. 138. See also Alain Tanguy, 'Troubles confessionnels: la difficile séparation de l'Eglise et de l'Etat au début du XXe siècle', *Ar Men*, 149 (2005), 32–7.
119 Julien Gracq, *La forme d'une ville* (Paris: José Corti, 1985), p. 151.
120 On the FNC, see James F. McMillan, 'Catholicism and nationalism in France: the case of the Fédération Nationale Catholique, 1924–39', in Frank Tallet and Nicholas Atkin (eds), *Catholicism in Britain and France since 1789* (London: Hambledon Press, 1996), pp. 151–63.
121 Figures from McMillan, 'Catholicism', p. 155.
122 Abbé Jean Desgranges, 'Les manifestations de Finistère', *Nouvelliste de Bretagne*, 17 December 1924.

123   ADCdA, 1/M/354, leaflet distributed in Plélo, January 1925.
124   ADCdA, 1/M/352, from a police report of a meeting in Saint-Brieuc, 12 December 1924.
125   'Avis aux catholiques des Côtes-du-Nord: à lire en chaire, le dimanche 11 janvier', *La Nouvelliste de Bretagne*, 10 January 1925.
126   'Une lettre de monsiegneur: avis aux catholiques des Côtes-du-Nord', *La Croix des Côtes-du-Nord*, 17 January 1925: The extract cited here comes from a journalist's commentary on the bishop's instructions.

5 The Politics of the State (1): People and Protests, 1830–52

1   See Mathilde Larrère, 'Ainsi paradait le roi des barricades: les grandes revues de la garde nationale, à Paris, sous la Monarchie de Juillet', *Mouvement social*, 179 (1997), 9–32.
2   A. Besnier, 'L'esprit public dans un département Breton en 1848', *Nouvelle Revue de Bretagne*, 2:2 (1948), 83–90.
3   See Charles F. Ramus (ed.), *Daumier: 120 Great Lithographs* (New York: Dover, 1978). Similar themes are present in Balzac's depiction of Crevel in the first pages of his *Cousine Bette*.
4   ADI&V, 1/M/113, report dated 13 May 1832.
5   ADLA, 1/M/509, letter dated 20 March 1832.
6   On *ancien régime* cérémonies, see the important works by Arlette Farge: *Vivre dans la rue à Paris au XVIIIe siècle* (Paris: Gallimard, 1992) and *La vie fragile: violence, pouvoirs et solidarités à Paris au XVIIIe siècle* (Paris: Hachette, 1986). For a useful case study of one *ancien régime* royal cérémony, see Penny Richards, 'Rouen and the golden age: the entry of Francis I, 2 August 1517', in Christopher Allmand (ed.), *Power, Culture and Religion in France, c.1350–c.1550* (London: Boydell, 1989), pp. 117–31.
7   Nolwenn Juhel, 'La pastorale d'un prêtre Breton dans la second moitié du XVIIIe siècle', *Annales de Bretagne et des Pays de l'Ouest*, 110:2 (2003), 77–109.
8   See Jo Burr Margadant, 'The Duchesse de Berry and royalist political culture in post-Revolutionary France', *History Workshop*, 43 (1997), 23–52 (33).
9   Jacques Godechot (ed.), *Les Constitutions de la France depuis 1789* (Paris: Garnier-Flammarion, 1979), p. 34; Claude Nicolet, *L'idée républicaine en France (1789–1924)* (Paris: Gallimard, 1994), p. 16.
10 Mona Ozouf, *La fête révolutionnaire, 1789–1799* (Paris: Gallimard, 1976), pp. 31–7.
11 On this point, see my *French Revolutions, 1815–1914* (Edinburgh: Edinburgh University Press, 1999), pp. 68–70. On restoration festivals, see Landric Raillat, 'Les manifestations à l'occasion du sacré de Charles X ou les ambiguïtés de la fête politique', in A. Corbin, N. Gérôme and D. Tartowsky (eds), *Les Usages politiques des fêtes aux XIXe–XXe siècle* (Paris: Publications de la Sorbonne, 1994), pp. 53–62.
12 On Guizot's thinking, see Pierre Rosanvallon, *Le moment Guizot* (Paris: Gallimard, 1985).
13 See Corbin, 'L'Impossible présence', in Corbin, Gérôme and Tartowsky (eds), *Les Usages politiques des fêtes*.

14 Details taken from report in ADM, 1/M/cérém/7, dated 3 August 1835.
15 ADM, 1/M/cérém/7, report dated 3 August 1835.
16 ADI&V, 1/M/112, report dated 12 August 1835.
17 ADCdA, 1/M/374, report dated 28 July 1834.
18 ADM, 1/M/cérém/7, report dated 2 May 1836.
19 'Politique: anniversaire des fêtes de Juillet', *Annales de la Société Royale Académique de Nantes*, 3 (1832), 341–2.
20 ADI&V, 1/M/112, report dated 3 August 1835.
21 ADCdA, 1/M/374, report dated 27 July 1834.
22 ADM, 1/M/cérém/7, report dated 2 May 1843; ADCdA, 1/M/374, report dated 28 July 1834.
23 ADI&V, 1/M/112, report dated 13 August 1835.
24 Ibid., report dated 12 August 1835.
25 ADLA, 1/M/515, report dated 28 July 1843.
26 ADM, M/680, report dated 7 July 1847.
27 ADI&V, 1/M/112, report dated 13 August 1835.
28 ADM, 1/M/cérém/7, report dated 2 May 1836.
29 ADM, M/2205, police report dated 15 September 1847.
30 ADM, 1/M/cérém/7, report dated 2 May 1836.
31 Ibid., report dated 22 March 1838.
32 Ibid., report dated 2 May 1843.
33 Ibid., report dated 12 August 1845.
34 The classic essay by E. P. Thompson remains an essential starting-point for any debates on this point. See his 'The moral economy of the English crowd in the eighteenth century', in his *Customs in Common* (Harmondsworth: Penguin, 1993), pp. 185–258. See also Steven L. Kaplan, *Bread, Politics and Political Economy in the Reign of Louis XV* (The Hague: Martinus Nijoff, 1976).
35 ADCdA, 1/M/330, mayor's report dated 31 January 1832.
36 The Morbihan Prefect also denied any political motive behind riots in 1840: see his letter to the Finistère Prefect, dated 22 April 1840, ADF, 1/M/159.
37 ADCdA, 1/M/330, report dated 7 February 1832.
38 ADCdA, 1/M/325, report dated 21 November 1845.
39 ADCdA, 1/M/330, reports dated 18 January 1847 and 6 March 1847.
40 Jean-Marie Déguignet, *Mémoires d'un paysan bas-Breton* (Releg-Kerhuon: An Here, 1999), p. 48.
41 Figures from ADF, 1/N/57, report dated 30 August 1847 and ADF 1/N/58, report dated 6 October 1848.
42 ADF, 1/M/159, letter dated 12 November 1846.
43 Ibid., report dated December 1846.
44 André Burguière, *Bretons de Plozévet* (Paris: Flammarion, 1977), pp. 111–12.
45 ADF, 1/M/159, report dated 14 November 1846.
46 Ibid., report dated 19 February 1847.
47 Déguinet, *Mémoires*, p. 55.
48 ADF, 1/M/159, letter dated 24 February 1847 and 1/M/178, letter dated 6 April 1847.
49 ADCdA, 1/M/330, report dated 24 January 1839.
50 ADM, M/2205, report dated 4 February 1847.

51 This was a traditional feature of such crises. See Kaplan, *Bread, Politics and Political Economy*, pp. 88–90.
52 See, for example, ADF, 1/M/159, letter dated 30 January 1847, ADCdA, 1/M/325, reports dated 20 and 21 November 1845.
53 Thompson, 'The moral economy', pp. 232–3.
54 ADF, 1/M/159, letter dated 30 January 1847.
55 ADCdA, 1/M/325, report dated 18 November 1845.
56 ADF, 1/M/159, letter dated 6 March 1847.
57 Ibid., letter dated 7 March 1847.
58 ADF, 1/M/139, letter dated 7 February 1847.
59 ADM, M/2205, report dated 26 March 1847.
60 ADCdA, 1/M/325, report dated 18 November 1845, and ADCdA, 1/M/330, report dated 17 November 1845.
61 ADF, 1/M/159, letters dated 14 November 1846 and 13 March 1847.
62 ADCdA, 1/M/330, report dated 18 November 1845.
63 Ibid., report dated 22 November 1845.
64 ADF, 1/M/159, poster dated 7 May 1840.
65 ADCdA, 1/M/325, report dated 18 November 1845. (Other posters appeared around Morlaix in March 1832: unfortunately, they were not transcribed. ADF, 1/M/159, report dated 4 March 1832.)
66 ADM, M/2205, anonymous letter addressed to the Gournin mayor, 29 January 1847.
67 ADF, 1/M/159, report dated 27 January 1847.
68 Ibid., prefect's report, dated 30 January 1847.
69 ADF, 1/M/159, report dated 2 May 1840.
70 ADCdA, 1/M/330, reports dated 16, 18 and 27 June 1832.
71 ADCdA, 1/M/325, report dated 20 November 1845; ADCdA, 1/M/330, report dated 24 January 1839, from Moncontour.
72 ADCdA, 1/M/330, report dated 23 October 1832, from Saint-Brandon, see also reports dated 18 November 1838 (Plérin) and 29 November 1838 (Moncontour) from the same file.
73 ADCdA, 1/M/330, report dated 14 January 1847, from Loudéac.
74 See Guy Hadebourg, *Mendiants et vagabonds en Bretagne au XIXe siècle* (Rennes: Presses Universitaires de Rennes, 1998).
75 ADCdA, 1/M/330, police report 12 February 1832.
76 Kaplan notes this tendency in his work on the *ancien régime*. See his *Bread, Politics and Political Economy*, pp. 424–37.
77 ADCdA, 1/M/325, report dated 26 November 1845.
78 Yvonne Le Brun, '"L'émeute" de Rennes dès 9 et 10 janvier 1847', *Annales de Bretagne*, 89:4 (1982), 479–503.
79 ADCdA, 1/M/330, report dated 18 March 1845.
80 ADF, 1/M/159, letter dated 7 March 1847.
81 ADCdA, 1/M/330, report dated 23 October 1832.
82 Ibid., report dated 18 March 1845.
83 ADF, 1/M/159, letter dated 11 p.m., 7 May 1847.
84 For example, see ADCdA, 1/M/330, letter from the Ministry of Commerce, dated 29 January 1839, concerning the Moncontour mayor.

85 ADCdA, 1/M/330, report dated 17 December 1838.
86 ADM, M/2205, report dated 25 January 1847.
87 Ibid., report dated 30 January 1847.
88 Ibid., report dated 15 March 1847.
89 ADF, 1/M/159, report dated 23 November 1846.
90 Ibid., report dated 30 January 1847.
91 ADCdA, 1/M/325, report dated 20 November 1845 concerning Lamballe and Châtelandreu.
92 ADF, 1/M/159, report dated 30 January 1847.
93 Ibid., circular dated 15 December 1846.
94 ADCdA, 1/M/330, letter dated 24 November 1845.
95 ADCdA, 1/M/325, report dated 20 November 1845 from Loudéac.
96 ADCdA, 1/M/330, reports dated 18 and 19 December 1838.
97 Kaplan, *Bread, Politics and Political Economy*, p. 5.
98 ADF, 1/M/159, circular from the Ministry of the Interior, 18 January 1847.
99 Ibid., poster dated 8 May 1847.
100 ADF, 1/N/57, report dated 30 August 1847.
101 ADCdA, 1/M/330, circular dated 24 January 1847.
102 For example, see ADF, 1/M/159, report dated 3 May 1840.
103 ADCdA, 1/M/325, report dated 20 November 1845.
104 ADF, 1/M/159, report dated 30 January 1847.
105 Ibid., report dated 8 February 1847.
106 ADCdA, 1/M/330, report dated 28 January 1847.
107 Jean Le Bihan and Yann Lagadec, 'Les sous-préfets de Bretagne sous la monarchie de Juillet (1830–48): une génération d'administrateurs à part?', *Annales de Bretagne et des Pays de l'Ouest*, 111:4 (2004), 47–70.
108 Déguignet, *Mémoires*, p. 61.
109 Jean Pascal, *Les députés bretons de 1789 à 1983* (Paris: PUF, 1983), pp. 207–11.
110 AN, BB/30/296, undated list. On the banquet campaign, see my *French Revolutions*, pp. 116–22.
111 See, for example, Eugène Corgné, 'Les Elections de 1848 en Bretagne', *Nouvelle Revue de Bretagne*, 2:2 (1898), 91–107 (95–6).
112 See Guy Frambourg, 'Un Commissaire du gouvernement provisoire de la République: Guépin', *Annales de Bretagne*, 66:3 (1959), 329–46.
113 Godechot (ed.), *Les Constitutions* p. 264.
114 AN, BB/30/364, document dated 8 October 1848.
115 ADM, M/2255, 29 February 1848
116 AN, C/939, letter from Soret to the Club de Clubs in Paris, 17 April 1848.
117 Georges Sand, *Politique et polémiques (1843–1850)* (Paris: Imprimerie nationale, 1997), p. 340.
118 George Fasel, 'The wrong revolution: French Republicanism in 1848', *French Historical Studies*, 8 (1973–4), 654–80 (660).
119 Christian Ménard (ed.), 'La Révolution de 1848 dans le Finistère: la correspondonce des commissaires de la République dans le département', *Bulletin de la Société Archéologique du Finistère*, 104 (1976), 239–97 (296).
120 Peter Amann makes a similar observation in relation to the clubs' political culture. See his *Revolutions and Mass Democracy: the Paris Club Movement in 1848* (Princeton, Princeton University Press, 1975).

121 ADM, M/2205, 20 September 1848.
122 ADM, M/2206, 25 February 1850
123 See anon., *Aux Paysans par un fils de paysan de Saint-Malo* (Paris: Desoye, 1849).
124 F. Guérin, *Au clergé* (Vannes: Lamarzelle, n.d. [1848?]).
125 Cited in Eugène Corgné, 'Les Elections de 1848 en Bretagne', *Nouvelle Revue de Bretagne*, 2:2 (1948), 91–107.
126 Michel Denis, 'Le christianisme bleu en Bretagne de la Révolution au Second Empire', in A. Droguet (ed.), *Les Bleus de Bretagne*, pp. 323–31.
127 Laurent Paubert, 'Les catholiques et l'élection présidentielle du 10 décembre 1848 dans le Morbihan et le Finistère', *Annales de Bretagne et des Pays de l'Ouest*, 107:4 (2000), 103–19.
128 Michel Lagrée, 'Evêques gallicans et diocèses ultramontain: Vannes (1848–1870)', in Michel Lagrée and Jacqueline Sainclivier (eds), *L'Ouest et la politique* (Rennes: PUR, 1996), pp. 113–28.
129 See Paubert, 'Les catholiques et l'élection présidentielle'.
130 ADF, 1/M/209, 10 April 1848.
131 Frambourg, 'Un Commissaire', p. 332, Henri Goallou, *Hamon: Commissaire du Gouvernement puis Préfet d'Ille-et-Vilaine* (Rennes: Institut Armoricain de Recherches historique de Rennes, 1973), pp. 52–4.
132 Gilbert Nicolas, *Instituteurs entre politique et religion: la première génération de normaliens en Bretagne au 19e siècle* (Rennes: Apogée, 1993), p. 177.
133 Pascal, *Députés bretons*, pp. 213–17.
134 See, for example, the letters exchanged between commissaires, reproduced in Ménard (ed.), 'La Révolution de 1848 dans le Finistère', pp. 281–2.
135 See Haudebourg, *Mendiants et Vagabonds*, p. 35
136 Goallou, *Hamon*, p. 123.
137 ADM, 1/M.cérém/8, 10 February 1851.
138 Ibid., 5 May 1850
139 ADM, 1/M.cérém/7, 25 November 1848
140 ADM/M/2205, 21 November 1848
141 Olivier Ihl, *La Fête républicaine* (Paris: Gallimard, 1996), notes the austerity and moralism of the Republican festivals of this period, but seems to ignore the particular political context in which these tendencies developed.
142 ADM, 1/M.cérém/8, 27 November 1850.
143 ADLA, 1/M/516, 5 May 1850. Such rigid distinctions between acceptable and unacceptable forms of Republicanism were quite typical in France in 1851–2. See John M. Merriman, *The Agony of the Republic: the Repression of the Left in Revolutionary France, 1848–51* (Yale: Yale University Press, 1978)
144 ADM, 1/M.cérém/8, 15 May 1851.
145 ADF, 1/M/209, 14 November 1848.

6 The Politics of the State (2): The Management of Democracy, 1850–1940

1 See Isser Woloch, *The New Regime: Transformations of the French Civic Order, 1789–1820s* (New York: Norton, 1994), pp. 81–3.
2 Similar concepts of democracy are discussed in my 'The Republic, the people and the writer: Victor Hugo's social and political writing', *French History*, 14:3 (2000), pp. 272–94.

3. On this feature of French political life, see Raymond Huard, *La Naissance du parti politique en France* (Paris: Presses de Sciences Politiques, 1996).
4. *Democracy*, second edition (Birmingham, 1994), p. 9.
5. Information from Jean Pascal, *Les Députés Bretons de 1789 à 1983* (Paris: PUR, 1983), p. 229.
6. Ibid., p. 242. The confused political conditions of December 1851 mean that it is not possible to determine exact participation levels.
7. Pascal, *Députés bretons*, p. 242.
8. Bernard Ménager, *Les Napoléon du Peuple* (Paris: Aubier, 1988), p. 432.
9. Pascal, *Députés bretons*, pp. 276–7.
10. Ibid., pp. 326–8.
11. Ibid., pp. 403–4.
12. Patrick Pierre, *Les Bretons et la République: la construction de l'identité bretonne sous la troisième République* (Rennes: PUR, 2001), p. 310.
13. For an incisive and informative survey of modern Breton political culture, see Jean-Jacques Monnier, *Le comportement politique des Bretons, 1945–94* (Rennes: PUR, 1994).
14. ADF, 1/M/328, 11 January 1852.
15. ADCdA, 1/M/330bis, report dated 7 July 1852.
16. ADF, 1/M/328, circular dated 8 January 1852.
17. ADLA, 1/M/100, report dated 24 June 1857.
18. ADLA, 3/Z/111, circular dated 18 December 1851.
19. Ibid., circular dated 16 November 1852.
20. ADM, 3/M/201, poster dated 15 December 1851.
21. ADM, 1/Z/23, letter dated 16 February 1852.
22. See Rosemonde Sanson, 'Le 15 août: fête nationale du Second Empire', in A. Corbin, N. Gérôme and D. Tartowsky (eds), *Les Usages politiques des fêtes aux XIXe – XXe siècle* (Paris: Publications de la Sorbonne, 1994), pp. 117–36.
23. AN, BB/30/335, document dated 6 March 1852.
24. See my *French Revolutions* (Edinburgh: Edinburgh University Press, 1999), chapter 7. For more detailed analyses of the peasant insurrections, see Peter McPhee, *The Politics of Rural Life: Political Mobilization in the French Countryside, 1846–52* (Oxford: Oxford University Press, 1992), and Ted W. Margadant, *French Peasants in Revolt: the Insurrection of 1851* (Princeton: Princeton University Press, 1979).
25. ADLA, 1/M/100, circular dated 18 June 1857.
26. Michel Lagrée, *Religion et cultures en Bretagne (1850–1950)*, (Paris: Fayard, 1992), p. 33.
27. ADM, 3/M/201, poster dated 15 December 1851.
28. Gilbert Nicholas, *Instituteurs entre politique et religion: la première génération de normaliens en Bretagne au 19e siècle* (Rennes: Apogée, 1993), p. 165.
29. ADLA, 1/M/100, JP's report dated 24 June 1857.
30. Ménager, *Les Napoléon*, pp. 145–9.
31. Ibid., p. 122.
32. ADLA, 1/M/100, Loroux JP's letter, 3 June 1863.
33. Yves Tanneau (ed.), 'Récits de voyages et correspondance cornouaillaise: la famille Gouzil, de Pouldergat (1838–69)', *Bulletin de la Société Archéologique du Finistère*, 96 (1970), 245–91 (266–8).
34. ADM, 1/Z/23, circular dated 12 September 1856.

35 See, for example, ADCdA, 1/M/265, report dated 24 March 1859.
36 ADI&V, 1/M/142, report from Redon, dated 31 October 1873.
37 Pierre, *Bretons*, p. 198.
38 Lagrée, *Religion*, pp. 160–2.
39 ADLA, 1/M/100, Loroux JP, report dated 3 June 1863.
40 Ibid., police report from Savenay, dated 29 May 1863.
41 Ibid., Loroux JP, 3 June 1863.
42 Ibid., Piriac mayor's letter, dated 15 June 1863.
43 ADM, 1/Z/23, Hennebont police report, 1 June 1863.
44 ADLA, 1/M/100, mayor's report, Saint-Nicolas-de-Redon, 29 May 1863; and Ancenis Sub-Prefect's report, 2 June 1863.
45 ADM, 1/Z/23, Auray mayor, 2 June 1863.
46 ADLA, 1/M/100, Loroux JP's report, 3 June 1863.
47 ADM, 1/Z/23, Auray police report, 14 June 1863.
48 ADLA, 1/M/100, police report from Carquefou, 1 June 1863.
49 Ibid., police report from Saint-Philibert, 2 June 1863.
50 Armand Fresneau, [Morbihan election address], (Vannes: Lamarzelle, n.d. [1863?]). Piedmont was the northern Italian region which led the Italian nationalist movement.
51 ADM, 1/Z/23, Prefect's circular dated 13 July 1863.
52 L. de Serbois, *Souvenirs de Voyages en Bretagne et en Grèce* (Paris: Le Clerc & Dillet, 1864), pp. 221–2.
53 François-Marie de Luzel, *Notes de voyage en Basse–Bretagne* (Rennes: PUR/Terre de Brume, 1997), p. 98.
54 Robert Tombs, *France, 1815–1914* (London: Longman, 1996), pp. 485–9.
55 Similar perspectives can be found in Theodore Zeldin, *France, 1848–1945: Politics and Anger* (Oxford: Oxford University Press, 1979).
56 AN, F/7/6780, police report dated 31 January 1832 and ADI&V, 1/M/116, police report dated 1 June 1833.
57 ADLA, 1/M/515, reports dated 12 and 19 October 1840.
58 Claude Geslin, 'La violence ouvrière en Bretagne au XIXe siècle', *Kreiz*, 13 (2000), 199–218 (200–1).
59 ADF, 1/M/134, police report dated 5 May 1833; ADF, 1/M/177, dated 11 October 1833.
60 A. Guépin and E. Bonamy, *Nantes au XIXe siècle* (Ivry and Nantes: Phénix and Maison des sciences de l'homme Ange Guépin, 2000 [1835]). On Guépin, see Pamela Pilbeam, 'A forgotten socialist and reminist: Ange Guépin', in M. Cornick and C. Crossley (eds), *Problems in French History* (Basingstoke: Palgrave, 2000), pp. 64–80.
61 André Siegfried, *Tableau politique de la France de l'Ouest* (Paris: Imprimerie nationale, 1995), p. 188. Plozévet could also be cited as an example of this tendency. See André Burguière, *Bretons de Plozévet* (Paris: Flammarion, 1977).
62 Pascal, *Députés*, pp. 276–7.
63 Olivier Ihl, 'Convivialité et citoyenneté: les banquets commémoratifs dans les campagnes républicaines à la fin du XIXe siècle', in A. Corbin, N. Gérôme and D. Tartowsky (eds), *Les Usages politiques des fêtes aux XIXe – XXe siècle* (Paris: Publications de la Sorbonne, 1994), pp. 137–57.
64 ADI&V, 1/M/142, St-Malo Sub-Prefect's report, dated 8 March 1875.

65 Pascal, *Députés*, pp. 300–1, and 314–16.
66 Déguignet, *Mémoires*, pp. 335–41.
67 Siegfried, *Tableau*, p. 42.
68 Déguignet has slightly exaggerated the number of voters. However, the point he makes about the substantial Republican vote remains correct.
69 Corbin, *Village Bells*, pp. 274–5. See also Jean-Clément Martin, 'Quatorze juillet 1880, quartorze juillet 1889, l'instauration de la fête nationale dans l'ouest', *Annales de Bretagne*, 91 (1984), 201–47.
70 Martin, 'Quatorze juillet', p. 205.
71 See, for example, ADLA, 2/Z/109, letters from Meilleraye-de Bretagne (6 May 1889), Sion (29 April 1889), and Cassoun (2 May 1889).
72 ADF, 1/M/136, Morlaix Sub-Prefect, 25 February 1888.
73 See, for example, ADF, 1/M/134, Brest Sub-Prefect, 30 November 1888. See also comments by Lagrée, *Religion*, p. 70.
74 ADI&V, 1/M/149, Fougères Sub-Prefect, July 1909.
75 ADF, 1/M/136, Morlaix Sub-Prefect, 1 November 1909.
76 Ibid., Morlaix Sub-Prefect, 12 July 1889.
77 ADI&V, 1/M/155, Vitré Sub-Prefect, 15 March 1923.
78 ADLA, 3/Z/111, report dated 3 August 1913.
79 ADI&V, 1/M/142, Prefect, 1 November 1906.
80 Jean-François Tanguy, 'La Bretagne entre conquête républicaine et intégration nationale, 1870–1914', *Annales de Bretagne et des Pays de l'Ouest*, 111:4 (2004), 71–95 (87).
81 ADLA, 3/Z/96, 15 July 1907.
82 See, for example, ADCdA, 1/M/363, Guingamp Sub-Prefect, 4 February 1925; ADI&V, 1/M/155, Redon Sub-Prefect, 10 March 1924.
83 See, for example, the observations in ADCdA, 1/M/363, undated report (1926?) on Republican committees in Dinan.
84 ADLA, 3/Z/111, Paimboeuf Sub-Prefect, 3 August 1913.
85 Hervé Baudru, 'Le Cercle Républicain d'Enseignement Laïque d'Ille-et-Vilaine, 1904–27', *Annales de Bretagne et des Pays de l'Ouest*, 109:2 (2002), 103–13.
86 In this respect, it can be compared to some of the Republican groups which developed in Spain in the same period. See Ramiro Reig, 'Entre la realidad y la ilusión: el fenómeno blasquisat en Valencia, 1898–1936', in Nigel Townson (ed.), *El Republicanismo en España (1830–1977)*, (Madrid: Alianza Editorial, 1994), pp. 395–424.
87 Maurice Lucas, 'A propos d'un cacique radical et bigouden: Georges Le Bail', in *Etudes sur la Bretagne et les pays celtiques* (Bannalec: CRBC, 1987), pp. 325–52.
88 ADLA, 3/Z/111, Paimboeuf Sub-Prefect, 3 August 1913.
89 ADI&V, 3/M/335, election address from 1928. Significantly, even a skilled and observant political commentator such as Siegfried preferred to use such simple categories as means by which to evaluate political practices. See his *Tableau*, pp. 54–5.
90 See, for example, ADI&V, 1/M/155, Prefect's reports dated March and April 1923.
91 ADF, 1/M/134, Brest Sub-Prefect, January 1907.
92 Emile Masson, *Les Bretons et le socialisme* ed. J.-Y. Guiomar (Paris: Maspero, 1972), p. 208.

93 ADF, 1/M/134, Brest Sub-Prefect's report dated January 1907.
94 ADF, 1/M/135, Châtealin Sub-Prefect's report dated 29 September 1906.
95 Henry Baüer, 'Au pays Breton', in his *Idée et réalité* (Paris: H. Simon, 1899), pp. 277–84.
96 ADF, 1/M/136, Morlaix Sub-Prefect, 30 August 1889.
97 Yves Kano, *Les populations bretonnes* (n.p.: SEPEC, 2000 [1886]), p. 33.
98 Denise Delouche, 'Le peuple noir (à propos du numéro de *l'Assiette au Beurre* du 3 octobre 1903)', in A. Draguet (ed.), *Les Bleus de Bretagne*, pp. 223–47 (p. 237).
99 Charles Le Goffic, 'Le Crucifié de Keraliès', in *Gens de Bretagne*, 2, ed. D. Besançon (Paris: Omnibus, 1998), pp. 57–152; Yves Le Fevre, *La Terre des prêtres* (Morlaix: Le Bouquiniste, 1999 [1924]).
100 AN, F/7/12738, police report, Brest, 5 January 1925.
101 ADI&V, 1/M/142, Vitré Sub-Prefect, 27 September 1906. See also the comments in Ford, *Nation*, p. 138.
102 ADI&V, 1/M/155, Fougères Sub-Prefect, 8 November 1923.
103 Siegfried, *Tableau*, p. 162. See also ADI&V, 1/M/142, Vitré Sub-Prefect, 27 September 1906.

7 The Politics of Brittany: Regionalism and Nationalism

1 For a useful survey of the Breton economy, see Claude Geslin, 'La vie économique: un siècle de mutations douloureuses', in J.-J. Monnier and J.-C. Cassard (eds), *Toute l'histoire de la Bretagne* (Morlaix: Skol Vreizh, 1997), pp. 427–50.
2 Le comte H. de Charency, H. Gaidoz and Charles de Gaulle, 'Pétition pour les langues provinciales au Corps Législatif de 1870', reproduced in M. Nicolas, *Le Séparatisme en Bretagne* (Brasparts: Beltan, 1986), pp. 216–24. See also Fañch Postic, 'Pétition pour le breton: une des premières initiatives pour les langues régionales', *Ar Men*, 140 (April 2004), pp. 26–31.
3 Jean-François Tanguy, 'La Bretagne entre conquête républicaine et intégration nationale, 1870–1914', *Annales de Bretagne et des Pays de l'Ouest*, 111:4 (2004), 71–95
4 Monseigneur David, 'Discours', *Association Bretonne: Comptes-Rendus, Procès-Verbaux, Mémoires*, 1876, pp. xxxii–xxxviii (p. xxxvi).
5 Max Nicol, *Sainte Anne d'Auray: histoire du pèlerinage* (Sainte-Anne-d'Auray: Libraire du Pèlerinage, 1877), pp. 81–4.
6 H. Gaidoz, 'La poésie bretonne pendant la guerre de 1870–71: etude de littérature provinciale', *Revue des deux mondes* (15 December 1871), pp. 923–36.
7 Jean-Yves Guiomar, *Le bretonisme: les historiens bretons au XIXe siècle* (NP: Société d'Histoire et d'Archéologie de Bretagne, 1987), p. 133.
8 Suzanne Berger, *Les paysans contre la politique: l'organisation rurale en Bretagne*, trans. J.-P. Huet (Paris: Seuil, 1975), p. 45
9 Guiomar, *Bretonisme*, p. 189.
10 Michel Denis, 'Arthur de La Borderie (1827–1901) ou, "l'histoire, science patriotique"', in N.-Y. Tonnerre (ed.), *Chroniqueurs et historiens de la Bretagne* (Rennes: PUR, 2001), pp. 143–55.
11 *Association Bretonne: Agriculture, Comptes-Rendus et Procès-Verbaux* (1887), pp. 81–102.

12 Guiomar, *Bretonisme*, p. 374.
13 Ibid., p. 387.
14 Alain Déniel, *Le mouvement breton, 1919–45* (Paris: Maspero, 1976), p. 21.
15 Louis de Kerjégu, 'Discours', *Association Bretonne: Comptes-Rendus, Procès-Verbaux, Mémoires* (1876), pp. vi–xii (p. vii).
16 Andreu de Kerdrel, 'Discours', *Association Bretonne: Agriculture* (1888), pp. vi–xv.
17 Kerjégu, 'Discours', pp. xi–xii.
18 Le baron de Jouvenel, 'Discours', *Association Bretonne: Comptes-Rendus, Procès-Verbaux, Mémoires* (1876), pp. xii–xiv.
19 Marquis de l'Estourbeillon, 'Discours', *Association Bretonne: Comptes-Rendus, Procès-Verbaux, Mémoires* 32 (1913), p. xxxv.
20 P. de Courcy, 'Guingamp et sa banlieue', *Bulletin Archéologique de l'Association Bretonne* (1876), pp. 45–63.
21 Jouvenel, 'Discours'.
22 Kersanté, 'Traitement des engrais de ferme', *Bulletin Agricole de l'Association Bretonne* (1876), pp. 6–14.
23 L.-A. Bourgault-Ducoudray, 'La musique au congrès du Guingamp', *Bulletin Agricole de l'Association Bretonne* (1876), pp. 41–4; F.-M. Luzel, 'Un conte populaire breton', *Bulletin Archéologique de l'Association Bretonne* (1876), pp. 274–88; Jézégou, 'Enseignement de la langue bretonne dans les écoles du Finistère', *Association Bretonne: Comptes-Rendus, Procès-Verbaux, Mémoires*, 32 (1913), pp. 251–2.
24 Jean-Yves Guiomar, 'Le celtisme chez les intellectuels français/Bretons de gauche au XIXe siècle', in Alain Droguet (ed.), *Les Bleus de Bretagne* (Saint-Brieuc: Fédération « Côtes-du-Nord, 1789 », 1991), pp. 283–92.
25 The title refers back to a Breton saying: 'Faith and Brittany are like sister and brother.'
26 Information from the extremely informative article by Fañch Elegoët, 'Prêtres, nobles et paysans en Léon au début du XXe siècle; notes sur un nationalisme Breton: *Feiz ha Breiz*, 1900–14', *Plurial*, 18 (1979), 39–90. The analysis in the following paragraphs owes much to this article.
27 Michel Lagrée, *Religion et cultures en Bretagne (1850–1950)* (Paris: Fayard, 1992), p. 274.
28 See Christian Brunel, 'Le public de *Feiz ha Breiz*', in M. Lagrée (ed.), *Bretagne et religion* (Rennes: Institut Culturel de Bretagne/Skol-Uhel ar Vro, 1990), pp. 99–116.
29 F. Broudic, 'La polémique entre Y. Le Febvre et E. Masson à propos de la langue bretonne', in *Etudes sur la Bretagne et les pays celtiques: mélanges offertes à Yves Le Gallo* (Bannelec: CRBC, 1987), pp. 47–56.
30 Lagrée, *Religion et cultures*, p. 235.
31 ADCdA, 1/M/354, police report of a meeting in Saint-Brieuc, 18 March 1935.
32 On these issues, see the interesting assessment presented by Hudson Meadwell, 'The Catholic Church and the Breton language in the Third Republic', *French History*, 5:3 (1991), 325–44.
33 Jean-Marie Déguignet, *Mémoires d'un paysan bas-breton* (Le Relecq-Kerhuon: An Here, 1998), p. 410.
34 Charles Le Goffic, 'Le mouvement panceltique', *L'Âme bretonne*, Vol I (Paris: Honoré Champion, 1908), pp. 372–434 (p. 421).

35 Charles Le Goffic, 'Le régionalisme breton', *L'Âme bretonne*, Vol II (Paris: Champion, 1912), pp. 149–58.
36 Figures from Jack E. Reece, *The Bretons Against France: Ethnic Minority Nationalism in Twentieth-Century Brittany* (Chapel Hill: University of North Carolina Press, 1977), p. 61. Data on social origins is not available for the entire membership: hence these figures do not add up to 100%.
37 Charles Le Goffic, 'Préface' to *L'Âme bretonne*, Vol II, p. vii.
38 Anatole Le Braz, 'Pour la vieille France', *Impressions de la Bretagne*, ed. Régis Louarn (Spezed: An Here, 2004), pp. 37–40.
39 Le Braz, 'La Bretagne poétique et légendaire: l'œuvre de M. Luzel', *Impressions*, pp. 45–55.
40 Le Braz, 'La famine en Bretagne', *Impressions*, pp. 197–9.
41 Le Braz, *Il était une voix*, ed. Yann-Ber Piriou (Rennes: Apogée, 1995), pp. 57–8.
42 Philippe Le Stum, 'Néo-druidisme et régionalisme en Bretagne, 1900–14', *Bulletin de la Société archéologique du Finistère*, 126 (1997), 441–66.
43 See, for example, Corinne Prével-Montagne, 'Armel Beaufils et la Bretagne', *Ar Men*, 132 (January 2003), pp. 50–7.
44 A. Batillat, 'Sur l'architecture bretonne', *Bulletin de l'Union Régionaliste Bretonne*, 1929, pp. 134–7.
45 Fred Orton and Griselda Pollock, 'Les données bretonnantes: la prairie de répresentation', *Art History*, 3:3 (1980), 314–44 (327).
46 On the 1937 Exposition see Elise M. Moentmann, 'Searching for French identity in the regions: national versus local visions of France in the 1930s', *French History*, 17:3 (2003), 307–27.
47 M. de l'Estourbeillon, 'Au secours de la patrie', *Bulletin de l'Union Régionaliste Bretonne* (1929), pp. 7–11; le Marquis de l'Estourbeillon, 'Le culte de la tradition', *Bulletin de l'Union Régionaliste Bretonne* (1930), pp. 55–8.
48 Joseph Surcouf, 'La Bretagne et son passé', *Bulletin de l'Union Régionaliste Bretonne* (1929), pp. 77–94.
49 Claude Geslin, 'Le mouvement ouvrier de 1815 à 1914', in J.-J. Monnier and J.-C. Cassard (eds), *Toute l'histoire de Bretagne* (Morlaix: Skol Vreizh, 1997), pp. 491–511 (p. 495).
50 René Bazin, *De toute son âme* (Paris: Nelson/Calmann-Lévy n.d. [1897?]), p. 43.
51 Lagrée, *Religion et cultures*, pp. 145–7.
52 Geslin, 'Mouvement ouvrier', pp. 496–9.
53 Jean Noël Retière, *Identités ouvrières: histoire sociale d'un fief ouvrier en Bretagne, 1909–90* (Paris: L'Harmatten, 1994), p. 26.
54 Jean Pascal, *Les députés bretons de 1789 à 1983* (Paris: Presses Universitaires de France, 1983), pp. 509–10.
55 Jean-Christophe Fichou, 'Le Front Populaire et les conserveurs de sardines de Bretagne', *Annales de Bretagne et des Pays de l'Ouest*, 111:1 (2004), 111–25.
56 Louis Guilloux, *La maison du people* (Paris: Bernard Grasset, 1953 [1927]), p. 32.
57 Guilloux, *Maison*, p. 140.
58 Jean-Yves Guiomar, *Emile Masson: les Bretons et le socialisme* (Paris: Maspero, 1972), p. 38.
59 See J. Didier Giraud and Marielle Giraud, *Emile Masson: professeur de liberté* (Chamalières: Canope, 1991) for an evocative, sympathetic and informative biography.

60 Guimoar, *Emile Masson*, p. 137.
61 Ibid., p. 177.
62 Ibid., p. 231.
63 Ibid., p. 206.
64 Ibid., p. 191.
65 Ibid., p. 269.
66 On these points, see the perceptive analysis of Michel Denis, 'Comment être Breton sous la troisième République', in J.-Didier Giraud and Marielle Giraud (eds), *Emile Masson: prophète et rebelle* (Rennes: PUR, 2005), pp. 199–210.
67 See, for example, the records in ADCdA, 1/M/350, Republican declaration, 19 January 1919.
68 See, for example, Louis Castel, 'La garde du foyer', *La Bretagne Nouvelle*, 18 (April 1918), pp. 11–14.
69 Roger Dupuy, 'Identité bretonne et République dans la première moitié du XXe siècle', *Annales de Bretagne et des Pays de l'Ouest*, 111:4 (2004), 97–102.
70 See the provocative letter by J.-P. Calloc'h, written in January 1915, and reproduced in the appendix to Alain Déniel, *Le Mouvement Breton, 1919–1945* (Paris: Maspero, 1976), pp. 335–6.
71 Hélias, *Le Cheval d'Orgueil*, pp. 216–17
72 This can be compared with Gérard Prémel's strongly argued essay, 'Anamnèse d'un dommage, ou comment le français est venu aux bretons', *Langage et Société*, 72 (1995), pp. 51–95.
73 On the effects of the First World War, see Klaus Theweleit, *Male Fantasies, Vol I: Women, Floods, Bodies, History*, trans. Stephen Conway (Cambridge: Polity, 1987), and J. M. Winter, *Sites of Memory, Sites of Mourning* (Cambridge: Cambridge Univrsity Press, 1995).
74 Alongside *La Brière*, Louis Guilloux's later *Le sang noir* (1935) should also be mentioned: a magnificent work of modernist literature using a Joycean technique to describe a single day in 1917.
75 Olier Mordrel, *'Breiz Atao': ou, histoire et actualité du nationalisme breton* (Paris: Alain Moreau, 1973), p. 49; 'Petite histoire du mouvement breton', *Breiz Atao*, 26 April 1936.
76 PNB, *Le Nationalisme Breton: aperçu doctrinal* (Rennes: Editions du Parti National Breton, 1932), p. 26.
77 On the origins of *Breiz Atao*, see Déniel, *Mouvement*, pp. 56–8.
78 Morvan Lebesque, *Comment peut-on être Breton?* (Paris: Seuil, 1970), p. 159, notes this common tendency to conflate the movement with the journal.
79 La Bénélais, 'La France en Bretagne: son œuvre', *Breiz Atao*, 15 November 1921.
80 PNB, *Le nationalisme Breton*, p. 14.
81 'A la jeunesse bretonne', *Breiz Atao*, 16 September 1934.
82 'Lettre ouverte au gouvernement', *Breiz Atao*, 21 April 1936.
83 *Appel à la jeunesse de Bretagne* (Paris: Groupe NB–UYB, n.d. [1922?]), p. 1.
84 Roparz Hemon and Olivier Mordrel, 'Premier et dernier manifeste de *Gwalarn* en langue française', reproduced in the appendix to Mordrel, *Breiz Atao*, pp. 515–17.
85 'Le programme Saga', Déniel, *Mouvement*, p. 380.
86 PNB, *Le nationalisme Breton*, pp. 8 and 33.

87 'Déclaration d'Olier Mordrel devant le tribunal correctionnel, à Rennes . . .', *Breiz Atao*, 18 December 1938.
88 'Le Front Breton', *Breiz Atao*, 21 October 1934.
89 'Manifeste de Guingamp', *Breiz Atao*, 4 September 1938.
90 F. Debauvais, *L'Intérêt breton et l'avenir de la Bretagne: essai d'un nationalisme positif* (Rennes: Edition de *Breiz Atao*, 1926), p. 1.
91 Morvan Marchal, 'Au congrès de Rosporden', *Breiz Atao*, 1 October 1927.
92 Bénelais, 'La France'.
93 'La Déclaration de Carhaix', (1929), reproduced in Déniel, *Mouvement*, pp. 343–9.
94 'Le Front Breton', *Breiz Atao*, 21 October 1934.
95 Patrick Dieudonné (ed.), *Bretagne: un siècle d'architectures* (n.p.: Terre de Brume/AMAB, 2001), pp. 94–5.
96 Mordrel, *Breiz Atao*, p. 72.
97 On the PCF and *Breiz Atao*, see the suggestive article by Hervé Le Goff, 'Le Parti communiste française et le mouvement autonomiste breton', *Cahiers d'histoire sociale*, 16 (2001), pp. 93–102.
98 Marchal, 'Au congrès'.
99 'Manifeste du Parti à Guingamp', *Breiz Atao*, 4 September 1938.
100 'Aux Electeurs', in Déniel, pp. 354–7.
101 PNB, *Nationalisme*, pp. 26–8.
102 For a fascinating analysis of these themes in a French context, see Richard F. Kuisel, *Capitalism and the State in Modern France* (Cambridge: Cambridge University Press, 1981).
103 'Crises en Bretagne', *Breiz Atao*, 6 July 1930.
104 'Le programme Saga', *Breiz Atao*, 12 March 1933.
105 F. Debauvais, 'Crises en Bretagne', *Breiz Atao*, 6 July 1930. See also Debauvais, *Intérêt*, pp. 4 and 9.
106 Mazéas, 'Aux Electeurs', p. 355.
107 Mazéas, 'Aux Electeurs', p. 356.
108 'Bretons, n'allez pas là-bas', *Breiz Atao*, 29 November 1936.
109 PNB, *Nationalisme*, p. 20.
110 'La Déclaration de Carhaix', *Breiz Atao*, 18 August 1929.
111 'Le programme Saga', p. 381.
112 O. Mordrel, 'La France nous a menti . . .', *Breiz Atao*, 18 September 1938.
113 PNB, *Nationalisme*, p. 24.
114 Coarer, 'Paysans bretons, avec nous dans la lutte contre impérialisme' [April 1934], in Déniel, pp. 385–6.
115 'Le Front Breton', *Breiz Atao*, 21 October 1934.
116 Mordrel, *Breiz Atao*, pp. 235 and 191.
117 [untitled], *Breiz Atao*, 16 May 1937.
118 See Déniel, *Mouvement*, pp. 199–200.
119 On this 'fascistization' of French political culture, see Robert Soucy, *French Fascism: The Second Wave, 1933–1939* (London: Yale University Press, 1995) and Zeev Sternhell, *Ni droite, ni gauche: l'idéologie fasciste en France* (Paris: Complexe, 1987). While these two works offer quite contrasting perspectives on the nature of fascism, it is significant that both authors concur that a fascist 'style' was growing more prevalent in French interwar politics.

120 'Le programme Saga', p. 383.
121 'Manifeste de Guingamp', *Breiz Atao*, 4 September 1938.
122 'Les voix amies', *La Pensée bretonne*, 15 August 1922; 'Echoes et controverses', *La Pensée bretonne*, 15 October 1922.
123 Lebesque, *Comment peut-on être Breton?*, p. 162.
124 Daniel Le Couédic, 'Une Pléaide bretonne: les temps des profits', in Daniel Le Couédic and Jean-Yves Veillard (eds), *Ar Seiz Breur* (Rennes: Terre de Brume & Musée de Bretagne, 2000) pp. 90–116 (pp. 96–8).
125 Pierre Jakez Hélias, *Le Quêteur de mémoire* (Paris: Plon, 1990), p. 127. The gap between Hélias's writing and nationalist writing is explored in Francis Favereau, 'L'évolution du discours bretonnant chez Pierre-Jakez Hélias', in Michel Lagrée and Jacqueline Sainclivier (eds), *L'Ouest et la politique* (Rennes: PUR, 1996), pp. 165–77.
126 AN, F/7/12.754, report from Lorient, 3 May 1928.
127 Ibid., report from Lorient, 31 October 1928.
128 AN, F/7/13.244, Minister of the Interior, citing the Finistère Prefect, 21 November 1927.
129 AN, F/7/13.244, Rennes police official, 28 March 1928.
130 AN, F/7/14.685, Ille-et-Vilaine Prefect, 31 July 1935.
131 Ibid., Ministry of the Interior report, undated [1933?].
132 Ibid., Ille-et-Vilaine Prefect, 31 July 1935.
133 Ibid., Rennes police official, 25 July 1935.
134 Déniel, *Mouvement*, p. 205.
135 Reece, *Bretons*, p. 113.
136 Déniel, *Mouvement*, p. 140.
137 Figures cited in Robert O. Paxton, *French Peasant Fascism: Henry Dorgères's Greenshirts and the Crises of French Agriculture, 1929–1939* (Oxford: Oxford University Press, 1997), p. 14.
138 Paxton, *Peasant Fascism*, pp. 38–40.
139 Ibid., p. 58.
140 Pascal Ory, 'Le Dorgèrisme: institution et discours d'une colère paysanne (1929–31)', *Revue d'histoire moderne et contemporaine*, 22 (1975), 168–90. Once again, these figures should be treated as generous, maximum estimates.
141 'Le péril de la propagande socialiste dans les milieux paysans', *Le Matin*, 27 April 1934.
142 'Périr ou s'unir', *Le Progrès agricole de l'Ouest*, 4 November 1934.
143 'Organisons-nous', *Le Progrès agricole de l'Ouest*, 5 January 1936.
144 On this point see Soucy, *French Fascism*, pp. 43–6.
145 While Morvan Lebesque does not use these terms, his analysis of *Breiz Atao* certainly suggests this perspective. See, for example, his *Comment peut-on être Breton?*, p. 166.
146 Françoise Morvan, *Le monde comme si: nationalisme et dérive identitaire en Bretagne* (Arles: Actes Sud, 2002), p. 174.
147 Morvan, *Le monde*, p. 215.
148 Ibid., p. 232.

8 The End of the Road? Breton Nationalism and Vichy France, 1940–5

1. To date, there is still no single, well-researched volume which one can recommend as a history of Brittany during the Second World War. However the collection edited by Christian Bourgeard, *Bretagne et identités Régionales* (Brest: CRBC, 2001), presents some perceptive and informative studies.
2. One excellent contribution to the debate is Robert Soucy, *French Fascism: The Second Wave, 1933–1939* (New Haven: Yale University Press, 1995). The first chapter of this work includes an extremely useful survey of recent debates.
3. See Eric Nadaud, 'Le renouvellement des pratiques militants de la SFIO au début du Front Populaire (1934–1936)', *Mouvement social*, 153 (1990), 9–32.
4. The term 'accommodation' is more complex than it might appear. See the subtle and perceptive arguments put forward by Philippe Burrin, *La France à l'heure allemande, 1940–1944* (Paris: Seuil, 1995).
5. Jean Airiau (ed.), *Odette Jolly: Sage-Femme* (Nantes: Siloë, 1999), p. 89.
6. Morvan Lebesque, *Comment peut-on être Breton?: essai sur la démocratie française* (Paris: Seuil, 1970), p. 165.
7. Michel Denis, 'Le mouvement Breton pendant la guerre: un bilan', in C. Bougeard (ed.), *Bretagne et identités régionales* (Brest: CRBC, 2001), pp. 151–66 (p. 166).
8. AN, F/1cIII/1130, report dated 20 March 1923.
9. ADCdA, 1.M.356, report dated 12 December 1925.
10. Ibid., report dated 21 June 1928.
11. AN, F/7/12.754, report dated 3 November 1928.
12. ADCdA, 1.M.355, reports dated 2 December 1934 and 30 June 1935.
13. ADI&V, 1.M.156, poster dated 18 January 1936 and ADCdA, 1.M.350, report dated 7 June 1933.
14. Jacqueline Sainclivier, *L'Ille-et-Vilaine, 1918–1958* (PUR, 1996), p. 90.
15. Ibid., p. 91; Claude Kahn and Jean Landais, *Nantes et le Front Populaire* (Nantes: Ouest-Editions and Université Permanente de Nantes, 1997) p. 23; ADI&V, 1.M.159, report dated 4 July 1935.
16. ADCdA, 1.M.356, report dated 8 April 1936.
17. Kahn and Landais, *Nantes*, p. 73.
18. Robert O. Paxton, *French Peasant Fascism: Henry Dorgères's Greenshirts and the Crises of French Agriculture, 1929–1939* (Oxford: Oxford University Press, 1997), pp. 112–13.
19. ADCdA, 1.M.355, report dated 30 June 1935. See also reports from the Loire-Inférieure prefect, dated 19 May and 25 June 1934, AN, F/7/13.026.
20. Ibid., report dated 12 November 1936.
21. ADLA, 2.Z.108, circular dated 21 December 1937.
22. ADCdA, 1.M.261, report dated 25 February 1939.
23. *Salido* (Paris: Gallimard, 1976), p. 36.
24. 'Manifeste de Guingamp', reproduced in Alain Déniel, *Le Mouvement breton, 1919–1945* (Paris: Maspero, 1976), pp. 401–5.
25. Père Amand Boulé, *De Dunkerque à la Liberté* (Saint-Brieuc: Les Presses bretonnes, 1976), p. 15.
26. 'Diskleriadur', reproduced in Déniel, *Mouvement*, pp. 408–9.

27 AN, F/7/14.685, Ministry of the Interior report, dated 4 August 1939.
28 Ibid., police report, dated 31 October 1939.
29 Christian Bougeard, 'La Bretagne et les Bretons face à l'Occupation', in his *Bretagne et Identités Régionales*, pp. 13–29 (p. 18).
30 Guy Haudebourg and Franck Liaigre, 'La Résistance communiste en Loire-Inférieure (juin 1940–juin 1944)', in Bougeard (ed.), *Bretagne*, pp. 89–102 (p. 90).
31 *Une jeunesse bretonne: an durzunell* (Rennes: Sareda, 1998), p. 22.
32 Boulé, *Dunkerque*, p. 16.
33 Gendreau, *Jeunesse*, p. 26.
34 Sainclivier, *Ille-et-Vilaine*, p. 219.
35 Monique Vérité, *Odette du Puigaudeau: une Bretonne au désert* (Paris: Payot and Rivages, 2001), p. 252.
36 Charles Le Quintrec, *Une Enfance bretonne* (Paris: Albin Michel, 2000), p. 75, and Gendreau, *Jeunesse*, p. 35.
37 Gendreau, *Jeunesse*, p. 35
38 Maurice Rajsfus, *Les Français de la débâcle: juin–septembre 1940, un si bel été* (Paris: Le Cherche Midi, 1997), p. 140.
39 Sainclivier, *Ille-et-Vilaine*, p. 221–2.
40 Soma Morgenstern, *Errance en France*, translated by Nicole Casanova (Paris: Liana Levi, 2002), pp. 147–9.
41 Gendreau, *Jeunesse*, p. 38.
42 Marie-Paul Salonne, *Fends la bise: Aïde, jeune bretonne agent de liaison* (Rennes: La Découvrance, 1997 [1945]), p. 55.
43 Christian Bourgeard, *René Pleven, un français libre en politique* (Rennes: PUR, 1994), p. 84.
44 Marc Bloch, 'L'Etrange Défaite', in his *L'Histoire, la Guerre, la Résistance* (Paris: Quarto-Gallimard, 2006), pp. 519–653 (539–40, 560–1).
45 Gendreau, *Jeunesse*, pp. 37–8.
46 Le Quintrec, *Enfance*, pp. 76–7.
47 Gendreau, *Jeunesse*, p. 62.
48 Roland de Kermadec, *1937–1946: De l'Orne au Finistère: ma drôle de guerre* (Spézet: Keltia, 1995), p. 108.
49 Pierre Jakez Hélias, *Le Quêteur de mémoire: quarante ans de recherche sur les mythes et la civilisation bretonne* (Paris: Plon, 1990), pp. 132–3.
50 Bougeard, 'La Bretagne', p. 15.
51 Michel Chaillou, *1945* (Paris: Seuil, 2004), p. 40.
52 Le Quintrec, *Enfance*, pp. 77–8.
53 See the excellent analysis of this event in Yvon Tranvouez, 'La mémoire d'un bombardement britannique: Notre-Dame-des-Anges (Morlaix, 1943–2003)', *Annales de Bretagne et des Pays de l'Ouest*, 111:1 (2004), 127–51.
54 Jean Guiffan, 'Les Bretons et la Perfide Albion', *Ar Men*, 147 (2005), pp. 28–37.
55 Vérité, *Odette du Puigaudeau*, pp. 260–5.
56 Suzanne Berger, *Les paysans contre la politique: l'organisation rurale en Bretagne, 1911–74*, trans. J.-P. Huet (Paris: Seuil, 1975), pp. 172–3.
57 Ronan Calvez, '1941: le breton, langue d'Etat', in Bougeard (ed.), *Bretagne et identités régionales*, pp. 207–21.

58 Marc Olivier Baruch, 'L'Etat français et la création des régions', in Bougeard, *Bretagne et identités régionales*, pp. 31–46.
59 Jean-Yves Carluer, 'Les protestants bretons pendant la Seconde Guerre mondiale', in Bougeard (ed.), *Bretagne et identités régionales*, pp. 271–84.
60 Bougeard, 'La Bretagne', p. 20.
61 Yvon Tranvouez, 'Les catholiques et la question bretonne (1940–44)', in Bougeard (ed.), *Bretagne et identités régionales*, pp. 285–306. The material presented in this paragraph is largely drawn from Tranvouez's valuable essay.
62 Olier Mordrel, *Breiz Atao: ou, Histoire et actualité du Nationalisme Breton* (Paris: Alain Moreau, 1973), p. 217.
63 Déniel, *Mouvement*, p. 224.
64 Lionel Boissou, 'L'Allemagne et le nationalisme breton (1939–45)', in Bougeard (ed.), *Bretagne et identités régionales*, pp. 321–36; AN, F/7/14.685, note by Himmler, 4 July 1940.
65 Denis, 'Le mouvement', p. 154.
66 Kristian Hamon, *Les Nationalistes bretons sous l'occupation* (Le Relecq-Kerhuon: An Here, 2001), p. 35.
67 Denis, 'Le mouvement', p. 158.
68 Mordrel, *Breiz Atao*, p. 261.
69 Ibid., p. 262.
70 Boulé, *Dunkerque*, p. 70.
71 Ibid., p. 80.
72 Mordrel, *Breiz Atao*, p. 268.
73 Déniel, *Mouvement*, p. 227.
74 Denis, 'Le mouvement', p. 156.
75 AN, F/7/15.144, report dated 2 October 1940.
76 Ibid., report dated 31 October 1940.
77 Mordrel, *Breiz Atao*, p. 287.
78 AN, F/7/15.144, report dated 22 June 1941.
79 Mordrel, *Breiz Atao*, p. 317.
80 AN, F/7/15.144, report dated 29 May 1942.
81 Hamon, *Nationalistes*, pp. 86–90.
82 Ibid., p. 119.
83 Ibid., p. 149.
84 Luc Capdevila, *Les Bretons au lendemain de l'Occupation* (Rennes: PUR, 1999), p. 50.
85 Ibid., p. 48.
86 See, for example, Déniel, *Mouvement*, p. 306, which suggests a membership of 60. Capdevila, *Les Bretons*, suggests 80 in December 1943, p. 47.
87 Kristian Hamon, *Le Bezen Perrot* (Fouesnant: Yoran Embanner, 2004), pp. 8 and 54.
88 Ibid., pp. 60–7.
89 Ibid., p. 25.
90 Déniel, *Mouvement*, p. 309.
91 Maen-Nevez, 'Reveil légitime', *Kad*, 4 (11,502 [sic – 1941?]), pp. 1–4.
92 Boissou, 'L'Allemagne'. This moment in Breton history is eloquently evoked in the novel by William Palmer, *The Pardon of Saint Anne* (London: Jonathan Cape, 1997).

93 Calvez, '1941'.
94 Georges G.-Toudouze, *Anne et le mystère Breton* (Paris: Hachette, 1942), p. 39.
95 *Anne*, p. 47.
96 Hamon, *Nationalistes*, p. 155.
97 Gilles Ragache, *Les enfants de la guerre: vivre, survivre, lire et jouer en France, 1939–49* (n.p.: Perrin, 1997), p. 163.
98 Jacqueline Lalouette, 'Vercingétorix: 1940–45. De Vichy au maquis', in Bougeard (ed.), *Bretagne et identités régionales*, pp. 47–62.
99 Angèle Jacq, *Les Hommes Libres, I: Ils n'avaient que leurs mains* ... (St-Evarzec: Palémon, 2003), p. 289.
100 Rajsfus, *Les Français*, p. 143.
101 Salonne, *Fends la bise*, p. 11.
102 Gendreau, *Jeunesse*, pp. 79–81.
103 Christopher Neumaier, 'The escalation of German reprisal policy in occupied France, 1941–42', *Journal of Contemporary History*, 41:1 (2006), 113–31 (120–1).
104 Haudebourg and Liaigre, 'La Résistance communiste', p. 96.
105 Jean-Jacques Monnier, 'Des militants bretons dans la Résistance', in Bougeard (ed.), *Bretagne et identités régionales*, pp. 103–19.
106 Carlier, 'Les protestants', p. 281.
107 Salonne, *Fends la Bise*, p. 149.
108 NA, WO/219/2367, report dated 8 September 1944.
109 Capdevila, *Bretons*, p. 23.
110 Luc Capdevila, *Les Bretons au lendemain de l'Occupation* (Rennes: PUR, 1999), p. 29; NA, WO/219/2367, report dated 8 September 1944.
111 Cornelius Ryan, 'Peasants' street battle with Nazi looters', *Daily Telegraph*, 9 August 1944.
112 Capdevila, *Les Bretons*, p. 60.
113 NA, WO/219/2365, report dated 6 August 1944.
114 Capdevila, *Les Bretons*, p. 95.
115 Ibid., p. 296.
116 Ibid., p. 28.
117 Françoise Rouxel, 'Brest en baraques (1945–1975)', *Ar Men*, 62 (October 1994), pp. 2–15.
118 Sainclivier, *Ille-et-Vilaine*, pp. 265–6.
119 Didier Guyvarc'h, 'Les cinquante otages dans la mémoire nantaise', in Bougeard (ed.), *Bretagne et identités régionales*, pp. 381–92.
120 See Sarah Farmer, *Martyred Village: Commemorating the 1944 Massacre at Oradour-sur-Glane* (Berkeley: University of California Press, 1999).
121 Capdevila, *Les Bretons*, p. 210.
122 NA, WO/219/5055, report dated 21 March 1945: transcript of witness's statement in English.
123 Louis Guilloux, *O.K., Joe!* (Paris: Gallimard, 1976), pp. 123–5.
124 Capdevila, *Les Bretons*, p. 101.
125 Salonne, *Fends la Bise*, p. 236.
126 Hanna Diamond, *Women and the Second World War in France, 1939–1948* (Harlow: Longman, 1999), p. 138.
127 Capdevila, *Les Bretons*, p. 241.

[128] Ibid., p. 374.
[129] Hélias, *Le Quêteur*, p. 145.
[130] Fañch Broudic, 'Du Breton au français; les années décisives de l'après-guerre', *Ar Men*, 47 (February 1996), pp. 20–9.
[131] Déniel, *Mouvement Breton*, pp. 314–16.
[132] Erwan Chartier, 'Morvan Lebesque: le masque et la plume d'un intellectuel breton', *Ar Men*, 143 (November 2004), pp. 24–31.
[133] Françoise Morvan, *Le Monde comme si: nationalisme et dérive identitaire en Bretagne* (Arles: Actes Sud, 2002).
[134] *Libération*, 11 May 2000.
[135] *Ouest-France*, 10 May 2000.
[136] *Télégramme*, 27 June 2000.
[137] Erwan Chartier, 'La Saint Loup à Guingamp', *Ar Men*, 147 (July 2005), pp. 20–7.
[138] Michel Philippe and Erwan Chartier, 'Le Bleun-Brug, 1950', *Ar Men*, 112 (May 2000), pp. 10–17.
[139] See my 'Roots, rock, Breizh: music and the politics of nationhood in contemporary Brittany', *Nations and Nationalism*, 11:1 (2005), 103–20.
[140] Georges Cadiou, 'Pierre Hervé et le projet de Loi du PCF sur la langue bretonne en 1947', *Peuple Breton*, 476 (Sep 2003), pp. 18–19.
[141] Martine Cocaud, 'Engagements en revendications féminines en Ille-et-Vilaine de 1945 aux années soixantes', *Annales de Bretagne et des Pays de l'Ouest*, 108:2 (2001), 85–101.
[142] Jean Pascal, *Les Députés bretons de 1789 à 1983* (Paris: PUR, 1983), pp. 529–30.
[143] Odette du Puigaudeau, *Grandeur des îles* (Paris: Payot & Rivages, 1996), p. 73.

Conclusion: Mordrel's Children

[1] Michel Denis, 'Le mouvement Breton pendant la guerre: un bilan', in C. Bougeard (ed.), *Bretagne et identités régionales* (Brest: CRBC, 2001), pp. 151–66 (p. 166).
[2] AN, F/7/15.144, report dated 31 October 1940.
[3] See, for example, Ronan Le Coadic, *L'identité bretonne* (Rennes: PUR and Terre de Brume, 1998), pp. 63, 195.

Bibliography

Archive sources

Archives départementales des Côtes d'Armor
1.M.261, 1/M/263, 1/M/265, 1/M/325, 1/M/330, 1/M/330bis, 1/M/350, 1/M/351, 1/M/352, 1/M/354, 1/M/355, 1/M/356, 1/M/363, 1/M/374.

Archives départementales du Finistère
1/M/134, 1/M/135, 1/M/136, 1/M/139, 1/M/159, 1/M/177, 1/M/178, 1/M/209, 1/M/328.
1/N/57, 1/N/58.

Archives départementales de l'Ille-et-Vilaine
L.449.
1/M/112, 1/M/113, 1/M/115, 1/M/116, 1/M/142, 1/M/143, 1/M/149, 1/M/155, 1.M.156, 1.M.159.
3/M/335, 3/M/344.
4/M/98bis.

Archives départementales de la Loire-Atlantique
1/M/100, 1/M/113, 1/M/150, 1/M/509, 1/M/510, 1/M/511, 1/M/515, 1/M/516.
2.Z.108, 2/Z/109.
3/Z/96, 3/Z/111.

Archives départementales du Morbihan
M/680, M/2205, M/2206, M/2255.
1/M/cérém/7, 1/M.cérém.8.
3/M/201.
1/Z/23.

Archives nationales (Paris)
BB/30/335, BB/30/364.
C/939.
F/1/C1 (III)/1127, F/1cIII/1130.
F/7/6780, F/7/12.738, F/7/12.754, F/7/13.026, F/7/13.244, F/7/14.685, F/7/15.144.

National Archives (Kew)
WO/219/2365, WO/219/2367, WO/219/5055.

Published primary sources

Adresse des citoyens de la ville de Brest à l'Assemblée Nationale sur les circonstances actuelles (Paris: Patriote française, n.d. [1792–3?]).
Airiau, Jean (ed.), *Odette Jolly: Sage-Femme* (Nantes: Siloë, 1999).
Ampère, J.-J., 'Des castes dans l'ancienne Egypte', *Revue des deux Mondes*, 14 September 1848, pp. 645–52 (p. 652).
Appel à la jeunesse de Bretagne (Paris: Groupe NB – UYB, n.d. [1922?]).
Aux Paysans par un fils de paysan de Saint-Malo (Paris: Desoye, 1849).
Balzac, Honoré de, *Les Chouans, ou la Bretagne en 1799* (Paris: Gallimard, 1972 [1829]).
—— *Un drame au bord de la mer* (Rezé: Séquences, 1993).
Barère, 'Rapport du comité de salut public sur les idiomes', *www.languefrancaise.net*, accessed 18 August 2005.
Barthélemy, Charles, *Histoire de la Bretagne Ancienne et Moderne* (Tours: Mame, 1853).
Batillat, A., 'Sur l'architecture bretonne', *Bulletin de l'Union Régionaliste Bretonne*, 1929, pp. 134–7.
Baude, J.-J., 'Les côtes de la Manche', *Revue des Deux Mondes*, 1 July 1851.
—— 'Les côtes de Bretagne: Saint-Malo et les malouins', *Revue des Deux Mondes*, 15 November 1851, pp. 651–90.
—— 'Les côtes de Bretagne: la baie de Saint-Brieuc', *Revue des Deux Mondes*, 15 September 1852, pp. 1053–79.
Baüer, Henry, 'Au pays Breton', in his *Idée et réalité* (Paris: H. Simon, 1899), pp. 277–84.
Bazin, René, *De toute son âme* (Paris: Nelson/Calmann-Lévy, n.d. [1897?]).
Blackburn, Henry, 'De Saint Malo à Dinan en 1880', trans. P. Galliou, *Ar Men*, 62 (October 1994), pp. 26–40.
Bloch, Marc, 'L'Etrange Défaite', in his *L'Histoire, la Guerre, la Résistance* (Paris: Quarto-Gallimard, 2006), pp. 519–653.
Boisgobey, Fortuné de, *Voyage en Bretagne, 1839* (Rennes: Ouest–France, 2001).
Botherel, de, *Protestations adressés au roi et au public*, ed. Loeiz Le Bec (Ar Relug–Kerhoun: An Here, 2000).
Boulé, Père Amand, *De Dunkerque à la Liberté* (Saint-Brieuc: Les Presses bretonnes, 1976).
Bourgault-Ducoudray, L.-A., 'La musique au congrès du Guingamp', *Bulletin Agricole de l'Association Bretonne* (1876), pp. 41–4.
Brizeux, A., *Les Bretons, deuxième édition* (Paris: Paul Masgana, 1848).
Brousmiche, J.-F., *Voyage dans le Finistère en 1829, 1830 et 1831* (Quimper: Morvan, 1977).
Bruno, G., *Le Tour de la France par deux enfants: devoir et patrie* (Paris: Eugène Blin: 1995 [1905?]).
Caesar, *The Gallic War*, trans. H. J. Edwards (Cambridge, MA: Harvard University Press, 1994).
Cambry, Jacques, *Voyage dans le Finistère* (Paris: Layeur, 2000 [1794–5]).
Castel, Louis, 'La garde du foyer', *La Bretagne Nouvelle*, 18 (April 1918), 11–14.
Chaillou, Michel, *1945* (Paris: Seuil, 2004).
Charency, Comte H. de, H. Gaidoz and Charles de Gaulle, 'Pétition pour les langues provinciales au Corps Législatif de 1870', reproduced in M. Nicolas, *Le Séparatisme en Bretagne* (Brasparts: Beltan, 1986), pp. 216–24.

Chateaubriand, François-René, *Mémoires d'outre-tombe*, Vol I (Paris: Librairie Générale Française, 1973).
—— *De La Vendée* (La Rochelle: Rumeur des Ages, 1990 [1819]).
Châteauneuf, Benoiston de and Villermé, *Rapport d'un voyage fait dans les cinq départements de la Bretagne, pendant les années 1840 et 1841* (Rennes: Tud ha Bro, 1982).
Clorivière, Pierre de, *Lettres de P. de Clorivière, 1787–1814*, Vol I (Paris: Durassié, 1948).
Cochut, André, 'L'Algérie et le budget', *Revue des Deux Mondes*, 15 March 1849, pp. 926–52.
Conan, *Les aventures extraordinaires du citoyen Conan*, trans. Paolig Combot (Morlaix: Skol Vreizh, 2001).
Courcy, P. de, 'Guingamp et sa banlieue', *Bulletin Archéologique de l'Association Bretonne* (1876), pp. 45–63.
Darsel, Joachim (ed.), *L'homme qui croyait en la République: livre de vie de Jean-Marie Jézéquel* (Morlaix: Le Bouquiniste, 2000).
David, Monseigneur, 'Discours', *Association bretonne: Comptes-Rendus, Procès-Verbaux, Mémoires* (1876), pp. xxxii–xxxviii.
Dawson, William Harbutt, *Across the Silver Streak: Holiday Rambles* (Plymouth: Latimer, 1884).
Debauvais, F., *L'Intérêt Breton et l'Avenir de la Bretagne: essai d'un nationalisme positif* (Rennes: Edition de *Breiz Atao*, 1926).
Déguignet, Jean-Marie, *Mémoires d'un paysan bas-Breton* (Ar Releg-Kerhuon: An Here, 1998).
Delzell, Charles F., *Mediterranean Fascism, 1919–45* (London: Walker, 1971).
Dubuisson-Aubenay, *Itinéraire de Bretagne en 1636*, two volumes (Paris: Layeur, 2000).
l'Estourbeillon, Marquis de, 'Discours', *Association Bretonne: Comptes-Rendus, Procès-Verbaux, Mémoires*, 32 (1913), p. xxxv.
—— 'Au secours de la patrie', *Bulletin de l'Union Régionaliste Bretonne* (1929), pp. 7–11.
—— 'Le Culte de la Tradition', *Bulletin de l'Union Régionaliste Bretonne* (1930), pp. 55–8.
Flaubert, Gustave, 'Par les champs et par les grèves: voyage en Bretagne, 1847', in *Œuvres complètes* II, ed. B. Masson (Paris: Seuil, 1964).
E. Fleury, 'Excursion dans l'arrondissement de Brest', *Bulletin de la Société Académique de Brest*, 1 (1858–60), pp. 422–66.
Fresneau, Armand, [Morbihan election address], (Vannes: Lamarzelle, n.d. [1863?]).
Gaidoz, H., 'La poésie bretonne pendant la guerre de 1870–71: etude de littérature provinciale', *Revue des deux mondes*, 15 December 1871, pp. 923–36.
Gautier, Théophile, *Le salon de 1847* (Paris: Le Livre à la carte, 1997).
Gendreau, Georges *Une jeunesse bretonne: an durzunell* (Rennes: Sareda, 1998).
Gernoux, Alfred (ed.), 'De Nantes à Brest en 1845: correspondance d'Armand Guérand, 1824–61', *Nouvelle Revue de Bretagne*, January–February 1950, pp. 50–9.
Gracq, Julien, *La forme d'une ville* (Paris: José Corti, 1985).
G.-Toudouze, Georges, *Anne et le mystère Breton* (Paris: Hachette, 1942).
Guépin, A. and E. Bonamy, *Nantes au XIXe siècle* (Ivry and Nantes: Phénix and Maison des sciences de l'homme Ange Guépin, 2000 [1835]).
Guérin, F., *Au clergé* (Vannes: Lamarzelle, n.d. [1848?]).

Guide Bleu: Bretagne (Paris: Hachette, 1920).
Guilloux, Louis, *La maison du people* (Paris: Bernard Grasset, 1953 [1927]).
—— *Ma Bretagne* (Bédée: Flolle Avoine, 1998 [1973]).
—— *Salido* (Paris: Gallimard, 1976).
—— *O.K., Joe!* (Paris: Gallimard, 1976).
Hélias, Piere-Jakez, *Le cheval d'orgueil: mémoires d'un Breton du pays bigouden* (Paris: Plon, 1975).
—— *Le Quêteur de mémoire* (Paris: Plon, 1990).
Hugo, Victor, *Quatrevingt-treize* (Paris: Gallimard, 1979 [1874]).
Jacq, Angèle, *Les Hommes Libres, I: Ils n'avaient que leurs mains . . .* (St-Evarzec: Palémon, 2003).
Jézégou, 'Enseignement de la langue bretonne dans les écoles du Finistère', *Association Bretonne: Comptes-Rendus, Procès-Verbaux, Mémoires*, 32 (1913), pp. 251–2.
Jouvenel, Baron de, 'Discours', *Association Bretonne: Comptes-Rendus, Procès-Verbaux, Mémoires*, 1876, pp. xii–xiv.
Justification des prêtres qui refusent de faire le serment civique ([Rennes?]: n.p., n. d. [1790?]).
Kano, Yves, *Les populations bretonnes* (n.p.: SEPEC, 2000 [1886]).
Keranflec'h, Charles de, *Voyage dans les montagnes du centre Bretagne et de Vendée, 1857* (Spézet: Keltia, 1998).
Kerdrel, Andreu de, 'Discours', *Association bretonne: Agriculture* (1888), pp. vi–xv.
Kerjégu, Louis de, 'Discours', *Association Bretonne: Comptes-Rendus, Procès-Verbaux, Mémoires* (1876), pp. vi–xii.
Kermadec, Roland de, *1937–1946: De l'Orne au Finistère; ma drôle de guerre* (Spézet: Keltia, 1995).
Kersanté, 'Traitement des engrais de ferme', *Bulletin Agricole de l'Association Bretonne* (1876), pp. 6–14.
La Rochejaquelein, Marquise de, *Mémoires* (Paris: Mercure de France, 2002).
Le Braz, Anatole, *Il était une voix . . . discours et conférences* (Rennes: Apogée, 1995).
—— *Au Pays des Pardons* (Rennes: Terre de Brume, 1998 [1894]).
—— *Impressions de la Bretagne*, ed. Régis Louarn (Spezed: An Here, 2004).
—— 'Le Gardien du feu', in *Gens de Bretagne*, 2, ed. D. Besançon (Paris: Omnibus, 1998).
Le Breton, *Lettre . . . à MM. les Ecclésiastiques du Département de Morbihan* (Paris: Imprimerie Nationale, 1791).
Le Fevre, Yves, *La Terre des prêtres* (Morlaix: Le Bouquiniste, 1999 [1924]).
Le Gendre, *Supplément à l'adresse au peuple breton par ses députés à l'Assemblée nationale* (n.p.: no publisher, 1790).
Le Goffic, Charles, 'Le Crucifié de Keraliès', in *Gens de Bretagne*, 2, ed. D. Besançon (Paris: Omnibus, 1998), pp. 57–152.
—— *L'Ame bretonne*, Vol I (Paris: Champion, 1908).
—— *L'Ame bretonne*, Vol II (Paris: Champion, 1912).
—— *L'Ame bretonne*, Vol III (Paris: Honoré Chapman, 1908).
Le Marchand d'Epinay, *Seconde Adresse de la ville de Rennes aux habitans des campagnes* (Rennes: Vatar, 1790).
Le Quintrec, Charles, *Une enfance bretonne* (Paris: Albin Michel, 2000).
Leroy-Beaulieu, Paul, *La Question de la population* (Paris: Alcan, 1913).

Lewis, Wyndham, *The Complete Wild Body*, ed. Bernard Lafoucade (Santa Barbara: Black Sparrow Press, 1982).
Lisle, Rouget de, *Historique et Souvenirs de Quiberon* (Rennes: La Découvrance, 1995 [1821]).
Loth, Joseph, 'Les langues romane et bretonne en Armorique', *Revue celtique*, 28 (1907), 374–403.
Luzel, François-Marie de, *Notes de voyage en Basse-Bretagne* (Rennes: PUR/Terre de Brume, 1997).
—— *Journal de route et lettres de mission* (Rennes: Presses Universitaires de Rennes/Terre de Brume, 1994 [1864]).
—— 'Un conte populaire breton', *Bulletin Archéologique de l'Association Bretonne* (1876), pp. 274–88.
Machiavelli, Niccolò, *The Prince*, trans. G. Ball (Harmondsworth: Penguin, 1999).
Masson, Emile, *Les Bretons et le socialisme*, ed. J.-Y. Guiomar (Paris: Maspero, 1972).
Ménard, Christian (ed.), 'La Révolution de 1848 dans le Finistère: la correspondance des commissaires de la République dans le département', *Bulletin de la Société Archéologique du Finistère*, 104 (1976), 239–97.
Ménétra, Jacques-Louis, *Journal of My Life* (New York: Columbia University Press, 1986), trans. A. Goldhammer.
Mérimée, Orain, Adolphe (ed.), *La Chouannerie en Pays Gallo* (Bouhet: La Decouvrance, 2002).
Mérimée, Prosper, *Notes d'un voyage dans l'Ouest de la France* (Paris: Adam Biro, 1989).
Michelet, Jules, *Tableau de la France* (Paris: Société des Belles Lettres, 1934).
Mill, J. S., *Considerations on Representative Government* (London: Dent, 1972).
Mirbeau, Octave, 'Le Nid de frelons', *Contes Cruels II*, ed. Pierre Michel and Jean-François Nivet (Paris: Séguier, 1990), pp. 455–60.
—— 'Au pays de la fièvre', in *Croquis bretons*, ed. Jean-François Nivet (Rezé: Séquences, 1993), pp. 83–94.
Mordrel, Olier, *'Breiz Atao': ou, histoire et actualité du nationalisme Breton* (Paris: Alain Moreau, 1973).
Morgenstern, Soma, *Errance en France*, trans. Nicole Casanova (Paris: Liana Levi, 2002), pp. 147–9.
Nicol, Max, *Sainte Anne d'Auray: histoire de pèlerinage* (Sainte-Anne-d'Auray: Librarie du Pèlerinage, 1877).
PNB, *Le Nationalisme Breton: aperçu doctrinal* (Rennes: Editions du Parti National Breton, 1932).
'Politique: anniversaire des fêtes de Juillet', *Annales de la Société Royale Académique de Nantes*, 3 (1832), 341–2.
Puigaudeau, Odette du, *Grandeur des îles* (Paris: Payot & Rivages, 1996).
Renan, Ernest, 'La poésie des races celtiques', in *Œuvres complètes*, vol II (Paris: Calmann-Lévy, 1948).
—— *Souvenirs d'enfance et de jeunesse* (Paris: Nelson, n.d. [1883]).
Richer, Edouard, *Description du Croisic et d'une partie de la côte voisine* (Paris: Res Universis, 1993 [1823]).
Ryan, Cornelius, 'Peasants' street battle with Nazi looters', *Daily Telegraph*, 9 August 1944.

Salonne, Marie-Paul, *Fends la bise: Aïde, jeune bretonne agent de liaison* (Rennes: La Découvrance, 1997 [1945]).
Sand, Georges, *Politique et polémiques (1843–50)* (Paris: Imprimerie nationale, 1997).
Sangnier, Marc, 'Appel à la Jeunesse', 1899, on *www.cardijn.net*; accessed 22 August 2002.
Saulcy, F. de, 'De l'étude des hiéroglyphes', *Revue des deux Mondes*, 14 June 1846, 603–21.
Schultz, Jeanne, *Jean de Kerdren* (Paris: Nelson, 1933 [1890]).
Scott, Walter, *Rob Roy* (London: Collins, n.d. [1818]).
Serbois, L. de, *Souvenirs de voyages en Bretagne et en Grèce* (Paris: Le Clerc & Dillet, 1864).
Siegfried, André, *Tableau politique de la France de l'Ouest* (Paris: Imprimerie nationale, 1995).
Souvestre, Emile, *Les Derniers Bretons* (Rennes: Terre de Brume, 1997 [1836]).
—— 'Les récits de la muse populaire: le sorcier du Petit-Haule', *Revue de Deux Mondes*, 15 February 1849, pp. 608–39.
—— 'Les récits de la muse populaire: la fileuse', *Revue de Deux Mondes*, 1 April 1849, pp. 102–33.
—— *Le Foyer breton: contes et récits populaires* (Paris: Nelson, n.d.).
Stendhal, *Mémoires d'un touriste* (Paris: Maspero, 1981).
Surcouf, Joseph, 'La Bretagne et son passé', *Bulletin de l'Union Régionaliste Bretonne* (1929), pp. 77–94.
Taine, Hippolyte, *Carnets de Voyage: notes sur la province, 1863–65* (Paris: Hachette, 1897).
Tanneau, Yves (ed.), 'Récits de voyages et correspondance cornouaillaise: la famille Gouzil, de Pouldergat (1838–69)', *Bulletin de la Société Archéologique du Finistère*, 96 (1970), 245–91.
Tench, Watkin *Letters from Revolutionary France*, ed. Gavin Edwards (Cardiff: University of Wales Press, 2001).
Thiers, A., *Histoire de la Révolution française*, thirteenth edition, vol. 6 (Paris: Furne, 1857).
Villemarqué, Théodore Hersart de La, *Barzhaz Breizh*, ed. Per Denez (Spézet: Coop Breizh, 1997).
Young, Arthur *Travels in France and Italy* (London: Dent, 1934).
Zola, Emile *Les coquillages de M. Chabre* (Nantes: Joca Seria, 1994).

Papers consulted

Breiz Atao
Libération
Le Monde
Nouvel Observateur
Ouest-France
La Pensée bretonne
Le Télégramme

Secondary sources: Brittany

Ar Beg, Loeiz *Les Bretons et leurs libertés* (Brasparts: Beltan, 1989).
Aumasson, Pascal and André Cariou, 'La peinture d'histoire et les Bleus', in Alain Droguet (ed.), *Les Bleus de Bretagne* (Saint-Brieuc: Fédération "Côtes-du-Nord, 1789", 1991), pp. 207–21.
Aupiais, Grégory, 'L'urbanisme à Guérande au XVIIIe siècle', *Annales de Bretagne et des Pays de l'Ouest*, 106:4 (1999), 65–78.
Badone, Ellen, 'Le folklore breton de l'anticléricalisme', *Annales de Bretagne*, 98 (1991), 423–45.
Baruch, Marc Olivier, 'L'Etat français et la creation des régions', in C. Bougeard (ed.), *Bretagne et identités régionales* (Brest: CRBC, 2001), pp. 31–46.
Baudru, Hervé, 'Le Cercle Républicain d'Enseignement Laïque d'Ille-et-Vilaine, 1904–27', *Annales de Bretagne et des Pays de l'Ouest*, 109:2 (2002), 103–13.
Bellevue, Marquis de, 'La conjuration de Pontallec dans le pays de Ploërmel', *Association Bretonne: Comptes-Rendus, Procès-Verbaux, Mémoires*, 28 (1909), pp. 44–55.
Bérest, E., 'Les voyageurs français en Bretagne', in J. Balcon and Y. Le Gallo, *Histoire littéraire et culturelle de la Bretagne*, Vol II (Paris – Spezed: Champion – Coop Breizh, 1997), pp. 177–218.
Berger, Suzanne, *Les Paysans contre la politique* (Paris: Seuil, 1975).
Besnier, A, 'L'esprit public dans un département Breton en 1848', *Nouvelle Revue de Bretagne*, 2:2 (1948), 83–90.
Bihan, Jean-Paul, 'L'urbanisme de Quimper au Moyen-Age', *Ar Men*, 125 (November 2001), pp. 2–13.
Boissou, Lionel, 'L'Allemagne et le nationalisme breton (1939–45)', in C. Bougeard (ed.), *Bretagne et identités régionales*, (Brest: CRBC, 2001), pp. 321–36.
Bougeard, Christian, *René Pleven, un français libre en politique* (Rennes: PUR, 1994).
―― 'Bleus, Blancs et Rouges en Bretagne dans l'entre-deux-guerres', in Alain Droguet (ed.), *Les Bleus de Bretagne* (Saint-Brieuc: Fédération 'Côtes-du-Nord 1989', 1991), pp. 403–17.
―― 'La Bretagne et les Bretons face à l'Occupation', in his *Bretagne et identités régionales* (Brest: CRBC, 2001), pp. 13–29.
Broudic, Fañch, 'La polémique entre Y. Le Febvre et E. Masson à propos de la langue bretonne', in *Etudes sur la Bretagne et les pays celtiques: mélanges offertes à Yves Le Gallo* (Bannelec: CRBC, 1987), pp. 47–56.
―― *La pratique du breton de l'Ancien Régime à nos jours* (Rennes: Presses Universitaires de Rennes, 1995).
―― 'Du Breton au français: les années décisives de l'après-guerre', *Ar Men*, 47 (February 1996), pp. 20–9.
―― *Qui parle Breton aujourd'hui?* (Brest: Brud Nevez, 1999).
Brunel, Christian, 'Le public de *Feiz ha Breiz*', in M. Lagrée (ed.), *Bretagne et religion* (Rennes: Institut Culturel de Bretagne/Skol-Uhel ar Vro, 1990), pp. 99–116.
Burguière, André, *Bretons de Plozévet* (Paris: Flammarion, 1977).
Cadiou, Georges, 'Pierre Hervé et le projet de Loi du PCF sur la langue bretonne en 1947', *Peuple breton*, 476 (September 2003), pp. 18–9.
Calvez, Ronan, '1941: le breton, langue d'Etat', in C. Bougeard (ed.), *Bretagne et identités régionales* (Brest: CRBC, 2001), pp. 207–21.

Capdevila, Luc, *Les Bretons au lendemain de l'Occupation* (Rennes: PUR, 1999).
Carluer, Jean-Yves, 'Les Protestants bretons pendant la Seconde Guerre mondiale', in C. Bougeard (ed.), *Bretagne et identités régionales* (Brest: CRBC, 2001), pp. 271–84.
Castel, Yves-Pascal, 'La fleur de lis aux fenestrages aux églises', *Ar Men*, 74 (February 1996), pp. 64–9.
—— 'La calvaire de Tronoën', *Ar Men*, 119 (March 2001), pp. 28–35.
Chadwick, Nora, *Early Brittany* (Cardiff: University of Wales Press, 1969).
Chappée, François, 'Les anticléricalismes "maritimes" à Paimpol, 1880–1914', in M. Lagrée (ed.), *Bretagne et religion* (Rennes: Institut Culturel de Bretagne/Skol-Uhel ar Vro, 1990), pp. 39–55.
Chartier, Erwan, 'Morvan Lebesque: le masque et la plume d'un intellectuel breton', *Ar Men*, 143 (November 2004), pp. 24–31.
—— 'La Saint Loup à Guingamp', *Ar Men*, 147 (July 2005), pp. 20–7.
Cocaud, Martine, 'Engagements et revendications féminines en Ille-et-Vilaine de 1945 aux années soixantes', *Annales de Bretagne et des Pays de l'Ouest*, 108:2 (2001), 85–101.
Collins, James B., *Classes, Estates and Order in Early Modern Brittany* (Cambridge: Cambridge University Press, 1994).
Collis, John, 'Celtic Myths', *Antiquity*, 71 (1997), 195–210.
Constantine, Mary-Ann, *Breton Ballads* (Aberystwyth: CMCS, 1996).
Corgné, Eugène, 'Les Elections de 1848 en Bretagne', *Nouvelle Revue de Bretagne*, 2:2 (1948), 91–107.
Croix, Alain, 'Blancs, Bleus et Doléances', in Alain Droguet (ed.), *Les Bleus de Bretagne* (Saint-Brieuc: Fédération 'Côtes-du-Nord 1989', 1991), pp. 23–43.
—— *L'Âge d'or de la Bretagne, 1532–1675* (Rennes: Ouest-France, 1993).
Davies, Wendy, *Small Worlds: The Village Community in Early Medieval Brittany* (London: Duckworth, 1988).
Delouche, Denise, 'Le peuple noir (à propos du numéro de *l'Assiette au Beurre* du 3 octobre 1903)', in Alain Droguet (ed.), *Les Bleus de Bretagne* (Saint-Brieuc: Fédération 'Côtes-du-Nord 1989', 1991), pp. 223–47.
Denefle, Sylvette, 'Croyances et pratiques aux fontaines en Cornouaille et Léon', in M. Lagrée (ed.), *Bretagne et religion* (Rennes: Institut Culturel de Bretagne/Skol-Uhel ar Vro, 1990), pp. 25–39.
Denez, Per, 'Le Barzhaz Breizh et la renaissance bretonne', in his edition of the *Barzhaz Breizh* (Spézet: Coop Breizh, 1997), pp. 9–31.
Déniel, Alain, *Le mouvement breton, 1919–45* (Paris: Maspero, 1976).
Denis, Michel, *Rennes, berceau de la liberté: revolution et démocratie, une ville à l'avant-garde* (Rennes: Ouest-France, 1989).
—— 'Le christianisme bleu en Bretagne de la Révolution au Second Empire', in Alain Droguet (ed.), *Les Bleus de Bretagne* (Saint-Brieuc: Fédération 'Côtes-du-Nord 1989', 1991), pp. 323–31.
—— 'Le mouvement Breton pendant la guerre: un bilan', in C. Bougeard (ed.), *Bretagne et identités régionales* (Brest: CRBC, 2001), pp. 151–66.
—— 'Arthur de La Borderie (1827–1901) ou, "l'histoire, science patriotique"', in N.-Y. Tonnerre (ed.), *Chroniqueurs et historiens de la Bretagne* (Rennes: PUR, 2001), pp. 143–55.
—— 'Comment être Breton sous la Troisième République', in J.-Didier Giraud and Marielle Giraud (eds), *Emile Masson: prophète et rebelle* (Rennes: PUR, 2005), pp. 199–210.

Denis, Michel and Claude Geslin, *La Bretagne des Blancs et des Bleus, 1815–1880* (Rennes: Quest-France, 2003).
Desfontaine, Muriel, 'Odette du Puigaudeau: à la croisée des regards, entre Bretagne et Mauritanie', *Plurial*, 8 (1999), pp. 31–9.
Dietler, Michael, '"Our ancestors the gauls": archaeology, ethnic nationalism, and the manipulation of Celtic identity in modern Europe', *American Anthropologist*, 96:3 (1994), 584–605.
Dieudonné, Patrick, (ed.), *Bretagne: un siècle d'architectures* (n.p.: Terre de Brume/AMAB, 2001).
Dillon, Myles and Nora Chadwick, *The Celtic Realms* (London: Phoenix, 2000).
Duchemin, Jacques, *Pardons bretons du temps passé* (Brussels: Sodim, 1997).
Duhamel, Maurice, *Histoire du peuple breton des origines à 1532* (Kergleuz: An Here, 2000 [1939]).
Duhem, Sophie, 'XVe–XVIIe: le "costume" des Bretons', *Ar Men*, 117 (December 2000), pp. 28–39.
Dupuy, Roger, 'Les Bleus de Bretagne (1789–1801): essai de typologie socio-politique', in Alain Droguet (ed.), *Les Bleus de Bretagne* (Saint-Brieuc: Fédération 'Côtes-du-Nord 1989', 1991), pp. 189–95.
—— *La Bretagne sous la Révolution et l'Empire (1789–1815)* (Rennes: Ouest-France, 2004).
'Identité bretonne et République dans la première moitié du XXe siècle', *Annales de Bretagne et des Pays de l'Ouest*, 111:4 (2004), 97–102.
Elegoët, Fañch, 'Prêtres, nobles et paysans en Léon au début du XXe siècle: notes sur un nationalisme Breton: *Feiz ha Breiz*, 1900–14', *Plurial*, 18 (1979), 39–90.
—— 'L'identité bretonne: notes sur la production de l'identité négative', *Plurial*, 24 (1980), 43–67.
Estienne, René, 'La correspondance de Joseph Delaville-Leroulx, député lorientais du Tiers aux Etats généraux', in Alain Droguet (ed.), *Les Bleus de Bretagne* (Saint-Brieuc: Fédération 'Côtes-du-Nord 1989', 1991), pp. 137–48.
Favereau, Francis, 'L'évolution du discours bretonnant chez Pierre-Jakez Hélias', in Michel Lagrée and Jacqueline Sainclivier (eds), *L'Ouest et la politique* (Rennes: PUR, 1996).
Fichou, Jean-Christophe, 'Le Front Populaire et les conserveurs de sardines de Bretagne', *Annales de Bretagne et des Pays de l'Ouest*, 111:1 (2004), 111–25.
Ford, Caroline, *Creating the Nation in Provincial France: Religion and Political Identity in Brittany* (Princeton: Princeton University Press, 1993).
Frambourg, Guy, 'Un Commissaire du gouvernement provisoire de la République: Guépin', *Annales de Bretagne*, 66:3 (1959), 329–46.
Frélaut, Bertrand, 'Les Bleus de Vannes (1791–95): naissance d'une classe politique', in Alain Droguet (ed.), *Les Bleus de Bretagne* (Saint-Brieuc: Fédération 'Côtes-du-Nord 1989', 1991), pp. 167–76.
Gabory, Emile, 'La Révolte des Cent-Jours en Loire-Inférieure', in G. Dottin (ed.), *Mélanges bretons et celtiques offerts à M. J. Loth* (Rennes and Paris: Plihon & Hommany, 1927), pp. 204–10.
Galliou, Patrick, and Michael Jones, *The Bretons* (Oxford: Blackwell, 1991).
Gemie, Sharif, 'The Marée noire, vintage 1999: ecology, regional identity and politics in contemporary France', *Modern and Contemporary France*, 9:1 (2001), 71–86.

—— 'The politics of language: debates and identities in contemporary Brittany', *French Cultural Studies*, 13:2 (2002), 145–64.

—— 'Roots, rock, Breizh: music and the politics of nationhood in contemporary Brittany', *Nations and Nationalism*, 11:1 (2005), 103–20.

—— 'The seed thrower's story', *Planet: The Welsh Internationalist*, 161 (October 2003), 52–64.

Gervais, P., 'L'Autre Bretagne: les clubs révolutionnaires, 1789–1795', *Archives historiques de la Révolution française*, 266 (1986), 422–47.

Geslin, Claude, 'La vie économique: un siècle de mutations douloureuses', in J.-J. Monnier and J.-C. Cassard (eds), *Toute l'histoire de la Bretagne* (Morlaix: Skol Vreizh, 1997), pp. 427–50.

—— 'Le mouvement ouvrier de 1815 à 1914', in J.-J. Monnier and J.-C. Cassard (eds), *Toute l'histoire de Bretagne* (Morlaix: Skol Vreizh, 1997), pp. 491–511.

—— 'La violence ouvrière en Bretagne au XIXe siècle', *Kreiz*, 13 (2000), 199–218.

Giraud, J. Didier and Marielle Giraud, *Emile Masson: professeur de liberté* (Chamalières: Canope, 1991).

Glon, Thierry, 'Ecrivains de la Recouvrance (de 1960 à 1980)', *Plurial*, 5 (1995), 33–52.

Goallou, Henri, *Hamon: Commissaire du Gouvernement puis Préfet d'Ille-et-Vilaine* (Rennes: Institut Armoricain de Recherches historique de Rennes, 1973).

Gourhand, Jean, 'L'abbé Joseph Mahé, premier érudit morbihannais', in N.-Y. Tonnerre (ed.), *Chroniques et historiens de la Bretagne* (Rennes: PUR, 2001), pp. 125–41.

Gourlay, Patrick, *Charles Daniélou, 1878–1953: Itinéraire politique d'un Finistérien* (Rennes: PUR, 1996), pp. 24–6.

Guiffan, Jean, 'Les Bretons et la Perfide Albion', *Ar Men*, 147 (2005), pp. 28–37.

Guiomar, Jean-Yves, *Emile Masson: Les Bretons et le socialisme* (Paris: Maspero, 1972).

—— *Le bretonisme: les historiens bretons au XIXe siècle* (n.p.: Société d'Histoire et d'Archéologie de Bretagne, 1987).

—— 'Le celtisme chez les intellectuels français/bretons de gauche au XIXe siècle', in A. Draguet (ed.), *Les bleus de Bretagne* (Saint-Brieuc: Fédération "Côtes-du-Nord, 1789"', 1991), pp. 283–92.

—— 'La Révolution Française et les origines celtiques de la France', *Annales historiques de la Révolution Française*, 1992, pp. 63–84.

—— 'Le bretonisme, une expression de la droite française', in M. Lagrée and J. Sainclivier (eds), *L'Ouest et la politique* (Rennes: PUR, 1996), pp. 129–40.

—— 'Le Barzaz Breiz de Théodore Hersart de La Villemarqué', in P. Nora (ed.), *Les Lieux de Mémoire*, Vol. III (Paris: Quarto – Gallimard, 1997), pp. 3479–514.

Gury, J., 'A la découverte de la Bretagne, dans la seconde moitié du XVIIIe siècle', in J. Balcon and Y. Le Gallo (eds), *Histoire culturelle et littéraire de la Bretagne*, Vol. I (Paris – Spezed: Champion – Coop Breizh, 1997), pp. 391–8.

Guyvarc'h, Didier, 'Les cinquante otages dans la mémoire nantaise', in C. Bougeard (ed.), *Bretagne et identités régionales*, (Brest: CRBC, 2001), pp. 381–92.

Hamon, Kristian, *Les Nationalistes bretons sous l'occupation* (Le Relecq-Kerhuon: An Here, 2001).

—— *Le Bezen Perrot* (Fouesnant: Yoran Embanner, 2004).

Haudebourg, Guy, *Mendiants et vagabonds en Bretagne au XIXe siècle* (Rennes: PUR, 1998).

Haudebourg Guy, and Franck Liaigre, 'La Résistance communiste en Loire-Inférieure (juin 1940–juin 1944)', in C. Bougeard (ed.), *Bretagne et identités régionales* (Brest: CRBC, 2001), pp. 89–102.

Hubert, Henri, *The Rise of the Celts*, trans. M. R. Dobie (London: Constable, 1987 [1934]).

—— *The Greatness and Decline of the Celts*, trans. M. R. Dobie (London: Constable, 1987 [1934]).

Hue, Bernard, 'Un Breton à la conquête des cœurs: Auguste Pavie face à l'identité Kmère et lao', *Plurial*, 8 (1999), 23–30.

Hurt, John, 'The Parlement of Brittany and the Crown: 1665–75', *French Historical Studies*, 4 (1965–6), 411–33.

Jones, Michael, *Ducal Brittany, 1364–99: Relations with England and France During the Reign of Duke John IV* (Oxford: Oxford University Press, 1970).

—— *The Creation of Brittany: A Late Medieval State* (London: Hambledon Press, 1988).

Jover, Manuel, 'Gauguin, la découverte', *L'œil*, hors-série (2003), pp. 18–31.

Nolwenn, Juhel, 'La pastorale d'un prêtre breton dans la seconde moitié du XVIIIe siècle: les sermons de René Cavaro de Kergorre', *Annales de Bretagne et des Pays de l'Ouest*, 110:2 (2003), 77–109.

Kahn, Claude and Jean Landais, *Nantes et le Front Populaire* (Nantes: Ouest-Editions and Université Permanente de Nantes, 1997).

Kerhervé, Jean, 'Ecriture et récriture de l'histoire "dans l'Histoire de Bretagne" de Bertrand d'Argentré: l'exemple du Livre XII', in N.-Y. Tonnerre (ed.), *Chroniques et historiens de la Bretagne* (Rennes: PUR, 2001), pp. 77–109.

Kermoal, Christian, *Les notables du Trégor: éveil à la culture politique et évolution dans les paroisses rurales (1770–1850)* (Rennes: PUR, 2002).

Lagrée, Michel, 'Le clergé Breton et le premier centenaire de la Révolution française', *Annales de Bretagne*, 91 (1984), 249–67.

—— *Religion et cultures en Bretagne* (Paris: Fayard, 1992).

—— 'Evêques gallicans et diocèses ultramontains: Vannes (1848–1870)', in Michel Lagrée and Jacqueline Sainclivier (eds), *L'Ouest et la politique* (Rennes: PUR, 1996), pp. 113–28.

Lalouette, Jacqueline, 'Vercingétorix: 1940–45, de Vichy au maquis', in C. Bougeard (ed.), *Bretagne et identités régionales* (Brest: CRBC, 2001), pp. 47–62.

Lebel, Anne, 'L'apprentissage de la citoyenneté à Saint-Brieuc de 1788 à 1795', in A. Draguet (ed.), *Les bleus de Bretagne* (Saint-Brieuc: Fédération "Côtes-du-Nord, 1789", 1991), pp. 105–16.

Lebesque, Morvan, *Comment peut-on être Breton?* (Paris: Seuil, 1970).

Le Bihan, Jean and Yann Lagadec, 'Les sous-préfets de Bretagne sous la monarchie de Juillet (1830–1848): une génération d'administrateurs à part?', *Annales de Bretagne et des Pays de l'Ouest*, 111:4 (2004), 47–70.

Le Boulanger, Jean-Michel, 'Réflexions sur l'identité de la Bretagne', *Hopala*, 3 (1999), 8–15.

Le Brun, Yvonne, '"L'émeute" de Rennes des 9 et 10 janvier 1847', *Annales de Bretagne*, 89:4 (1982), 479–503.

Le Coadic, Ronan, *L'identité bretonne* (Rennes: PUR and Terre de Brume, 1998).

Le Couédic, Daniel, 'Une Pléiade bretonne: les temps des profits', in Daniel Le Couédic and Jean-Yves Veillard (eds), *Ar Seiz Breur* (Rennes: Terre de Brume & Musée de Bretagne, 2000), pp. 90–116.

Le Douget, Annick, *Juges, esclaves et négriers en Basse-Bretagne, 1750–1850* (Spézet: Unesco, 2000).
Le Gall, Jean André, *Charles Le Goffic (1863–1932), ou: de la difficulté d'être breton* (Guingamp: La Planée, 2002).
Le Goff, Hervé, 'Le Parti communiste française et le mouvement autonomiste breton', *Cahiers d'histoire sociale*, 16 (2001), 93–102.
Le Goff, T. J. A., *Vannes and Its Region: A Study of Town and Country in Eighteenth-Century France* (Oxford: Clarendon Press, 1981).
Leloup, Daniel, 'Protection des monuments: les premiers classements en Bretagne', *Ar Men*, 115 (October 2000), pp. 12–19.
Lespagnol, André, *Entre l'argent et la gloire: la course malouine au temps de Louis XIV* (Rennes: Apogée, 1995).
Le Stum, Philippe, 'Néo-druidisme et régionalisme en Bretagne, 1900–14', *Bulletin de la Société archéologique du Finistère*, 126 (1997), 441–66.
Lucas, Maurice, 'A propos d'un cacique radical et bigouden: Georges Le Bail', in (no ed.) *Etudes sur la Bretagne et les pays celtiques* (Bannalec: CRBC, 1987), 325–52.
Mathan, Anne de, 'Les insurrections girondistes de Bretagne en 1793: premiers résultats', *Annales de Bretagne et des Pays de l'Ouest*, 111:4 (2004), 29–42.
Markale, Jean, *Identité de Bretagne* (Paris: Entente, 1985).
Martin, Jean-Clément, *La Vendée et la France* (Paris: Seuil, 1978).
—— 'Quatorze juillet 1880, quartorze juillet 1889, l'instauration de la fête nationale dans l'ouest', *Annales de Bretagne*, 91 (1984), pp. 201–47.
—— *La Vendée de la mémoire (1800–1980)*, (Paris: Seuil, 1989).
McDonald, Maryon, *'We are not French!': Language, Culture and Identity in Brittany* (London: Routledge, 1989).
Meadwell, Hudson, 'The Catholic Church and the Breton language in the Third Republic', *French History*, 5:3 (1991), 325–44.
Meyer, Jean, *La Noblesse bretonne au XVIIIe siècle* (Paris: Flammarion, 1972).
Meyer, J., 'L'environnement intellectuelle de la Bretagne au XVIIIe siècle', in J. Balcon and Y. Le Gallo, *Histoire littéraire et culturelle de la Bretagne*, vol I (Paris – Spezed: Champion – Coop Breizh, 1997), pp. 345–58.
Minois, Georges, 'Anne de Bretagne: un portrait sans concessions', *Ar Men*, 106 (Sepember 1999), pp. 14–23.
Moal, Stefan, 'Breton: Construire un avenir', *Ar Men*, 150 (January 2006), pp. 44–53.
Monnier, Jean-Jacques, *Le Comportement politique des Bretons, 1945–94* (Rennes: PUR, 1994).
—— 'Des militants bretons dans la Résistance', in C. Bougeard (ed.), *Bretagne et identités régionales* (Brest: CRBC, 2001), pp. 103–19.
Morvan, Françoise, *Le Monde comme si: nationalisme et dérive identitaire en Bretagne* (Arles: Actes Sud, 2002).
Musgrave, Elizabeth, 'Momento Mori: the function and meaning of Breton ossuaries, 1450–1750', in P. C. Jupp and G. Howarth (eds), *The Changing Face of Death* (London: Macmillan, 1995), pp. 62–75.
Nicolas, Gilbert, *Instituteurs entre politique et religion* (Rennes: Apogée, 1993).
Nicolas, Michel, 'Les Bretons et la politique: entre suivisme et particularisme', *Ar Men*, 150 (January 2006), pp. 54–61.

Nières, Claude 'Le pouvoir municipal en Bretagne en 1789 d'après les cahiers de doléances', in Alain Droguet (ed.), *Les Bleus de Bretagne* (Saint-Brieuc: Fédération 'Côtes-du-Nord 1989', 1991), pp. 13–22.

Orton, Fred and Griselda Pollock, 'Les données bretonnantes: la prairie de répresentation', *Art History*, 3:3 (1980), pp. 314–44.

Palmer, William, *The Pardon of Saint Anne* (London: Jonathan Cape, 1997).

Pascal, Jean, *Les Députés bretons de 1789 à 1983* (Paris: Presses Universitaires de France, 1983).

Paubert, Laurent, 'Les catholiques et l'élection présidentielle du 10 décembre 1848 dans le Morbihan et le Finistère', *Annales de Bretagne et des Pays de l'Ouest*, 107:4 (2000), pp. 103–19.

Pennec, Alain, 'La Bretagne pendant la Révolution', in Jean-Jacques Monnier and Jean-Christophe Cassed (eds), *Toute l'histoire de Bretagne* (Morlaix: Skol Vreizh, 1997), pp. 394–426.

Perazzi, Jean-Charles, *Diwan: vingt ans d'enthousiasme, de doute et d'espoir* (Spézet: Coop Breizh, 1998).

Pétré-Grenouilleau, Olivier, *Nantes au temps de la traite des Noirs* (Paris: Hachette, 1998).

Philippe, Michel and Erwan Chantier, 'Le Bleun-Brug, 1950', *Ar Men*, 112 (May 2000), pp. 10–17.

Pierre, Patrick, *Les Bretons et la République: la construction de l'identité bretonne sous la troisième République* (Rennes: PUR, 2001).

Pilbeam, Pamela, 'A forgotten socialist and feminist: Ange Guépin', in M. Cornick and C. Crossley (eds), *Problems in French History* (Basingstoke: Palgrave, 2000), pp. 64–80.

Pomian, Krystof, 'Franks et Gauls', in P. Nora (ed.), *Les Lieux de Mémoire* II (Paris: Quarto/Gallimard, 1997), pp. 2245–300.

Poisson, Henri and Jean-Pierre Le Mat, *Histoire de Bretagne* (Spézet: Coop Briezh, 2000).

Postic, Fañch, 'Pétition pour le breton: une des premières initiatives pour les langues régionales', *Ar Men*, 140 (April 2004), pp. 26–31.

Postic, Fañch and François de Beaulieu, 'Le nouvel essor de la littérature orale', *Ar Men*, 1998 (hors série), pp. 40–9.

Prémel, Gérard, 'Anamnèse d'un dommage, ou comment le français est venu aux bretons', *Langage et Société*, 72 (1995), pp. 51–95.

Prével-Montagne, Corinne, 'Armel Beaufils et la Bretagne', *Ar Men*, 132 (January 2003), pp. 50–7.

Provost, George, 'Entre cantiques et penn-baz: les pardons du Centre-Bretagne, XVIIe–XIXe siècle', *Kreiz Breizh*, 10 (2004), 13–20.

Quéniart, Jean, *Le Grand Chapelletout: violence, normes et comportements en Bretagne rurale au 18e siècle* (Rennes: Apogée, 1993).

—— 'Les mauristes et l'historiographie bretonne', in N.-Y. Tonnerre (ed.), *Chroniques et historiens de la Bretagne* (Rennes: PUR, 2001), pp. 111–23.

—— *La Bretagne au XVIIIe siècle (1675–1789)* (Rennes: Ouest-France, 2004).

Rajsfus, Maurice, *Les Français de la débâcle: juin–septembre 1940, un si bel été* (Paris: Le Cherche Midi, 1997).

Reece, Jack E., *The Bretons Against France: Ethnic Minority Nationalism in Twentieth-Century Brittany* (Chapel Hill: University of North Carolina Press, 1977).

Retière, Jean Noël, *Identités ouvrières: histoire sociale d'un fief ouvrier en Bretagne, 1909–90* (Paris: L' Harmattan 1994).
Rio, Joseph, *Mythes fondateurs de la Bretagne: aux origines de la celtomanie* (Rennes: Editions Ouest-France, 2000).
Rochard, Yvon, 'Le bagne de Brest', *Ar Men*, 58 (April 1994), pp. 12–25.
—— 'Lannion et la Trégor Valley', *Ar Men*, 124 (September 2001), pp. 2–13.
Rogard, Vincent, *Les Catholiques et la question sociale: Morlaix, 1840–1914* (Rennes: PUR, 1997).
Rouxel, Françoise, 'Brest en baraques (1945–1975)', *Ar Men*, 62 (October 1994), pp. 2–15.
Ruellan, Jean, 'Moncontour dans la Révolution: une ville bleue au cœur d'un pays chouan', in Alain Droguet (ed.), *Les Bleus de Bretagne* (Saint-Brieuc: Fédération 'Côtes-du-Nord 1989', 1991), pp. 79–92.
Sainclivier, Jacqueline, *L'Ille-et-Vilaine, 1918–1958: vie politique et sociale* (Rennes: PUR, 1996).
Soubigou, Gilbert, 'Les auteurs bretons dans l'écriture exotique et coloniale', *Plurial*, 8 (1999), 13–21.
Stephens, Meic, 'An empty chair in Lorient; the thirtieth Interceltic Festival', *Planet*, 143 (October 2000), 86–91.
Stoll, Stéphanie, 'La déferlante des micro-brasseries', *Ar Men*, 99 (December 1998), pp. 56–9.
Sutherland, Donald, *The Chouans: The Social Origins of Popular Counter-Revolution in Upper Brittany, 1790–96* (Oxford: Clarendon Press, 1982).
Tanguy, Alain, 'Troubles confessionnels: la difficile séparation de l'Eglise et de l'Etat au début du XXe siècle', *Ar Men*, 149 (2005), pp. 32–7.
Tanguy, Bernard, *Aux origines du nationalisme breton*, vol I (Paris: Union générale d'éditions, 1977).
Tanguy, Jean-François, 'La Bretagne entre conquête républicaine et intégration nationale, 1870–1914', *Annales de Bretagne et des Pays de l'Ouest*, 111:4 (2004), 71–95.
Tranvouez, Yvon, 'Les catholiques et la question bretonne (1940–44)', in C. Bougeard (ed.), *Bretagne et identités régionales* (Brest: CRBC, 2001), pp. 285–306.
—— 'La mémoire d'un bombardement britannique: Notre-Dame-des-Anges (Morlaix, 1943–2003), *Annales de Bretagne et des Pays de l'Ouest*, 111:1 (2004), 127–51.
Trenard, Louis, 'Images de Bretagne dans la presse du XVIIIe siècle', *Annales de Bretagne et des Pays de l'Ouest*, 54:4 (1976), 585–604.
Vallerie, Erwan, *Nous barbares locaux: théorie de la nation et autres textes de 'Sav Breizh'* (Le Relecq-Kerhoun: An Here, 1997).
Veillard, Jean-Yves, 'La Bretagne, cible des humoristes à la Belle Epoque', in M. Lagrée and Jacqueline Sainclivier (eds), *L'Ouest et le politique* (Rennes: PUR, 1996).
Vérité, Monique, *Odette du Puigaudeau: une Bretonne au désert* (Paris: Payot and Rivages, 2001).
Williams, Heather, 'Le voyage transculturel de Brizeux', *Seuils et traverses, enjeux de l'écriture de voyage*, 2 vols, ed. Jean-Yves Le Disez (Brest: CRBC, 2002), I, pp. 275–85.
—— 'Une sauvagerie très douce', in N. Harkness, P. Rowe, T. Unwin and J. Yee (eds), *Visions/Revisions* (Oxford: Peter Lang, 2003), pp. 99–106.

Secondary sources: historiography, nationalism and other topics

Alexander, R. S., *Bonapartism and Revolutionary Tradition in France: the 'fédérés' of 1815* (Cambridge: Cambridge University Press, 1991).

Alloula, Malek, *The Colonial Harem*, trans. M. Godzich and W. Godzich (Chicago: University of Minnesota Press, 1986).

Amann, Peter, *Revolutions and Mass Democracy: The Paris Club Movement in 1848* (Princeton: Princeton University Press, 1975).

Anderson, Benedict, *Imagined Communities: Reflections on the Origin and Spread of Nationalism*, revised edition (London: Verso, 1994).

Antliff, Mark, 'Cubism, Celtism and the Body Politic', *Art Bulletin*, 74:4 (1992), 655–8.

Arblaster, Anthony, *Democracy*, second edition (Birmingham: Open University Press, 1994).

Aaron, Jane and Chris Williams (eds), *Postcolonial Wales* (Cardiff: University of Wales Press, 2005).

Belmont, Nicole, 'L'Académie celtique et George Sand', *Romantisme*, 9 (1975), 29–38.

Bertho, Catherine, 'L'invention de la Bretagne: génèse sociale d'un stéréotype', *Actes de la recherche en sciences sociales*, 35 (1980), 45–62.

Billig, Michael, *Banal Nationalism* (London: Sage, 1995).

Bloom, William, *Personal Identity, National Identity and International Relations* (Cambridge: Cambridge University Press, 1990), pp. 38–40.

Bouloiseau, Marc, *La République jacobine* (Paris: Seuil, 1972).

Bourget, M.-N., 'Race et folklore: l'image officielle de la France en 1800', *Annales ESC*, 31 (1976), pp. 802–33.

Breuilly, John, *Nationalism and the State* (Manchester: Manchester University Press, 1985).

Buchsenschutz, Olivier and Alain Schnapp, 'Alésia', in P. Nora (ed.), *Les Lieux de Mémoire*, III (Paris: Quarto/Gallimard, 1997), pp. 4103–40.

Burke, Peter, 'Did Europe exist before 1700?', *History of European Ideas*, 1 (1980), pp. 21–9.

—— '*Hen domine, adsunt Turcae*: a sketch for a social history of post-medieval Latin', in P. Burke and R. Porter (eds), *Language, Self and Society* (Cambridge: Polity, 1994), pp. 23–50.

Burrin, Philippe, *La France à l'heure allemande, 1940–1944* (Paris: Seuil, 1995).

Carrer, Philippe *L'envers du décor: ethnopsychiatrie en Bretagne et autres terres celtes* (Spézet: Coop Breizh, 1999).

Castoriadis, Cornelius, 'La crise du processus identificatoire', in his *La Montée de l'insignificance* (Paris: Seuil, 1996), pp. 125–39.

Chapman, Timothy, 'The Celt in archaeology', in Terence Brown (ed.), *Celticism* (Amsterdam: Rodopi, 1996), pp. 61–78.

Chickering, Roger, '"Casting their gaze more broadly": women's patriotic activism in imperial Germany', *Past and Present*, 118 (1988), 156–86.

Cohen, Paul, 'Heroes and dilettantes: the Action française, Le Sillon and the generation of 1905–14', *French Historical Studies*, 15:4 (1988), 673–87.

—— 'Of Linguistic Jacobinism and cultural Balkanization: contemporary French linguistic politics in historical context', *French Politics, Culture and Society*, 18:2 (2000), 21–48.

Collis, John, 'Celts and politics', in P. Graves-Brown, S. James and C. Gamble (eds), *Cultural Identity and Archaeology* (London: Routledge, 1996), pp. 167–78.
Corbin, Alain, 'Paris-Province', in P. Nora (ed.), *Les Lieux de Mémoire*, II (Paris: Quarto-Gallimard, 1997), pp. 2851–88.
────── *Villages Bells: Sound and Meaning in the 19th century French Countryside*, trans. M. Thom (London: Papermac, 1999).
────── 'L'Impossible présence', in A. Corbin, N. Gérôme and D. Tartowsky (eds), *Les Usages politiques des fêtes aux XIXe–XXe siècle* (Paris: Publications de la Sorbonne, 1994).
Davis, Natalie Z., 'Proverbial wisdom and popular errors', in her *Society and Culture in Early Modern France* (Cambridge: Polity, 1987), pp. 227–70.
Delbreil, Jean-Claude, *Centrisme et Démocratie Chrétienne en France: le Parti Démocrate Populaire: des origines au MRP* (Paris: Publications de la Sorbonne, 1990).
Diamond, Hanna, *Women and the Second World War in France, 1939–1948* (Harlow: Longman, 1999).
Dietler, Michael, 'A tale of three sites', *World Archaeology*, 30:1 (1998), 72–89.
Ellis, Peter Beresford, *The Celtic Dawn: A History of Pan-Celticism* (London: Constable, 1993).
Elshtain, Jean Bethke, 'Sovereignty, identity and sacrifice', in *Real Politics: at the Centre of Everyday Life* (Baltimore: Johns Hopkins University Press, 1997), pp. 126–44.
Fanon, Frantz, *Les damnés de la terre* (Paris: Maspero, 1968).
Farge, Arlette, *Vivre dans la rue à Paris au XVIIIe siècle* (Paris: Gallimard, 1992).
────── *La vie fragile: violence, pouvoirs et solidarités à Paris au XVIIIe siècle* (Paris: Hachette, 1986).
Farmer, Sarah, *Martyred Village: Commemorating the 1944 Massacre at Oradour-sur-Glane* (Berkeley: University of California Press, 1999).
Fasel, George, 'The wrong revolution: French Republicanism in 1848', *French Historical Studies*, 8 (1973–74), 654–80.
Fitzpatrick, Andrew P., '"Celtic" Iron Age Europe: the theoretical basis', in P. Graves-Brown, S. James and C. Gamble (eds), *Cultural Identity and Archaeology* (London: Routledge, 1996), pp. 238–55.
Fleury-Ilett, Béatrice, 'The identity of France: archetypes in Iron Age studies', in P. Graves-Brown, S. James and C. Gamble (eds), *Cultural Identity and Archaeology* (London: Routledge, 1996), pp. 196–208.
Fontana, Josep, *The Distorted Past: A Reinterpretation of Europe*, trans. Colin Smith (Oxford: Blackwell, 1995).
Geary, Patrick J., *The Myth of Nations: The Medieval Origins of Nations* (Princeton: Princeton University Press, 2002).
Gellner, Ernest, *Nationalism* (London: Weidenfeld and Nicolson, 1997).
Gemie, Sharif, 'What is a school?: defining and controlling primary schooling in early nineteenth-century France', *History of Education*, 21:2 (1992), 129–47.
────── *Women and Schooling: Gender, Authority and Identity in the Female Schooling Sector, France, 1815–1914* (Keele: Keele University Press, 1995).
────── 'France, Orientalism and Algeria: fifty-four articles from the *Revue des Deux Mondes*, 1846–1852,' *Journal of Algerian Studies*, 3 (1998), 48–70.
────── *French Revolutions, 1815–1914* (Edinburgh: Edinburgh University Press, 1999).
────── 'The Republic, the people and the writer: Victor Hugo's social and political writing', *French History*, 14:3 (2000), 272–94.

—— 'Loti, Orientalism and the French colonial experience', *Journal of European Area Studies*, 8:2 (2000), 149–66.

—— 'An extremism of the center: Jean-Pierre Chevènement, French presidential candidate, 2002', *French Politics, Culture and Society*, 22:1 (2004), 76–97.

Godechot, Jacques (ed.), *Les Constitutions de la France depuis 1789* (Paris: Garnier-Flammarion, 1979).

Goubert, Pierre, *The Ancien Regime: French Society, 1600–1750*, trans. S. Cox (London: Weidenfeld and Nicolson, 1976).

Green, Miranda, *Celtic Art: Reading the Messages* (London: Weidenfeld and Nicolson, 1996).

Green, Miranda (ed.), *The Celtic World* (London: Routledge, 1995).

Guibernau, Montserrat, *Nations without States: Political Communities in a Global Age* (Cambridge: Polity, 1999).

Guenée, Bernard, *States and Rulers in Later Medieval Europe*, trans. J. Vale (Oxford: Oxford University Press, 1985).

—— 'Les "Grandes Chroniques de France": le Roman aux roys, 1274–1518', in P. Nora (ed.), *Les Lieux de Mémoire*, I (Paris: Quarto/Gallimard, 1997), pp. 739–58.

Guiomar, Jean-Yves, *La nation entre l'histoire et la raison* (Paris: La Découverte, 1990).

Hampson, Norman, 'From regeneration to terror: the ideology of the French Revolution', in Noel O'Sullivan (ed.), *Terrorism, Ideology and Revolution* (Brighton: Wheatsheaf, 1986), pp. 49–66.

Huard, Raymond, *La Naissance du parti politique en France* (Paris: Presses de la fondation nationale des Sciences Politiques, 1996).

Hunt, Lynn, *Politics, Culture and Class in the French Revolution* (London: Methuen, 1984).

Hutchinson, John, and Anthony D. Smith, *Nationalism* (Oxford: Oxford University Press, 1994).

Ihl, Olivier, 'Convivialité et citoyenneté: les banquets commémoratifs dans les campagnes républicaines à la fin du XIXe siècle', in A. Corbin, N. Gérôme and D. Tartowsky (eds), *Les Usages politiques des fêtes aux XIXe–XXe siècle* (Paris: Publications de la Sorbonne, 1994), pp. 137–57.

—— *La fête républicaine* (Paris: Gallimard, 1996).

James, Simon, *The Atlantic Celts: Ancient People or Modern Invention?* (London: British Museum Press, 1999).

Jefferies, Matthew, 'The age of historicism', in S. Berger (ed.), *A Companion to Nineteenth-Century Europe* (Oxford: Blackwell, 2006), pp. 316–32.

Jones, Siân and Paul Graves-Brown, 'Introduction: archaeology and cultural identity in Europe', in their *Cultural Identity and Archaeology* (London: Routledge, 1996), pp. 1–24.

Jourdan, Annie, 'The image of Gaul during the French Revolution', in Terence Brown (ed.), *Celticism* (Amsterdam: Rodopi, 1996), pp. 183–206.

Kabbani, Rana, *Imperial Fictions: Europe's Myths of the Orient* (London: Pandora, 1994).

Kaplan, Steven L., *Bread, Politics and Political Economy in the Reign of Louis XV* (The Hague: Martinus Nijoff, 1976).

Kneafsey, Moya, 'Tourism images and the construction of Celticity in Ireland and Brittany', in D. C. Harvey, R. Jones, N. McInroy and C. Milligan (eds), *Celtic Geographies: Old Cultures, New Times* (London: Routledge, 2002), pp. 123–38.

Kuisel, Richard F., *Capitalism and the State in Modern France* (Cambridge: Cambridge University Press, 1981).
Landick, Marie, 'French courts and language legislation', *French Cultural Studies*, 11 (2000), pp. 131–48.
Larrère, Mathilde, 'Ainsi paradait le roi des barricades: les grandes revues de la garde nationale, à Paris, sous la Monarchie de Juillet', *Mouvement social*, 179 (1997), pp. 9–32.
Leerssen, Josep, 'Celticism', in Terence Brown (ed.), *Celticism* (Amsterdam: Rodopi, 1996), pp. 1–20.
Lyons, Martyn, 'The audience for Romantism: Walter Scott in France', *European History Quarterly*, 14 (1984), 21–46.
—— 'Fires of expiation: book-burnings and Catholic missions in restoration France', *French History*, 10:2 (1996), 240–66.
Margadant, Jo Burr, 'The Duchesse de Berry and Royalist political culture in post-revolutionary France', *History Workshop*, 43 (1997), 23–52.
Margadant, Ted W., *French Peasants in Revolt: The Insurrection of 1851* (Princeton: Princeton University Press, 1979).
McCrone, David, *The Sociology of Nationalism: Tomorrow's Ancestors* (London and New York: Routledge, 1998).
McMillan, James F., 'Catholicism and nationalism in France: the case of the Fédération Nationale Catholique, 1924–39', in Frank Tallet and Nicholas Atkin (eds), *Catholicism in Britain and France since 1789* (London: Hambledon Press, 1996), pp. 151–63.
McPhee, Peter, *The Politics of Rural Life: Political Mobilization in the French Countryside, 1846–52* (Oxford: Oxford University Press, 1992).
Ménager, Bernard, *Les Napoléon du Peuple* (Paris: Aubier, 1988).
Merriman, John M., *The Agony of the Republic: The Repression of the Left in Revolutionary France, 1848–51* (Yale: Yale University Press. 1978).
Moentmann, Elise M., 'Searching for French identity in the regions: national versus local visions of France in the 1930s', *French History*, 17:3 (2003), 307–27.
Mohen, Jean-Pierre, *Standing Stones: Stonehenge, Carnac and the World of Megaliths*, trans. Harry N. Abrams (London: Thames and Hudson, 1998).
Mosse, George L., *Nationalism and Sexuality: Middle-Class Morality and Sexual Norms in Modern Europe* (Madison: University of Wisconsin Press, 1985).
Nadaud, Eric, 'Le renouvellement des pratiques militants de la SFIO au début du Front Populaire (1934–1936)', *Mouvement social*, 153 (1990), pp. 9–32.
Nairn, Tom, *The Break-Up of Britain: Crisis and Neo-Nationalism*, second edition (London: Verso, 1981).
Neumaier, Christopher, 'The escalation of German reprisal policy in occupied France, 1941–42', *Journal of Contemporary History*, 41:1 (2006), 113–31.
Nicolet, Claude, *L'idée républicaine en France (1789–1924)* (Paris: Gallimard, 1994).
Nières, Claude, 'Rivalités France-Angleterre vue de Bretagne au XVIII siècle', in Robert Chaguy (ed.), *La Révolution française* (Grenoble: Presses Universitaire de Grenoble, 2002), pp. 21–34.
Nochlin, Linda, 'The imaginary Orient', in her *The Politics of Vision* (London: Thames and Hudson, 1991), p. 33–59.
O'Halloran, Clare, 'Irish re-creations of the Gaelic past: the challenge of MacPherson's Ossian', *Past and Present*, 124 (1989), pp. 69–95.

Ong, Walter J., *Orality and Literacy: The Technologizing of the Word* (London: Routledge, 1982).
Ory, Pascal 'Le Dorgèrisme: institution et discours d'une colère paysanne (1929–31)', *Revue d'histoire moderne et contemporaine*, 22 (1975), 168–90.
Ozouf, Jacques and Mona Ozouf, '*La Tour de la France par deux enfants*: le petit livre rouge de la République', in P. Nora (ed.), *Les Lieux de Mémoire*, I (Paris: Gallimard, 1997), pp. 277–302.
Ozouf, Mona, *La fête révolutionnaire, 1789–1799* (Paris: Gallimard, 1976).
—— 'L'invention de l'ethnographie française: le questionnaire de l'Académie celtique', *Annales ESC*, 36 (1981), pp. 210–30.
Paxton, Robert O., *French Peasant Fascism: Henry Dorgères's Greenshirts and the Crises of French Agriculture, 1929–1939* (Oxford: Oxford University Press, 1997).
Ragache, Gilles, *Les Enfants de la guerre: vivre, survivre, lire et jouer en France, 1939–49* (n.p.: Perrin, 1997).
Raillat, Landric, 'Les manifestations à l'occasion du sacré de Charles X ou les ambiguïtés de la fête politique', in A. Corbin, N. Gérôme and D. Tartowsky (eds), *Les Usages politiques des fêtes aux XIXe–XXe siècle* (Paris: Publications de la Sorbonne, 1994), pp. 53–62.
Ramus, Charles F., (ed.), *Daumier: 120 Great Lithographs* (New York: Dover, 1978).
Rankin, David, 'The Celts through Classical eyes', in M. Green (ed.), *The Celtic World* (London: Routledge, 1995), pp. 21–33.
Reardon, Bernard, *Religion in the Age of Romanticism: Studies in Early Nineteenth-Century Thought* (Cambridge: Cambridge University Press, 1985).
Reece, Jack E., *The Bretons Against France: Ethnic Minority Nationalism in Twentieth-Century Brittany* (Chapel Hill: University of North Carolina Press, 1977).
Reig, Ramiro, 'Entre la realidad y la ilusión: el fenómeno blasquisat en Valencia, 1898–1936', in Nigel Townson (ed.), *El Republicanismo en España (1830–1977)* (Madrid: Alianza Editorial, 1994), pp. 395–424.
Renfrew, Colin, 'Prehistory and the identity of Europe', in Siân Jones and Paul Graves-Brown (eds), *Cultural Identity and Archaeology* (London: Routledge, 1996).
Richards, Penny, 'Rouen and the Golden Age: the entry of Francis I, 2 August 1517', in Christopher Allmand (ed.), *Power, Culture and Religion in France, c.1350–c.1550* (London: Boydell, 1989), pp. 117–131.
Rigney, Ann, 'Immemorial routines: the Celts and their resistance to history', in Terence Brown (ed.), *Celticism* (Amsterdam: Rodopi, 1996), pp. 159–81.
Rosanvallon, Pierre, *Le moment Guizot* (Paris: Gallimard, 1985).
Said, Edward, *Orientalism* (Harmondsworth: Penguin, 1978).
—— *Culture and Imperialism* (London: Verso, 1994).
Sanson, Rosemonde, 'Le 15 août: fête nationale du Second Empire', in A. Corbin, N. Gérôme and D. Tartowsky (eds), *Les Usages politiques des fêtes aux XIXe–XXe siècle* (Paris: Publications de la Sorbonne, 1994).
Schöpflin, George, *Nations, Identity, Power: The New Politics of Europe* (London: Hurst, 2000).
Sewell, William H., *A Rhetoric of Bourgeois Revolution: The Abbé Sieyes* (Durham: Duke University Press, 1994).
Sims-Williams, Patrick, 'Celtomania and Celtoscepticism', *Cambrian Medieval Celtic Studies*, 36 (1998), 1–35.

Smith, Anthony D., *Nationalism: Theory, Ideology, History* (Cambridge: Polity, 2001).
Soucy, Robert, *French Fascism: The Second Wave, 1933–1939* (London: Yale University Press, 1995).
Sternhell, Zeev, *Ni droite, ni gauche: l'idéologie fasciste en France* (Paris: Complexe, 1987).
Tagore, Rabindranath, *Nationalism* (London: Macmillan, 1991 [1917]).
Theweleit, Klaus, *Male Fantasies, Vol I: Women, Floods, Bodies, History*, trans. Stephen Conway (Cambridge: Polity, 1987).
Thompson, E. P., *The Making of the English Working Class* (Harmondsworth: Penguin, 1993).
—— 'The Moral economy of the English crowd in the eighteenth century', in his *Customs in Common* (Harmondsworth: Penguin, 1993), pp. 185–258.
Todorov, Tzvetan, *Nous et les autres: la réflexion française sur la diversité humaine* (Paris: Seuil, 1989).
—— *On Human Diversity: Nationalism, Racism and Exoticism in French Thought*, trans. C. Porter (Cambridge, MA: Harvard University Press, 1993).
Tombs, Robert, *France, 1815–1914* (London: Longman, 1996).
Trumpener, Katie, *Bardic Nationalism: The Romantic Novel and the British Empire* (Princeton: Princeton University Press, 1997).
Wilcox, Lynne, '*Coup de langue*: the amendment to Article 2 of the Constitution: an equivocal interpretation of linguistic pluralism', *Modern and Contemporary France*, 2:3 (1994), 269–78.
Whitney, Sarah, 'Gender, class and generation in interwar French Catholicism: the case of the Jeunesse Ouvrière Chrétienne Féminine', *Journal of Family History*, 26:4 (2001), 480–507.
Winter, J. M., *Sites of Memory, Sites of Mourning* (Cambridge: Cambridge University Press, 1995).
Woloch, Isser, *The New Regime: Transformations of the French Civic Order, 1789–1820s* (New York: Norton, 1994).
Woolf, Stuart, *Napoleon's Integration of Europe* (London: Routledge, 1991).
Woolf, Stuart (ed.), *Nationalism in Europe, 1815 to the Present* (London: Routledge, 1996).
Zeldin, Theodore, *France, 1848–1945: Politics and Anger* (Oxford: Oxford University Press, 1979).

Websites

www.asterix.tm.fr
www.cardijn.net
www.languefrancaise.net

Index

AB (Association Bretonne) 44, 186–188
Académie Celtique 41–43
Act of Union (1532) 4, 64
Action française 33, 51, 208, 212–213
Action Libéral populaire (ALP) 125–126
administration, local 59
agriculture 8, 55, 123, 186, 188, 206–207
air-raids 218
Alsace-Lorraine 198
alcoholism 180–181
Alésia, battle of 44
Algeria 202
ALP (Action Libéral populaire) 125–126
Ancenis 111
ancien régime 35, 54–60, 134, 148
Anderson, Benedict 27, 32
Anne, Duchess of Brittany 4, 50
Anne et le mystère Breton (Toudouze) 225
anticlericalism 96, 163, 164, 181, 189
Antliff, Mark 51
Ar Beg, Loeiz 54
Arblaster, Anthony 160
archaeology 186, 225
aristocracy *see* nobility
Armorique 18
art 9, 39, 94, 192
artillery, British 76
Arouet, François-Marie *see* Voltaire
Association Bretonne (AB) 44, 186–188

Astérix 11
authorities 146–147, 167–168, 205
Azeglio, Massimo d' 28

Badone, Ellen 119
Balzac, Honoré de 9–10, 91, 95–97, 108, 116, 151
Barère 79, 85
Barthélemy, Charles 78, 117
Bazin, René 193
Barzaz Breiz (Villemarqué) 47–49, 101–102, 186–187, 191, 238
Bastianelli, Auguste 127
Batillat, A. 192
Baude, J.-J. 89, 95, 97, 104
Béatrix (Balzac) 151
Belgium, refugees from 215–216
Bergson, Henri 51
Berry, Duchess de 109–110, 134
Bertho, Catherine 60
Besnier, A. 133
Bezen Perrot (BP) 224
Billig, Michael 27
Blackburn, Robin 99–100, 104
blatiers 143
Bloc National 128
Bloom, William 31, 32
Bleun-Brug 189, 232
Blues de Bretagne, Les (Droguet) 53
Blues, the (Republican Society) 78–84, 154, 158
'Blues de Bretagne' 193

Index 301

Boisgobey, Fortuné de 9, 91, 98, 99, 100, 104
Botherel, Comte de, pamphlet of 64–66
Boulainvilliers, comte de 34
Boulé, Père Amand 215, 222
BP (Bezen Perrot) 224
Breiz Atao 198–206, 208, 210{–}211, 212, 214, 215, 236
Brest 57
Breton Association 71
Breton Club 68
Bretonism 104
bretonnitude 47, 98–100, 189–190, 191, 200, 209, 216, 236–239
Bretons against France, The (Reece) 14
Breuilly, John 27
Brière, La (Châteaubriant) 197–198
Britain, influence of 76, 82
Brittany
  compared with Scotland 237–238
  negative interpretation of 12–13, 36, 50, 87–89, 96–97
Brizeux, Auguste 50, 93, 104
Broudic, Fañch 5, 6, 231
Brousmiche, J.-F. 46, 49, 94, 95, 103, 117–118
Bruno, G. 50–51
Buchanan 35
Buchsenschutz, Olivier 44
Burke, Peter 30

Caesar, Julius 18, 33–34, 36–37, 44
cahiers, peasant 66–69, 78
calvaires 119
Cambry, Jacques 18, 43, 57, 83, 84, 86–87, 89–90, 91, 92, 95, 95
Camelots du Roi 212–213
Capdevila, Luc 230
Cardiff 191
Carhaix 7
Carnac 2–3, 95
Carolingian Empire 20
Carrier, citoyen 82
Cartel, the 128
Castelnau, General du 128

Catholic Church 69, 153, 156, 182, 189–190
Catholicism 55, 95–96, 103–104
  political 122–130, 154, 193
  under the Second Empire 167, 168
Cavaignac 160
CELIB (Comité d'Etudes et de Liaison des Intérêts Bretons) 8, 18, 234, 235
'Celtic amoralism' 232
Celtic identity 10, 25, 38–41, 202, 208
Celtic Studies 224 –226
Celticism 85, 158, 182–183, 186–187, 188, 200
  and Orientalism 91–104
Celtoscepticism 39–40
Celts 18, 35, 35–49
Chadwick, Nora K. 37, 38–39, 93
Champollion, Jean-François 98
Chapman, Timothy 35
Charlemagne 20, 45
Châteaneuf, Benoiston de 89, 97
Chateaubriand, François-René 62, 77–78, 101
Châteaubriant 157
Châteaubriant, Alphonse de 197–198
Cheval d'Orgueil, Le (Hélias) 121–122, 196–197
Chouannerie 108–117, 140, 238
Chouans 74–77, 81, 85, 95–96
Chouans, Les (Balzac) 9–10, 12, 96–97, 108
Chroniques 33–34
church, and state 168–169, 198
clerical-Bonapartist alliance 168, 170
Clorivière, Pierre-Joseph de 70
clubs, political 79–84, 153
CNB (National Breton Committee) 222, 223
Cochut, André 91
cod-fishing 57
Cohen, Paul 60
Colbert, Jean-Baptiste 55
collaboration 218, 220–226, 230–231, 232, 238–239
Combourg 56
Comédie humaine (Balzac) 9

302 Index

comices agricoles 123, 186
colony 237
Comité d'Etudes et de Liaison des Intérêts Bretons (CELIB) 8, 18, 234, 235
Comités de Défense paysanne 207–208, 213
Comment peut-on être Breton? (Lebesque) 15, 212
commerce 8–9, 58–59, 60
Commissaires 155
Communism 215
Conan, citoyen 81
conscription 63, 72, 108–110. 186, 214–215
conservatism 188, 220
Constantine, Mary-Ann 47, 93–94
Constitution
    Breton 62–64, 66–68
    Republican 134, 156–157
Constitutional Church 69–71
Corporation Paysanne 218–219
costume 60
Côtes d'Armor 5
Courrier du Finistère 219
Creating the Nation in Provincial France (Ford) 16–17
Croix, Alain 16, 58
Croix de Feu 213–214
crosses, mission 115–116
Crucifié de Keralies, Le (Le Goffic) 181
Cubism 51
culture 35, 36–37, 101, 122–123, 232–233, 238
Czechoslovakia 203

dance 89
Daumier, Honoré 133
Davies, Wendy 20, 22
Dawson, William H. 88, 104
Debauvais, F. 201, 215, 221, 222
De Bello Gallico (Caesar) 34, 36–37, 44
De toute son âme (Bazin) 193
decentralization 185, 186, 188
Déguignet, Jean-Marie 88, 98, 141, 142, 149, 173–175, 177, 180, 190
Delaporte, Raymond 222 –223, 224

Delaville-Leroulx, Joseph 69, 79
democracy 159, 161
    Breiz Atao 203{–}204
    under the Republicans 171–182
    Second Empire 164–171
demography 8, 57
    Association Bretonne 187–188
    Chouans 76, 112–114
    July Monarchy festivals 136–139
    Republican Society 80
    Union Régionalist Bretonne 190–192
Denefle, Sylvette 118
Denez, Per 47, 231
Déniel, Alain 206
Denis, Michel 16, 53–54, 66, 212, 236
Derniers Bretons, Les (Souvestre) 99
Desfontaine, Muriel 101
Desgranges, Jean-Marie 128–129, 189–190
Diamond, Hanna 230
Dietler, Michael 44, 45
Dillon, Myles 38–39
Dinan 212, 213
dirt 87–90
Diwan 6, 232
Domine Salvum 138
Dorgères, Henry 207–208, 212, 213
Dottin, Georges 178–179
Dreyfus Affair 163
Droguet, Alain 53
druidism 37, 43, 95, 225
Dubreuil, Léon 204
Dubuisson-Aubenay 87
Duhamel, Maurice 35, 201
Duparc, Monseigneur 189, 219–220, 223
Dupuy, Roger 76, 78, 196

economy 8–9, 55–58, 123, 185, 186, 206–207
education 56–57, 102, 122–123, 167
    see also schools
Eisteddfod 191
elections 159–164
    April 1848 155
    Breiz Atao 206

Second Empire 165–167, 169–170
Third Republic 173–175
Elegoët, Fañch 88
Elgasse, Charles 154
Ellis, Peter B. 39
Elshtain, Jean Bethke 31–32
emsav 184, 231–234
England, and the nobility 21
Enlightenment, the 34–35, 41, 59, 64
Ergué-Armel 173–175
Estates of Brittany 22, 61–62, 64
evacuation 215

'Faith and Brittany' 124, 189–190
Falloux Law 167
Fanon, Franz 25, 27, 31
fascism 14, 28–29, 202, 203–204, 207, 234
  Breiz Atao 210–211, 212
  and nationalism 210–214
Fasel, George 152
Fédération Nationale Catholique (FNC) 128–130
Fédéderation Régionaliste de Bretagne (FRB) 209
Feiz ha Breiz 124, 189–190, 204
Festival Interceltique (FIL) 7
festivals 133–139, 150–158, 164–165, 166, 175
festoù-noz 7
feudalism 20–21
FIL (Festival Interceltique) 7
Finistère 5, 10, 118
fishing 124
sardines 142
Fitzpatrick, Andrew 39
flags *see* tricolour; white flag
Flaubert, Gustave 9, 100, 104
FLB (Front de Libération de la Bretagne) 203
fleur-de-lys 116
Fleury, E. 92
FNC (Fédération Nationale Catholique) 128–130
food riots 140–148
Ford, Caroline 16–17

France
  Occupation of 211–212, 218, 221, 229–231
  origins of 32–35
FRB (Fédéderation Régionaliste de Bretagne) 209
Freemasons 223, 224
Frélaut, Bertrand 80
French Revolution, origins 54
Front de Libération de la Bretagne (FLB) 203

Gallic War, The (Caesar) 34, 36–37, 44
Galliou, Patrick 39
Gascony 21
Gauguin, Paul 9
Gaulle, Charles de 216, 217, 223, 229
Gauls *see* Celts
Gautier, Théophile 50
Gendreau, Georges 215, 216, 227
'General Will' (Rousseau) 159
Gerbe, La 218
Germany, Nazi 210, 220
  Occupation of France 14, 211–212, 218, 229–231
Gervais, P. 79
Girondins 83
Gleizes, Albert 51
Glézen, Jean-Marie 67–68
Gracq, Julien 128
grain 114, 141, 143
Green, Miranda 39
Greenshirts 207, 208, 211, 212
Group Régionliste breton 198
Guépin, Ange 172
Guérand, Armand 95, 118
Guérande 151
Guérin, F. 153
Guide Bleu 121
Guilloux, Louis 11, 193, 214, 230
Guingamp 81
Guiomar, Jean-Yves 16, 47
Guizot, François Pierre Guillaume 135
Gwalarn 199

Hamon, Kristian 223, 224
Hampson, Norman 82

Hélias, Pierre-Jakez 121–122, 196–197, 204, 217, 230–231
Hémon, Roparz 225, 232
Henri V 109, 110, 186
Hervé, Pierre 233
Hervilly, Comte d' 76
Heure Bretonne, l' 222, 224, 231
Himmler, Heinrich 221
Histoire des Celtes (Pelloutier) 18, 35
history 18–35
Holy Roman Empire 34
hommes libres, Les (Jacq) 226
houses, illumination of 137, 139, 150, 153
Hubert, Henri 19, 46
Hue, Bernard 101
Hugo, Victor 88, 104
Humanité, L' 5
Hunt, Lynn 41

'Icelandic Pardon' 124
Icelanding Fisherman (Loti) 86, 91–92
Imagined Communities (Anderson) 27
independence 3–5
Islam 95

Jacobins 159
Jacq, Angèle 226
James, Simon 40
Jean III, duke 21–22
Jeuness Etudiante Chrétienne 227
Jeunesses patriotes 213
Jews 223, 224
Jézéquel, Jean-Marie 78, 81
Jolly, Odette 211
Jones, Michael 21, 39
Jouvenel, Baron de 188
July Monarchy 132–139, 149

Kabbani, Rana 94
Kad 225
Kano, Yves 100, 181
Keranflec'h, Charles de 93, 103
Kerdrel, Audren de 162
Kergorre, René Cavaro de 134
Kerjégu, Louis de 188

Kermadec, Roland de 217
Kornog 204

La Borderie, Arthur de 186–187
La Parfaite Amitié 59
La Parfaite Union 59
La Riboisière, Count de 176–177
La Rochejaquelein, Marquise de 73, 77
La Roüerie, Tuffin de 71
La Vendée 72–78
Lagrée, Michel 122, 154, 189, 193
Lainé, Célestin 203, 222, 224
Lamennais, Hugues-Felicité Robert de 48
language
   Breton 5–6, 15, 21, 46, 47, 60, 88, 91, 93, 97, 101–102, 157, 185, 188, 194–195, 196–197, 199, 225, 226, 231
   Gallo 6
   Celtic 37, 39, 40, 98
   French 6, 34, 41–42, 60, 196–197
Last Chouan, The (Balzac) 108
Latin tradition 32–33
law 60, 67
Le Bail, Georges 179
Le Boulanger, Jean-Michel 7
Le Braz, Anatole 2, 92–93, 104, 118, 121, 191
Le Breton, Pierre-Jean 70
Le Coadic, Ronan 16
Le Febvre, Yves 181, 193–194, 195, 204
Le Goffic, Charles 45, 92, 98, 99, 103, 104, 121, 181, 190, 209
Le Quintrec, Charles 2
League of Patriotic Frenchwomen (LFFP) 125
Lebesque, Morvan 15, 212, 231, 235
Legendre, Laurent-Françios 68, 85
Legitimism 48, 103–104, 185–186
Leo XIII 179
Léon region 117, 124, 189
l'Estourbeillon de la Garnache, Marquis de 188, 191, 192, 210
Lewis, Wyndham 10
LFB (Ligue Fédéraliste Breton) 199, 209

LFFP (League of Patriotic
    Frenchwomen) 125
Liberation 229–231, 232
liberty 125
Liberty Trees 150, 153–154, 158
Ligue de la Patrie française (LPF) 125
Ligue Fédéraliste Breton (LFB) 199, 209
Lincoln, Andrew 232
literature 9–11, 15, 42–43, 46–49, 73,
    77–78, 102
Locronan 232
Loth, Joseph 98
Loti, Pierre 86, 91–92, 94, 104
Loucher Law (1928) 207
Loudéac 123–124
Louis-Napoleon 154, 160, 161, 162,
    165, 166, 170
Louis the Pious 20
Louis XIV 55, 59
Lower Brittany 5–6
LPF (Ligue de la Patrie française) 125
Luckenwalde 222
Luzel, François-Marie 92, 93, 99, 104,
    170, 191

Machiavelli, Niccolò 4
MacPherson, James 18, 35, 41, 49
Magnier, Brutus 82
Mahé, Joseph 2–3, 123
*Making of the English Working Class,
    The* (Thompson) 17
Manifeste de Guimgamp (*Breiz Atao*) 214
Marchal, Morvan 201
marches 136–137
markets 145–146
Marseillaise 157, 171, 226
Martin, Jean-Clément 81
Masson, Emile 180, 194–195, 196, 209
Maurras, Charles 33, 51, 208
Mazéas, G. 201, 202, 206
McDonald, Maryon 12–13
megaliths 225
Mémoires (Déguignet) 88
Mérimée, Prosper 43, 50, 87, 95, 117
Michelet, Jules 5, 10, 99, 104, 210
migration 8, 19–20
Mill, J.S. 4, 28

Millon, Abbé 124
Ministry of the Interior 141, 148,
    171–172
Mirbeau, Octave 91, 96
Moal, Stefan 5
modernity 189, 193, 204
Mon frère Yves (Loti) 94
monarchy 21, 33, 55, 68, 148, 163,
    167, 172–175
    see also July Monarchy
Monde comme si, Le (Morvan) 13–14
Monnier, Jean-Jacques 15–16
Montcontour 83–84
monuments, prehistoric 1–3, 186, 225
Morbihan 5
Mordrel, Olier 201, 203, 215, 220, 221,
    223, 232
Morgenstern, Soma 216
Morlaix 176
Morvan, Françoise 13–14, 208–209
MRP (Popular Republican Movement)
    233, 234
Mun, Albert de 125, 126
music 6–7
Muzillac 156

Nairn, Tom 29
Nantes 8, 21, 58, 82, 171, 227–228
Nantes au XIXe siècle (Guépin et al) 172
Napoleon 41
Napoleon III 44
National Assembly 66, 69, 70, 172
National Breton Committee (CNB)
    222, 223
National Guard 68, 81, 132–133,
    136, 156
National Sozialistische Volkswohlfahrt
    218
nationalism 12–17, 26–32, 236–239
    and fascism 210–214
    German 220
    Italian 168
Nazis *see* Germany, Nazi
new PNB 220–224, 226, 230, 231, 234
Nicol, Max 120, 124
Nicolet, Claude 134
Nivillac, July Monarchy festival in 139

nobility 20–21, 33–34, 58–59
  and Counter-Revolutionary
    movements 76, 77
  and politics 61–66, 67, 123–124
Nochlin, Linda 94
Nomenoë 20
Nous barbares locaux (Vallerie) 15
Nouvel Observateur 25
noyades 82

O Lo Lê 220
Old Regime *see ancien régime*
Orientalism 86–104
Orleanist regime 115, 154, 158
  reaction to food riots 143–144, 147–149
Orton, Fred 192
Ossian (MacPherson) 18, 35, 41, 49
Ouest-Éclair 125, 180
Ozouf, Jacques 50
Ozouf, Mona 50, 134–135

PAB (Parti Autonomiste Breton) 198–199, 200, 201, 202
pardons 118–122, 234
Paris 55, 155–156
Parlement, of Brittany 61
Parti Autonomiste Breton (PAB) 198–199, 200, 201, 202
Parti Communiste de France (PCF) 215, 233, 235
Parti Démocratique Populaire (PDP) 126–127, 219
Parti National Breton (PNB) 199, 200, 201, 203, 204, 206, 215, 220
  see also new PNB
Parti Populaire Français 224
Parti Social Français 213–214
Pascal, Jean 155
patriotism 78–79, 116, 145
patronage 124–125
Pavie, Auguste 101
PCF (Parti Communiste de France) 215, 233, 235
PDP (Parti Démocratique Populaire) 126–127, 219
peasantry *see* Third Estate

Peasants into Frenchmen (Weber) 14–15
Pêcheur d'Islande (Loti) 86, 91–92, 94
Pellerin, Joseph-Michel 66
Pelloutier, Simon 18, 35
Pénestin 136
Pennec, Alain 54
Pensée bretonne, La (Le Febvre) 192, 195
'people, the', at Second Republic festivals 152–153
Perrot, J.-M. 189, 220, 224
Pétain, Marshal 217–218, 219, 220
Peuple Breton, Le 86
Pivert, Marcel 211, 212
Pleven, René 233–234
Ploërmel 139, 157
Plouarzel, *menhir* at 49
PNB (Parti National Breton) 199, 200, 201, 203, 204, 206, 215, 220
  see also new PNB
poetry 93–94, 188
politics 9, 79–84, 233–234
  Breiz Atao 200–202
  Catholic 122–130, 154, 193
  Chouannerie 114–115
  international 34
  and the nobility 61–66
Pollock, Griselda 192
Pontcallec, Marquise de 63, 77
Popular Front 127, 206, 213
Popular Republican Movement (MRP) 233, 234
population 56
poverty 142
press, the 166
priests 69–71, 122–123, 138, 161, 181
prisoners 216, 221–222
privateers 57–58
Protestants 179, 228
Province, La 213
Provost, Georges 120
publications, *Breiz Atao* 201, 204
Puigaudeau, Odette du 101, 218, 219, 234

Quatrevingt-treize (Hugo) 89
Queffélec, Henri 225–226
Quimper 19

racism 202–203
Radical Party 128, 130, 160
rebellion 63, 66–69, 72–78
Recteur de l'île de Sein (Queffélec) 225–226
Reece, Jack 14
reformation 96–97, 102–103
refugees 11, 214, 215–216
Regionalism 190–192
religion 37, 95–96, 117–122, 138–139, 153–154
Remonstrance (1788) 64
Renan, Ernest 83, 92, 99, 123
Renfrew, Colin 39–40
Rennes 21, 56, 62, 171, 217
Rennes, berceau de la liberté (Denis) 53–54
Republican Society (the Blues) 78–84, 154, 158
Republicans 104, 171–182, 182
Resistance, the 224, 226–228
revolt, June 1848 155–156
Ribbentrop, Ulrich Freidrich 221
Richer, Edouard 92
riots, food 114, 140–149
Romanticism 43, 46, 48–49
Rousseau, Jean-Jacques 159
Royal Catholic Army 72–73
royal customs houses 66–67
Russians, white 224

Sabbatine library 59
Saga programme 201–202, 203, 204
Said, Edward 86, 90–91
Sainclivier, Jacqueline 15
Saint-Brieuc 193, 215
Saint-Malo 57–58
Saint-Pol-de-Léon 232
Sainte Anne 118, 120
Sainte-Anne-d'Auray 120, 186
Sainte-Geneviève 164–171
Salonne, Marie-Paule 216, 227, 228, 230
salt 62
Sand, George 151, 153
Sangnier, Marc 126
sardines, fisheries 142

Sarzeau 136
Schnapp, Alain S. 44
schools 176, 177, 178–179
Schöpflin, George 32
Schultz, Jeanne 121
science 97–98, 103
Scotland, compared with Brittany 237–238
Scott, Walter 10, 43
Second Empire 164–171, 172, 182
Second Republic 149–158, 162
Section Française de l'Internationale Ouvrière (SFIO) 128, 211, 233
seigneural system 66–69
Sein, island of 216
Seiz Breur 208, 209
Serbois, L. de 96, 99, 104, 170
Service feminine français (SFF) 218
sexuality 94–95
SFF (Service feminine français) 218
SFIO (Section Française de l'Internationale Ouvrière) 128, 211, 233
Siegfried, André 172, 181
Sillon 126, 127
Sims-Williams, Patrick 40–41
slave trade 58
Smith, Anthony D. 30–31
socialism 164, 193–195, 207–208, 211
Socialist Youth 211, 212
songs 153
Soret 150–152
Souben, Monique 75, 76
Souvestre, Emile 2, 42–43, 91, 92, 96, 99, 104, 117
Spain, refugees from 214
standing stones 1–3
state, and church 168–169, 198
Stendhal 87
Stivell, Alan 6
Stonehenge, A temple Restor'd to the British Druids (Stukeley) 18, 35
studies, academic 15–16
Stukeley, William 18, 35
suffrage 160, 162
Sutherland, Donald 76

Tableau de la France (Michelet) 10
Tagore, Rabindranath 26
Taine, Hippolyte 87–88, 104
Tanguy, Jean-François 178
taxes 62, 63, 64
telecommunications 8
Temps nouveaux 194
Tench, Walkin 71, 84
Tène, La 18
Terre des Prêtres, La (Febvre) 181, 204
terrorism 203
texts, classical 36
Thebault, Léon 179
Thiers, A. 96
Third Estate 35, 66–69
Third Republic 162–164, 172–181, 182, 186
Thompson E. P. 17, 143
timelessness 92–94
Todorov, Tzvetan 86, 103
Tombs, Robert 170–171
Toudouze, Georges 225
Tour de la France par deux enfants, Le (Bruno) 50–51
tourists 104
towns 99–100
tradition, Latin 32–33
Tranvouez, Yvon 219
Trégor Valley 8
Tréguier 123
tricolour 115, 116
trojans 33–34
Trumpener, Katie 10
Ty Kodaks 201
typhus 56

UDB (Union démocratique bretonne) 3–4, 86, 104
Union démocratique bretonne (UDB) 3–4, 86, 104
Union Régionaliste Brettone (URB) 190–192, 209
Upper Brittany 6
URB (Union Régionaliste Bretonne) 190–192, 209

Vallerie, Erwan 15, 29–30
Vercingetorix 44–45, 238
Vichy, government 217, 218–219
Vieilles Charrues 7
Villemarqué, Théodore Hersart de la 47–51, 88, 92, 93, 101–102, 103, 185, 186–187, 188, 191, 200, 210, 238
Villermé, Louis-René 89, 97
Villers-Cotterêts decree (1539) 60
Voltaire 33
Voyage dans le Finistère (Cambry) 18, 86–87, 89–90

Wagner, Hans-Otto 220–221
We are not French! (McDonald) 12–13
Weber, Eugen 14–15
white flag 109–110
Wild Body (Lewis) 10
women 135, 237
Woolfe, Stuart 27
World War I 196–198, 215
World War II 214–219

Young, Arthur 56